Sustainable Development Goals

We dedicate this book to our families and friends, spanning the world but all affected by our common fate

Sustainable Development Goals

Law, Theory and Implementation

Edited by

Duncan French

Professor of International Law, University of Lincoln, UK

Louis J. Kotzé

Research Professor, North-West University, South Africa

Edward Elgar
PUBLISHING

Cheltenham, UK • Northampton, MA, USA

Published by
Edward Elgar Publishing Limited
The Lypiatts
15 Lansdown Road
Cheltenham
Glos GL50 2JA
UK

Edward Elgar Publishing, Inc.
William Pratt House
9 Dewey Court
Northampton
Massachusetts 01060
USA

A catalogue record for this book
is available from the British Library

Library of Congress Control Number: 2018931780

This book is available electronically in the **Elgar**online
Law subject collection
DOI 10.4337/9781786438768

ISBN 978 1 78643 875 1 (cased)
ISBN 978 1 78643 876 8 (eBook)

Typeset by Columns Design XML Ltd, Reading
Printed on FSC approved paper
Printed and bound in Great Britain by Marston Book Services Ltd, Oxfordshire

Contents

Contributors

Sam Adelman is Associate Professor at the School of Law, University of Warwick, United Kingdom

Helmut Philipp Aust is Professor at the Faculty of Law, Freie Universität Berlin, Germany

Michelle Barnard is Senior Lecturer at the Faculty of Law, North-West University, South Africa

Lynda M. Collins is Professor with the Centre for Environmental Law and Global Sustainability at the University of Ottawa, Canada

Nathan Cooper is Associate Professor at the Faculty of Law, University of Waikato, New Zealand

Anél du Plessis is Professor at the Faculty of Law, North-West University, South Africa

Duncan French is Professor of International Law and Head of Lincoln Law School, United Kingdom

Louis J. Kotzé is Research Professor at the Faculty of Law, North-West University, South Africa; and Visiting Professor of Environmental Law at the University of Lincoln, United Kingdom

Graham Long is Senior Lecturer at the School of Geography, Politics and Sociology, Newcastle University, United Kingdom

Owen McIntyre is Professor at the School of Law, University College Cork, Ireland

Karen Morrow is Professor at the Hillary Rodham Clinton School of Law, Swansea University, United Kingdom

Nadia Sánchez Castillo-Winckels is a lawyer admitted to the Chilean Bar and a doctoral candidate affiliated to the Grotius Centre for International Legal Studies at Leiden University, the Netherlands

Werner Scholtz is Professor at the Faculty of Law, University of the Western Cape, South Africa

Niko Soininen is a postdoctoral researcher at the Gothenburg University Law School, Sweden; and Senior Lecturer at the School of Law, University of Eastern Finland, Finland

Acknowledgements

We have had the immense pleasure over the course of two years to collaborate with leading scholars across the globe in producing this book. We are grateful for this privilege and for the honour to have been able to convene such an illustrious group of scholars around the theme of law and the Sustainable Development Goals.

We wish to thank in particular Jean Claude Ashukem and Caiphas Soyapi from the North-West University, South Africa for their assistance in the editorial management and proofreading processes.

Colleagues at both our respective institutions, North-West University and the University of Lincoln, United Kingdom, have supported us in this project. In particular, Professor French wishes to thank those colleagues who participate in the Lincoln Centre for Environmental Law and Justice for providing a base for such rich discussion on environmental matters in Lincoln.

Finally, we wish to extend a special word of thanks to our outstanding publishing team at Edward Elgar Publishing, which has guided the conceptualisation, execution and publication of this book according to the highest professional standards of care.

1. Introduction

Duncan French and Louis J. Kotzé

The negotiation, and adoption in September 2015, of the Sustainable Development Goals (SDGs)[1] within the framework of the United Nations (UN) has been heralded as a notable step in the international community's ongoing, if uneven, commitment to global development. More than just a continuation of the Millennium Development Goals (MDGs), which ran from 2000 to 2015, the SDGs – more rhetorically known as the 'Global Goals' – seek to encapsulate and promote global aspirations across a wide array of topic areas broadly associated with sustainable development.

First proposed at the 2012 UN Conference on Sustainable Development (the 'Rio +20' Summit), the Global Goals were finally reduced through intergovernmental negotiation, following more open-ended dialogues with civil society, interest groups, business and others, to 17 Goals, though within that reflecting 169 targets and many more indicators. Unlike the MDGs, which were numerically limited to eight goals, the Global Goals ultimately adopted contain a plurality of objectives. The 2015 UN General Assembly document, *Transforming our world: the 2030 Agenda for Sustainable Development*, which adopted the Global Goals, sets out very much in the usual way of UN documents high rhetoric around international cooperation, development and the onward progression of humanity. Nevertheless, within such rhetoric, there is also a level, if not quite precision, of detail around what the international community should strive to achieve over the next 15 years. Noticeably less on how, and by what means.

[1] The terms SDGs and Global Goals are used interchangeably in the book, reflecting much of the practice surrounding the goals; though equally we must acknowledge that some UN bodies have been more scrupulous in exclusively referring to them as the SDGs. When referring to a particular goal, the book more commonly refers to them as SDG 1, or Global Goal 2. Both for reasons of neatness and, more importantly, because it is not common practice, we have avoided the shorthand of GG 3.

The Goals included range from those rather similar in overview (if differing in quite a lot of respects as regards content and detail) from those set out in the MDGs, such as SDG 1 on the eradication of poverty, SDG 2 on zero hunger and SDG 4 on education, to those much newer to the SDGs, including SDG 11 on sustainable cities and SDG 16 focusing on access to justice and the rule of law. Of particular note is the inclusion of numerous 'green' Goals, namely on climate (SDG 13), life below water (SDG 14) and life on land (SDG 15). This is in contrast to the rather more summary, vague – and indeed cursory – MDG 7 on environmental sustainability.

Also notable is the inclusion of what might be termed overtly polycentric issues, such as good health and well-being (SDG 3), gender equality (SDG 5) and decent work (SDG 8). Such Goals – like the environmental cluster – are polycentric not simply because they require a complex mix of policy actions (which might be said to be a hallmark of all the Goals), but because they cannot be achieved, whether directly or indirectly, by simple improvements in economic growth and industrialisation. Indeed, unlike the MDGs, which were purposely directed at 'supporting' the Global South, the SDGs are targeted at all States, including more developed Northern States. Perhaps this is the reason why there are multiple tensions at the heart of the Goals; progress towards some risks jeopardising, at least without the imposition of appropriate measures and integrated planning, progress on others. The promotion of sustainable industry and infrastructure (SDG 9) sits uneasily against not only the environmental Goals, but also sustainable consumption and production targets (SDG 12); or, at least, might do. To that extent, the Global Goals present a complex and problematic agenda of transformative social change.

The objective of this edited collection is to consider this complexity through one particular lens, namely the relationship between law, human rights and the Global Goals. There are, of course, many others: education, the role of civil society, the importance of research and development in technology, and the like. This book touches upon these – and other – forces where necessary, but the focus very much is on the role, influence and interlinkages between law (in all its many guises) and the Global Goals. This is not a new topic; law and development as a field of scholarship and methodology has sought to capture the complexity of such debates for decades. And within the specific topic of UN Goals, previous publications have sought to interrogate the relevance of law, and particularly of human rights, to the achievement of the MDGs.[2] Most commentary has focused on international law, and to a lesser extent domestic (i.e. public law) implementation.[3] Both are of essential relevance. But it is equally important not to neglect the increasing significance of other 'typologies'; notably corporate, private, local government and transnational law, as well as soft law and mixed systems.

In unduly simplified form, the relationship between law and the Goals can be formulated in several distinct, and yet almost invariably overlapping, ways. At its most foundational, lies the question of the status of the Goals, present and future. In short, are the Goals binding in legal terms? Or might they become so over time? Much of the emphasis here is on their status in international law, though there is no reason why similar questions cannot be raised at the domestic level.[4] A more nuanced argument, discussed in several of the chapters, is how far the Goals (and especially the targets set thereunder) correspond with, are symmetrical to, or a deviation of present obligations set out in law, most noticeably human rights standards or obligations in environmental law. There are few, if any, examples of where the Goals might be said to deviate from current law or policy in an upwards trajectory; rather the usual argument is how far (and to what extent) such Goals and targets differ negatively in content, timing, coverage or in all respects from previous standards set.

Second, is the question of the role (or absence) of law in the implementation of the Global Goals. The Goals are, by their nature, policy objectives, but within them they contain measures that can either very specifically or more obliquely be promoted (or harmful activity proscribed) by the adoption of laws and regulations. Within this, of course, is a multitude of possibilities, encompassing both public law and administration, rights-based approaches and the encouragement of contractual and other private forms of law-making. In this context, law is easily reduced to an instrumental form, merely seeing it as a question as to how it can assist in the achievement of the Goals. Putting to one side

---

[2] See, for example, J. Castellino 'The MDGs and International Human Rights Law: A View from the Perspective of Minorities and Vulnerable Groups' (2009) 13(1) *The International Journal of Human Rights* 10–28.

[3] See, for example, 'Part 7: International Law and the Millennium Development Goals' in H. Ruiz Fabri, R. Wolfrum and J. Gogolin (eds) *Select Proceedings of the European Society of International Law: Volume 2, 2008* (Hart, 2008) 461–526.

[4] See, on the normative status of the SDGs, D. French, 'The Global Goals: Formalism Foregone, Contested Legality and "Re-Imaginings of International Law"' (2017) *Ethiopian Yearbook of International Law* 151–178.

the alternative – the capacity of law to inhibit the Goals (which is considered below) – there are nevertheless other, pertinent issues around law and implementation. One is existential and conceptual; the very function of law in the achievement of sustainable development. That has been widely debated, perhaps too much so. There is a general consensus – at least among lawyers – that law can play a pivotal role in improving development. And when the Global Goals are placed within their proper context of sustainable development, law has been central to its progress since it was first endorsed internationally in 1987.[5] While the debate continues as to what are essential and what are contextual factors to ensure successful legal implementation in the matter of development, there is nevertheless a general sense that law, if properly devised, can be an instrument of change.[6]

A further, positive, analysis – building on this understanding – would be to affirm the constitutive role of law in the achievement of the Goals. Law as a social construction provides one, and by no means the most effective, form of political action and social mobilisation. Nevertheless, because of the authority in which it is held, measures taken by accepted means of legality often have a definitive quality to them. Though this is a quality often surpassing their actual capacity to achieve the level of societal change desired, the fact that such change is enshrined in law has a catalysing impact, beyond its immediate effect. The promotion of gender equality and eradication of racism are perhaps good examples of such a positive role for law. It is incapable of achieving fully the objective itself, but beyond its pure instrumentalism it has a constitutive effect in changing social understandings and challenging previous assumptions. To that extent, law in this area can be both instrumental and constitutive.

Nevertheless, there are more critical questions around the implementation of the Goals through law. Law has its own culture, its own way of seeing things – beyond the aspiration of human rights, regulatory law is often narrow and constrained. Private law more so. To say that law can implement the Goals says little about the relative power, and conflicting and diverse interests of the rule- and decision-makers. Even more than that, law can be a hindrance to the achievement of development, and there is often little movement against the most entrenched political and economic interests. The Goals themselves say little about tax evasion, the

---

[5] Report of the World Commission on Environment and Development: *Our Common Future* (Brundtland Report, 1987).

[6] See, for example, S. Roach Anleu, *Law and Social Change*, 2nd edn (Sage Publishing, 2010).

regulation of multinational corporations or the prohibition of those activities truly destructive of global Earth system integrity. Law as a means of implementation of the Goals should be neither preferred nor unquestioned. Moreover, as an instrument of political choices, it must equally be acknowledged that law may be used as much as to deny progress on the Goals as to promote them.

The final caricature of law that might be posited here is specifically related to human rights. There is an invariable assumption that human rights and development goals are mutually compatible and supportive.[7] But as several chapters in this book demonstrate, the relationship should not be subject to such reductionist analysis. True, there is significant overlap with many of the (especially social) Global Goals – just as there were with the MDGs – and yet the points of tension are numerous. As already indicated, such Goals may fall short of the standards set in human rights; in other words, the level of political ambition negotiated is a regression of that already set in human rights law. But beyond this, there are wider questions of scope (both scope of action and scope of responsibility), divergent time lines and inconsistent coverage, as well as more administrative questions of supervision, reporting and monitoring. Of particular interest is the extent to which the Goals phrase themselves in human rights terms at all, or seek to avoid, as far as possible, such language. While the UN earnestly seeks to place the SDGs and the International Bill of Rights[8] as synergistic, the clear intention of many of the intergovernmental negotiators would seem to be to keep them apart. And this is not simply a static question at the time of negotiation and adoption. How are such Goals (and indeed the corresponding human rights) interpreted and implemented going forward, both at the international and domestic levels, in legislative, policy and importantly, *judicial* fora? There is a traction between the Goals and human rights, but it should not be readily assumed as symmetrical and analogous; the potential for tension is significant.

* * *

[7] See for a critique, M. Langford, A. Sumner and A. Ely Yamin (eds) *The Millennium Development Goals and Human Rights: Past, Present and Future* (Cambridge University Press, 2013).

[8] Seen as including the Universal Declaration of Human Rights of 1948; the International Covenant on Civil and Political Rights of 1966; and the International Covenant on Economic, Social and Cultural Rights of 1966.

The book is divided into two parts. Part I explores various general themes relating to the Global Goals (for instance, their ontology, the relevance of human rights, the politics that lie behind the Goals). Part II then considers, in turn, eight of the Goals themselves (including gender equality, access to water and sanitation, the 'environmental' Goals, access to justice and the rule of law). It would, of course, have been possible to have included a chapter on each of the 17 Goals, but for two related reasons the editors felt a more selective process was both permissible and, in fact, warranted. First, while the chapters are directly linked to specific Goals, most of the chapters invariably touch on elements of many of the other Goals; one of the partial successes of the SDGs is that they do make some linkage between themselves. Not completely, and not without notable challenges, however. But intellectually, one can interpret and read the Goals corporately as well as individually. Second, as editors we chose Goals about which we felt there were important, significant and/or new to things to say from a legal perspective. For instance, the inclusion of a chapter on SDG 11 on sustainable cities was both necessary and added conspicuously to the literature.

The collection begins with a searing attack on the Goals themselves by Sam Adelman. In particular, he critiques the underlying existential assumptions on which the Goals are premised. The Goals continue the neoliberal sustainable development myth that economic growth and respecting environmental constraints are mutually compatible. As he argues, sustainable development remains a dangerous illusion, which jeopardises long-term social justice and environmental protection. Moreover, the SDGs are deeply anthropocentric and thus fail to give precedence to those measures truly necessary to prevent global Earth system harm, as captured in the move towards the Anthropocene. As he pertinently records, 'The SDGs bring to mind an Irish joke in which a lost tourist rolls down her car window and asks a local for directions to Dublin. He rubs his chin, thinks for a moment, and says "I wouldn't start from here." In the Anthropocene, the point of departure for the goals should surely have been ecological sustainability rather than development.'

The following chapter by Louis J. Kotzé, takes forward this critique and subjects the Goals to what he refers to as three 'new-millennial analytical paradigms', namely the Anthropocene, Planetary Boundaries theory and Earth system governance theory. Each poses existential challenges for the Goals, and all reveal the current limitations of the Goals. The Goals are designed around incremental changes in international society and the global environment. But, as this chapter reveals, the enormity of the problems facing the Earth, and more particularly,

Earth system integrity, demand much more radical change. Of particular importance are the insights of Earth system governance, which pushes us towards considering normative and institutional realignment in the face of the enormity of global environmental change. The author concludes that the Goals as presently written will not only not prevent such harm, but will also exacerbate negative change. Moreover, the appearance of doing something through the Goals pushes back what is much more necessary; namely, a wider and deeper dialogue as to fundamental societal change.

This chapter is followed by a deeply analytical chapter by Lynda M. Collins on the relationship between human rights and the Global Goals. While recognising the traditional dichotomy between human rights and development, Collins suggests that the suspicion, and indeed animosity, among many human rights advocates of the Goals is (perhaps) misplaced. While of course the real test is in the process of implementation, there is no denying that the 2030 Agenda for Sustainable Development is a powerful document in the eyes of governments, business and civil society. Of course, there remain genuine questions as to how far human rights and the Goals are co-extensive, complementary or conflicting, but this neglects a broader reality. As she notes,

> [I]t is possible that SDGs will supplant human rights as the focal point for global cooperation and implementation efforts. On the other hand, the SDGs explicitly endorse a human rights approach and would certainly achieve a huge step forward in the realization of human rights, particularly economic, environmental and social rights, if they are fully realized. Even a partial achievement of the SDGs would advance the goals of human rights, particularly with respect to social, environmental and economic rights, which have so far lagged behind the civil and political rights.

The following chapter by Graham Long considers the transformative effect of the Goals. As he himself notes, his chapter may be taken as a defence of the Goals. In particular, he seeks to draw out what he terms cross-cutting 'commitments' with the Agenda, namely that the Goals are universal, that the Goals and targets are interconnected and indivisible, and that they are premised on the understanding that 'no-one should be left behind'. As he says,

> If the SDGs indeed represent a new model of "governing through goals", then their underpinning principles – in effect, attributes of the whole goal framework – are crucial to understanding how such governance might operate, and its prospects for success.

While recognising that implementation of the Goals will present their own challenges, his aim is to contextualise our understanding of the Goals; indeed, in his own words, to 'usefully complicate' them.

The final chapter in Part I considers the application of the Global Goals to one of the more intractable problems of international law, namely effective and sustainable ocean governance. Nadia Sánchez Castillo-Winckels reviews the ongoing difficulties of developing a workable and sustainable regime. She argues that the SDGs have the potential to play a key role in enhancing public access to information and participation in institutions managing these resources, notably regional fisheries management organisations and the International Seabed Authority. In particular, the SDGs emphasise the participation of civil society, something altogether missing so far in ocean governance. The Goals build upon other initiatives to ensure institutional transparency, accountability and effectiveness. As an exemplar of what might be achieved (and be achievable), the chapter raises the intriguing proposition that the Goals have merit in empowering civil society organisations to join States and industry organisations as principal actors in achieving sustainable development, in this case in an area which was previously strictly intergovernmental in nature and form, namely the governance of high seas fisheries and deep seabed minerals.

The book then moves into Part II to reflect on particular Goals. Part II begins with a chapter by Karen Morrow on gender equality. Morrow examines the development of gender as an issue within the Goals, reflecting on the perceived advantages and systemic challenges of a discrete Goal on gender equality, rather than a more pervasive and integrated approach. The chapter considers, in particular, the weakening of gender issues within SDG 5 in contrast to established human rights law; something that is of concern not just textually but, much more importantly, in relation to the message that this sends and its impact on the ground. Separating gender empowerment in the Goals from human rights law risks, in particular, divorcing (in)action from the supervisory and legal mechanisms that already exist to promote and protect gender equality. In short, as Morrow concludes,

> goals-based approaches, if they continue on the present trajectory, will come to be viewed as otiose by the human rights and gender constituencies, prompting them to disengage and shift focus to other areas where their efforts are more likely to avail.

The next chapter by Owen McIntyre on SDG 6 on access to water and sanitation continues to reflect on the challenges of reconciling the Goal with pre-existing legal frameworks. Similar to Morrow, he recognises the political importance of the Goal and how it has the potential to now determine and dominate future activity around the issue. For McIntyre, however, the relationship between Goal 6 and its concomitant legal framework has the potential to be much more positive and mutually supportive. He sees Goal 6 and present actions as a two-way relationship, whereby the former will influence the ongoing development and implementation of relevant legal measures and approaches. In particular, the SDGs place greater emphasis on transboundary water cooperation. As he notes:

> While the existing rules and principles of international water will clearly have a significant role to play in achieving the Targets set out under SDG 6, it is equally apparent that SDG 6 will shine an important spotlight on the need to improve transboundary water governance in order to render it 'fit for purpose' in the twenty-first century.

The following chapter by Helmut Philipp Aust and Anél du Plessis moves on to focus on one of the more innovative Goals adopted, namely Goal 11 on sustainable cities. As the authors note, its inclusion is further evidence of 'the thickening layer of international normative guidance on questions of "good urban governance"' or, more colloquially put, the urban turn in global governance. While generally supportive of the inclusion of a goal around sustainable cities, recognising the importance such urban centres now play socially, economically and environmentally, the Goal itself is not without paradoxes and is subject to criticism. In attempting to be comprehensive, the Goal has set within itself internal conflicts and conundrums: how to ensure cities are safe, for instance, while also making them as inclusive as possible. Beyond this, the Goal is silent on some of the most challenging aspects, notably the institutional role played by cities in national and global governance. Goal 11 is thus a first step, but as the authors say, 'one would have expected Goal 11 to be much clearer on the fact that the countries of the world may have to define, among others, realistic institutional improvements at the city scale and in national urban development plans and budgets'.

The next chapter considers the environmental cluster of Goals, namely those pertaining to the climate (SDG 13), water resources – both fresh (SDG 6) and marine (SDG 14) – as well as biodiversity (SDG 15). Werner Scholtz and Michelle Barnard reflect on the inclusion of such Goals, and how far they represent, take forward or backtrack on current environmental obligations. They find the situation rather mixed; neither altogether negative nor unduly progressive. Indeed, they see scope for reflection of the Goals (and, in particular, certain targets) in customary environmental norms and the practice of Conferences of the Parties of certain treaties. Moreover, they argue that the inclusion of the ecosystem approach to water management in SDG 6 is to be welcomed. And yet, as they move to the conclusion, their chapter resonates concerns in earlier chapters that the environmental agenda in the Global Goals is secondary to the economic push. Thus despite evidence of normativity, it may well not be enough to prevent environmental harm at the expense of more paradigmatic growth considerations.

The penultimate chapter by Niko Soininen reflects on Global Goal 16 on the rule of law, access to justice and the imperative of having strong and accountable institutions. The inclusion of the rule of law would seem to be a legal 'win' as regards the Global Goals, and yet as Soininen argues, there is an inherent – if unseen – tension between the rule of law (as principally understood and applied by lawyers) and socio-economic and scientific reality. After discussing the principal understandings of the rule of law, namely formal, procedural and substantive, Soininen questions the relevance of such traditional approaches to the Goals. As he notes,

> One of the main problems with all the rule of law theories is that they impose certainty on an uncertain socio-ecological world … All these three rule of law theories require different kinds of certainty that is at odds with the uncertainty of the socio-ecological 'real' world … The clash between (legal) certainty and socio-ecological uncertainty may at times be the single greatest obstacle for effectively achieving environmental goals, such as the SDGs.

Nevertheless, not all is lost. What is required is flexibility – by lawyers – in how the rule of law is understood and applied. Soininen posits two lines of inquiry to counter this, namely that the law needs to find ways to be adaptable and that courts need greater flexibility to weigh and interpret scientific evidence.

The final chapter by Nathan Cooper and Duncan French focuses on SDG 17 on international partnerships as key to the implementation of the other Goals. It includes targets in such areas as overseas development assistance, debt sustainability, technology transfer, capacity-building and international trade. And yet the Goal also reveals many of the contradictions within the primarily voluntarist nature of the international community's approach to development: namely, grand words and moral injunction yet weak normative commitment. Moreover, the chapter notes that the Goal weakens yet further the traditional normative argument of the South as to the existence of a positive obligation in international law on development cooperation. Indeed, even where the Goal seeks new ground in diversifying partnerships (such as to include civil society), there remains little support for the view that the Goals will provide either clarity or certainty, particularly within a domestic context. The authors conclude that the innate voluntarism within international partnerships as the driving mechanism supporting implementation of the Goals ultimately puts at risk their effective attainment. Global solidarity, either as a legal principle or political commitment, remains inchoate.

* * *

What lessons can be taken from the collection? As always, each chapter makes its own contribution to the broader debate. But perhaps as editors we might be privileged to suggest three emerging themes, which if we may be so bold, should also prompt further work and reflection. The first is the locus of law (and the insight of the lawyer) in mediating between the politics of the Goals and their aspiration. Many of the chapters highlight challenges in the wording of the Goals: a lack of clarity, or a divergence from the law as it is presently stated. Elsewhere, there is discussion of problems of implementation and monitoring. Finally, some seek to conceptualise how the Goals might be strengthened by greater integration into the normative framework, or through judicial activism. What is largely absent is the ongoing, and circular, sterile debate about the status of the Goals. Implementation is a key focus of many of the chapters and law's contribution to that. Thus, the first key theme is proactive ontology: asserting a particularly clear role for law and the lawyer in understanding, critiquing and giving effect to the Goals; not having to apologise for invading the academic space of others, but revealing how law as a discipline is continually evolving to give it insight and tools on the most social, political and global of topics.

Second, many of the chapters place the Goals within a broader, and a more structural, context. The Goals raise wide-ranging questions of rights, responsibilities, power and alienation. They reveal systems that seemingly remain desensitised to popular claims to change. Corporate power held by too few; political, legal and bureaucratic processes that remain premised on outdated notions of rights; and cultures that marginalise the other. Few suspect the Goals will bring about transformative change, though many worry that the aspirations there are in the Goals will be stymied by the systems presently in place. This is particularly evident in terms of the language and use of human rights in the Goals, which has already been alluded to. In addition, one might point to the dichotomy of the rhetoric of civil society and the continuing fragility by which civil society is able to exercise influence in many States and over global political processes. There are many other instances illustrated throughout the book. Thus, whatever they might promise, the Goals cannot change society. Whether society – in its many guises – changes the Goals is something all should be worried about.

Third, despite the claimed role of the lawyer in bringing analytical rigour to the Goals, this is no fiefdom. Above all, the Goals demand interdisciplinarity in implementation and interdisciplinarity in analysis, including aspects related to the politics of the Goals; the law surrounding them; necessary changes in technology; economic models and accountancy practices; and the sociological insights to prompt social change. These – and so many other – disciplines all have something to bring to the Goals. Each brings its own particular lens, but also its own particular baggage. But also with each, there is something to learn. As lawyers, we think we bring structure, clarity of language and a focus on implementation. Indeed we might. But ours is not the only toolkit available.

Nevertheless, a question: are we merely observers or are we (also) practitioners who, through our work, must seek to achieve real change where it is most critically required? How far do our insights contribute merely to the debate, and, more importantly, how far can they prompt real change? Interdisciplinarity is not an end in itself, a dialogue merely for the sake of a dialogue. True interdisciplinarity also has the potential for change and impact. This is not to dismiss the value of critique and analysis as a good in its own right, but if we accept – as most do – the underlying aims of the Goals (if not necessarily the Goals themselves), then our analysis should also seek to prompt wider debate and conversations; to reopen closed dialogues and epistemologies where necessary, and to broaden others. Academic inquiry has the freedom to say things which politics and deeply embedded exclusionary and marginalising neoliberal (corporate) narratives have often closed down. More so, where there is an apparent consensus. So it is with the Goals. There is arguably too much at stake not to question that which is taken for granted.

PART I

General themes

2. The Sustainable Development Goals, anthropocentrism and neoliberalism

Sam Adelman

2.1 INTRODUCTION

This chapter provides an existential critique of the Sustainable Development Goals (SDGs), also known as the Global Goals. With this aim in mind, I interrogate the meaning of sustainability, development and their concatenation in the idea of sustainable development from the Brundtland Commission's promotion of the concept in *Our Common Future* in 1987 to its current incarnation as a neoliberal form of green capitalism.[1] My critique is developed in two parts: first, through an analysis of the differences between sustainable development and ecological sustainability – sustainable development is widely embraced as a process that promotes sustainability despite the history of extractive, ecologically unsustainable economic development that prioritises economic growth over environmental protection;[2] and second, through a critique of anthropocentrism.

Endless economic growth is not sustainable if it breaches absolute biophysical limits and planetary boundaries, and ignores the rupture of the Earth system in the Anthropocene,[3] the first geological epoch in which the activities of a single species, *Homo sapiens*, have irreversibly

[1] World Commission on Environment and Development (WCED), *Our Common Future* (Oxford University Press, 1987).

[2] 'Extractivism is a nonreciprocal, dominance-based relationship with the earth, one purely of taking. It is the opposite of stewardship, which involves taking but also taking care that regeneration and future life continue.' N. Klein, *This Changes Everything: Capitalism vs. the Climate* (Simon and Schuster, 2014) 149.

[3] On planetary boundaries, see J. Rockström, W. Steffen, K. Noone et al, 'Planetary Boundaries: Exploring the Safe Operating Space for Humanity' (2009) *Ecology and Society* 14(2), 32–55; W. Steffen, K. Richardson, J. Rockström et al, 'Planetary Boundaries: Guiding Human Development on a Changing Planet' (2015) *Science* 347(6223), 1–10.

altered the geological structure of the planet. Human disturbance of the Earth system during the Great Acceleration following World War II is clear and connects the geohistory to human history with fateful consequences for all species.[4] The Anthropocene is a rupture of the Earth system that poses fundamental epistemological and ontological challenges to humankind.[5] This rupture affects all forms of development, including the mainstream understanding of sustainable development provided by the World Commission on Environment and Development 1987. I argue that ecological sustainability is incompatible with contemporary patterns of production and consumption and models of development that prioritise economic growth. The SDGs reproduce growth fetishism by promoting an intrinsically anthropocentric approach to sustainability that reinforces the long-standing criticism that sustainable development is an oxymoron. Herman Daly, a former World Bank economist and proponent of steady state economics, argues that '[t]he term sustainable growth should be rejected as a bad oxymoron'.[6]

In Section 2.2, I discuss the troubled history of sustainable development. This is followed in Section 3 by a discussion of the intrinsic anthropocentrism in international environmental and climate law reflected in the SDGs. The fourth section provides an immanent critique of the SDGs that leads to the conclusion that just as sustainable development fosters the illusion that it is possible to achieve endless economic growth and social justice while protecting the environment, so the SDGs promote the delusion that capitalism is the solution rather than

---

[4] Earth system thinking systematically and systemically conceives the planet as a single unified, integrated and constantly changing entity rather than a collection of ecosystems. See J. Zalasiewicz, P. Crutzen and W. Steffen, 'The Anthropocene' in F.M. Gladstein, J.G. Ogg, M. Schmitz and G. Ogg (eds), *The Geologic Time Scale* (Elsevier, 2012), 1033–1040 and J. Zalasiewicz, M. Williams, W. Steffen and P. Crutzen, 'The New World of the Anthropocene' (2010) *Environmental Science and Technology* 44(7), 2228–2231. On history in the Anthropocene, see D. Chakrabarty, 'The Climate of History: Four Theses' (2009) *Critical Inquiry* 35, 197–222.

[5] P.J. Crutzen, 'Geology of Mankind' (2002) *Nature* 415.6867, 23, at 23.

[6] H.E. Daly, 'Toward Some Operational Principles of Sustainable Development' (1990) *Ecological Economics* 2(1), 1. See also W. Sachs, 'Sustainable Development: On the Political Anatomy of an Oxymoron' in W. Sachs, *Planet Dialectics: Explorations in Environment and Development* (Zed Books, 1999); M. Redclift, 'Sustainable Development (1987–2005): An Oxymoron Comes of Age' (2005) *Sustainable Development* 13(4), 212–227; U. Brand, 'Green Economy – the Next Oxymoron? No Lessons Learned from Failures of Implementing Sustainable Development' (2012) *GAIA* 21(1), 28–32.

the cause of the rupture in the Earth system and the ecological degradation and destruction that accompanies it.

2.2 THE PATH FROM DEVELOPMENT TO SUSTAINABLE DEVELOPMENT

After World War II, development was promoted as the means whereby what was then referred to as the Third World could achieve economic growth, reduce poverty and promote social justice. In principle, development is a process of social change designed to improve the well-being of people. In practice, it has regularly manifested itself as underdevelopment or maldevelopment so that its scope and rationale have been vigorously contested. As Björn Hettne observes, it is 'one of the oldest and most powerful of all Western ideas' and is closely associated with growth and progress from backwardness to modernity,[7] and an almost teleological process of modernisation.[8] As Westernisation, it was designed to incorporate developing countries into global capitalism; in the Soviet model, it was the path to socialism. Ecological sustainability was not a priority in either paradigm. In the 1970s and 1980s, dependency and world systems theorists cogently argued that the development of the West depended upon long histories of colonialism and imperialism that incorporated what was then called the Third World into the global political economy on unequal terms.[9] Walter Rodney famously argued that Europe 'underdeveloped' Africa in pursuit of raw materials and profits, creating structural inequalities that persist to the present day.[10] Such arguments reflected the significant anti-development or post-development backlash that emerged in the last quarter of the twentieth century. For example, Arturo Escobar deployed Michel Foucault's concept of power to argue that development is a power–knowledge nexus ostensibly designed to save the victims of underdevelopment from themselves while protecting the interests of the superpowers during the Cold War. Developmentalism

---

[7] B. Hettne, *Development Theory and the Three Worlds: Towards an International Political Economy of Development* (Longman, 1995) 29.

[8] See W.W. Rostow, *The Stages of Economic Growth: A Non-Communist Manifesto* (Cambridge University Press, 1999).

[9] A.G. Frank, 'The Development of Underdevelopment' in S.M. Wheeler and T. Beatley (eds), *The Sustainable Urban Development Reader* (Routledge, 2004).

[10] W. Rodney, *How Europe Underdeveloped Africa* (Bogle-L'Ouverture, 1972).

became an almost evangelical ideology of salvation through industrialisation, modernisation and integration into the global political economy through free trade and the exploitation of natural resources.[11] It was a process that Wolfgang Sachs described as intrinsically and inexorably destructive of the environment and, we might add, that heightens risks to vulnerable communities.[12]

Hettne writes that '[d]evelopment is a contested concept, which implies that it has meant different things from one historical situation to another and from one actor to another'.[13] One of the major criticisms levelled against the concept is that it has seldom been 'owned' by those subjected to it and too often been imposed on populations through violent forms of neo-colonialism and imperialism that repeatedly resulted in chronic socio-political, economic and environmental crises. Gustavo Esteva argues that '[t]he metaphor of development gave global hegemony to a purely Western genealogy of history, robbing peoples of different cultures of the opportunity to define the forms of their social life'. It is a concept that cannot 'delink itself from the words with which it was formed-growth, evolution, maturation' and has become totemic – a magic solution to the problems that confront us. But for many people 'this positive meaning of the word "development" … is a reminder of what they are not … To escape from it, they need to be enslaved to others' experiences and dreams.'[14] To the objects of development in the global South, it has always been a Eurocentric, technocratic, depoliticising concept.

In response to persistent criticism, the dominant idea of development metamorphosed under the aegis of the World Bank, the International Monetary Fund (IMF) and the World Trade Organization (WTO) into human-centred development (influenced by Amartya Sen's conception of development as freedom) and latterly as sustainable development, but

---

[11] A. Escobar, *Encountering Development: The Making and Unmaking of the Third World* (Princeton University Press, 2011). See also G. Esteva, 'Development' in W. Sachs (ed), *The Development Dictionary: A Guide to Knowledge as Power* (Zed Books, 1992).

[12] W. Sachs, 'Environment' in W. Sachs (ed), *The Development Dictionary: A Guide to Knowledge as Power* (Zed Books, 1992) 24–37.

[13] B. Hettne, *Thinking About Development: Development Matters* (Zed Books, 2009) 1.

[14] Esteva, above n 11, 9, 10.

economic growth has remained central.[15] The emergence of neoliberalism in the early 1980s marked a crucial turning point. Hitherto, development had generally been understood as a state-driven process; afterwards, the so-called Washington consensus promoted dogmatic market fundamentalism, which demanded privatisation, deregulation, free trade in pursuit of endless economic growth, the sanctity of private protection, and protection of contractual and investor rights.[16] Eduardo Gudynas's argument that the classical Western idea of development has been declared dead several times in the last decades but persists in a zombie form applies equally to the neoliberal ideology that infects sustainable development.[17]

Neoclassical (especially neoliberal) economists view economic growth as essential and inevitable. Well-being is clearly linked to economic activity, but it is quality rather than the quantity that is crucial. As Kate Raworth observes, nothing in nature grows forever;[18] uncontrollable growth is cancerous. Since growth is hardwired into the logic of capitalism, we are confronted with a conundrum: whether it is possible to achieve ecological sustainability in a mode of production that impels the breaching of planetary boundaries and if so, whether capitalism can be sufficiently reformed to permit this. 'The development mentality is the daily manifestation of growth fetishism',[19] as Clive Hamilton argues, because the hegemonic conception of development cannot countenance non-capitalist economic activity or commons governance.

Ramírez-Cendrero distinguishes between 'pure' post-developmental proposals such as *buen vivir* (roughly translated as living well) or those based on the rights of nature, identifies possible spaces for an alternative

[15] A. Sen, *Development as Freedom* (Oxford University Press, 2013). Sen attempted to shift the focus of development from growth to freedom and human capacities.

[16] See Baxi's analysis of the emergence of trade-related, market-friendly human rights: U. Baxi, *The Future of Human Rights* (Oxford University Press, 2012).

[17] E. Gudynas, 'Buen Vivir: Today's Tomorrow' (2011) *Development* 54(4), 441.

[18] K. Raworth, *Doughnut Economics: Seven Ways to Think Like a 21st-Century Economist* (Random House, 2017). Raworth rehearses the overwhelming arguments against using GDP as the primary measure of development, not least because of the danger this poses to the Earth system. She advocates a form of economics that addresses impoverishment within planetary limits.

[19] C. Hamilton, *Growth Fetish* (Allen and Unwin, 2003) 184.

to capitalist development, and clarifies the differences between alternatives to development and alternatives to capitalism.[20] He is sceptical that post-development models can transcend capitalism, although he recognises that 'post-developmentalist criticism has contributed decisively to the awareness of the physical and environmental limits of capitalism's production and consumption patterns … and the risks of neo-extractivism associated with new development strategies in some Latin American countries as merely new forms of capitalist modernization'.[21]

In Latin America, alternatives *to* development have emerged based upon Andean cosmovisions such as *buen vivir*. Many indigenous knowledges have no concept similar to the Western idea of development. *Buen vivir* takes several forms but all seek to dissolve the society–nature dualism in Eurocentric rationality, to overturn the notion that human beings are the only source of values, and to move beyond modernity's obsessions with growth and progress. It

> moves away from the prevalence of instrumental and manipulative rationality. It rejects the modern stance that almost everything should be dominated and controlled, either persons or Nature, so as to become a means to our ends. Furthermore, the Buen Vivir does not endorse the classical understanding of a unidirectional linear progression of history, following a precise path, as several directions are possible.[22]

Buen vivir is intrinsically pluralistic and rejects the hierarchies and dualisms that characterise Western philosophy, but has nevertheless evolved to incorporate aspects of Western thinking where they are not antithetical, such as Western science. Its salience to sustainability flows from the conviction that well-being is only possible within a community in harmony with nature, symbolised by the centrality in its axiology of *Pachamama* (Mother Earth), the source of life. *Buen vivir* 'calls for a "biocentric" understanding of life in which Nature has rights of its own and an intrinsic significance regardless of its value for human life'.[23] As

---

[20] There is a significant difference between alternative development and alternatives to development. Whereas the former envisages development in a different form, the latter rejects the concept of development as irredeemable.

[21] J.M. Ramírez-Cendrero, 'Limits and Contradictions of Post-developmentalism as a Heterodox Approach to Capitalist Development' (2017) *Capitalism Nature Socialism*, <https://doi.org/10.1080/10455752.2017.1334220> at 15.

[22] Gudynas, above n 17, 445.

[23] R. Ramírez, 'La Transición Ecuatoriana Hacía El Buen Vivir' in I. León (ed), *Sumak Kawsay/Buen Vivir y Cambios Civilizatorios* (FEDAEPS, 2010) 24.

such, it provides a coherent critique of modernity and hegemonic theories of development that rejects the reduction of human identity to a *homo economicus* defined by material consumption. It has a strong communitarian ethos that promotes substantive participatory democracy and progressive visions of social, environmental and climate justice.[24] *Buen vivir* has been incorporated into the constitutions of Ecuador (2008) and Bolivia (2009), albeit in contradictory ways.[25] Above all, it promotes a conception of what sustainable development might mean that is markedly different to mainstream Western understandings.

2.2.1 Sustainable Development

Sustainable development is a deceptively simple idea that is widely incorporated in domestic and international environmental law, but its meaning is contested. An obvious reading is that it is development that is sustained in the sense that it endures over a period of time, but it is more commonly understood as development 'causing little or no damage to the environment and therefore able to continue for a long time'.[26] The widespread purchase of this inaccurate perception illustrates the extent to which it has successfully been inculcated in public consciousness as an environmentally friendly process.

Sustainable development emerged, albeit indirectly, at the 1972 UN Conference on the Human Environment in Stockholm. The preamble is notably anthropocentric, linking the importance of protecting the environment to its impact on 'the well-being of peoples and economic

---

[24] A. Acosta, 'El Buen (con) Vivir, Una Utopıa Por (Re)construir: Alcances de la Constitucion de Montecristi' (2010) OBETS. *Revista de Ciencias Sociales*, 6(1), 35–67; A. Acosta and E. Gudynas, 'La Renovacion de la Crıtica al Desarrollo y El Buen Vivircomo Alternativa' (2011) *Utopıa y Praxis Latinoamericana* 16(53), 71–83 <http://www.gudynas.com/publicaciones/GudynasAcostaCriticaDesarrolloBVivirUtopia11.pdf> accessed 15 May 2017; A. Escobar, 'Sustainability: Design for the Pluriverse' (2011) *Development* 54(2), 137–140.

[25] The Ecuadorian Constitution guarantees the rights of *buen vivir* (articles 12–34) and grants rights to nature (articles 71–74). *Constitución Política de la República del Ecuador*, 20 October 2008. In Bolivia, *buen vivir* informs the 2009 Constitution, which does not grant rights to nature. However, *Pachamama* is protected under the Law of the Rights of Mother Earth (Law 071 of the Plurinational State) passed by the Plurinational Legislative Assembly on 21 December 2010.

[26] Cambridge English Dictionary <http://dictionary.cambridge.org/dictionary/englısh/sustaınable> accessed 5 May 2017.

development throughout the world'.[27] It became a leitmotif in *Our Common Future* in 1987 and the centrepiece of Agenda 21, a non-binding document adopted at the 1992 United Nations Conference on Environment and Development in Rio de Janeiro, from which the Convention on Biological Diversity, the United Nations Convention to Combat Desertification and the UN Framework Convention on Climate Change emerged. In 2002, the World Summit on Sustainable Development held in Johannesburg produced non-binding declarations on sustainable consumption and production, water and sanitation, and energy. Principle 4 in the Rio Declaration makes it clear that '[i]n order to achieve sustainable development, environmental protection shall constitute an integral part of the development process and cannot be considered in isolation from it', but Principle 12 requires states to 'cooperate to promote a supportive and open international economic system that would lead to economic growth and sustainable development in all countries'. Twenty years later, the 'Common Vision' of the Rio+20 summit in 2012 reaffirmed 'the need to achieve sustainable development by: promoting sustained, inclusive and equitable economic growth'.[28]

The Brundtland Commission defined sustainable development as 'development that meets the needs of present generations without compromising the ability of future generations to meet their own needs',[29] and this has become the dominant framing in a formulation that proffered the possibility of integrating 'economic development, social justice and environmental protection in a virtuous circle on the one hand, and a means of overcoming the physical limits of the biosphere through market solutions on the other'.[30] Within five years of the publication of *Our Common Future*, more than 70 definitions of sustainable development had been proposed, demonstrating the chameleon-like capacity of the concept to mean all things to all people, but it is this vague capaciousness that enables states and transnational corporations to greenwash unsustainable activities by misleading the public about the environmental impacts

---

[27] Stockholm Declaration of the United Nations Conference on the Human Environment, UN Doc. A/Conf.48/14/Rev. 1(1973); 11 ILM 1416 (1972).

[28] Emphases supplied. Rio Declaration on Environment and Development (A/CONF.151/26, vol. I) and Agenda 21 (A/CONF.151/26, vol. II), adopted by the United Nations Conference on Environment and Development, 14 June 1992; United Nations Conference on Sustainable Development Outcome Document: The Future We Want, 20 to 22 June 2012. A/RES/66/288.

[29] WCED, above n 1, 43.

[30] S. Adelman, 'Rio+20: Sustainable Injustice in a Time of Crises' (2013) *Journal of Human Rights and the Environment* 4(1), 6–31 at 11.

of their products or services.[31] Most of these definitions perpetuate instrumental rationality, progress and economic growth and they conceive nature as capital. Sustainable development has been described as 'economic development that is complementary to environment and society, as a process of development that emphasises intergenerational equity or as a process of ensuring environmental services on a very long-term basis';[32] but as Ruth Gordon argues, it 'appears to address what is essentially an enigma without meaningfully challenging existing power structures or the impact that the modern quest for a higher material standard of living has had on the natural world'.[33]

The Commission treated development and sustainability as commensurate and interchangeable, and viewed poverty rather than unrestrained extractive industrialisation as the main enemy of sustainable ecosystems. It viewed poverty as a cause rather than a symptom of unsustainability and its solution was to encompass environmental issues within sustainable development rather than changing the dominant model of development. This is explicit from the outset: 'What is needed now is a new era of economic growth – growth that is forceful and at the same time socially and environmentally sustainable'.[34] The Brundtland Report focused on the core concepts of needs and 'limitations imposed by the state of technology and social organization on the environment's ability to meet present and future needs' rather than biophysical limits and planetary boundaries.[35] It considered the needs of current and future generations but not those of other species. In the view of Imran et al, its

---

[31] J. Holmberg and R. Sandbrook, 'Sustainable Development: What Is To Be Done?' in J. Holmberg (ed), *Policies for a Small Planet* (Earthscan, 1992) 19–38. A notorious recent example is the measures taken by car manufacturers to defeat emissions tests for diesel cars: J.K. Lynes, 'Volkswagen Committed the Cardinal Sin of Greenwashing: Lying', *The Globe and Mail*, 24 September 2015 <https://www.theglobeandmail.com/report-on-business/rob-commentary/volkswagen-committed-the-cardinal-sin-of-greenwashing-lying/article26500698/> accessed 27 June 2017.

[32] E. Kumi, A.A. Arhin and T. Yeboah, 'Can Post-2015 Sustainable Development Goals Survive Neoliberalism? A Critical Examination of the Sustainable Development-Nexus in Developing Countries' (2014) *Environment Development and Sustainability* 16, 539–554 at 544.

[33] R. Gordon, 'Unsustainable Development' in S. Alam, S. Atapattu, C.G. Gonzalez and J. Razzaque (eds), *International Environmental Law and the Global South* (Cambridge University Press, 2015) 63.

[34] WCED, above n 1, xii.

[35] *Ibid* at 43.

'anthropocentric approach fails to adequately acknowledge the relationship of environmental crises to environmental ethics and values ... [and] it does not adequately recognize the ecological limits of natural capital – i.e. the boundary beyond which exploitation of a natural resource will have significant irreversible impacts'.[36] This anthropocentrism is reflected in the report's treatment of species and ecosystems as resources for development in assertions such as 'Conservation of living natural resources is ... crucial for development.'[37] The report accepts that conservation 'is not only justified in economic terms'[38] but the aesthetic, ethical, cultural and scientific justifications it provides are also markedly anthropocentric.

The Brundtland Commission sought to reconcile economic growth, social equity and environmental protection (the so-called the triple bottom line) in a single concept. Four decades later, in a world scarred by inequality, looming climate catastrophe and the rupture to the Earth system, sustainable development's 'success' is still predominantly measured in terms of economic growth. The concept has been condemned for fostering the illusion that endless growth is possible on a finite planet but as Haydn Washington argues, '[i]n a finite world, we need to accept once and for all that sustainability *cannot* be about further growth. This challenge remains critical, though still denied.'[39]

Escobar argues that sustainable development emerged through the

> problematization of global survival, a process which induces a re-working of the relationship between nature and society. This problematization appeared as a response to the destructive character of development, on the one hand, and the rise of environmental movements in both the North and the South, on the other ... [t]he ecodevelopmentalist vision expressed in mainstream versions of sustainable development reproduces central aspects of economism and developmentalism.[40]

---

[36] S. Imran, K. Alam and N. Beaumont, 'Reinterpreting the Definition of Sustainable Development for a More Ecocentric Reorientation' (2014) *Sustainable Development* 22, 134–144 at 135.

[37] WCED, above n 1, 147.

[38] *Ibid* at 155.

[39] H. Washington, *Demystifying Sustainability: Towards Real Solutions* (Earthscan, 2015) 36 (emphasis in original).

[40] A. Escobar, 'Constructing Nature: Elements for a Post-structural Political Ecology' in R. Peet and M. Watts (eds), *Liberation Ecologies: Environment, Development, Social Movements* (Routledge, 1996) 51–52.

He argues that it 'focuses not so much on the negative consequences of economic growth on the environment, as on the effects of environmental degradation on growth and the potential for growth'.[41] Redclift contends that sustainable development 'was coined in the 1980s to meet contradictions in policy and practice, and to "square the circle" of resource conservation and economic growth … [but in practice] has been advocated primarily as a means of subordinating nature to economic growth'.[42] In a similar vein, Sachs writes that it 'promises nothing less than to square the circle: to identify a type of development that promotes both ecological sustainability and international justice' in a formula 'designed to maximize consensus rather than clarity'.[43] Sachs argues that the Brundtland Report failed to address the crisis of justice arising from unsustainable development and moved quickly from the conservation of nature to the conservation of growth.[44] Seeking to maximise acceptance of the concept, the World Commission on Environment and Development provided capitalism with a conceptual basis and an ethical/normative justification for the commodification and monetisation of nature.

Withering criticism of this kind has not deterred proponents of ecomodern developmentalism such as Jeffrey Sachs, who declaims that we have entered the era of 'the Age of Sustainable Development', 'a world in which economic progress is widespread; extreme poverty is eliminated; social trust is encouraged … and the environment is protected from human-induced degradation'.[45] Sachs believes that salvation does not require trade-offs between getting rich and saving the planet, but instead lies in the virtuous synergies that technology can deliver. A more realistic perspective is provided by advocates of degrowth who disparage the faith that discourses of ecological modernisation place in the role of markets, pointing to the deficiencies of carbon markets and the likelihood that decarbonisation will be cancelled out by unceasing economic growth. They argue that it is possible to achieve sustainable degrowth

---

41 *Ibid* at 54.

42 M. Redclift and G. Woodgate, 'Sustainable Development and Nature: The Social and the Material' (2013) *Sustainable Development* 21(2), 92–100 at 92.

43 W. Sachs, 'Sustainable Development and the Crisis of Nature: On the Political Anatomy of an Oxymoron' in F. Fisher and M.A. Hajer (eds), *Living with Nature: Environmental Politics as Cultural Discourse* (Oxford University Press, 1999) 25–26.

44 *Ibid* at 29.

45 J. Sachs, *The Age of Sustainable Development* (University of Columbia Press, 2015) 3. The term Anthropocene appears three times in 543 pages.

through the 'equitable downscaling of production and consumption that increases human well-being and enhances ecological conditions at the local and global level, in the short and long term'.[46] Healy et al write that

> [t]he promises of ecological modernization (i.e. dematerialization of the economy, economic growth linked to lower environmental impacts, win–win sustainable economic development) cannot be fulfilled. On the contrary, these promises and the assumptions on which they are based have evolved into discourses that legitimize the opening up of new spheres of capital circulation and accumulation. The ascendancy of the rhetoric of the 'green economy' or even 'green growth', and the promotion of markets for carbon and ecosystem services, illustrate this well.[47]

As a core discourse of ecological modernisation, sustainable development frames eco-political issues such as climate change, biodiversity loss and ecological degradation 'as matters of scientific knowledge, technological innovation, and managerial perfection – an effort that has always been central to the paradigm of sustainability and the policy approaches of ecological modernization' as a means of depoliticising them.[48] In Erik Swyngedouw's words, 'Vague concepts like climate change policy, biodiversity policy or "sustainability" replace proper names in politics' so that '[p]ost-political climate governance does not solve problems; it

---

[46] F. Schneider, G. Kallis and J. Martínez-Alier, 'Crisis or Opportunity? Economic Degrowth for Social Equity and Ecological Sustainability. Introduction to this Special Issue' (2010) *Journal of Cleaner Production* 18(6), 511–518 at 512. See also A. Escobar, 'De-growth, Post-development, and Transitions: A Preliminary Conversation' (2015) *Sustainability Science* 10(3), 451–462; J. Martínez-Alier, U. Pascual, F.D. Vivien and E. Zaccai, 'Sustainable De-growth: Mapping the Context, Criticisms and Future Prospects of an Emergent Paradigm' (2010) *Ecological Economics* 69(9), 1741–1747; T. Jackson, *Prosperity Without Growth: Economics for a Finite Planet* (Earthscan, 2009).

[47] H. Healy, J. Martínez-Alier and G. Kallis, 'From Ecological Modernization to Socially Sustainable Economic De-growth: Lessons from Ecological Economics' in R.L. Bryant (ed), *The International Handbook of Political Ecology* (Edward Elgar Publishing, 2015) 586. Ecomodernists are prominent among those celebrating the possibility of a 'good' Anthropocene made possible by techno-fixes such as geoengineering, terraforming, etc. See C. Hamilton, 'The Theodicy of the "Good Anthropocene"' (2015) *Environmental Humanities* 7(1), 233–238. On green economy, see Adelman, above n 30.

[48] I. Blühdorn, 'Sustainability – Post-sustainability – Unsustainability' in T. Gabrielson, C. Hall, J.M. Meyer and D. Schlosberg (eds), *The Oxford Handbook of Environmental Political Theory* (Oxford University Press, 2016) 268.

moves them around'.[49] Environmental problems are addressed through environmental legislation or technological fixes frequently accompanied by market-based instruments.[50] Maarten Hajer, a leading ecological modernisation theorist, acknowledges that sustainable development does not call for structural change and is 'basically a modernist and technocratic approach to the environment that suggests that there is a techno-institutional fix for the present problems ... [it] does not address the systemic features of capitalism that make the system inherently wasteful and unmanageable.'[51]

A decade after the euphemistically styled Great Recession, neoliberalism lives on zombie-like, incapable of providing viable responses to either sustainability or development, but seemingly incapable of being consigned to the dustbin of history.[52] David Harvey describes neoliberal economics as an ideological smokescreen designed to conceal a more fundamental class project of accumulation by dispossession through private appropriation of the commons.[53] Ecological sustainability will not be delivered by neoliberalism and it cannot be achieved through the dystopian anthropocentrism that disfigured the Holocene but is perpetuated by the SDGs.

---

49 E. Swyngedouw, 'Depoliticized Environment and the Promises of the Anthropocene' in R.L. Bryant (ed), *The International Handbook of Political Ecology* (Edward Elgar Publishing, 2015) 140.

50 I. Bailey, A. Gouldson and P. Newell, 'Ecological Modernisation and the Governance of Carbon: A Critical Analysis' (2011) *Antipode* 43, 682–703.

51 A.P.J. Mol and D.A. Sonnenfeld, 'Ecological Modernisation Theory in Debate' in A.P.J. Mol and D.A. Sonnenfeld (eds), *Ecological Modernisation Around the World: Perspectives and Critical Debates* (Psychology Press, 2000) 17–49 at 22. Mol and Hajer quoted in O. Langhelle, 'Why Ecological Modernisation and Sustainable Development Should Not Be Conflated' in G. Spaargaren, D.A. Sonnenfeld and A.P.J. Mol (eds), *The Ecological Modernisation Reader: Environmental Reform in Theory and Practice* (Routledge, 2010) 402–405, at 414.

52 C. Crouch, *The Strange Non-Death of Neoliberalism* (Polity, 2011).

53 D. Harvey, *A Brief History of Neoliberalism* (Oxford University Press, 2007).

2.3 ANTHROPOCENTRISM

Law is deeply, intrinsically and persistently anthropocentric.[54] As Klaus Bosselmann puts it, 'The law cements the view that only humans matter and the environment has just instrumental value – a view with grave ecological blindness.'[55] Law has been instrumental in naturalising the idea of nature as property over which human beings have dominion. Private property is a foundational concept in Western domestic law and international law, a consistent trope in which land and nature are primarily conceived as objects of ownership. Burdon argues that property rights epitomise Eurocentric approaches to the environment that justify humanity's right to exploit and expropriate nature.[56] In short, law legitimises the idea that nature exists solely to serve the needs of human beings. Earth jurisprudence, Wild Law and Law for Nature are prominent among emergent legal philosophies that seek to correct the deep anthropocentrism of law.[57]

Anthropocentrism is the 'idea that human interests, human goods and/or human values are the focal point of any moral evaluation of environmental policy and the idea that these human interests, goods and values are the basis of any justification of an environmental ethic'.[58] Human beings exploit nature because they have come to conceive it as existing for their own personal benefit through unsustainable epistemologies of mastery and ideologies such as neoliberalism that are legitimated by anthropocentric legal systems.[59] We may perforce think as *Anthropos*

---

[54] On mechanical jurisprudence, see F. Capra and U. Mattei, *The Ecology of Law: Toward a Legal System in Tune with Nature and Community* (Berrett-Koehler, 2015).

[55] K. Bosselmann, *The Principle of Sustainability: Transforming Law and Governance* (Ashgate, 2008) 135.

[56] C. Cullinan, *Wild Law: A Manifesto for Earth Justice* (Siber Ink, 2002); P.D Burdon (ed), *Exploring Wild Law: The Philosophy of Earth Jurisprudence* (Wakefield Press, 2011); P.D. Burdon, *Earth Jurisprudence: Private Property and the Environment* (Routledge, 2015). See also A. Grear, 'Human Rights, Property and the Search for "Worlds Other"' (2012) *Journal of Human Rights and the Environment* 3(2), 173–195.

[57] V. De Lucia, 'Towards an Ecological Philosophy of Law: A Comparative Discussion' (2013) *Journal of Human Rights and the Environment* 4(2), 167–190.

[58] E. Katz, 'A Pragmatic Reconsideration of Anthropocentrism' (1999) *Environmental Ethics* 21, 377–390 at 377–378.

[59] S. Adelman, 'Epistemologies of Mastery' in A. Grear and L.J. Kotzé (eds), *Research Handbook on Human Rights and the Environment* (Edward Elgar Publishing, 2015) 9–27.

but human cognitive abilities do not lead ineluctably either to anthropocentrism or the correct identification of long-term human needs and interests.[60] Indeed, the plethora of onto-epistemologies and the differential power to materialise illustrates the danger of treating *Anthropos* as a homogeneous, undifferentiated entity.[61] Moreover, it is not inevitable that anthropocentrism will result in speciesism on the one hand or misanthropy on the other.[62] The freedom to reason enables *Homo sapiens* to choose to embrace onto-epistemologies that give precedence to Gaia.[63]

Despite these caveats, anthropocentrism is generally regarded as problematic on several grounds. Deontological thinkers believe it is wrong when it is negatively motivated, for example harming other species. Immanuel Kant argued that right action is motivated by a sense of duty derived from the categorical imperative. Virtue ethics holds that actions may not be negatively motivated but may still be regarded as intrinsically wrong if they fail to give equal value to the needs and interests of other species and the biosphere. Arguments for sustainability are made on the

---

[60] On the nature of Anthropos, see A. Grear, 'Deconstructing Anthropos: A Critical Legal Reflection on "Anthropocentric" Law and Anthropocene "Humanity"' (2015) *Law and Critique* 26(3), 225–249; A. Grear, '"Anthropocene, Capitalocene, Chthulucene": Re-encountering Environmental Law and its "Subject" with Haraway and New Materialism' in L.J. Kotzé (ed), *Environmental Law and Governance for the Anthropocene* (Hart, 2017) 77–96.

[61] J. Moore is among those who argue that the idea of the Anthropocene is problematic because it does not give sufficient weight to the reality that a particular mode of production has successfully reinforced anthropocentric epistemologies already at work in religious, economic and political philosophies: J.W. Moore, 'The Capitalocene, Part I: On the Nature and Origins of Our Ecological Crisis' (2017) *The Journal of Peasant Studies* 44(3), 594–630. I agree with this position but use Anthropocene for the reason advanced by Donna Haraway, that it is well entrenched and seems less controversial than Capitalocene for many important players: D.J. Haraway, 'Staying with the Trouble: Anthropocene, Capitalocene, Chthulucene' in J.W. Moore (ed), *Anthropocene or Capitalocene? Nature, History, and the Crisis of Capitalism* (PM Press, 2016) 34–76.

[62] See O. O'Neill, 'Environmental Values, Anthropocentrism and Speciesism' (1997) *Environmental Values* 6, 127–142.

[63] J. Lovelock, *The Revenge of Gaia* (Allen Lane, 2006). The Gaia hypothesis was initially proposed by Lovelock in the 1970s. Named after the Greek goddess of the Earth, it argues that the advent of life on the planet generated a homeostatic tendency to regulate the biosphere in ways favourable to the development and maintenance of life. It gained wide public traction but is scientifically controversial. See M. Ruse, *The Gaia Hypothesis: Science on a Pagan Planet* (University of Chicago Press, 2013).

basis of obligation and virtue but the literature on sustainability, climate change and the Anthropocene increasingly reflects consequentialist perspectives buttressed by Earth and climate science in which actions are considered right or wrong in light of their actual or probable effects.[64] Utilitarianism may be viewed as an anthropocentric version of consequentialism in which the pleasure, happiness, preferences and interests of human beings are the only relevant factors in assessing the correctness of actions.[65] In the Brundtland Report, sustainable development is 'explicitly rooted in a utilitarian and social philosophy that reflects a form of enlightened self-interest, conserving land and resources for later human use'.[66] As neoliberal economics has demonstrated, this is a short step away from cost-benefit analyses that put a price on nature but cannot value it in non-monetary terms.

Consequentialist theories differ according to the ways in which they deem actions to be right or wrong, whether such actions are evaluated on individual or collective bases, and the knowledge that agents have about potential consequences. The negative ecological consequences of the Anthropocene orient much philosophical thinking but consequentialism does not offer simple answers to unsustainability. As we have seen, ecomodernists who comprehend the scale of the planetary emergency nevertheless resist the contention that anthropocentrism is the source of climate and environmental harms.

---

64 There is a difference between actual and expected consequentialism, i.e. between effects or harms that have already occurred and those that can reasonably be expected to occur. Stephen Gardiner argues that virtue ethics rather than consequentialist or deontological approaches are most appropriate to climate change because ethics is 'not only about our relationships with other morally important entities, it is also about *who we are*'. S.M. Gardiner, 'Are We the Scum of the Earth? Climate Change, Geoengineering and Humanity's Challenge' in A. Thompson and J. Bendik-Meyer (eds), *Ethical Adaptation to Climate Change: Human Virtues of the Future* (The MIT Press, 2012) 241–259, at 242; emphasis in original. On geoengineering and consequentialism, see S. Adelman, 'Geoengineering: Rights, Risks and Ethics' (2017) *Journal of Human Rights and the Environment* 8(1), 119–138.

65 The work of Peter Singer demonstrates that this form of consequentialism is not necessarily confined to human beings but can be extended to sentient beings. See for example, P. Singer, *Practical Ethics* (Cambridge University Press, 2011). Jeremy Bentham and John Stuart Mill gave consideration to other species but remained resolutely anthropocentric: P.G. Brown, 'Are There Any Natural Resources?' (2004) *Politics and the Life Sciences* 23(1), 12–21.

66 Imran et al, above n 36, 136.

Ecocentrism seeks to overcome the inherent anthropocentrism of Western modernity arising from the Cartesian separation of society and nature and the Baconian treatment of the environment as a set of resources that exist to service humanity.[67] It sees intrinsic and moral value in nature, on which all living beings depend for survival, and views the Earth and the universe as an interconnected and interdependent web of sub-systems.[68] Because human history and the geohistory are now inextricably linked and human agency has epochal geological consequences, it follows that anthropocentrism that correctly identifies the interests of current and future generations must paradoxically be premised upon a radical ecocentrism because human well-being is contingent upon the health of the Earth system. In this perspective, ecocentrism becomes a form of anthropocentrism.[69]

For Donna Haraway, counterposing anthropocentrism and ecocentrism reflects a failure to comprehend the scale of the harms and changes we confront. Thinking in terms of the Anthropocene is *too* anthropocentric because it privileges 'human exceptionalism' in ways that occlude the nature of the problem as well as possible solutions. Haraway rejects both Anthropocene and Capitalocene in favour of thinking about and beyond the human, the non-human and the inhuman on the Chthulucene, the new Earth that requires new thinking.[70] Haraway excoriates those who naively fetishise technoscience, climate change catastrophists who foreclose possibilities, and those who do not adequately respect other species, the optimists who threaten to unleash hubristic anthropocentric techno-fixes such as geoengineering in pursuit of illusions of mastery, and the

---

[67] See Adelman, above n 59.

[68] 'Ecocentrism goes beyond biocentrism (ethics that sees inherent value to all living things) by including environmental systems as wholes, and their abiotic aspects. It also goes beyond zoocentrism (seeing value in animals) on account of explicitly including flora and the ecological contexts for organisms', H. Washington, B. Taylor, H.N. Kopnina, et al, 'Why Ecocentrism is the Key Pathway to Sustainability' (2017) *The Ecological Citizen* 1. Kopnina argues that 'moral ecocentrism is necessary if the interests of nonhumans are to be protected outside of utilitarian interests': H. Kopnina, 'The Victims of Unsustainability: A Challenge to Sustainable Development Goals' (2016) *International Journal of Sustainable Development and World Ecology* 23(2), 113–121 at 4.

[69] On the relationship between ecocentrism and deep ecology, see H. Kopnina, 'The Lorax Complex: Deep Ecology, Ecocentrism and Exclusion' (2012) *Journal of Integrative Environmental Sciences* 9(4), 235–254.

[70] A concept derived from the Greek *khthon*, 'of the earth' and *kainos*, 'completely new'.

pessimists who are unwilling to think sympoietically about systems that are complex, self-organising, collectively producing and boundaryless.[71]

A more conventional approach is taken by Clive Hamilton, who argues that it is now too late to think about anthropocentrism with the intellectual tools of the Holocene because the Anthropocene has fundamentally altered what it means to be human. Since *Anthropos* has misidentified its interests, a new, reconceptualised anthropocentrism is required because the only way to promote human interests is by protecting the Earth system through a more rigorous, self-conscious anthropocentrism.[72] More rather than less anthropocentrism is required to grasp both the immensity of the power humankind has accrued and the enormity of the obligations this imposes. Critiquing post-humanist thinking, Hamilton distinguishes between anthropocentrism as scientific fact and as normative claim and argues that the rupture to the Earth system means that it is too late to abandon anthropocentrism even if it were possible to do so. 'The original fault in the growth-driven techno-industrial system is its *monstrous* anthropocentrism rather than its anthropocentrism as such. The problem is not that human beings are anthropocentric, but that *we are not anthropocentric enough*.'[73]

Hamilton contends that only by recognising the super-agency that humankind has acquired as a geological agent can *Homo sapiens* accept the consequences of its behaviour and a commensurate level of responsibility needed to protect the biosphere and its biota. This new anthropocentrism, which can only emanate from an acknowledgement of the embeddedness of *Anthropos* in nature-as-a-whole, offers hope that it is still possible that human beings may use their immense, planetary-changing powers to enhance rather than destroy the Earth system. The singular prize of the Enlightenment, our freedom to reason, is also freedom to choose to turn away from the calamitous path of capitalism. Hamilton counterposes his anthropocentrism to hubristic Promethean ecomodernist thinking, which he regards as misanthropic rather than

---

[71] D.J. Haraway, *Staying with the Trouble: Making Kin in the Chthulucene* (Duke University Press, 2016). See also Grear, above n 60.

[72] C. Hamilton, *Defiant Earth: The Fate of Humans in the Anthropocene* (Polity, 2017). I paraphrase Hamilton's terminology, which tends to treat human beings in an undifferentiated manner that ascribes equal agency and historical responsibility for the Anthropocene.

[73] *Ibid* at 43; emphases in original.

anthropocentric when it advocates solutions such as geoengineering that threaten the interests of humankind.[74]

In Hamilton's new anthropocentrism, the SDGs fail because they are both insufficiently yet also, too anthropocentric. On the one hand, they continue to propagate an anthropocentric conception of development that does not adequately address the nature and scale of the rupture of the Anthropocene. On the other, they are not anthropocentric enough because they fail to acknowledge and accept the responsibilities that come with human agency on a geological scale and the irrefragable logic that follows now that the interests of the Earth system and humanity coincide completely, if temporarily, with the collision of human history and geohistory. The following section analyses the SDGs as a Holocene anachronism.

2.4 THE SUSTAINABLE DEVELOPMENT GOALS

With the Millennium Development Goals (MDGs) due to expire in 2015, preparatory work on the SDGs began at the Rio+20 summit in 2012. The outcome document, 'The Future We Want', called for the creation of an open Working Group to prepare a geographically 'fair, equitable and balanced' proposal for the SDGs.[75] In September 2015, the non-binding SDGs were unanimously adopted by 193 members states in the UN General Assembly. Whereas the MDGs applied only to developing countries, the SDGs are global and extend the focus of international development beyond poverty to sustainability. And whereas the MDGs contained eight goals and met with mixed success, the SDGs contain 17 goals, 169 targets and 304 indicators. One study found less than a third (29 per cent) of the 169 targets to be well defined and consistent with the latest scientific evidence, that 54 per cent could be more specific, and 17 per cent to be weak.[76] Economic growth is still envisaged as the primary means of reducing poverty. Since the size of national income is valued more than the quality of economic activity and its relationship to human and ecological well-being, the SDGs hold fast to neoliberalism and thus

---

[74] Some ecomodernists terrifyingly speak about a 'good Anthropocene' in which profit can be made by using unproven technologies. Hamilton, above n 47, 233–238.

[75] UN General Assembly, 'The Future We Want', General Assembly Resolution A/RES/66/288, 27 July 2012, 64.

[76] ICSU/ISSC, *Review of the Sustainable Development Goals. The Science Perspective* (International Council for Science, 2015) 6.

fail to reconcile the contradiction between growth and sustainability at the core of sustainable development. They promote an anthropocentric approach to poverty reduction in which environmental protection is necessary only to the extent that it is consistent with growth in an extremely weak form of sustainable development.[77] Paragraph 48 in *Transforming our world: the 2030 Agenda for Sustainable Development* states that the signatory states 'are committed to developing broader measures of progress to complement gross domestic product' but it is not clear how ecological sustainability is to be measured.[78] The phrase 'harmony with nature' appears three times in a document that is resolutely anthropocentric and envisages economic growth on a scale incompatible with such harmony.[79] Samir Amin argued that the MDGs were a discourse 'intended to legitimize the policies and practices implemented by dominant capital and those who support it', a charge equally applicable to the SDGs.[80] The 2030 Agenda contains lofty ambitions and stirring rhetoric but no enforcement mechanisms.[81] The signatories

> envisage a world in which every country enjoys sustained, inclusive and sustainable economic growth and decent work for all. A world in which consumption and production patterns and use of all natural resources – from air to land, from rivers, lakes and aquifers to oceans and seas – are sustainable ... One in which humanity lives in harmony with nature and in which wildlife and other living species are protected.[82]

---

[77] On weak and strong forms of sustainable development, see B. Hopwood, M. Mellor and G. O'Brien, 'Sustainable Development: Mapping Different Approaches' (2005) *Sustainable Development* 13, 38–52.

[78] UN General Assembly, Transforming our world: the 2030 Agenda for Sustainable Development, 21 October 2015, A/RES/70/1 <http://www.refworld.org/docid/57b6e3e44.html> accessed 8 February 2017. All the paragraphs referred to in this section are from this document.

[79] The aim of Goal 12.8 is to 'ensure that people everywhere have the relevant information and awareness for sustainable development and lifestyles in harmony with nature' by 2030.

[80] S. Amin, 'The Millennium Development Goals: A Critique from the South' (2006) *Monthly Review* 57(10), 6.

[81] J.H. Spangenberg, 'Hot Air or Comprehensive Progress? A Critical Assessment of the SDGs' (2016) *Sustainable Development* 25(4), 311–321. Like the Paris Agreement, the SDGs reflect the voluntarist nature and increasingly *à la carte* nature of international law.

[82] Para 9; emphasis supplied.

On face value, the goals are praiseworthy. They include the restoration of water-related ecosystems, a halt to the loss of biodiversity, ending overfishing, deforestation and desertification, achieving sustainable cities, and combating climate change – all undoubtedly necessary for ecological sustainability. The problem lies in the implicit underlying messages in the Agenda about the aims and meaning of development, and the many contradictions between its parts and its broader aspirations.

The solutions offered ultimately fall short of effective regulation. They include 'environmentally sound management and safe use of chemicals, the reduction and recycling of waste and the more efficient use of water and energy' (para 34), halving 'capita global food waste at the retail and consumer levels' by 2030 (Goal 12.3); and encouraging 'companies, especially large and transnational companies, to adopt sustainable practices' (Goal 12.6). The overall aim of Goal 12 is to achieve 'sustainable patterns of production and consumption', which is worthy but inconsistent with the cognitively dissonant ways in which the Agenda promotes more consumption and production elsewhere.[83] The underlying logic seems to be that the failure of extractive, growth-driven development to deliver sustainability is because it has not been imposed with sufficient rigour. Thus, Goal 8 calls for increased annual GDP growth in least developed countries and higher levels of economic productivity everywhere. Remarkably, sustained unsustainability is combined in a single sentence in the call for '*sustained*, inclusive and *sustainable* economic growth, full and productive employment and decent work for all'.[84] The targets further complicate the aim of this goal. Goal 8.1 aims to '[s]ustain per capita economic growth in accordance with national circumstances and, in particular, at least 7 per cent gross domestic product growth per annum in the least developed countries' but says nothing about the logical corollary that growth in developed countries will need to substantially decrease to have any chance of meeting the 2°C target or the

---

[83] There is substantial evidence of the negative impacts of unfettered consumption on the environment. See, for example, J.B. Foster, B. Clark and R. York, *The Ecological Rift: Capitalism's War on the Earth* (Monthly Review Press, 2010); I. Angus, *Facing the Anthropocene: Fossil Capitalism and the Crisis of the Earth System* (Monthly Review Press, 2016). P. Ekins argues that a sustainable consumer society is another oxymoron: 'The Sustainable Consumer Society: A Contradiction in Terms?' (1991) *International Environmental Affairs* 3, 243–257. It has been calculated that 4.1 Earths would be required if everyone on the planet consumed as much as an average US citizen: C. McDonald, 'How Many Earths Do We Need? *BBC News*, 16 June 2015 <http://www.bbc.co.uk/news/magazine-33133712> accessed 14 February 2017.

[84] Emphases supplied.

exhortation to keep the increase in average global temperature below 1.5°C in Article 2 of the Paris Agreement on climate change (the latter being more consistent with climate science and the needs of least developed countries).

Goal 8.4 calls upon states to endeavour to decouple economic growth from environmental degradation through improvements in 'global resource efficiency in consumption and production', which is essential because, as Fletcher and Rammelt argue, 'without decoupling, the goals themselves will be unlikely to be achievable'.[85] However, there is much scepticism about the likelihood of decoupling. Ward et al use historical data and modelled projections to demonstrate how difficult it is to decouple GDP growth from increases in material and energy and argue that it 'is therefore misleading to develop growth-oriented policy around the expectation that decoupling is possible'.[86]

Paragraph 68 states that '[i]nternational trade is an engine for inclusive economic growth and poverty reduction, and contributes to the promotion of sustainable development'. It is also an engine for skewed globalisation and massive inequality, and incompatible with sustainable production and consumption. Goal 17.10 calls for *more* trade liberalisation and *more* power for the WTO. Goal 17.13 vaguely mentions the need to 'enhance global macroeconomic stability' through 'policy coordination' but provides neither specific targets nor the means for achieving this. The goal makes no mention of tax avoidance and evasion or debt service, which drain developing countries of vast amounts of income that could be spent on poverty reduction.[87] The SDGs call for 'debt financing, debt relief,

---

[85] R. Fletcher and C. Rammelt, 'Decoupling: A Key Fantasy of the Post-2015 Sustainable Development Agenda' (2016) *Globalizations* 2. T. Jackson regards decoupling as a myth that is not economically feasible. Thomas Wanner describes it as a central myth of the Green Economy agenda. Jackson, above n 46. T. Wanner, 'The New "Passive Revolution" of the Green Economy and Growth Discourse: Maintaining the "Sustainable Development" of Neoliberal Capitalism' (2015) *New Political Economy* 20(1), 21–41.

[86] J.D. Ward, P.C. Sutton, A.D. Werner et al, 'Is Decoupling GDP Growth from Environmental Impact Possible?' (2016) *PloS One* 11(10), 10 and 14.

[87] Developing countries lose about $100 billion annually due to tax avoidance by transnational corporations: Tax Justice Network, 'UNCTAD: multinational tax avoidance costs developing countries $100 billion+', 26 March 2015 <http://www.taxjustice.net/2015/03/26/unctad-multinational-tax-avoidance-costs-developing-countries-100-billion/> accessed 25 May 2017. See also C. Fuest and N. Riedel, 'Tax Evasion and Tax Avoidance in Developing Countries: The Role of International Profit Shifting' (Oxford University Centre for Business Taxation, 2010). The World Bank estimates that developing countries have paid more than

and debt restructuring, as appropriate' but not *cancellation*. Parts of the Agenda clearly read as if they were written by groups that had not been introduced to each other.

The aim of Goal 10 is to reduce inequality within and between countries but the means of achieving this envisaged goal is likely to result in ecological catastrophe. Goal 10.1 aims to 'progressively achieve and sustain income growth of the bottom 40 per cent of the population at a rate higher than the national average' by 2030, but the SDGs do not address the causes of inequality or drivers of poverty such as free trade and the structural inequalities hardwired into the global economy.[88] Goal 1.1 aims to 'eradicate extreme poverty for all people everywhere, currently measured as people living on less than $1.25 a day' by 2030 but as Jason Hickel points out, it is not possible to escape poverty on £1.25 per day.[89] Although global GDP has increased by 271 per cent since 1990, the number of people living on less than $5 a day has increased by more than 370 million, demonstrating that the link between growth and poverty reduction is tenuous. The problem is not a lack of wealth but how it is distributed, and the SDGs offer no conception of distributive justice – nor, for that matter, environmental or climate justice – although the aim of Goal 5 is to achieve 'gender equality and empower all women and girls'. The poorest 60 per cent of the global population received just 5 per cent of all new income generated by global growth between 1999 and 2008.[90] Oxfam calculates that the richest 1 per cent has owned more wealth than everybody else on the planet since 2015, eight men own the same amount of wealth as the poorest half of the world, and the incomes of the poorest 10 per cent of people grew by less than $3 a year between 1988 and 2011, while those of the richest 1 per cent increased 182 times

---

$4.2tn in interest payments since 1980 <http://data.worldbank.org/indicator/DT.INT.DECT.CD?locations=XO> accessed 25 May 2017.

[88] I.M. Wallerstein, 'After Developmentalism and Globalization, What?' (2005) *Social Forces* 83(3), 1263–1278; J. Rice, 'Ecological Unequal Exchange: Consumption, Equity, and Unsustainable Structural Relationships within the Global Economy' (2007) *International Journal of Comparative Sociology* 48(1), 43–72.

[89] J. Hickel, 'Five Reasons to Think Twice about the UN's Sustainable Development Goals' <http://blogs.lse.ac.uk/africaatlse/2015/09/23/five-reasons-to-think-twice-about-the-uns-sustainable-development-goals/> accessed 25 May 2017.

[90] The Story of Poverty <https://therules.org/campaign/the-story-of-poverty/> accessed 24 May 2017.

as much.[91] A recent study estimated that eradicating poverty will take at least 100 years at $1.25 per day and 200 years at $5 per day, and global GDP will have to exceed $100,000 per capita.[92] As Hickel argues, 'To eradicate poverty global GDP would have to increase to 175 times its present size if we go with $5/day. In other words, if we want to eradicate poverty with our current model of economic development, we need to extract, produce, and consume 175 times more commodities than we presently do.'[93] Maldevelopment of this kind that fails to address pathologies of accumulation and consumption will wreak ever greater ecological destruction and increase impoverishment as humanity hurtles down the path to madness and self-destruction.

Ariel Salleh argues that '[t]he SDG proposals are not just unrealistic but undemocratic, since the goals are to be realised by growing gross domestic product (GDP), increasing market liberalisation and free trade, as well as according more power to the World Trade Organization'.[94] In a similar vein, Heloise Weber argues that neoliberal policies are explicit goals in a 'framework that privileges commercial interests over commitments to provide universal entitlements to address fundamental life-sustaining needs. Political struggles over development will continue *against* the ideology of the SDG project and for transformative shifts for actually sustainable development.'[95]

The SDGs bring to mind an Irish joke in which a lost tourist rolls down her car window and asks a local for directions to Dublin. He rubs

---

[91] D. Hardoon, 'An Economy for the 99%: It's Time to Build a Human Economy that Benefits Everyone, Not Just the Privileged Few' (Oxfam International, 2017) <https://oxfam.app.box.com/v/an-economy-for-99-percent/1/15862322999/122574711571/1> accessed 14 February 2017, 2.

[92] D. Woodward, '*Incrementum ad Absurdum*: Global Growth, Inequality and Poverty Eradication in a Carbon-Constrained World' (2015) *World Economic Review* 4, 43–62. 'The new global poverty line is set at $1.90 using 2011 prices. Just over 900 million people globally lived under this line in 2012 (based on the latest available data), and we project that in 2015, just over 700 million are living in extreme poverty.' The World Bank <http://www.worldbank.org/en/topic/poverty/brief/global-poverty-line-faq> accessed 25 May 2017.

[93] J. Hickel, 'It Will Take 100 Years for the World's Poorest People to Earn $1.25 a Day', *The Guardian*, 30 March 2015 <https://www.theguardian.com/global-development-professionals-network/2015/mar/30/it-will-take-100-years-for-the-worlds-poorest-people-to-earn-125-a-day> accessed 24 May 2017.

[94] A. Salleh, 'Climate, Water, and Livelihood Skills: A Post-Development Reading of the SDGs' (2016) *Globalizations* 13(6), 952–959 at 953.

[95] H. Weber, 'Politics of "Leaving No One Behind": Contesting the 2030 Sustainable Development Goals Agenda' (2017) *Globalizations* 1–16 at 1 (emphasis in original).

his chin, thinks for a moment, and says 'I wouldn't start from here.' In the Anthropocene, the point of departure for the goals should surely have been ecological sustainability rather than development. Starting with development as growth precludes ecological sustainability; starting with sustainability opens up a range of alternatives more likely to reduce poverty and promote social justice. Starting from 'here' with development subordinates the Earth system, most of the global population and all other species to the 'needs' of the economy. After all, it is possible to measure the health of the atmosphere, ecosystems, oceans and species with increasing precision and to set targets in international environmental governance instruments such as the SDGs.[96] Starting from 'here' reproduces the fallacies of modernity and Holocene thinking. Starting from 'here' reinforces neoliberal dogma and market fundamentalism by insisting that economic development requires free trade, protection of investor rights and the privatisation of commons, when what is most needed is a new global 'Grundnorm', an organising principle for global governance enforced through a deceptively simple but utterly profound test for all economic activity: is it ecologically sustainable?

2.5 CONCLUSION

The SDGs are incommensurate with the scale and urgency of the unfolding planetary catastrophe and offer no real possibility of global, climate or social justice for current or future generations. They promote a weak, anthropocentric form of sustainable development that ignores ecological reality and continues to prioritise economic growth above social justice and environmental protection. They contain a 'lack of consideration given to the need for radical change in people's demands on the Earth', and 'a perpetuation of the view that nature is merely a collection of natural resources that can be subdued by the human race'.[97] Hickel maintains that the SDGs 'lock in the global development agenda for the next 15 years around a failing economic model that requires urgent and deep structural changes'.[98]

---

[96] For example, the targets in articles 2 and 4 in the Paris Agreement.

[97] C.C. Williams and A.C. Millington, 'The Diverse and Contested Meanings of Sustainable Development' (2004) *The Geographical Journal* 170(2), 101.

[98] J. Hickel, 'Why the New Sustainable Development Goals Won't Make the World a Fairer Place' <http://theconversation.com/why-the-new-sustainable-development-goals-wont-make-the-world-a-fairer-place-46374> accessed 2 June 2017.

As Haydn Washington argues, development cannot be sustainable if it ignores ecological limits and planetary boundaries. Extractive, fossil-fuelled growth is the driving force of *un*sustainability. Development cannot be sustainable and prioritise endless economic growth while leaving contemporary patterns of production, consumption and accumulation unchanged because the commodification and monetisation of nature are anathema to sustainability.[99] To be ecologically sustainable, economic activity cannot replicate the anthropocentric shortcomings of Eurocentric rationality predicated upon dominium over nature; it cannot be an alternative form of development rebadged as sustainable development but an alternative *to* development.

The MDGs enjoyed mixed success.[100] When commentators review the SDGs in 2030, hopefully they will not find that global poverty was reduced in a series of pyrrhic victories that came at the cost of widespread ecological destruction, species extinction and growing injustice from climatic harms because the goals were based on Holocene thinking. If not, they may lament the failure to move beyond the contradictions of a conception of development that could never have been sustainable and belatedly accept that ecological sustainability should have been the starting point, the focus and the central goal of Agenda 2030 rather than an optional extra because sustainability is a precondition for all attempts to reduce poverty in the Anthropocene.

---

99 H. Washington, above n 39, 193–194.

100 Despite a decline during the 15 years of the MDGs, approximately 700 million people remain in extreme poverty: World Food Programme <https://www.wfp.org/climate-change/climate-impacts> accessed 1 November 2016. These numbers would be substantially higher but for China's dramatic growth since 1979.

3. The Sustainable Development Goals: an existential critique alongside three new-millennial analytical paradigms

Louis J. Kotzé

3.1 INTRODUCTION

Member States of the United Nations (UN) have been setting global goals since at least the UN Development Decade in the 1960s. While the specifics vary, commentators generally agree that global goals are non-binding, quantitative, time-bound objectives, mostly related to human development issues (broadly conceived), which governments collectively agree upon and aim to systematically implement and monitor progress towards achievement.[1] Several sets of global goals have been created over the past decades around the following issues: ending colonialism; accelerating economic development and growth in developing and least developed countries; expanding education; eradicating smallpox; expanding immunisation to reduce child mortality and the incidence of several diseases; improving the situation of children and women; and adopting various human rights instruments globally.[2]

Continuing along this path, countries committed more recently in 2000 to achieve the Millennium Development Goals (MDGs) by 2015. Consisting of eight goals predominantly geared towards the interests of the developing world, the MDGs specifically aimed at galvanising efforts to meet the needs of the world's poorest. This much is evident from the type of objectives they pursued, including: eradicate extreme poverty and hunger; achieve universal primary education; promote gender equality

[1] R. Jolly, 'Global Goals: The UN Experience', *Background Paper: Human Development Report 2003* (United Nations Development Programme, 2003) 1–22 at 2.

[2] *Ibid*, at 3.

and empower women; reduce child mortality; improve maternal health; combat HIV/Aids, malaria and other diseases; ensure environmental sustainability; and build global partnerships for development. The general view is that most of the eight MDGs have been achieved to a greater or lesser extent, despite concerns that existed at the time of their adoption related to, among other things, their scope and focus. Chasek et al, for example, argue that the MDGs considered neither the root causes of poverty and gender equality, nor the underlying environmental issues related to development and improvement of the human condition.[3] They have nevertheless been hailed (rightly or wrongly) to represent the 'most successful anti-poverty movement in history',[4] and (perhaps more realistically) they are considered to 'have provided a common vision and have contributed to remarkable progress'.[5]

On the back of these achievements, and in an effort to further build on the global political momentum instigated by the MDGs, states agreed on and committed to the achievement of 17 Sustainable Development Goals (SDGs) in 2015.[6] Setting out 169 specific targets under the 17 goals, the SDGs currently constitute the principal roadmap for development around the world for the next 15 years. Also known as the *2030 Agenda for Sustainable Development*, the SDGs are altogether a much more comprehensive and ambitious initiative, which aims to extend the almost exclusive developing country and poverty alleviation focus of the MDGs to include, in a more multifaceted way, other pertinent global concerns such as climate change. A further significant difference between the two agendas is the explicit inclusion of and focus on *sustainable* development in the SDGs. While MDG 7 was specifically aimed at ensuring environmental sustainability, the prominence of *sustainable* development in the name of the SDGs, and as a leitmotif throughout the SDGs, arguably suggests an expanded understanding of socio-economic development to

---

[3] P.S. Chasek, L.M. Wagner, F. Leone et al, 'Getting to 2030: Negotiating the Post-2015 Sustainable Development Agenda' (2016) *Review of European Community and International Environmental Law* 25(1), 5–14 at 7.

[4] United Nations, *The Millennium Development Goals Report* (United Nations, New York, 2015) at 3 <http://www.un.org/millenniumgoals/2015_MDG_Report/pdf/MDG%202015%20rev%20(July%201).pdf> accessed 25 January 2018.

[5] United Nations General Assembly, 'Outcome Document of the Special Event to Follow up Efforts Made Towards Achieving the Millennium Development Goals', A/68/L.4 (1 October 2013); and more generally, United Nations, *The Millennium Development Goals Report*, above n 4.

[6] United Nations General Assembly, 'Transforming our world: the 2030 Agenda for Sustainable Development', A/RES/70/1 (21 October 2015).

also include environmental concerns. Presumably at initial face value, the progression from development to sustainable development as expressed through the SDGs might signal a recognition by the world of the need to ensure that whatever type of development is fostered by the goals, their benefits must be able to last in perpetuity.

If one accepts that the SDGs are the roadmap for the world to achieve sustainable development until 2030, and if one accepts that the only way human and non-human life on Earth can continue is if demands to sustain all life can never exceed the carrying capacity or impact the ecological integrity of the Earth system, then the following question arises: are the SDGs in fact appropriate and able to guide humanity along a road of sustainability that is possible *ad infinitum*? Building on Sam Adelman's incisive critique of the SDGs in light of anthropocentrism and neo-liberalism in this volume,[7] I offer here a related existential critique of the SDGs through three contemporary analytical lenses of (i) the Anthropocene, (ii) the planetary boundaries theory, and (iii) the Earth system governance theory. These lenses could be described as new-millennial analytical paradigms that respectively seek:

(i) to emphasise the primacy of *Anthropos* and the extent of the human impact on the environment, while offering an ecological alternative to the prevailing destructive anthropocentrism that permeates virtually all governance institutions, norms and processes, and which diminishes global Earth system integrity;
(ii) to offer a new and much clearer quantified vision of the limitations of the planet (expressed as boundaries) to sustain all human and non-human life in the wake of increasing anthropogenic pressures; and
(iii) to emphasise the critical need for a normative realignment in the face of planetary shifts and to offer a new perspective on an integrated, but fragile, Earth system that should be governed by norms, institutions and processes that are better aligned with and able to respond to the integrated Earth system.

It is my hypothesis that the SDGs, when they are critically evaluated through these three new-millennial analytical paradigms, are not a suitable roadmap for the type of truly *sustainable* present and future development that must ensure the continuation of all (not only human) life on Earth. The main reason for this, I believe, is that despite their

[7] See Chapter 2.

reference to, and shallow alignment with, the three-pillared approach to sustainable development (environmental, social and economic concerns), the SDGs mostly push environmental interests to the periphery of their concern while prioritising human-focused social and economic development at the expense of global Earth system integrity. This simply amounts, at best, to a continuation of the MDG approach and experience, with the SDGs likely to exacerbate Anthropocene-inducing conditions and to push humanity further across planetary boundaries.

In order to prove this hypothesis, the discussion commences in Section 3.2 with a brief description of the SDGs as the latest incarnation of anthropocentric (un)sustainable development. Section 3.3 describes each of the three new-millennial analytical paradigms. In conclusion, Section 3.4 offers an existential critique of the SDGs in light of these analytical paradigms with a view to evaluating the suitability and appropriateness of the SDGs as the latest global development vision on which much of the future of all life on Earth could hinge.

3.2 THE 2030 AGENDA FOR SUSTAINABLE DEVELOPMENT

The SDGs were adopted by the United Nations General Assembly (UNGA) through a formal Resolution titled *Transforming our World: the 2030 Agenda for Sustainable Development* on 25 September 2015.[8] On a plain reading of this constitutive document, the SDGs, like the preceding MDGs, is a wish list setting out a grand and ambitious vision of an idealistic future. It is, in its own poetic words, 'a plan of action for people, planet and prosperity … to free the human race from the tyranny of poverty and want and to heal and secure our planet'.[9] The SDGs are clearly cast in aspirational language which seeks to convey the 'determination' of the world to improve the lives of people; protect the planet; ensure that everyone enjoys prosperous and fulfilling lives; foster peaceful, just and inclusive societies free from fear and violence; and to revitalise the global partnership for sustainable development to ensure the achievement of the goals.[10]

Normatively speaking, like all the global goals preceding them, the SDGs are of a non-binding political nature. They are therefore not

---

[8] United Nations General Assembly 'Transforming our world, above n 6. A/RES/70/1 (21 October 2015).

[9] *Ibid*, Preamble.

[10] *Ibid*.

binding legal norms in their own right, although, as Kim says, 'they are grounded in international law and made consistent with existing commitments expressed in various [binding] international agreements and other soft law instruments'.[11] Because many of the SDGs are already reflected in various juridical instruments, international (environmental) law provides the normative context in which (some of) the SDGs should operate and interact with each other, as well as the binding normative means to achieve some of these targets in practice.[12] The fact that the SDGs are political non-legal aspirations does not, however, diminish the significance that states themselves attribute to the eventual fulfilment of the goals. With reference to the creation of the UN in the aftermath of the Second World War, states declared in *Transforming our world*: 'Today we are also taking a decision of great historic significance. We resolve to build a better future for all people, including the millions who have been denied the chance to lead decent, dignified and rewarding lives and to achieve their full human potential.'[13] To this end, the SDGs are obviously not meant to be a mere declaration of sorts that is useful for window-dressing and that might perhaps gain the normative power of soft law over time. There is at least some sense of deeper commitment to achieving the goals and their respective targets. This much is further evidenced by the inclusion of several 'means of implementation'.[14] Moreover, if the level of seriousness, broad commitment and state involvement during the final determination of the MDGs' achievements are anything to go by, including the considerable public displays of victory following the publication of the Millennium Development Goals Report in 2015,[15] one could reasonably expect a similar, if not greater, resolve of commitment from states to achieving the SDGs and to showcasing their achievements in this respect. Admittedly, whether this would simply amount to worthless window-dressing, remains to be seen.

A further significant consideration in trying to understand what the SDGs are and what they could mean to the world is the concept of sustainable development, which appears both as the centrepiece of the SDGs *and* as the historic and prevailing cornerstone of international

---

[11] R. Kim 'The Nexus between International Law and the Sustainable Development Goals' (2016) *Review of European, Comparative and International Environmental Law* 25(1), 15.

[12] *Ibid*, 17.

[13] *Ibid*, para 50.

[14] *Ibid*, paras 39–46.

[15] See, for example, <http://www.un.org/millenniumgoals/2015_MDG_Report/pdf/MDG%202015%20PR%20Global.pdf> accessed 25 January 2018.

environmental law and global environmental politics and governance. The gradual rise of sustainable development began with the 1972 Stockholm Conference on the Human Environment. The underlying ethos of this global gathering was that the human environment belongs exclusively to humans; it exists for, and must therefore be protected for, the utilisation of humans, their health, well-being and prosperity. As the first global environmental conference, Stockholm provided the anthropocentric context for the ensuing deliberations and the context for the subsequent development of global environmental norms by placing human beings centre-stage and elevating human entitlements to the environment.

In 1982, the UNGA adopted the World Charter for Nature with a majority vote (111 votes, with the United States casting the only dissenting vote).[16] As a far more radical counterpoint to the Stockholm Conference and Declaration, the World Charter for Nature is premised on the idea that human development is possible only if ecological limits are respected, with the notion of safeguarding ecological integrity at the core of virtually all of the provisions of the Charter. In the preamble of the Charter, the UNGA acknowledges that benefits from nature depend on 'the maintenance of natural processes and on the diversity of life forms', as well as 'the crucial importance attached by the international community to the promotion and development of co-operation aimed at protecting and safeguarding the balance and quality of nature'. To this end, the Charter clearly supports a stronger form of ecological sustainability, i.e., an approach which would appear to prioritise ecological integrity and environmental care above other considerations, and as a prerequisite to achieving efficient economic growth and social equity.[17] Intriguingly, the World Charter for Nature is almost entirely disregarded in the ensuing paradigm narrative of sustainable development, with states probably shying away from the Charter's explicit ecological approach because they viewed it as being deleterious to neoliberal economic development and growth.[18]

---

[16] United Nations General Assembly, A/RES/37/7 adopted at the 48th Plenary Meeting on 28 October 1982.

[17] See generally, K. Bosselmann, *The Principle of Sustainability: Transforming Law and Governance*, 2nd edn (Routledge, 2017).

[18] See further L. Kotzé and D. French, 'The Anthropocentric Ontology of International Environmental Law and the Sustainable Development Goals: Towards an Ecocentric Rule of Law in the Anthropocene' (2018) *Global Journal of Comparative Law* 7(1), 5–36.

What followed instead with far greater fanfare and support from states, was the highly influential Brundtland Report of 1987, which formally introduced the concept of sustainable development to the world. It defined sustainable development as 'development that meets the needs of the present generation without compromising the ability of future generations to meet their own needs'.[19] Instead of continuing down the strong ecological sustainability route of the World Charter for Nature, the Report essentially introduced the much weaker anthropocentric three-pillared approach to sustainable development into global environmental and developmental law, politics and governance; an approach that continues to hold sway, as we shall see below.

The Rio Declaration on Environment and Development of 1992 reaffirmed the Stockholm Declaration's provisions, embraced the Brundtland definition of sustainable development, and further emphasised in anthropocentric terms that '[H]uman beings are at the centre of concerns for sustainable development'.[20] Principle 3 of the Declaration affords people a 'right to development' (notably not a duty to conserve), which 'must be fulfilled so as to equitably meet developmental and environmental needs of present and future generations'. Such terminology implies an environment subjugated to human developmental needs instead of an ecologically intact environment where human and non-human needs are equally recognised and which functions in harmony over the long term.

Although states later recognised rhetorically in the Johannesburg Declaration on Sustainable Development of 2002 that 'humankind is at a crossroads' and that the global community of states must 'make a determined effort to respond positively to the need to produce a practical and visible plan to bring about poverty eradication and human development',[21] the substance of sustainable development remained grounded in the *status quo ante*.

Similarly, Rio +20's outcome document, *The Future We Want*, was exclusively focused on human development concerns, with the world recognising that '[E]radicating poverty is the greatest global challenge facing the world today and an indispensable requirement for sustainable development';[22] a central leitmotif that is also repeated in the SDGs as indicated below. Critically important as it is for the world to eradicate

---

[19] Chapter 2, para 1 <http://www.un-documents.net/our-common-future.pdf> accessed 25 January 2018.

[20] Principle 1.

[21] Para 7.

[22] Para 2.

poverty in its efforts to address inter-human hierarchies and injustices, the equally important issue of intra-species justice is absent from this key document. The document also ignores the fact that poverty cannot be eradicated sustainably and continuously if the integrity of the Earth system is not kept intact. In a stark affirmation of their support for an anthropocentric ethic, and in relation to the latter commitment, states instead recognised that 'people are at the center of sustainable development';[23] while the future *we* want clearly excludes non-humans and their interests.

In addition to revealing the pervasive anthropocentric ontology of global environmental and developmental law, governance and politics, the foregoing historical trajectory of sustainable development is particularly instructive when attempting to determine the significance of the SDGs and their potential impact. When reading *Transforming our world*, it becomes clear that the SDGs are simply a continuation of development policies past; regurgitating as they do a deeply engrained notion of weak anthropocentric sustainable development that has been popularised and perpetuated through consecutive global conferences, their accompanying soft law instruments, and a single high-level report.[24] Even during the negotiation process preceding the SDGs, influential commentators warned about the real and potential pitfalls if the SDGs were to be based on a weak anthropocentric approach to sustainable development (as opposed to a strong, ecocentric approach),[25] which merely sees it as a balancing of social, economic and environmental interests while ignoring the critical need to respect Earth system integrity and ecological limits. Griggs et al proposed in the run-up to the finalisation of the SDGs that:

> The [SDGs'] definition of sustainable development, as laid out in the 1987 report from the UN World Commission on Environment and Development (the Brundtland Commission), should therefore be redefined to 'development

---

[23] Para 6.

[24] This much is further evident from states' reaffirmation of 'the outcomes of all major United Nations conferences and summits which have laid a solid foundation for sustainable development and have helped to shape the new [SDG] Agenda.' Para 11.

[25] For a critical account of the differences between the (anthropocentric) weak and the (ecocentric) strong approach to sustainable development, see E. Neumayer, *Weak versus Strong Sustainability: Exploring the Limits of Two Opposing Paradigms* (Edward Elgar Publishing, 2003).

> that meets the needs of the present while safeguarding Earth's life-support system, on which the welfare of current and future generations depends'.[26]

Regrettably, the SDGs never ventured beyond the axiomatic confines of weak anthropocentric sustainable development, and in their final iteration merely reinforce the anthropocentric sustainable human development agenda that has been pivotal in the global environmental law and governance framework for the past 50 years. For example, in its preamble, *Transforming our world* states that the SDGs 'are integrated and indivisible and balance the three dimensions of sustainable development: the economic, social and environmental'. While the inclusion of environmental concerns into development is laudable, it is accomplished through a weak anthropocentric paradigm that is squarely aimed at improving human development at whatever ecological cost, and in terms of which environmental concerns are all too easily relegated to the sidelines. This much is evident from states' proud declaration that they 'have adopted a historic decision on a comprehensive, far-reaching and *people-centred* set of universal and transformative Goals and targets'.[27]

In a nutshell then, the SDGs in essence represent simply the next iteration of a tired development vision tried before. This vision is squarely based on the trite, decades-old notion of sustainable development which has been incorporated virtually verbatim into the SDGs from various existing global declarations and from the Brundtland Report. The SDGs therefore provide nothing new or radical in terms of the type of development they seek to achieve; the developmental paradigm they pursue remains a weak, anthropocentric one where socio-economic interests of (certain privileged) human beings reign supreme. While the SDGs themselves set out non-binding objectives and targets, some of these are encapsulated in binding international law instruments which could eventually contribute to the success of the SDGs' implementation. There is also at least some level of commitment to achieve the goals and if the past experience with the MDGs is anything to go by, the SDGs would probably achieve a measured degree of success with respect to their socio-economic-oriented goals and targets. Given its anthropocentric orientation, however, it is highly unlikely that any significant advances will be made as far as environmental interests are concerned – an issue I return to in greater detail below.

---

[26] See further D. Griggs, M. Stafford Smith, O. Gaffney et al, 'Sustainable Development Goals for People and Planet' (2013) *Nature* 495, 306.

[27] Own emphasis. Para 2.

3.3 NEW-MILLENNIAL ANALYTICAL PARADIGMS

I have sought to briefly describe above the meaning and significance of the SDGs. While I have argued they are important to guide development into the next 15 years despite their being non-binding, I now turn more fully to the question of whether they are *appropriate* to serve this crucial role. I commence the analysis in this part with a description of what I term three 'new-millennial analytical paradigms', i.e., the Anthropocene, the planetary boundaries framework, and the Earth system governance framework. Partly acting as lenses through which to view the state of the world today, and alongside which regulatory responses could be designed to better respond to present global challenges, they have emerged since around 2000 and, when measured against trite paradigms such as sustainable development, potentially provide more comprehensive, current and critical paradigms for analysing the human–environment interface.

3.3.1 Anthropocene

While the Earth has been impacted and altered before, this is the first time in its history that humans are considered to act as geological agents capable of changing Earth and its natural system: humans have the potential 'to transform Earth rapidly and irreversibly into a state unknown in human experience'.[28] The Anthropocene was first introduced in a 2000 publication by Eugene Stoermer and Paul Crutzen as a term of art expressing the geological significance of this anthropogenic change.[29] Emphasising the central role of mankind as a major driving force in modifying the biosphere, the term Anthropocene suggests that the Earth is rapidly moving into a critically unstable state, with the Earth system gradually becoming less predictable, non-stationary and less harmonious as a result of the global human imprint on the biosphere.[30] In the Anthropocene, humanity has become a geological agent in much the

---

[28] A.D. Barnosky, E.A. Hadly, J. Bascompte et al, 'Approaching a State Shift in Earth's Biosphere' (2012) *Nature* 486, 52.

[29] P.J. Crutzen and E.F. Stoermer, 'The 'Anthropocene' (2000) *IGBP Global Change Newsletter* 41, 17–18.

[30] L. Kotzé, 'Rethinking Global Environmental Law and Governance in the Anthropocene' (2014) *Journal of Energy and Natural Resources Law* 32(2), 121–156.

same way as a volcano or meteor – able to change the Earth and its system, and possibly even to cause a mass extinction.[31]

Several commentators have ventured definitions of the Anthropocene. For example, Steffen, Crutzen and McNeill state:

> The term *Anthropocene* … suggests that the Earth has now left its natural geological epoch, the present interglacial state called the Holocene. Human activities have become so pervasive and profound that they rival the great forces of Nature and are pushing the Earth into planetary *terra incognita*. The Earth is rapidly moving into a less biologically diverse, less forested, much warmer, and probably wetter and stormier state.[32]

In a later paper, the authors (with Grinevald) propose:

> The term Anthropocene suggests: (i) that the Earth is now moving out of its current geological epoch, called the Holocene and (ii) that human activity is largely responsible for this exit from the Holocene, that is, that humankind has become a global geological force in its own right.[33]

The existence of a boundary that separates the current relatively harmonious Holocene epoch from the human-dominated and unstable Anthropocene has not been officially defined though.[34] A proposal to formalise the Anthropocene as an epoch of the geological time scale is currently being prepared by the Anthropocene Working Group for consideration by the International Commission on Stratigraphy in the near future.[35]

Whether the Anthropocene is formally accepted as the new geological epoch is arguably less important than recognising its epistemological qualities and potential. Baskin recently opined that the Anthropocene is a 'paradigm dressed as epoch', that it has entered the *zeitgeist* in spectacular fashion, and that it has 'scientific respectability despite not yet being

---

[31] M. Hodson and S. Marvin, 'Urbanism in the Anthropocene: Ecological Urbanism or Premium Ecological Enclaves?' (2010) *City* 14, 299–313.

[32] W. Steffen, P.J. Crutzen and J. McNeill, 'The Anthropocene: Are Humans Now Overwhelming the Great Forces of Nature?' (2007) *Ambio* 36, 614.

[33] W. Steffen, J. Grinevald, P. Crutzen et al, 'The Anthropocene: Conceptual and Historical Perspectives' (2011) *Philosophical Transactions of the Royal Society* 369, 843.

[34] A.D. Barnosky, J.H. Brown, G.C. Daily et al, 'Introducing the Scientific Consensus on Maintaining Humanity's Life Support Systems in the 21st Century: Information for Policy Makers' (2014) *The Anthropocene Review* 1(1), 78.

[35] See <http://quaternary.stratigraphy.org/workinggroups/anthropocene/>, accessed 25 January 2018.

an accepted scientific term'.[36] The Anthropocene is capturing the popular and scientific imagination of those who concern themselves with the global socio-ecological crisis, acting as it does as a mindset that emphasises human responsibility for causing *and* for responding to the global socio-ecological crisis: '[It] radically unsettles the philosophical, epistemological and ontological ground on which both the natural sciences and the social sciences/humanities have traditionally stood.'[37] To this end, the Anthropocene:

> … is not simply a neutral characterisation of a new geological epoch, but it is also a particular way of understanding the world and a normative guide to action. It is … more usefully understood as an ideology – in that it provides the ideational underpinning for a particular view of the world, which it, in turn, helps to legitimate.[38]

Because such a new world view or ideology 'heralds an opening of sorts, a clarion call for change',[39] as Baker argues, this change must also be reflected in, and carried through, our regulatory institutions in all their various binding and non-binding forms, including the SDGs.

3.3.2 Planetary Boundaries

The extent of anthropogenic encroachments on the biosphere, as suggested by the Anthropocene, is further exemplified in terms of planetary boundaries that determine the self-regulating capacity of the Earth system (otherwise understood as biophysical thresholds). Developed by Rockström and colleagues,[40] the boundary theory seeks to refocus our attention on the non-negotiable planetary preconditions that humanity needs to respect in order to avoid the risk of calamitous global environmental change. The boundary theory further serves to visualise multiple and growing human demands on limited and decreasing Earth system resources in concrete, appreciable terms. As a global environmental

---

[36] J. Baskin, 'Paradigm Dressed as Epoch: The Ideology of the Anthropocene' (2015) *Environmental Values* 24, 10.

[37] *Ibid.*

[38] *Ibid*, 10–11.

[39] S. Baker, 'Adaptive Law in the Anthropocene' (2015) *Chicago-Kent Law Review* 90(2), 567.

[40] J. Rockström, W. Steffen, K. Noone et al, 'Planetary Boundaries: Exploring the Safe Operating Space for Humanity' (2009) *Ecology and Society* 14(2), 1–33.

change threshold reference framework, planetary boundaries are signalling the fact that life on Earth is venturing into uncharted territory as far as the Earth system is concerned,[41] or an 'unsafe operating space' for all life in the Earth system.[42] A 'safe space', on the other hand, is a value judgement based on how societies deal with risk and uncertainty and it expresses the current Holocene 'space' we live in, which has more or less safely enveloped life on Earth for centuries. In terms of the boundary theory, when a boundary or biophysical threshold is crossed, we are entering an unsafe operating space,[43] which implies a risk of damaging or catastrophic loss of existing ecosystem integrity across the biosphere.[44] Of the nine planetary boundaries,[45] it is estimated that three have already been crossed, i.e., climate change, rate of biodiversity loss and the nitrogen cycle.[46]

As we are approaching and/or crossing these boundaries, we are simultaneously instigating a state shift in the Earth's biosphere that could cause critical planetary scale transitions as a result of threshold effects that could change life on Earth as we know it.[47] While terms such as the Anthropocene have emerged as useful frameworks to conceptualise and understand anthropogenic impacts on the complex Earth system, and to appreciate the limits of this system and the extent to which it can sustain human and non-human life, the planetary boundary framework, acting as it does to emphasise the existence of limits to Earth's carrying capacity, provides a potentially powerful concretisation of the ecological limits within which development (broadly conceived in this instance as human existence and aptly expressed through development goals such as the SDGs) must be allowed to occur. Remaining within these boundaries would indicate that we are respecting the ecological limits and integrity of the Earth system. We are encroaching on ecological limits and integrity where we transgress them.

---

41 Crutzen and Stoermer, above n 29, 17.

42 Rockström et al, above n 40.

43 Steffen et al, above n 33, 860.

44 B.W. Brook, E.C. Ellis, M.P. Perring et al, 'Does the Terrestrial Biosphere have Planetary Tipping Points?' (2012) *Trends in Ecology and Evolution* 1–6 at 1.

45 Climate change; rate of biodiversity loss (terrestrial and marine); interference with the nitrogen and phosphorus cycles; stratospheric ozone depletion; ocean acidification; global freshwater use; change in land use; chemical pollution; and atmospheric aerosol loading.

46 J. Rockström, W. Steffen, K. Noone et al, 'A Safe Operating Space for Humanity' (2009) *Nature* 461, 472–475.

47 Barnosky et al, above n 28, 52–58.

3.3.3 Earth System Governance

It has been argued above that the Anthropocene presents a new living reality characterised by the hitherto unacknowledged complexity of the Earth system, making it all but impossible to establish simple, clear, linear links between causes and effects, and making it crucially necessary, if challenging, to craft and execute future regulatory interventions.[48] The arrival of the Anthropocene therefore arguably would require of us to start thinking about law, politics and social ordering in planetary terms: 'discussions of the Anthropocene necessarily require thinking at the scale of the biosphere and over the long term. This is a planetary issue, matters at the large scale require some consideration of ethical connection and, perhaps, the implicit invocation of a single polity, however inchoate.'[49]

More importantly for present purposes, the Anthropocene would also require of us to start contemplating global environmental law and politics in terms of systems thinking. Recognising the connectivity, nonlinearity and complexity of socio-ecological processes, Earth system science is concerned with the 'study of the Earth's environment as an integrated system in order to understand how and why it is changing, and to explore the implications of these changes for global and regional sustainability'.[50] Our efforts to facilitate a sustainable future, to maximise equitable choices and to identify and enable those options that would keep us within safe operating spaces away from critical tipping points in the Earth system, will require our better understanding, mediating and responding to human interference with an increasingly unpredictable and complex Earth system.[51] While this would probably be the ultimate regulatory challenge of the Anthropocene, a systems approach simultaneously provides us with the cognitive framework to contemplate

---

48 F. Oldfield, A.D. Barnosky, J. Dearing et al, 'The Anthropocene Review: Its Significance, Implications and the Rationale for a New Transdisciplinary Journal' (2014) *The Anthropocene Review* 1(1), 3.

49 S. Dalby, 'Anthropocene Ethics: Rethinking "The Political" after Environment'. Paper presented at International Studies Annual Convention, Montreal, Canada, 2004. Available at <https://www.yumpu.com/en/document/view/42485216/anthropocene-ethics-rethinking-the-political-after-environment/3> accessed 26 January 2018.

50 A. Ignaciuk, M. Rice, J. Bogardi et al, 'Responding to Complex Societal Challenges: A Decade of Earth System Science Partnership (ESSP) Interdisciplinary Research' (2012) *Current Opinion in Environmental Sustainability* 4, 147–158 at 147.

51 Oldfield et al, above n 48, 3.

global socio-ecological change and to devise appropriate responses to such change.

As a response to the need for a systems approach, Biermann developed the concept of Earth system governance, which offers a new model for planet-wide environmental politics and governance.[52] Fundamentally rooted in Earth system science, Earth system governance is a reactive counter-narrative to localised, state-based, narrowly focused, and fragmented regulatory approaches to environmental issues through the trite application of an issue-specific environmental governance regime that focuses on, for example, pollution control, nature conservation and water protection, and that predominantly employs formal, state-based law and state institutions. Taking a much broader and integrated view, Earth system governance is a way of thinking about global environmental politics and governance which recognises, for example, that climate change is not only a matter of rising temperatures in Africa; it is also a matter of water governance, trade, armed conflict and nutrition; it impacts everyone everywhere and could be addressed by multiple state and non-state actors through a whole range of binding and non-binding regulatory interventions.

With reference to a more open, holistic, flexible, multi-scalar and multi-actor regulatory approach that is better able to capture and address the many complex global developments that transform the bio-geophysical cycles and processes of the Earth, the complex relations between global transformations of social and natural systems, and the multi-scale consequences of ecological transformation, Biermann et al define Earth system governance as

> … the interrelated and increasingly integrated system of formal and informal rules, rule-making systems and actor networks at all levels of human society (from local to global) that are set up to steer societies towards preventing, mitigating and adapting to global and local environmental change and, in particular, earth system transformation.[53]

---

[52] See among others, F. Biermann, *Earth System Governance: World Politics in the Anthropocene* (MIT Press, 2014).

[53] F. Biermann, M.M. Betsill, S. Camargo Vieira et al, 'Navigating the Anthropocene: the Earth System Governance Project Strategy Paper' (2010) *Current Opinion in Environmental Sustainability* 2, 203. See also for a more detailed conceptual analysis, F. Biermann '"Earth System Governance" as a Cross-cutting Theme of Global Change Research' (2007) *Global Environmental Change* 17, 326–337.

Earth system governance clearly is not only concerned with ways to influence and direct the Earth system: 'Earth System governance is [also] about the human impact on planetary systems. It is about the societal steering of human activities with regard to the longterm stability of geobiophysical systems.'[54] Any Earth system governance-based regulatory response, including its juridical elements such as international environmental law and its political instruments setting forth developmental aspirations (such as the SDGs), must respond to persistent Earth system uncertainty; nurture new responsibilities and modes of co-operation as a result of generational, spatial and socio-ecological interdependence between people, countries and species; respond to the functional interdependence of the Earth system and Earth system transformations; respond to the needs of an increasingly integrated globalised society; and respond to extraordinary degrees of socio-ecological harm.[55]

Ultimately, through the Earth system governance lens, it becomes possible to envision an intermeshed global regulatory space that must address a whole range of multi-level, reciprocal and interconnected regulatory socio-ecological challenges. This regulatory space includes various governance levels, normative arrangements and multiple state and non-state actors, which manifest in a multi-level spatial (geographic), temporal (applicable to present and future generations), and causal setting (interacting Earth system processes). Typical characteristics of this global regulatory space could include: global hybrid law (including interacting legal and quasi-legal structures);[56] multi-scalarity where a range of actors in a variety of interactions contribute to internalise norms transnationally through a process of interpretation, internalisation and enforcement; and ultimately, greater regulatory responsiveness to more effectively address the type of socio-ecological transformations that characterise the Anthropocene.[57] The extent to which the SDGs play a

---

54 F. Biermann, 'The Anthropocene: A Governance Perspective' (2014) *The Anthropocene Review* 1(1), 59.

55 Biermann et al, above n 53, 329–330.

56 Law could be 'hybrid' to the extent that it is state orchestrated rather than state centred; decentralised rather than centralised; based on dispersed rather than bureaucratic expertise; and integrating a mix of hard and soft law rather than focusing solely on mandatory rules. H. Osofsky, *Scales of Law: Rethinking Climate Change Governance* (PhD Dissertation, Oregon University, 2013) 39. Available at <https://scholarsbank.uoregon.edu/xmlui/bitstream/handle/1794/13297/Osofsky_oregon_0171A_10730.pdf?sequence=1> accessed 26 January 2018. The SDGs, while not law, could be an important part of such a hybrid body of law.

57 *Ibid*, 45–49.

meaningful role in, and are suited for, the Earth system governance paradigm is investigated below.

3.4 AN EXISTENTIAL CRITIQUE

In this section, I offer an existential critique of the SDGs in light of the analytical paradigms discussed immediately above, specifically with a view to evaluating the suitability and appropriateness of the SDGs. I do not claim this discussion to be exhaustive, and while I seek to highlight those issues I deem most pertinent, there will obviously be numerous others.

3.4.1 The Anthropocene

I have already indicated above that the Anthropocene is rapidly transcending its initial use as a 'mere rhetorical device',[58] permitting deeper epistemological enquiries into our regulatory interventions that seek to mediate the human–environment interface.[59] In doing so, the Anthropocene fulfils a useful function to the extent that it could assist in solidifying the idea of humanity as an Earth system driver, aiding understanding of anthropogenic Earth system processes[60] and fostering deeper political, social and cultural awareness of human-induced environmental changes.[61] Realising within this context that '[n]avigating the anthropocene [sic] has ... become a key challenge for policy-makers at all levels of decision-making ... to prepare – politically, legally, socially and economically – for the adaptation to those global environmental changes that can no longer be avoided'[62] provides a central impetus and motivation to also commence with a wholesale re-evaluation of the socio-political, legal and broader regulatory interventions that humans use to mediate our relations with one another and with other non-human Earth system entities. The SDGs, as the latest developmental roadmap for

---

[58] K. Scott, 'International Law in the Anthropocene: Responding to the Geoengineering Challenge' (2013) *Michigan Journal of International Law* 34(2), 309–358 at 312.

[59] Kotzé, above n 30, 121–156.

[60] W. Autin and J. Holbrook, 'Is the Anthropocene an Issue of Stratigraphy or Pop Culture?', July 2012, *GSA Today* 60–61 at 61.

[61] *Ibid*, 60.

[62] Biermann et al, above n 53, 202.

the following 15 years, must invariably be considered as part and parcel of these regulatory interventions.

The global socio-ecological crisis of the Anthropocene provides a convincing normative justification to strive towards the urgent development of a far more radical framework for development than the one the SDGs currently offer. What would instead be required is a framework for ecological sustainable development that can only be achieved if planetary boundaries are not crossed and if global Earth system integrity is respected. Based as they are on the perpetuation of growth without limits in an anthropocentric and weak sustainable development paradigm, in their current incarnation, the SDGs aim to do nothing of these and only serve to promote an already deeply entrenched anthropocentric agenda. Gillespie says in this regard that anthropocentrism and its instrumentalist rationality

> … assumes a mandate to experiment, operate, or to manipulate Earthly Nature as humans see fit … the organic unity of Earthly Nature was replaced by the notion of the world as a machine with dimensions susceptible to measurement and control … the inertness of matter, the asserted lack of sentience and lack of inherent value in all that is not human, absolves humanity of any guilt regarding the apparent damage that humans may inflict upon individual animals or complete ecosystems.[63]

Anthropocentrism, particularly to the extent that it is embedded in the SDGs, is seen to allow, legitimise and reinforce the type of unrestricted anthropocentric behaviour that is pushing the Earth system into the Anthropocene.[64] On this point, as a result, I believe that the SDGs fall far short in providing the type of future developmental roadmap that would be necessary to address the socio-ecological crisis of the Anthropocene.

The socio-ecological crisis of the Anthropocene requires a balanced consideration of social and economic interests, with particular weight being afforded to environmental interests, if the integrity of the Earth system were to be kept intact. Yet, as was the case with the MDGs, while it is plausible that some of the socio-economic-related SDGs might be achieved in full or in part in the short term, it is arguably far less certain that any of the SDGs' environmental objectives will be achieved and/or that the environment will be a crucial underlying consideration when

---

[63] A. Gillespie, *International Environmental Law, Policy and Ethics* (Oxford University Press, 1997) 9.

[64] R. Kim and K. Bosselmann, 'International Environmental Law in the Anthropocene: Towards a Purposive System of Multilateral Environmental Agreements' (2013) *Transnational Environmental Law* 2(2), 285–309.

contemplating the realisation of the socio-economic oriented SDGs. (And it is equally uncertain that the SDGs' socio-economic oriented objectives will be achieved over the long term if there is no sound continuing environmental base for their achievement). MDG 7 set out to 'ensure environmental sustainability', but in the end rather few of its achievements actually dealt with environmental sustainability, instead focusing on improving access to environmental services and conditions necessary for human welfare such as access to water, housing and sanitation.[65] While 2.6 billion people have gained access to improved drinking water since 1990, 2.1 billion people have gained access to improved sanitation, and the proportion of urban population living in slums in the developing country regions fell from approximately 39.4 per cent in 2000 to 29.7 per cent in 2014, MDG 7 is entirely silent on water protection and the improvement of water quality worldwide. The socio-economic achievements of the MDGs will be impossible without simultaneously protecting the ecological basis that support them – a critical consideration that was absent in MDG 7.

The same is arguably bound to happen with the SDGs. SDGs 1 and 2, for example, aim to end poverty in all its forms everywhere, to end hunger, achieve food security and improved nutrition, and promote sustainable agriculture, but do not recognise that this can occur sustainably only if Earth system limits are respected. SDG 6 aims to ensure the availability and sustainable management of water and sanitation for all, but says little about the need to protect aquatic systems as an integral part of the Earth system that is also crucial for the functional integrity of this system. SDGs 8 and 9 are geared towards promoting sustained, inclusive and sustainable economic growth, full and productive employment and decent work for all, and towards building resilient infrastructure, promoting inclusive and sustainable industrialisation and fostering innovation, but they are conspicuously silent on the extent to which these economic activities will inevitably impact Earth system integrity. In a similar vein, SDG 12 aims to ensure sustainable consumption and production patterns, but it is thin on the details related to what sustainable consumption and production actually would entail and how it is to be achieved in a world with an ever-growing population and dwindling resources.

Through the lens of the Anthropocene one is also able to more accurately situate and appreciate the existence of humans on Earth and as part of the Earth system in the context of the very long geological history of the Earth. It is generally believed that the Earth is approximately 4.5

---

65 United Nations, *The Millennium Development Goals Report*, above n 4, 7.

billion years old and that humans, in our present form, evolved approximately 200,000 years ago. By this account, it is clear that human history is far shorter than Earth history, which is significant for two reasons. First, while humans have been a part of the Earth's history for an almost negligible period of time, they have managed and continue to significantly alter and upset the harmony of the Earth system, despite such a brief period of time. This shows how powerful humanity has become, metamorphosing from insignificant inhabitants (co-)living with the Earth, to powerful and aggressive geological agents capable of changing the Earth in a very short period of time. Second, what the imagery of the Anthropocene requires is a significant expansion of our sense of time that is more attuned to 'Earth time'.[66] This would arguably foster a deeper appreciation of the short-, medium- and long-term nature of human impacts on the Earth system, and simultaneously could open up possibilities to devise mitigation and adaptation strategies that last and have an impact far further ahead in the future than those we currently have.

In the bigger 'Earth time' scheme of things, being only geared towards the next 15 years and despite their focus on present and future generations, the SDGs are decidedly short term and therefore inappropriate to guide the current generation to devise, adopt and implement those regulatory interventions that would be required to stay within a safe operating space well into the future. For this and all the other reasons set out above, I must conclude that the SDGs are wholly inappropriate to provide any truly sustainable future for humans and non-humans in the Anthropocene.

3.4.2 Planetary Boundaries

As already argued above, the anthropocentrism inherent in the ontological orientation of the SDGs risks exacerbating Anthropocene-like events, and a more ecological orientation for the SDGs is urgently required. The arrival of the Anthropocene clearly makes out a case in support of ecological sustainability as the only logical choice to ensure that the post-2015 UN development agenda remains within Earth system limits. These limits are usefully conceptualised by the nine planetary boundaries.[67] Respect for ecological limits, and therefore implicitly these planetary boundaries, which are touted as a 'new approach to global

---

[66] See, for a discussion, B. Richardson, 'Doing Time: The Temporalities of Environmental Law' in L. Kotzé (ed), *Environmental Law and Governance for the Anthropocene* (Hart, 2017) 55–74.

[67] Rockström et al, above n 40, 1.

sustainability',[68] is the only way in which humankind, acting as principal global agents of care, will be able to ensure a sustainable future for human and non-human constituents of the Earth community. It has already been explicitly recognised by Earth system scientists that visions of future developmental paradigms, such as the SDGs, must consider that

> ... the stable functioning of the Earth system is a prerequisite for thriving societies around the world. This approach implies that the PB [planetary boundaries] framework, or something like it, will need to be implemented alongside the achievement of targets aimed at more immediate human needs, such as provision of clean, affordable, and accessible energy and the adequate supply of food.[69]

Even though they have been created to 'stimulate action over the next 15 years in areas of critical importance for humanity and the planet',[70] the SDGs do not cover all the aspects addressed by the planetary boundary framework. For example, no goal or target for stratospheric ozone depletion has been included, despite the Ozone Secretariat's efforts, most probably because the international ozone law and governance regime has been marginally successful with ozone depletion moving out of the periphery of an area of critical importance as a result.[71] One would presume that while the drafters of the planetary boundaries framework could have chosen various other boundaries, they have carefully selected the nine boundaries because they cover the most prominent aspects critical for the proper functioning of the Earth system. If they were truly meant to promote Earth system integrity, the SDGs at the very least should have included all nine planetary boundaries, either as targets and/or in the goals more generally.

It has been shown above that the SDGs simply manage to rehash the trite and weak anthropocentric sustainable development agenda that has taken root in the global environmental law, politics and governance regime since 1972. Despite a noble but ultimately unsuccessful attempt

---

[68] *Ibid*, 1.

[69] W. Steffen, K. Richardson, J. Rockström et al, 'Planetary Boundaries: Guiding Human Development on a Changing Planet' (2015) *Science* 347(6223), 744.

[70] United Nations General Assembly, *Transforming our world*, above n 6, Preamble.

[71] Kim, above n 11, 16. Not everyone is as optimistic about the achievements and successes of the ozone regime: see, for example <http://www.smithsonianmag.com/science-nature/the-ozone-problem-is-back-and-worse-than-ever-136717745/>, accessed 26 January 2018.

by the World Charter for Nature of 1982 to counter neoliberal anthropocentrism, strong ecological sustainability has been largely absent from this regime. By pursuing anthropocentric sustainable development, the SDGs merely reinforce the prevailing conviction that there is a duty to protect environmental resources not for the benefit of environmental resources and their integrity, but purely for the sake of human development, needs and survival. To this end, sustainable development, through its normative vehicles such as the SDGs, is used to window-dress the neoliberal growth-without-limits paradigm,[72] a paradigm which has been central in pushing humanity towards and across planetary boundaries. For all these reasons, I must conclude that the SDGs would most probably be unable to keep humanity in the planetary boundaries' safe operating space, and that, if achieved to their fullest extent, they could even push humanity further across these critical planetary boundaries.

3.4.3 Earth System Governance

As was shown above, based as it is on systems thinking, one of the main rationales behind the idea of Earth system governance is to foster a normative realignment in the face of planetary shifts with a view, among other things, to improving the effectiveness of a fragmented global environmental law and governance regime. To this end, a systems approach would require the current fragmented and silo-ist global environmental law and governance regime to become more reflexive and integrated, and to be better aligned to an integrated Earth system. Similarly, considering their significant reciprocal relationship, one would expect associated development blueprints such as the SDGs, which act in tandem with binding international law, to be equally integrated in order to better respond to the regulatory challenges posed by an integrated Earth system. SDG 17 on global partnerships for sustainable development sounds appealing as an integrationist model but fails almost at the first hurdle of creating effective and meaningful linkages, a point which is illustrated in some detail by Cooper and French in this volume.[73] It appears then, as Kim says:

> … the SDGs themselves are presented using a silo approach. The drafters did not employ systems thinking when goal-setting and ended up forming a list of equally important global priorities. The non-hierarchical organization of the SDGs is problematic because the goals and targets interact. While some

---

72 See Adelman, Chapter 2 in this volume.

73 Cooper and French, Chapter 12 in this volume.

> targets are interdependent or reinforce each other, some impose constraints on others. Critical trade-offs will not be uncommon. Just like different objectives of international agreements point in different directions and may come into conflict, some of the SDGs and targets themselves are likely to compete for scarce resources or shift, rather than solve, problems.[74]

For example, ending hunger, achieving food security, improving nutrition and promoting sustainable agriculture (SDG 2) is a noble goal; so is the goal to ensure sustainable consumption and production patterns (SDG 12). But if one were to assume that increased agriculture demands more land and fertilisers, SDGs 2 and 12 may potentially conflict with SDG 15, which aims, among other things, to halt and reverse land degradation and halt biodiversity loss. On the issue of hierarchy, one would have expected that some goals should assume higher importance than others, particularly those that must provide a supporting base for the achievement of others. It could be argued, for example, that SDGs 14 and 15, which aim to conserve and sustainably use the oceans, seas and marine resources and to protect, restore and promote sustainable use of terrestrial ecosystems, sustainably manage forests, combat desertification, and halt and reverse land degradation and halt biodiversity loss, must be afforded a higher priority than, say, SDGs 8 and 12, which aim to promote sustained, inclusive and sustainable economic growth and to ensure sustainable consumption and production patterns. Sustained economic growth, consumption and production are, after all, entirely dependent on marine and terrestrial resources being intact and conserved sustainably. The most obvious second example is SDG 13, which aims to take urgent action to combat climate change and its impacts. None of the other 16 SDGs will arguably be achieved, at least not in the long term, in a world plagued by climate disruption.

As in all the instances above, collectively these concerns also relate to the specific understanding and meaning of sustainable development as it is embedded in the SDGs. It was indicated that the SDGs fully embrace an anthropocentric or weak form of sustainable development which prioritises socio-economic development at the cost of environmental integrity. Had the SDGs instead embraced a strong notion of ecological sustainability, they would arguably automatically have had to import some form of hierarchy between the 17 goals, especially to the extent that those goals aiming to protect Earth system integrity must be afforded a higher ranking than all the others if we are to remain in a 'safe operating space'. The SDGs therefore fail to 'speak to one another' in the

---

[74] Kim, above n 11, 17.

way that an integrated vision of Earth system governance demands, and they fail to prioritise protection of those critical elements of the Earth system upon which all other components depend. Being fragmented, silo-ist and non-hierarchical merely reinforces the potential of the SDGs to be used by states as a legitimating and justificatory foundation to prioritise socio-economic growth over environmental protection. The fallacies and false promises of weak sustainable development that were started by the Stockholm Declaration and subsequent events and instruments thus continue, and the world is nowhere closer to extricating itself from the process of self-destruction that it has inevitably embarked upon.

3.5 CONCLUSION

I have been particularly critical of the SDGs in my analysis above. This is because none of the three new-millennial analytical paradigms through which I have viewed the SDGs actually support, justify or legitimise the current purpose, focus, form and ontology of the SDGs. This is worrying considering that, as I have shown, the SDGs have some measure of normative authority and significance, while states have at least some sense of obligation to achieve the 17 goals and 169 targets. The SDGs clearly are therefore not insignificant in the larger global law, politics and governance scheme of things.

If the SDGs are the principal roadmap for development until 2030, they represent a lost opportunity as they will likely continue to advance socio-economic growth at the expense of ecological considerations, much like the MDGs before them. Socio-economic growth that is aimed at alleviating poverty and creating more inclusive societies, among other things, is critically important, but the extent to which this can be achieved is entirely dependent on Earth system integrity being safeguarded well into the future. The short-term successes of the SDGs might very well be significant, but it is hard to believe that they would be able meaningfully to address in the much longer term Anthropocene-inducing causes and events; prevent humanity from approaching and crossing planetary boundaries; and properly respond to an integrated but fragile Earth system in a coherent and effective way.

The analysis suggests that not only will the SDGs not address the ecological imperatives identified throughout; their failure to fully reflect these ecological concerns ultimately risks exacerbating the Anthropocene's multiple socio-ecological crises and the many problems these create by delaying (at least for 15 years) a critical political conversation about the challenges ahead. We also risk delaying a conversation, and more importantly, political, legal and governance actions, that would be needed to counter the likely impacts of the SDGs, which, in their present guise, are rhetorically ambitious but simultaneously destructive. Paradoxically, their successful attainment may further bifurcate human development agenda-setting and the demands on global ecological integrity. It would therefore also be essential to address this inherent paradox of the SDGs and their likely successors.

ACKNOWLEDGEMENT

Research for this chapter was supported in part by the author's European Union Marie Sklodowska Curie project titled: 'Global Ecological Custodianship: Innovative International Environmental Law for the Anthropocene' (GLEC-LAW) under grant agreement No. 751782 and it was completed in February 2018.

4. Sustainable Development Goals and human rights: challenges and opportunities

Lynda M. Collins*

> What we are announcing today – an Agenda for global action for the next 15 years – is a charter for people and the planet in the twenty-first century.[1]

4.1 INTRODUCTION

The UN General Assembly has compared the historic significance of the *2030 Agenda for Sustainable Development* to that of the Charter of the United Nations.[2] Many scholars and stakeholders agree that the promulgation of the *2030 Agenda* is indeed 'a decision of great historic significance'[3] – an unprecedented, multi-sectorial focusing of global resources and attention in a collaboration that seeks to transform the world as we know it. The Sustainable Development Goals (SDGs) articulated in the *2030 Agenda* have arguably become the primary unifying narrative among global actors, including governments, international agencies (such as the World Bank), civil society, and multinational business. Whether one is a fan or a critic, there is no denying that the SDGs have already succeeded in catching the world's attention and holding it. Literally millions of people were involved in producing

* The author is grateful to Madiha Vallani, Pooja Naidu and Meera Karunananthan for their very helpful contributions.

1 UN General Assembly, *Transforming our world: the 2030 Agenda for Sustainable Development*, 21 October 2015, A/RES/70/1 [*2030 Agenda*], Preamble, para 51.

2 Charter of the United Nations 24 October 1945, 1 UNTS XVI; *2030 Agenda*, above n 1, paras 49–53.

3 *2030 Agenda*, above n 1, para 50.

the SDGs and billions will benefit if they are achieved.[4] While no one would dispute the laudable aims of the *2030 Agenda*, it is possible that this new approach may be a disruptive discourse, potentially undermining or even supplanting the human rights paradigm. In the alternative, the *2030 Agenda* may be the best thing to happen to human rights in the twenty-first century.

This chapter will evaluate the challenges and opportunities for human rights in the context of the SDGs. It will begin by exploring the pragmatic and conceptual relationship between the SDGs and the human rights paradigm and will then analyse four distinct policy fields to interrogate the extent to which the SDGs serve or subvert human rights in these key areas: poverty; environment; equality and non-discrimination; and civil and political rights. The author will argue that while SDGs fall short of human rights norms in a number of instances, they have the real potential to advance the human rights agenda in unprecedented ways.

4.2 FROM HUMAN RIGHTS TO SDGS: A NEW ERA?

The SDGs and their associated Targets constitute a blueprint for a new world. This is a comprehensive and ambitious vision of development that seeks to eradicate a stunning list of long-standing social ills, including poverty, hunger, water scarcity, unemployment, inequality (both local and global), corruption and illiteracy. As it lifts the current generation out of poverty and suffering, the *2030 Agenda* simultaneously seeks to decouple economic growth from environmental degradation and secure clean air, sustainable agricultural systems, thriving oceans and healthy forests and freshwater ecosystems for the future. Remarkably, this comprehensive agenda for global transformation is not only broad, but also deep. All of the SDGs are intended to be implemented in a manner that leaves no one behind,[5] a clear mandate that is reflected throughout the specific language of the goals and targets. Goal 4, for example, is not just to ensure education for all, but to 'Ensure inclusive and equitable quality education and promote lifelong learning opportunities for all.' It includes Target 4.5: 'By 2030, eliminate gender disparities in education and ensure equal access to all levels of education and vocational training for the vulnerable, including persons with disabilities, indigenous peoples and children in vulnerable situations.' This pattern of increasing the granularity of goals to meaningful levels of specificity in their related targets is

[4] *Ibid*, paras 6, 52.

[5] *Ibid*, para 4.

repeated many times throughout the *2030 Agenda*, though there is certainly room for improvement.

As a whole, the *2030 Agenda* reflects a vision of profound global transformation, from the highest level of state–state relations to the daily, lived experience of the poorest people in the least developed countries of the world. Nevertheless, this stunningly ambitious global consensus has mixed implications for human rights discourse and practice.[6] Unlike its predecessor, the *Millennium Declaration*,[7] the *2030 Agenda* repeatedly references the importance of human rights,[8] and claims to be grounded in a human rights approach. However, if indeed the SDGs mark a global paradigm shift, then this could arguably undermine human rights as a hitherto hegemonic global narrative.[9] If rights were 'the currency of political and legal discourse' in the twentieth century,[10] it may be that global development goals are the currency of the twenty-first. It is possible, then, that the global concentration of efforts towards attaining the *2030 Agenda* will actually draw time, energy, financing and focus away from human rights both in theory and practice.

Certainly the *2030 Agenda* has been criticized for its failure to explicitly adopt various human rights norms, even though it references human rights.[11] Many SDGs are weaker than their human rights counterparts, and many fail to reference specific, binding human rights standards

---

[6] The term 'human rights' will be used broadly in this chapter to refer to rights enshrined in international human rights law, including Declarations and Conventions as interpreted by treaty bodies and authoritative tribunals and also domestic applications of such rights through constitutionalization and judicial interpretations by national courts. The term 'human rights system' denotes the whole panoply of international and national mechanisms for articulating and effectuating human rights, including the relevant international treaty bodies, international tribunals, UN Special Procedures, the UN Universal Periodic Review Process, international human rights NGOs, and domestic human rights actors (in both government and civil society).

[7] UN General Assembly, *United Nations Millennium Declaration, Resolution Adopted by the General Assembly*, 18 September 2000, A/RES/55/2.

[8] See V.P. Nanda, 'The Journey from the Millennium Development Goals to Sustainable Development Goals' (2016) *Denver Journal of International Law and Policy* 44, 389; J.D Sachs, 'From Millennium Development Goals to Sustainable Development Goals' (2012) *The Lancet* 379, 2206.

[9] See generally, L. Henkin, *The Age of Rights* (Columbia University Press, 1990).

[10] L. Trakman and S. Gatien, *Rights and Responsibilities* (University of Toronto Press, 1999) 3.

[11] See for example, J.H. Knox, 'Human Rights, Environmental Protection and the Sustainable Development Goals' (2015) *Washington International Law*

and instruments. The SDG and Targets related to water and sanitation, for example, fail to adopt the sufficiency criterion that has been recognized by the Committee on Economic, Social and Cultural Rights as an aspect of the right to water.[12] The *2030 Agenda* altogether fails to address the unique rights of Indigenous peoples, and there is no mention of the United Nations Declaration on the Rights of Indigenous Peoples.[13] Moreover, despite its multiple and laudable goals and targets addressing the rights of women and girls, and its explicit reference to the Convention on the Rights of the Child,[14] the *Agenda* makes no mention of the Convention on the Elimination of All Forms of Discrimination Against Women.[15] Finally, and perhaps most fundamentally, the *Agenda* has modified the basic language describing states' human rights obligations, affirming 'the responsibilities of all States … to respect, protect and *promote* human rights'.[16] Though 'promote' has sometimes been added as a fourth state obligation in the literature, the replacement of 'fulfill' with 'promote' suggests a weakening of this basic canon of international human rights law.[17]

Journal 24, 517; *Spotlight on Sustainable Development 2016* <http://www.socialwatch.org/node/17211> accessed 26 January 2018; *Joint Statement of the Chairpersons of the United Nations Human Rights Treaty Bodies on the Post-2015 Development Agenda* at 1 (18 January 2015) <http://www.ohchr.org/EN/NewsEvents/Pages/DisplayNews.aspx?NewsID=15505> accessed 26 January 2018.

[12] See M. Karunananthan, 'Whose Rights to Water Will the 2030 Agenda Promote?' in *Spotlight on Sustainable Development 2016* <https://www.2030spotlight.org/sites/default/files/contentpix/spotlight/pdfs/spotlight_ch2_6.pdf> accessed 26 January 2018.

[13] United Nations Declaration on the Rights of Indigenous Peoples, GA Res 61/295, UNGAOR, 61st Sess, Supp No 49, UN Doc. A/61/295 (2007).

[14] Convention on Rights of the Child, UNTS, vol 1577, p. 3.

[15] Target 5.6 (sexual and reproductive health and reproductive rights) does, however, reference the non-binding *Beijing Platform for Action.* United Nations, *Beijing Declaration and Platform of Action*, adopted at the Fourth World Conference on Women, 27 October 1995 <http://www.refworld.org/docid/3dde04324.html> accessed 26 January 2018.

[16] *2030 Agenda*, above n 1, at para 19 (italics added).

[17] See D. Shelton and A. Gould, 'Positive and Negative Obligations' in Dinah Shelton (ed), *Oxford Handbook of International Human Rights Law* (Oxford University Press, 2013) at 23–24; United Nations Human Rights Committee, *General Comment 31, Nature of the General Legal Obligation on States Parties to the Covenant*, Human Rights Committee, UN Doc. CCPR/C/21/Rev.1/Add.13 (2004).

Despite these legitimate concerns, there is reason to hope that the *2030 Agenda* will have a positive impact on the enjoyment of human rights around the globe. While most SDGs lack the specificity of human rights norms, and none enjoy binding status within an adjudicative process, if the gains envisioned by the SDGs are actually achieved, they will simultaneously do much to discharge states' obligations to respect, protect and fulfil human rights.

4.3 CO-EXTENSIVE, COMPLEMENTARY OR CONFLICTING? HUMAN RIGHTS VERSUS SDGS

One thing that is certain is that there is no SDG that can be said to be co-extensive with its analogous human right.[18] Sometimes the two will overlap or may act in a complementary fashion and sometimes the relevant SDG may be viewed as potentially weaker than, and thus undermining, a particular human rights norm. Collectively considered, it is fair to say that the SDGs fall short of the 'full coherence' with international human rights standards recommended by the UN Secretary General.[19] However, as noted above, the SDGs involve a massive global mobilization of resources and attention that is arguably unprecedented in human history. This alone may make them a more effective tool for realizing human rights than the formal human rights system itself. Even where an SDG falls short of a human rights norm, the massive push to achieve SDGs (should it continue) is a major advantage. To use an extreme hypothetical, 100 per cent attainment of a modest SDG would be more meaningful than 0 per cent attainment of an ambitious human rights standard.[20]

---

[18] The Danish Institute for Human Rights has developed an invaluable online *Human Rights Guide to the Sustainable Development Goals*, which allows users to correlate the various SDGs with pertinent human rights norms. Users can search SDGs to find relevant human rights provisions, or vice versa. See <http://sdg.humanrights.dk/en> accessed 26 January 2018.

[19] UN Secretary General, *The Road to Dignity by 2030: Ending Poverty, Transforming All Lives and Protecting the Planet: Synthesis Report of the Secretary-General on the Post-2015 Sustainable Development Agenda*, UN Doc. A/69/700 (4 December 2014), para 65.

[20] Indeed, Fellmeth argues that in some states, '[e]xtensive positive [human] rights may also play a role [that is] insidiously subversive of human dignity. The professed inability of the state to guarantee widespread positive rights may become a pretext for failing to implement modest improvements in positive

The complexity of the relationship between the *2030 Agenda* and human rights is reflected at all levels. On the meta-narrative level, the *2030 Agenda* states that the SDGs 'seek to realize the human rights of all' and note that they are 'indivisible', a core precept of international human rights law.[21] The *2030 Agenda* also states that it is 'grounded in the Universal Declaration of Human Rights [and] international human rights treaties',[22] but these treaties are largely conspicuous by their absence in the SDGs themselves. Interestingly, the SDGs reference five non-human rights treaties,[23] but the only human rights treaty that is explicitly mentioned is the Convention on the Rights of the Child.[24] The term 'human rights' appears only once within the actual SDGs and Targets (in Target 4.7 relating to education for sustainable development, including 'human rights') though there are references to 'equal rights' to economic resources,[25] 'labour rights'[26] and the 'rights' of women and girls.[27] Nevertheless, most of the SDGs overlap to some extent with human rights such that a comprehensive analysis of each intersection would merit its own volume. This chapter will therefore focus on four

---

rights well within the resources of the state …'. A.X. Fellmeth, *Paradigms of International Human Rights Law* (Oxford University Press, 2016) at 261.

[21] See for example, UN General Assembly, *Optional Protocol to the International Covenant on Economic, Social and Cultural Rights*, Preamble, 5 March 2009, A/RES/63/117, available at <http://www.refworld.org/docid/49c226dd0.html> accessed 27 January 2017; P. Gilabert, 'The Importance of Linkage Arguments for the Theory and Practice of Human Rights' (2010) *Human Rights Quarterly* 32, 425.

[22] *2030 Agenda*, above n 1, para 10.

[23] World Health Organization Framework Convention on Tobacco Control (SDG 3.a); Doha Declaration on the TRIPS Agreement and Public Health (3.b); Agreement on Trade-Related Aspects of Intellectual Property Rights (3.b); Convention on the Law of the Sea (14.c); United Nations Framework Convention on Climate Change (13.a).

[24] Convention on the Rights of the Child, UNTS, vol 1577, no 27531.

[25] Target 1.4.

[26] Target 8.8.

[27] Targets 5.6, 5.a. It is also noteworthy that the Indicators, developed to track progress with the SDGs and Targets, include additional references to 'human rights' in 10.3.1 (repeated in 16.b.1) 'Proportion of population reporting having personally felt discriminated against or harassed in the previous 12 months on the basis of a ground of discrimination prohibited under international human rights law'; 16.a.1 'Existence of independent national human rights institutions in compliance with the Paris Principles' and 16.10.1 'Number of verified cases of killing, kidnapping, enforced disappearance, arbitrary detention and torture of … human rights advocates in the previous 12 months'.

distinct policy areas: poverty, environment, equality and non-discrimination, and civil and political rights.

4.3.1 Poverty

The SDGs and Targets on poverty can be seen as the latest evolution in a chain of international instruments beginning with the Charter of the United Nations[28] itself. If it is true that 'the opposite of poverty is not wealth [but rather] justice',[29] then a concern with poverty eradication can be seen as pervading human rights theory and practice from its inception. Article 55 of the UN Charter states that the UN 'shall promote … higher standards of living, full employment, and conditions of economic and social progress and development'. Articles 22–26 of the Universal Declaration of Human Rights[30] recognize the right to social security, the right to work, the right to leisure, the right to an adequate standard of living 'including food, clothing, housing and medical care and necessary social services' and the right to education. These rights were codified in the International Covenant on Economic, Social and Cultural Rights[31] and have been elaborated over the years by the Committee on Economic, Social and Cultural Rights and various UN Special Procedures.[32] The UN General Assembly recognized the human right to development in the 1986 Declaration on the Right to Development,[33] defining it as 'comprehensive economic, social, cultural and political process, which aims at the constant improvement of the well-being of the entire population and of all individuals on the basis of their active, free and meaningful

---

[28] 1 UNTS XVI.

[29] B. Stevenson, *Just Mercy: A Story of Justice and Redemption* (Spiegel and Grau, 2014) 18.

[30] Universal Declaration of Human Rights, GA Res. 217A (III) A, Preamble, UN Doc. A/RES/217 (III) (10 December 1948).

[31] International Covenant on Economic, Social and Cultural Rights, 16 December 1966, 993 UNTS 3 art 15(1)(a) (entered into force 3 January 1976, accession by Canada 19 May 1976).

[32] See for example, the Special Rapporteur on the right to food: <http://www.ohchr.org/EN/Issues/Food/Pages/FoodIndex.aspx>; the Special Rapporteur on the right to housing as an aspect of the right to an adequate standard of living: <http://www.ohchr.org/EN/Issues/Housing/Pages/HousingIndex.aspx>; Special Rapporteur on the Right to Development: <http://www.ohchr.org/EN/NewsEvents/Pages/DisplayNews.aspx?NewsID=20616&LangID=E> all accessed 26 January 2018.

[33] UN GAOR, 41st Sess., Supp. No. 53, at 183, UN Doc. A/RES/41/128 (1986).

participation in development and in the fair distribution of benefits resulting therefrom'.[34] The right to development was elaborated in the 1992 Rio Declaration on Environment and Development[35] and the 1993 Vienna Declaration and Programme of Action,[36] the latter describing it as 'a universal and inalienable right and an integral part of fundamental human rights'. Development encompasses but goes beyond poverty alleviation; it concerns quality of life as well as standard of living, and is centrally concerned with both dignity and freedom.[37]

Although the SDGs as a whole, and those specifically directed at poverty eradication, are arguably the descendants of the economic, social and cultural rights and the right to development, and despite the *2030 Agenda's* professed adherence to a human rights approach, the SDGs and Targets in this area make no reference to the right to an adequate standard of living, the right to housing, the right to food, the right to water and sanitation (which is mentioned in the Declaration portion of the *2030 Agenda* but not in the SDGs or Targets), and indeed to the right to development itself (though the right to development is mentioned in the Preamble).[38] It seems clear, however, that the *2030 Agenda* nonetheless seeks to advance the substance of these rights to a significant degree. Nevertheless, the relative efficacy of the SDGs compared with the traditional human rights approach remains to be seen. It is possible that the non-binding nature of the SDGs will increase state buy-in and implementation, thus achieving some of the goals of human rights through an indirect (but more politically palatable) route. While SDG implementation efforts (or the lack thereof) will no doubt answer these questions in time, for some authors and activists, the human rights paradigm is viewed as inherently more effective than that of development.

Pogge and Sengupta suggest that the governments of the world should have chosen as their goal the full realization of human rights everywhere. Indeed, one can imagine a hypothetical *2030 Human Rights Agenda* that collects and elaborates the full suite of human rights, including all three

---

[34] *Declaration on the Right to Development*, GA Res. 41/128, UN Doc. A/RES/41/128, at 1 (4 December 1986).

[35] UN Doc. A/CONF.151/26 (vol I).

[36] UN Doc. A/CONF.157/23 (1993).

[37] A Sen, *Development as Freedom* (Oxford University Press, 1999); L.B. Sohn, 'The New International Law: Protection of the Rights of Individuals Rather than States' (1982) *American University Law Review* 32, 1; E. Daly, *Dignity Rights: Courts, Constitutions, and the Worth of the Human Person* (University of Pennsylvania Press, 2012).

[38] *2030 Agenda*, above n 1, Preamble, para 10, page 4/35.

generations of rights, as they have been articulated by binding and non-binding human rights instruments, UN treaty bodies, Special Procedures and agencies, regional judicial institutions and domestic constitutional and other courts. For Pogge and Sengupta, the adoption of a development paradigm in lieu of traditional human rights reflects a desire to delay implementation. They argue that the relative inferiority of development goals, as compared with human rights, is inherent in their very nature:[39]

> The discourse of development goals draws our attention to *diachronic comparisons* with historical benchmarks: we look at the trend since 1990 or 1960 or 1830, and we invariably find evidence that things have become better than they had been earlier. The language of human rights draws our attention to *synchronic comparisons* with what would now be possible and, if we cared to make such comparisons, we would invariably find that the extent of present deprivations is far greater than would be unavoidable. It is not surprising, then, that our national politicians and international officials, Western media and the world's affluent people prefer the former mode of presentation. But it does not fit with the language of rights. It does not fit with the recognition that all human beings have human rights to a life in dignity, a life in which they can meet their basic needs.[40]

Whatever the merits of this argument may be on the level of discourse analysis, the condition of 'progressive realization' attached to economic, social and cultural rights has probably already blurred the distinction between rights and goals in this context.[41] The right to development, moreover, is primarily located in soft law instruments, with the result that it is virtually unenforceable. Acharya elaborates:

> Current systems and international law provide for a moral sense of duty through soft law yet miss very important elements: the acceptance of an inherent right of every individual to the means of basic survival, a historical context of the relationship of developed countries with underdeveloped countries, and a notion of legal responsibility for development in the system of laws and remedies. Without these elements, human development fails on a

---

[39] T. Pogge and M. Sengupta, 'Assessing the Sustainable Development Goals from a Human Rights Perspective' (2016) *Journal of International and Comparative Social Policy* 32, 83.

[40] *Ibid*, at 85 (emphasis in original).

[41] See U.E. Effeh, 'A Case Study on How Not to Realize Economic, Social and Cultural Rights and a Proposal for Change' (2005) *Northwestern Journal of International Human Rights* 3, 2; M. Robinson, 'Advancing Economic, Social and Cultural Rights' (2004) *Human Rights Quarterly* 26, 866.

basic level because it becomes a notion of international charity and not a truth of human rights.[42]

Acharya argues that what is needed is a revitalization of human rights to make them more effective and enforceable in the area of poverty eradication, which he views as a right to survival.

Setting aside the larger debate as to whether international human rights law as a whole has succeeded in improving human rights practice around the world,[43] most scholars would agree that the human rights approach has not done a particularly good job of realizing economic, social and cultural rights (nor the right to development) thus far.[44] The international human rights system has tended to privilege civil and political rights and many national courts have held economic, social and cultural rights to be non-justiciable.[45] Where courts have held such rights to be justiciable, they have sometimes adopted narrow interpretations thwarting the meaningful achievement of the right in question.[46] As a result, in many cases, '[t]hese "rights" failed to make a meaningful contribution to poverty eradication'.[47] The very needs underlying the *2030 Agenda* could in fact be viewed as proof of the failure of economic, social and cultural rights. The right to an adequate standard of living has failed to reach 836 million people living in extreme poverty,[48] and 795 million undernourished

---

[42] FAO, IFAD and WFP, *The State of Food Insecurity in the World 2015. Meeting the 2015 international hunger targets: taking stock of uneven progress* (Rome, FAO, 2015) <http://www.fao.org/3/a-i4646e.pdf> accessed 13 February 2018.

[43] See for example, O.A. Hathaway, 'Do Human Rights Treaties Make a Difference?' (2002) *Yale Law Journal* 111, 1935; E. Neumayer, 'Do International Human Rights Treaties Improve Respect for Human Rights?' (2005) *Journal of Conflict Resolution* 49(6), 925; C. Dommen, 'The UN Human Rights Regime: Is It Effective?' (1997) *American Society of International Law Proceedings* 91, 460.

[44] See D.J. Whelan and J. Donnelly, 'The West, Economic and Social Rights and the Global Human Rights Regime: Setting the Record Straight, (2007) *Human Rights Quarterly* 29, 908; Effeh, above n 41; Robinson, above n 41.

[45] J. Castellino and S. Bradshaw, 'Sustainable Development and Social Inclusion: Why a Changed Approach is Central to Combatting Vulnerability' (2015) *Washington International Law Journal Association* 24(3), 459.

[46] See for example, N.J. Cooper, 'After *Mazibuko*: Exploring the Responses of Communities Excluded from South Africa's Water Experiment' (2017) *Journal of African Law* 61(1), 57.

[47] Castellino and Bradshaw, above n 45, 461.

[48] United Nations, *The Millennium Development Goals Report, 2015* <http://www.un.org/millenniumgoals/2015 MDG Report/pdf/MDG%202015%20 rev%20(July%201).pdf> at 4, accessed 26 January 2018.

people are still waiting for the realization of their right to food.[49] International human rights law has provided no effective remedies for violations of the right to development[50] and may in fact be structurally ill-suited to the task.

In this respect, Castellino and Bradshaw identify a number of 'core failures' in the international human rights system, including an over-emphasis on individual, civil and political rights and the use of formal legislative and adjudicative processes to enforce them.[51] Further,

> the use of human rights as a 'naming and shaming' tool with uncertain political support from many countries alienates states and effectively ends their engagement with prospective solutions ... [and] an over-emphasis on states as the primary liable actors for rights violations has resulted in missed opportunities with others who may be more sensitive to public pressure, such as the corporate sector.[52]

If in fact the human rights system in its current state of evolution is poorly adapted to the realization of socio-economic rights, then the SDGs may be very good news indeed for the world's 'bottom billion'.[53]

Unlike the human rights approach, the SDGs represent a collaborative process, supported (to a significant degree) by all regions of the world and multiple sectors, including governments, civil society and multi-national business. They do not rely on formal legislation and litigation and they provide states with the 'policy space' to develop and implement locally appropriate solutions.[54] Because the agreement is non-binding and its implementation is envisaged as a non-confrontational, cooperative effort, states may be more willing to embark on ambitious plans and programmes.[55] Moreover, the SDGs and Targets contain a clear timeline for eliminating extreme poverty and hunger (2030), in sharp contrast to the vague requirement of 'progressive realization' in the human rights

---

49 FAO, IFAD and WFP, above n 42.

50 See generally, S. Marks, 'The Right to Development: Between Rhetoric and Reality' (2004) *Harvard Human Rights Journal* 17, 137 (noting that 'The right to development (RTD) has been part of the international debate on human rights for over thirty years but has not yet entered the practical realm of development planning and implementation. States tend to express rhetorical support for this right but neglect its basic precepts in development practice').

51 Castellino and Bradshaw, above n 45, 465–466.

52 *Ibid*, at 466.

53 P. Collier, *The Bottom Billion, Why the Poorest Countries are Failing and What Can Be Done About It* (Oxford University Press, 2007).

54 Target 17.15.

55 Pogge and Sengupta, above n 39, 83.

context. Similarly, unlike formal human rights instruments, the Targets provide helpful guidance as to how states can realize the relevant goals. SDG 2 on hunger, for example, includes Target 2.3 to 'double the agricultural productivity and incomes of small-scale food producers, in particular women, indigenous peoples, family farmers, pastoralists and fishers …'. SDG 1 on poverty includes Target 1.3 'Implement nationally appropriate social protection systems and measures for all, including floors, and by 2030 achieve substantial coverage of the poor and the vulnerable'. Although this level of specificity may also be found in the reports of UN treaty bodies and Special Procedures, the obvious advantage of the SDGs here is that they are the product of global consultation and consensus.

On the question of poverty, SDG 1 states a far-reaching goal, unprecedented in its level of ambition and universality: 'End poverty in all its forms everywhere'. In addition to the goal of eradicating extreme poverty (defined as living on less than US$1.25/day) by 2030, the Targets include halving poverty, defined by national standards. In other words, the poverty goal applies to all nations. Given the concentration of poverty in the global south, this almost certainly implies an obligation on wealthy states to provide assistance to developing countries. This goal is also noteworthy for its incorporation of environmental resilience in Target 1.5: 'By 2030, build the resilience of the poor and those in vulnerable situations and reduce their exposure and vulnerability to climate-related extreme events and other economic, social and environmental shocks and disasters.' Bissio concludes that 'SDG 1 and its targets are thus a major departure from conventional thinking: they address poverty in all countries and in its multiple dimensions … they link the elimination of poverty to human rights and climate change and they point to the means that need to be mobilized to make it all happen'.[56]

In addition to SDG 1 and its related Targets, the SDGs also address hunger (SDG 2); health (SDG 3); education (SDG 4); water and sanitation (SDG 6); energy (SDG 7); employment (SDG 8); and global and local inequalities (SDG 10). These are all part of the irreducible core necessary to combat poverty in all its dimensions. The environmental SDGs (discussed in more detail below) would ensure access to crucial natural resources and the preservation of such resources in order to prevent widespread poverty in the future. In addition to this very

---

[56] R. Bissio, 'The New Goal on Poverty: A Welcome Paradigm Shift' in *Spotlight on Sustainable Development*, <https://www.2030spotlight.org/sites/default/files/contentpix/spotlight/pdfs/spotlight_ch2_1.pdf> accessed 31 January 2017.

impressive and multi-dimensional suite of goals and targets relating to poverty, the SDGs go well beyond poverty eradication to embrace a progressive vision of human development. SDG 9, for example, includes targets related to sustainable infrastructure,[57] access to financial markets for small-scale enterprises,[58] and universal and affordable access to the Internet (by 2020).[59] The SDGs contemplate development entitlements and obligations on a collective scale that have been difficult to capture in the human rights context. Collectively, the SDGs call for inclusive social protection systems, universal health coverage, energy infrastructure, job creation, and robust education systems (among other things). Moreover, they include multiple and integrated measures to advance equality and non-discrimination, another key aspect of the right to development. Taken together, the SDGs and Targets certainly have the potential to advance the right to development more than any other single initiative since its recognition by the international community.

Perhaps the most serious criticism of the *2030 Agenda* in this area is that it contemplates the continuation and expansion of a liberal, capitalist growth economy,[60] which many view as a root cause of poverty and environmental degradation. However, the human rights system has never attempted or succeeded in changing global macroeconomics, so this criterion is neutral as between the two approaches. In practice the SDGs and the human rights system (including treaty bodies, national constitutional courts, and human rights-focused NGOs) will hopefully collaborate to achieve the eradication of poverty and the attainment of development, however that project is framed.

4.3.2 Environment

The relationship between human rights and the SDGs is particularly nuanced in the area of environment since the application of a human rights approach to environmental matters is a relatively new and still evolving concept. Environmental human rights are generally understood to include three interrelated categories: procedural environmental rights (including access to information, public participation, and access to

---

57 Target 9.a.

58 Target 9.3.

59 Target 9.c.

60 See SDG 8 and *2030 Agenda*, above n 1, paras 3, 9, 13, 21, 27, 29; see also U. Acharya, 'The Future of Human Development: The Right to Survive as a Fundamental Element of the Right to Development' (2014) *Denver Journal of International Law and Policy* 42(3), 345, 362–366.

justice in environmental matters), the recognition of environmental deprivations of existing rights (for example, the rights to life and health), and the free-standing right to a healthy environment (sometimes framed as a 'healthy and ecologically balanced', 'safe', 'clean' or 'adequate' environment).[61]

4.3.2.1 Procedural environmental rights

There are a number of SDGs and Targets relevant to procedural environmental rights but they are generally weaker than their rights-based analogues. There are two provisions on access to information: Target 12.8 'By 2030, ensure that people everywhere have the relevant information and awareness for sustainable development and lifestyles in harmony with nature'; and Target 16.10 'Ensure public access to information and protect fundamental freedoms, in accordance with national legislation and international agreements'. The United Nations Special Rapporteur on Human Rights and the Environment has observed that both of these Targets state laudable goals but neither one equals the strength and specificity of analogous formulations found in relevant environmental instruments such as the Aarhus Convention[62] and Principle 10 of the Rio Declaration. Principle 10, for example, states: 'At the national level, each individual shall have appropriate access to information concerning the environment that is held by public authorities, including information on hazardous materials and activities in their communities ... States shall facilitate and encourage public awareness and participation by making information widely available.' This level of detail is absent in the SDGs and Targets: 'Worse, the phrase "in accordance with national legislation" [in Target 16.10] could be read as limiting the scope of Target 12.8 to a commitment to provide information only to the extent that national laws already require, which would make it almost a nullity.'[63]

Regarding the right of public participation in environmental decision-making, the relevant Target is 16.7, which states: 'Ensure responsive, inclusive, participatory and representative decision-making at all levels.' Once again this is substantially weaker than its counterpart in Principle

---

[61] See D.R. Boyd, *The Environmental Rights Revolution: A Global Study of Constitutions, Human Rights, and the Environment* (UBC Press, 2012); M. Burger, 'Bi-Polar and Polycentric Approaches to Human Rights and the Environment' (2003) *Columbia Journal of Environmental Law* 28(2), 371 at 376.

[62] Convention on Access to Information, Public Participation in Decision-Making and Access to Justice in Environmental Matters, 2161 UNTS 447; 38 ILM 517 (1999).

[63] Knox, above n 11, 517, 527.

10 of the Rio Declaration. Indeed, the Special Rapporteur states that '[w]hile the sentiment is again praiseworthy, the language could be much clearer'.[64] In particular, the Target should clarify that all people have the right to participate in decision-making and specifically that this includes women, children, people with disabilities, elders, poor people, minorities, migrants and Indigenous peoples.[65] In the third sub-category of procedural environmental rights – access to justice in environmental matters – Target 16.3 ('Promote the rule of law at the national and international levels and ensure equal access to justice for all') is once again 'too vague to be of much use'.[66] The Special Rapporteur also notes that access to justice is not meaningful if environmental advocates face the threat of state reprisals, and recommends that the SDGs specifically address the needs of human rights defenders.

4.3.2.2 Environmental deprivations of existing rights

With respect to the recognition of and redress for environmental deprivations of existing rights, the SDGs – if implemented – have tremendous potential. National, regional and international tribunals and treaty bodies have recognized that environmental degradation can violate the rights to life, health, privacy and family life, and culture, among others.[67] These bodies have also recognized environmental violations of the unique rights of Indigenous peoples, women and children.[68] The existing rights approach has tended to focus on the worst forms of environmental harm – the most polluted areas in a given nation with the most severe impacts on human well-being. If the SDGs and Targets on health, agriculture, and marine and terrestrial ecosystems are implemented, particularly in accordance with the *2030 Agenda's* injunction to 'leave no-one behind', they promise to go well beyond the elimination of the most extreme

---

[64] *Ibid*, at 517, 528.

[65] *Ibid*, citing *Joint Statement of the Chairpersons of the United Nations Human Rights Treaty Bodies on the Post-2015 Development Agenda*, at 1 (18 January 2015).

[66] *Ibid*, at 517, 529.

[67] See generally D.K Anton and D. Shelton, *Environmental Protection and Human Rights* (Cambridge University Press, 2011); D. Shelton (ed), *Human Rights and the Environment* (Edward Elgar Publishing, 2011); S. Kravchenko, 'Environmental Rights in International Law: Explicitly Recognized or Creatively Interpreted' (2012) *Florida Agricultural and Mechanical University Law Review* 7(2), 163.

[68] See generally L.M. Collins, 'The United Nations, Human Rights and the Environment' in A. Grear and L. Kotzé (eds), *Research Handbook on Human Rights and the Environment* (Edward Elgar Publishing, 2015) 219.

environmental problems and their resulting violations of existing rights. The SDGs could also promise an even greater impact on the right to a healthy environment.

4.3.2.3 The independent right to a healthy environment

The multiple, concrete and far-reaching environmental goals and targets contained in the *2030 Agenda* constitute a potentially game-changing elaboration of the scope and content of the human right to a healthy environment.[69] Empirical evidence suggests that enforceable environmental rights at the domestic level make a meaningful difference in improving legislation, litigation outcomes and environmental performance.[70] On the international level, however, the absence of any environmental rights convention (or international environmental court) has created some difficulty in defining the content of the independent right to a healthy environment. Scholars have proposed the precautionary principle, intergenerational equity, and protection of aesthetic interests as unique aspects of the free-standing right to a healthy environment; but these concepts are themselves highly abstract and hotly contested.[71] The substantive environmental SDGs and Targets, in contrast, are far more specific and prescriptive. If the right to a healthy environment does indeed exist as a norm of customary international law, then it should surely be interpreted in accordance with the *2030 Agenda*, which arguably represents the most cohesive global policy consensus since the Universal Declaration of Human Rights.

While some of the environmental SDGs and Targets are unhelpfully vague,[72] a few are remarkably specific, notably Target 14.5: 'By 2020, conserve at least 10 per cent of coastal and marine areas, consistent with national and international law and based on the best available scientific information'; and Target 12.3 'By 2030, halve per capita global food

---

69 Knox, above n 11.

70 Boyd, above n 61, *The Environmental Rights Revolution: A Global Study of Constitutions, Human Rights, and the Environment* (UBC Press, 2012); E. Daly and J.R May, *Global Environmental Constitutionalism* (Cambridge University Press, 2014); C. Jeffords and J. Gellers, 'Constitutionalizing Environmental Rights: A Practical Guide' (2017) *Journal of Human Rights Practice* 9(1), 136–145.

71 L.M. Collins, 'Are We There Yet? The Right to Environment in International and European Law' (2007) *McGill International Journal of Sustainable Development Law and Policy* 119; L.M. Collins, 'Security of the Person, Peace of Mind: A Precautionary Approach to Environmental Uncertainty' (2013) *Journal of Human Rights and the Environment* 4(1), 79.

72 Knox, above n 11, 517.

waste at the retail and consumer levels and reduce food losses along production and supply chains, including post-harvest losses'. Others set out specific policy tools for achieving environmental objectives, such as the use of seed banks to preserve biodiversity,[73] the elimination of fisheries subsidies that encourage over-fishing or illegal fishing;[74] and rationalization of 'inefficient fossil-fuel subsidies that encourage wasteful consumption by removing market distortions ... including by restructuring taxation and phasing out those harmful subsidies ...'.[75] Within the SDGs and Targets as a whole, there is a critical mass of meaningfully concrete provisions that are relevant both to the substance of the right to environment and the means by which states can fulfil it.

Should decision-makers look to the *2030 Agenda* for guidance in defining the scope and content of environmental rights, they might reasonably conclude that the right to a healthy environment includes, among other things: access to safe water and sanitation for all, including the protection and restoration of 'water-related ecosystems, including mountains, forests, wetlands, rivers, aquifers and lakes';[76] 'sustainable food production systems ... that help maintain ecosystems, that strengthen capacity for adaptation to climate change, extreme weather, drought, flooding and other disasters and that progressively improve land and soil quality';[77] protection from 'hazardous chemicals and air, water and soil pollution and contamination';[78] and 'universal access to safe, inclusive and accessible, green and public spaces, in particular for women and children, older persons and persons with disabilities'.[79] An environmental rights approach informed by the SDGs also suggests an obligation on states to 'build the resilience of the poor and those in vulnerable situations and reduce their exposure and vulnerability to climate-related extreme events and other ... environmental shocks and disasters';[80] take meaningful action to reduce greenhouse gas emissions within available resources;[81] 'substantially reduce the number of deaths and illnesses from hazardous chemicals and air, water and soil pollution

---

[73] Target 2.5.
[74] Target 14.6.
[75] Target 12.c.
[76] SDG 6; Target 6.6.
[77] Target 2.4.
[78] Target 3.9.
[79] Target 11.7.
[80] Target 1.5.
[81] A. Lehman, 'The Case for the Creation of an International Environmental Court: Non-State Actors and International Environmental Dispute Resolution'

and contamination';[82] and 'sustainably manage and protect marine and coastal ecosystems to avoid significant adverse impacts, including by strengthening their resilience, and take action for their restoration in order to achieve healthy and productive oceans'.[83] Furthermore, states must realize these rights on a non-discriminatory basis that addresses the needs of the most vulnerable first.[84]

The elaboration of the right to a healthy environment provided by the *2030 Agenda* is of more than academic interest. Successful litigation in a number of countries around the world has forced national governments to improve their environmental performance as a result of constitutional environmental rights.[85] Many countries automatically incorporate customary international law into their domestic law and others might at least be influenced by the international legal position. Similarly, as international actors continue to push for a global treaty or declaration on environmental rights and an international environmental court, they can be guided by the very helpful content provided by the SDGs and Targets. If the SDGs succeed in putting flesh on the bones of the right to a healthy environment, they might one day be viewed as the most significant development in the 'environmental rights revolution',[86] since the Stockholm Declaration of 1972.

4.3.3 Equality and Non-discrimination

The treatment of equality and non-discrimination in the *2030 Agenda* is a complex and multifaceted topic that cannot adequately be covered in the space available here. It is equally impossible to omit discussion of equality and non-discrimination in an analysis of human rights in the SDGs. This section will therefore take a middle road, selectively highlighting a few key aspects of the SDGs in this area. The primary observation to be made in this respect is that the *2030 Agenda* evinces a high-level commitment to integrate equality and non-discrimination into every aspect of sustainable development policy. It is a leitmotif running throughout the SDGs and Targets. Furthermore, the notion of equality embodied in the SDGs is arguably more robust than that codified in

---

(2015) *Colombia Natural Resources, Energy and Environmental Law Review* 26(2), 179.

[82] Target 3.9.

[83] Target 14.2.

[84] *2030 Agenda*, above n 1, para 4.

[85] Boyd, above n 61.

[86] *Ibid.*

human rights law, embracing a broader range of actors and interests. In particular, the SDGs address two objectives that arguably cannot be captured by human rights law in its current state of evolution. First, the SDGs seek to eliminate inequalities *among* states (SDG 10), for example by encouraging official development assistance to least developed countries (Target 10.b), and by ensuring 'enhanced representation and voice for developing countries in decision-making in global international economic and financial institutions …' (Target 10.6). Second, through the suite of environmental provisions discussed above (and by the very nature of sustainable development), the SDGs attempt to protect the interests of future generations – a population that is infinitely vulnerable to the consequences of present-day decision-making, yet lacks any formal rights or remedies within the international human rights system.

Thus, when the Preamble to the SDGs states the intention to leave no one behind, and to reach the most vulnerable first, this applies domestically, internationally and inter-generationally. In keeping with this very strong vision of equality, Target 10.2 goes beyond the minimum obligation of non-discrimination, committing states to 'empower and promote the social, economic and political inclusion of all irrespective of age, sex, disability, race, ethnicity, origin, religion or economic or other status'. This broad commitment to equality and social inclusion is evident in the specifics of most of the SDGs. A good example is Target 1.4: 'By 2030, ensure that all men and women, in particular the poor and the vulnerable, have equal rights to economic resources …'. Concern for the most vulnerable populations pervades all policy areas in the *2030 Agenda* and is undoubtedly most successful with respect to women and gender.

4.3.3.1 Women and gender

The SDGs and Targets set out multiple, integrated provisions advancing the rights of women and girls. The stand-alone goal, SDG 5, calls on states to 'achieve gender equality and empower all women and girls' and includes the ambitious Target 5.1 to 'end all forms of discrimination against women and girls everywhere'. Other Targets seek to eradicate: violence against women and girls,[87] sexual exploitation,[88] forced marriage,[89] and female genital mutilation.[90] In addition to these Targets, correlating roughly with 'negative rights', the Targets also include a

---

[87] Target 5.2.
[88] *Ibid.*
[89] Target 5.3.
[90] *Ibid.*

number of significant 'positive rights',[91] including state support for women's unpaid domestic labour (Target 5.4); equal opportunities for leadership in political, economic and public life (Target 5.5); 'universal access to sexual and reproductive health and reproductive rights' (Target 5.6); equal rights to economic resources (including land and natural resources) (Target 5.a); and access to technology to promote women's empowerment (Target 5.b). Target 5.c evinces a traditional human rights approach in its admonition to 'adopt and strengthen ... enforceable legislation for the promotion of gender equality'.

Although the 2030 Agenda arguably does not go as far as the rights-based regimes embodied in the Convention on the Elimination of All Forms of Discrimination Against Women and the Beijing Platform for Action,[92] the SDGs and Targets do present a truly integrated approach to gender equality (unlike the Millennium Development Goals). In addition to SDG 5 and its associated Targets, 10 other SDGs include Targets specifically directed at the interests of women and girls: SDGs 1, 2, 3, 4, 6, 8, 10, 11, 13, 17. Targets outside SDG 5 provide for a wide range of measures relevant to gender equality, including, for example: gender-sensitive development policies (Target 1.b); reducing maternal mortality (Target 3.1); universal access to sexual and reproductive health-care (Target 3.7); gender equality in education and vocational training (Target 4.5); protection for women migrants (Target 8.8); and special attention to the needs of women and girls with respect to sanitation and hygiene (Target 6.2), public transit (11.2), green and public spaces (11.7), and climate change (Target 13.b). In addition to these gender-specific provisions, several Targets apply explicitly to 'all women and men'[93] or 'all girls and boys'.[94]

Despite this ground-breaking progress on the integration of women's rights in the *2030 Agenda*, there is a glaring failure to address sexual orientation or gender identity.[95] While there may be cultural, religious

---

[91] Shelton and Gould, above n 18, at 562.

[92] Development Alternatives with Women for a new Era (DAWN), 'II.5 Overcoming Global Structural Obstacles and Preventing Negative Spill-over Effects for Realizing Women's Human Rights', in *Spotlight on Sustainable Development* <https://www.2030spotlight.org/en/book/605/chapter/ii5-overcoming-global-structural-obstacles-and-preventing-negative-spill-over50> accessed 13 February 2018.

[93] Targets 4.3, 8.5.

[94] Targets 4.1, 4.2.

[95] See generally, E. Mills, *Leave No One Behind: Gender, Sexuality and the Sustainable Development Goals* (Institute for Development Studies, 2015).

and/or political reasons accounting for this omission, they do not excuse it. If the SDGs are truly designed to leave no one behind and reach the most vulnerable first, then it is illogical and counterproductive to neglect sexual minorities, who are generally among the most marginalized populations in any community. Moreover, though sexual minorities have historically been disadvantaged in all nations, they are currently far more marginalized in developing than in developed countries, making them among the most vulnerable populations in the world.[96] However, though explicit references to sexual orientation and gender identity should have been made, it is possible that the term 'gender' will be treated as encompassing these concepts as the SDGs are implemented. The overarching policy to leave no one behind, and the comprehensive social inclusion language of Target 10.2 (in particular the phrase 'other status') strengthen this argument.[97] Similarly, many of the Targets are general and comprehensive enough to catch sexual orientation and gender identity. Target 4.a, for example, is potentially broad enough to encourage educational policies aimed at ending bullying based on sexual orientation: '... provide *safe*, *non-violent*, *inclusive* and effective learning environments *for all*'.[98] Clearly, however, the lack of express reference to sexual orientation leaves the question open to interpretation by states with the result that those most likely to take an inclusive approach to 'gender' in the SDGs are those who are already doing a better job at protecting the rights of sexual minorities. This is a serious defect which can only be addressed through implementation efforts that are more progressive than the text of the SDGs and Targets themselves. A similar observation may be made with respect to the *2030 Agenda's* treatment of Indigenous rights.

---

[96] See for example, P. Narayan, 'Somewhere Over the Rainbow ... International Human Rights Protections for Sexual Minorities in the New Millennium' (2006) *Boston University International Law Journal* 24(313), 320–324; H. Lau, 'Sexual Orientation: Testing the Universality of International Human Rights Law' (2004) *The University of Chicago Law Review* 71(1689); S. MacGuire, 'The Human Rights of Sexual Minorities in Africa' (2004) *California Western International Law Journal* 35(1); I. Saiz, *Bracketing Sexuality: Human Rights and Sexual Orientation – A Decade of Development and Denial at the UN* (Sexual Policy Watch, 2002); *Human Rights Protection for Sexual Minorities in Insular South-East Asia: Issues and Implications for Effective HIV Prevention* (UNESCO, 2013).

[97] Mills, above n 95, at 8–9.

[98] Emphasis added.

4.3.3.2 Indigenous rights

Perhaps the most shocking weakness in the *2030 Agenda* in the area of equality and non-discrimination is its failure to address the unique rights and vulnerabilities of Indigenous peoples. Like sexual minorities, Indigenous peoples suffer disproportionate poverty, social exclusion and human rights abuses in every nation of the world.[99] Many are still recovering from state-sponsored genocide or cultural genocide, and most face discrimination on multiple levels, including language, education, employment, access to government services, land tenure, control over natural resources, and environmental protection. Indigenous peoples have been treated as an impediment to economic development in many contexts and many face ongoing human rights abuses by the very entities that have been tasked with implementing the SDGs: states, corporations and occasionally even NGOs.[100] The SDGs and Targets make only two references to Indigenous peoples, in Target 2.3 concerning agricultural productivity and Target 4.5 concerning equal access to education. There is no reference to ILO Convention 169[101] nor to the United Nations Declaration on the Rights of Indigenous Peoples.[102] More importantly, many of the rights contained in these instruments are not reflected in the substance of the SDGs and Targets. There is no mention of the Indigenous right of 'free, prior and informed consent' to development activities, despite the recommendation of the UN human rights treaty body chairpersons.[103] The UN Special Rapporteur on Human Rights and the Environment has similarly stated that the SDGs should have included Indigenous rights Targets, including states' obligation to 'recognize the rights of indigenous peoples in the territory that they have traditionally occupied, including the natural resources on which they rely; provide

99 See *Addendum – Index of reports of the Special Rapporteur on the rights of indigenous peoples, James Anaya, by theme and by region* <http://www.ohchr.org/EN/Issues/IPeoples/SRIndigenousPeoples/Pages/SpecialReports.aspx> accessed 26 January 2018.

100 See for example, Report A/HRC/24/41, *Extractive industries and indigenous peoples. Report of the Special Rapporteur on the rights of indigenous peoples* <http://unsr.jamesanaya.org/study/report-a-hrc-24-41-extractive-industries-and-indigenous-peoples-report-of-the-special-rapporteur-on-the-rights-of-indigenous-peoples> accessed 26 January 2018.

101 International Labour Organization (ILO), *Indigenous and Tribal Peoples Convention, C169*, 27 June 1989, C169.

102 United Nations Declaration on the Rights of Indigenous Peoples, above n 14.

103 *Joint Statement of the Chairpersons of the United Nations Human Rights Treaty Bodies on the Post-2015 Development Agenda*, above n 11, 1.

them a reasonable benefit from any development in their traditionally occupied territories; and provide them access to legal remedies for harm caused by the development activities'.[104] Acknowledgment of these rights is particularly important in light of the *2030 Agenda's* emphasis on economic growth and industrialization. Without the necessary guarantees of Indigenous rights, there is a real risk that the *2030 Agenda* could lead to increased development of Indigenous territory at the expense of Indigenous well-being.[105] This would seriously undermine the *2030 Agenda's* commitment to 'the human rights of all' and clearly contravenes its stated intent to reach the most vulnerable segments of societies and leave no one behind. One can only hope that these overarching commitments will guide implementation efforts in ways that include and empower Indigenous communities.

4.3.4 Civil and Political Rights

While it may reasonably be said that the SDGs and Targets reflect and even buttress economic, environmental and social rights, the situation is less clear with respect to civil and political rights. Perhaps the reason for this is the perceived strengths of the human rights system with respect to these hegemonic 'first generation' rights. However, despite their very successful entrenchment in legal systems around the world, it is clear that widespread and serious violations of civil and political rights persist globally.[106] If the *2030 Agenda* is indeed the charter for the twenty-first century, then it should have addressed civil and political rights more fully. The chairs of the UN treaty bodies recommended the explicit inclusion of 'freedoms of expression, association and peaceful assembly'.[107] In addition, the SDGs should have addressed the unique vulnerability of human rights defenders. As the Special Rapporteur on Human Rights and the Environment has noted:

---

[104] At 19.

[105] For examples of these kinds of threats to Indigenous interests, see for example, J. Plummer, 'The Yanomami: Illegal Mining, Law and Indigenous Rights in the Brazilian Amazon' (2015) *Georgetown International Environmental Law Review* 27, 479; M.F. Jaska, 'Putting the "Sustainable" Back in Sustainable Development: Recognizing and Enforcing Indigenous Property Rights as a Pathway to Global Environmental Sustainability' (2006) *Journal of Environmental Law and Litigation* 21, 157.

[106] Hathaway, above n 43; Neumayer, above n 43; Dommen, above n 43.

[107] *Joint Statement of the Chairpersons of the United Nations Human Rights Treaty Bodies on the Post-2015 Development Agenda*, above n 11, cited in Knox, above n 11.

> States have obligations not only to refrain from violating the rights of free expression and association directly, but also to protect the life, liberty, and security of individuals exercising those rights. Although the targets under Goal 16 include some language relevant to those obligations, it is too general to be of much practical use.[108]

This concern has been addressed to some degree by Indicator 16.10.1, which will require states to track the '[n]umber of verified cases of killing, kidnapping, enforced disappearance, arbitrary detention and torture of journalists, associated media personnel, trade unionists and human rights advocates'. Again, as implementation unfolds, it will be important to ensure that civil and political rights are not neglected in the roll-out of the SDGs.

4.4 CONCLUSION

On the level of global policy, the *2030 Agenda for Sustainable Development* poses both challenges and opportunities for human rights. It is possible that SDGs will supplant human rights as the focal point for global cooperation and implementation efforts. On the other hand, the SDGs explicitly endorse a human rights approach and would certainly achieve a huge step forward in the realization of human rights, particularly economic, environmental and social rights, if they are fully realized. Even a partial achievement of the SDGs would advance the goals of human rights, particularly with respect to social, environmental and economic rights, which have so far lagged behind the civil and political rights. Ideally, human rights and the SDGs could be mutually reinforcing. Formal human rights mechanisms may act as a safety net or spur to implementation of the SDGs where there is delay or resistance on the part of states and/or non-state actors. SDGs and associated Targets may in turn advance the substance of particular human rights or even clarify and extend the scope of human rights, as in the case of the right to a healthy environment and the right to energy.

While debates may persist regarding the merits of each approach, there can be no doubt that the SDGs and human rights share a common centre in their concern for human happiness and well-being. In one respect, the SDGs attempt a crucial task that has so far proven to be beyond the reach of international human rights law; they seek to preserve the planet for

---

[108] Knox, above n 11, 521.

future generations. Indeed, at this critical juncture in global history it may be that the SDGs represent the best hope for human rights into the future.

5. Underpinning commitments of the Sustainable Development Goals: indivisibility, universality, leaving no one behind

Graham Long

5.1 INTRODUCTION

The new United Nations (UN) Sustainable Development Goals (SDGs) – or 'global goals' – comprise 17 goals and 169 targets. But they are underpinned and circumscribed by a wider framework of elements, including institutions, indicators and overarching principles. It is the last of these elements that is the topic for this chapter. In what follows I sketch the content and import of three commitments in and surrounding the goals: (i) that the goals are universal, but should be differentiated in country contexts; (ii) that the goals and targets are interconnected and indivisible; and (iii) that 'no one should be left behind'. These three elements are, I hope to show, crucial in understanding the SDGs as a framework, and in assessing implementation of the goals.

The significance of this exercise arises from the way that these commitments *usefully complicate* analysis of the goals. Much early academic treatment of the SDGs either offers theoretical and statistical modelling of interlinkages or prospects for global success,[1] or else passes

[1] See, for example, R. Costanza, L. Daly, L. Fioramonti et al, 'Modelling and Measuring Sustainable Wellbeing in Connection with the UN Sustainable Development Goals' (2016) *Ecological Economics* 130, 350–355; V. Spaiser, S. Ranganathan, R. Bali Swain et al, 'The Sustainable Development Oxymoron: Quantifying and Modelling the Incompatibility of Sustainable Development Goals' (2016) *International Journal of Sustainable Development and World Ecology* 457–470; C. Richert, F. Boschetti, I. Walker et al, 'Testing the Consistency Between Goals and Policies for Sustainable Development' (2016) *Sustainability Science* 12, 45–64.

judgement on whether, crudely put, the goals are 'good' or 'bad'.[2] These two strands of work have, by and large, focused on the content on the goals and targets themselves. This chapter sets out to address what might have been lost or missed in not addressing the presence and meaning of these wider commitments. For example, if the goals are to be assessed and critiqued in terms of how far they express or fail to express individual human rights, then a commitment to 'leave no one behind' surely bears on such an assessment. If the goals are deemed too distant, or prescriptive to work, then an intervening level of state adaptation and ownership bears on their chances of success. If our concern is with modelling the SDGs, their interactions and chances of success, it might be that these guiding principles constitute additional desiderata or constraints, and so matter for these models.

A third strand of academic work assesses the SDGs as an innovation in global governance. If the SDGs indeed represent a new model of 'governing through goals',[3] then their underpinning principles – in effect, attributes of the whole goal framework – are crucial to understanding how such governance might operate, and its prospects for success. I seek to consider, too, what these principles might mean for nascent efforts at SDG implementation. Commitments to nationally differentiated implementation of a universal agenda, to realising the goals in a way that respects their integrated character, and to a focus on the most marginalised, can serve to shape policies and frame how such efforts should be judged.

The chapter treats these principles as *underpinning* and *overarching* normative commitments of the SDGs. They are *commitments* in the sense that the SDG agreement signed by states – UN Resolution a/70/1, *Transforming our world: the 2030 Agenda for Sustainable Development* – emphasises them in the preamble, and elsewhere, as 'pledges', 'resolutions' or characteristics of the whole goals framework (and, as I show, they are reflected in the wider framework of supporting institutions, initiatives and discourses). I use the term *normative* here for three reasons. First, to denote that these principles are action guiding. They

---

[2] See, for example, E. Holden, K. Linnerud and D. Banister, 'The Imperatives of Sustainable Development' (2016) *Sustainable Development* 213–226; T. Pogge and M. Sengupta, 'The Sustainable Development Goals as Drafted: Nice Idea, Poor Execution' (2015) *Washington International Law Journal* 24(3), 571–587; H. Moore, 'Global Prosperity and Sustainable Development Goals' (2015) *Journal of International Development* 27(6), 801–815.

[3] N. Kanie and F. Biermann (eds), *Governing Through Goals: Sustainable Development Goals as Governance Innovation* (MIT Press, 2017).

determine, constitute and constrain successful implementation of the goals. Second, to note the connection of SDGs with wider currents of moral and political normative thought – for example, accounts of social justice and cosmopolitanism. Third, to highlight the evolving status of sustainable development as a 'norm' in international politics,[4] and explore how these commitments contribute to the constitution of that norm.[5]

The assessment of these normative commitments, in turn, contributes to three significant wider questions. First, what do the SDGs do for – or *to* – the concept of sustainable development? The contested understanding of sustainable development emerging from the 1992 UN Conference on Environment and Development specifies sustainable development as having social, environmental and economic components. This in itself went beyond – and perhaps away – from the Brundtland Report's framing of sustainable development as 'development that meets the needs of the present without compromising the ability of future generations to meet their own needs'.[6] The precise balance between, on the one hand, an idea of sustainability foregrounding the need to develop within planetary boundaries and on the other, a focus on poverty alleviation realised through economic growth, is unclear. There is disagreement about how far peace, and civil and political human rights, are core features of sustainable development rather than enablers. For some, this flexibility makes the idea of sustainable development useful; others have deemed it meaningless.[7]

---

[4] See M. Finnemore and K. Sikkink, 'International Norm Dynamics and Political Change' (1998) *International Organisation* 52(4), 886–917. I cannot undertake a full analysis of the norms in the SDGs – for example, where these norms sit within Finnemore and Sikkink's 'lifecycle' here.

[5] And, further, to prompt the question of whether they become norms themselves, in international politics and other related contexts (for example, development assistance, environmental policy).

[6] UN World Commission on Environment and Development, *Our Common Future* (Oxford University Press, 1987) 40.

[7] For an overview of these and other issues, see, for example, S.M. Lele, 'Sustainable Development: A Critical Review' (1991) *World Development* 19(6), 607–621; C. Sneddon, R. Howard and R. Norgaard, 'Sustainable Development in a Post-Brundtland World' (2006) *Ecological Economics* 57, 253–268. For an allegation of 'green wash', see B. Adams, 'Sustainable Development and the Greening of Development Theory' in F.J. Schuurman (ed), *Beyond the Impasse: New Directions in Development Theory* (Zed Books, 1993) 207–222. For a more positive view, see J. Meadowcroft, 'Sustainable Development: A New(ish) Idea for a New Century' (2000) *Political Studies* 48(2) 370–387.

Sustainable development, then, has been the subject of vigorous debate. But, the SDGs may have shifted the target and context of this debate in ways not yet fully appreciated. Adopting SDGs as a *replacement* for the Millennium Development Goals (MDGs) agenda fuses development and environmental concerns. Does this represent a shift in the content of sustainable development, or do these two agendas fit together without remainder? More than one recent assessment of the SDGs holds that the goals risk diluting the sustainability agenda,[8] but without fully understanding the normative agenda of the SDGs, it is hard to see how this could be accurately appraised. This chapter, then, contributes to a revised assessment of 'the concept's ethical and political possibilities', as measured against the SDG framework.[9]

Second, these norms are important for accountability. The SDGs admit of a range of discretion in how states respond to the achievement of their targets. If the goals are to be met, they are to be met through the voluntary development of 'ambitious national responses' (alongside responses from non-state actors such as cities, non-governmental organisations (NGOs), multi-stakeholder partnerships etc).[10] In this respect, the SDGs are similar to the Paris Agreement on Climate Change, which adopts the same global-yet-voluntary, universal-yet-national compromise.[11] It has been widely charged that the SDGs have ended up vague or weak[12] – perhaps even more so than in the context of the Paris Agreement, since the SDGs are so wide ranging. Certainly, they offer no clear set of standards for assessing country efforts at implementation, and since standards are crucial for any effort at making authorities answer for action or inaction, they offer no prospect of easy accountability.[13] But a focus on these three ideas enables exploration of whether these cross-cutting commitments offer the prospect of recovering standards, or at

---

[8] See, for example, Holden et al, above n 2.

[9] W. Lafferty, 'The Politics of Sustainable Development: Global Norms for National Implementation (1996) *Environmental Politics* 185–208, 190.

[10] United Nations General Assembly Resolution A/Res/70/1. *Transforming our world: the 2030 Agenda for Sustainable Development* (September 2015), para 78 <http://www.un.org/ga/search/view_doc.asp?symbol=A/RES/70/1&Lang=E>, accessed 23 January 2017.

[11] For further discussion, see S. Andresen, 'International Climate Negotiations: Top-down, Bottom-up or a Combination of Both?' (2015) *International Spectator* 50(1), 15–30.

[12] Holden et al, above n 2; Spaiser et al, above n 1.

[13] See, for example, R. Grant and R. Keohane, 'Accountability and Abuses of Power in World Politics' (2005) *American Political Science Review* 99(1), 29–43.

least the *genesis* of some standards, that would enable more meaningful and rigorous accountability.

Third, identifying these norms prompts an important research question about how they grew out of, and informed, the negotiation process – in effect, developing alongside it. A recent strand of work has attempted to analyse and take lessons from the process of securing multilateral agreement on the SDGs.[14] It might be that the emergence of these principles, and their invocation as reasons in the negotiations, deserves a richer analysis. This, it should be noted, is not a project for this chapter, but one that could run parallel to it.

The chapter is structured in four sections. The first offers an introduction to the SDGs and prefaces my analysis with some discussion of how these three commitments fit alongside the goals. In each of the subsequent sections, I take one of these commitments, locate it within and around the goals, and discuss it, paying mind to the three senses of 'normativity' I discussed above – fixing its content, asking about its implications for action to realise the goals, and showing its connection to larger debates in moral and political theory.

5.2 UNDERSTANDING THE FRAMEWORK OF THE GOALS

On the understanding of the SDGs I advance here, the SDG framework is composed of 'aspirational' and 'global' goals,[15] each of which has further targets beneath them which are meant to be more precise and action guiding in nature. Each target is, in turn, associated with particular indicators: metrics and yardsticks that will be used to monitor and assess progress against the goals. An initial set of indicators, though not yet robust or unproblematic, has been agreed by the UN Statistical Commission, along with governance and review arrangements for further modifications to the indicator framework. Clearly, indicators are important, serving both as interpretations of the targets and their intent, and also as ways to focus attention and action. But three further elements of the SDG framework should also be considered if we are to understand the SDGs fully.

---

[14] See, for example, P. Chasek and L. Wagner, 'Breaking the Mold: A New Type of Multilateral Sustainable Development Negotiation' (2016) *International Environmental Agreements: Politics, Law and Economics* 16(3), 397–413.

[15] UNGA A/res/70/1, above n 10, para 55.

The first are the means specified for implementing the goals. Goal 17 is conceptually different from the other goals by being focused on global means of implementation – overarching and underpinning issues such as trade and finance for development. But means of implementation are also specified goal by goal (arising from the negotiating position of the G77+China Bloc). In effect, these constitute targets, though a rather different kind of target – often tracking the presence of a specific process or enabler rather than an outcome. These offer direction on the actions taken to achieve the goals, and are reinforced by a separate section of the agreement detailing and reinforcing aspects of these means, focusing on global finance for development. The limited character of specified means of implementation is one reason why the SDGs cannot be said to amount to a strategy or 'roadmap'; nevertheless, they do represent some guidelines for implementation.

Second, the creation, reformatting and reinvigoration of institutions is also part of the SDGs. Specifically, the UN High Level Political Forum (HLPF) was created alongside the SDGs as a 'capstone' body for the SDG process. Its creation as a *forum*, though, is salient – the SDGs are not a treaty, and reflecting this, the HLPF is not a treaty body. Instead, it is an informal multilateral institution, and it is currently difficult to project how far it will establish itself as a significant site of global governance. The HLPF is specifically charged with review and follow-up of sustainable development.[16] Clearly, though, the scope of the HLPF as a vehicle for accountability is limited, given the absence of sanctions and standards in the SDGs. The SDGs are also accompanied by global fora and platforms concerned with partnerships. Furthermore, they may prove to invigorate UN regional bodies, such as the UN Economic Commission for Europe (UN-ECE) and for Latin America and the Caribbean (UN-ECLAC) given their role in a burgeoning set of initiatives and 'peer-learning' spaces. The SDGs are also creating or reinforcing national-level SDG bodies, and new networks of actors, including cities and private sector actors – for example, by giving increased focus to the activities of the UN Global Compact.[17]

---

[16] UNGA Resolution A/RES/67/290, *Format and Organizational Aspects of the High-Level Political Forum on Sustainable Development* (9 July 2013) <www.un.org/ga/search/view_doc.asp?symbol=A/RES/67/290&Lang=E> accessed 30 July 2017.

[17] The UN Global Compact is an initiative for business, aiming to encourage and support businesses commitment to – and reporting on – human rights and sustainable development principles, currently with around 9,000 business signatories. See <https://www.unglobalcompact.org/> accessed 25 July 2017.

The third element is composed of the principles discussed in this chapter. These principles, I will show, can be found not only within the SDGs, but also across these other aspects of the framework. They affect not just how the goals should be understood, but also what the institutions are tasked with, and how means of implementation are interpreted and constrained. Furthermore, as noted above, they guide deliberation on the content of the SDGs throughout the negotiating process. The content and shape of the SDGs, I would contend, arises partly from the agreement reached early in negotiations that the goals should be conceived of as universal and integrated. Lastly, their *rhetorical* importance should be noted, especially seeing as the SDG agenda resists easy summation. These ideas, of 'leaving no one behind' and that these goals are 'universal' or 'indivisible', are invoked as quick ways to characterise the particular appeal, the normative urgency or the transformative potential of the SDGs.

5.3 UNIVERSALITY

> [This framework] is accepted by all countries and is applicable to all, taking into account different national realities, capacities and levels of development and respecting national policies and priorities. These are universal goals and targets which involve the entire world, developed and developing countries alike.[18]

The first commitment I want to examine, then, is the idea that the SDGs are universal – accepted by all, and applicable to all. Universality is a key difference from the MDGs, which were oriented squarely towards developing countries. The SDGs explicitly apply to developed countries too, and by being action guiding *globally*, the SDGs might be transformative in a way that the MDGs were not. This in turn prompts a set of questions about how expectations and responsibilities are to be shared among countries, as I address below.

As spelt out in the agenda's formulation, universality – in the sense of being applicable to all – is a claim about scope. I show here, though, that it is through balance with the idea of national differentiation that the action-guiding power of the framework, and its universal acceptance, is best understood. Here we can readily see how the *status* of the SDG framework is important. For all countries to accept and commit to work towards targets on pro-poor growth, ending gender inequality, halving

---

[18] UNGA A/res/70/1, above n 10, para 5.

relative poverty, and having their progress regularly reviewed by other states, would indeed be a transformative shift in global politics. But such a shift is *prima facie* unrealistic – how could such a shift have been accepted by states almost universally wary, for different reasons, about interference, external control and imperialism? The answer on this question of acceptability lies in the scope built into the goals for national differentiation in response to these global targets.

5.3.1 Universal in Application

To be universal in application – 'applicable to all' – is simply to say that the goals apply to all countries. But what application *means*, and exactly *what* applies, are both important considerations. Universal application finds expression in the content of the SDGs, guiding them towards issues that affect all. The European Union (EU) position during negotiations is indicative of this approach – that a 'universal agenda should be built around goals and targets that are of concern and relevance to all countries'.[19] Here the stipulation of universality constrains the list of goals, insisting that the issues addressed must be significant global ones. Universal goals also necessarily have implications for ambition and action in all countries. To set a universal global goal is to set a goal for all countries, aggregated together, at the level required to achieve the global goal; 'global goals become de facto national goals too'.[20]

Universality, then, finds expression in the framing of many targets in the SDGs as *zero-based* targets. These are designed to be stretching for developed countries as well as developing ones. Phrased as 'eliminate' or 'ensure for all', at least some SDG targets are directly applicable to developed countries. As an example, the target specified as 'eliminating violence against women' (target 5.2) is readily applicable to developed countries such as the United Kingdom (UK). Since one in five women in the UK between the ages of 16 and 58 reports being the victim of sexual assault or attempted sexual assault, the relevance of a target to eliminate violence against women has not been lost on, among other bodies, the

[19] European Commission, *A Decent Life for All: From Vision to Collective Action* (2014), 3, ec.europa.eu/europeaid/sites/devco/files/part1-a-decent-life-for-all.pdf, accessed 30 July 2017.

[20] Global Agenda Council on Benchmarking Progress (GAC), *Getting to Zero: Finishing the Job the MDGs Started* (2012), 15 <www.brookings.edu/~/media/research/files/papers/2012/4/17%20millennium%20dev%20goals%20mcarthur/0417%20millennium%20dev%20goals%20mcarthur.pdf> accessed 30 July 2017.

UK parliamentary inquiry into implementation of SDG 5 in the UK.[21] Targets phrased as proportional reductions also apply readily to developed country contexts – for example, the target to reduce mortality from non-communicable disease (target 3.4). Universality as a commitment also guides the review framework, which should 'include both developed and developing countries'.[22] Indeed, during the first two years of Voluntary National Reviews (VNRs), both developed and developing countries have reported.[23]

To say that the agenda is applicable to all, though, is not to say that all of the agenda is *equally* applicable. In some cases, the wording of particular targets specifies groupings of countries or situations. In other cases, the agenda is less relevant to developed countries simply by virtue of how the ambition expressed in some targets has been framed. The maternal mortality target, for example (target 3.1), is still *applicable* to countries that surpass the target ambition, but it is not relevant in the sense of creating a demand for future policy (except, perhaps, for a constraint that maternal mortality should be prevented from increasing). Conversely, some targets expressly identify developed countries as taking the lead, for example in the context of SDG 12 on Sustainable Consumption and Production (most obviously, target 12.1). During negotiations, some maintained that this specific goal was key to the universality of the SDGs precisely because it generates demands for action more from developed countries.[24] On this understanding, the demand for the framework as a whole to be universal is compatible with particular goals and targets addressed more at one set of countries or another.

---

[21] Women and Equalities Committee of the UK Parliament, *Implementation of Sustainable Development Goal 5 in the UK* <https://publications.parliament.uk/pa/cm201617/cmselect/cmwomeq/885/885.pdf> accessed 26 January 2018.

[22] UNGA Resolution 67/290 (9 July 2013), 'Format and Organizational Aspects of the High-Level Political Forum on Sustainable Development', UN Doc. A/RES/67/290 <www.un.org/ga/search/view_doc.asp?symbol=A/RES/67/290&Lang=E> accessed 26 January 2018.

[23] The HLPF website <https://sustainabledevelopment.un.org/vnrs/> accessed 26 January 2018, details reporting countries in 2016 and 2017.

[24] G-77 and China, *Poverty Eradication, Building Shared Prosperity and Promoting Equality* (Presentation to Open Working Group, New York, 5 May 2014) <www.g77.org/statement/getstatement.php?id=140505c> accessed 30 July 2017.

5.3.2 Differentiation and Universal Acceptability

As outlined earlier, the universality of this framework is adopted simultaneously with the principle of national differentiation, that is, the need to '[take] into account different national realities, capacities and levels of development and [respect] national policies and priorities'.[25] Elsewhere, the document affirms: '[W]e will respect each country's policy space and leadership to implement policies for poverty eradication and sustainable development.'[26]

The agenda is not, then, something to be taken wholesale and applied in every country context. Though the agenda is universal, it is clearly differentiated: that is, it permits countries to respond with their own level of ambition, tailored to their national circumstances. If the agenda is indeed meaningfully 'accepted by all', it has been accepted in full awareness of the scope for national-level discretion in how to approach distant, non-specific targets. Reflecting this, the first two rounds of VNRs, and countries' national plans for implementation, offer differences in approach.

To take one country as an illustration, Sierra Leone's VNR from 2016 was focused on the question of how to align the SDGs with other national and international plans and programmes,[27] notably the National Agenda for Prosperity and the National Ebola Recovery Strategy. As a result, policy priorities are mapped onto priority areas of these plans. A selective approach is taken to which SDG indicators will be measured, and together these result in salient differences in emphasis – away from land tenure and outcomes for small-scale farmers, for example, to national food self-sufficiency; or away from measuring means of implementation that realise women's sexual and reproductive health and rights, to measuring outcomes in terms of reductions in teen pregnancies. Other aspects of goal 3 – mental well-being, alcohol and substance abuse, non-communicable disease – and the idea of environmental sustainability in agriculture, do not make the list of national 'priority' indicators. Clearly, this is not an exhaustive analysis, and the aim here is not necessarily to critique these decisions. What all this highlights, though, is that the Sierra Leone VNR document, is, as titled, a 'National *Adaptation* Report'.

---

25 UNGA A/res/70/1, above n 10, para 5.

26 *Ibid*, at para 63.

27 See Government of Sierra Leone, *Advanced Draft Report on Adaptation of the Goals in Sierra Leone* (2016) <https://sustainabledevelopment.un.org/content/documents/10720sierraleone.pdf> accessed 30 July 2017.

There is clearly a tension between the idea of the SDGs as being universal and indivisible, and the affirmation that countries can legitimately prioritise in their responses. If, on the one hand, cherry picking of SDG targets and goals is problematic – perhaps even self-defeating if the agenda is *truly* indivisible as a matter of fact – it is also invited by this focus on national ownership and national control. It is only with the latter that the agenda is 'accepted by all'. It is too early, yet, to say how far states can effectively wholly ignore the pieces of the agenda that they do not like: this is partly a function of how the accountability architecture for the SDGs develops.

Such apparently legitimate difference has implications both for how the implementation or progress of this agenda might be measured, and also for how success is assessed. It also poses the question of how this selectivity can be legitimated – among whom, and on what grounds. Hence, the reaffirmation of a state level of control over the agenda has, as I discuss later, implications for how far the agenda might be viewed as cosmopolitan in spirit or intent.

This also complicates modelling of the interactions between SDGs or conditions and prospects for their realisation, since individual countries can judge success differently, fulfil different shares of global zero targets, and make their own trade-offs among routes to implementation. In effect, the prospects for (and costs of) meeting the SDGs globally depend on the country level: the targets chosen, the interpretation of the goals, the policies enacted and how far the other commitments discussed here are upheld. Hence, as in the recent analysis by the International Council of Scientific Unions, exactly how the targets are interpreted, what level of ambition is attempted, and which policy routes will be enacted, should influence any assessment of how far targets reinforce or oppose each other.[28] While analyses have been keen to identify 'nexuses' of coherent goals to provide starting points for optimal implementation,[29]

---

[28] ICSU, *A Guide to SDG Interactions: From Science to Implementation* (2017) for example, 21–22, 26–27 <https://www.icsu.org/cms/2017/05/SDGs-Guide-to-Interactions.pdf> accessed 31 July 2017. While the ICSU Report does note some methodological limitations and the importance of some place- and time-specific variables, the coverage of these issues is sharply limited, and the analysis remains at a high level of generality. See also M. Nilsson, D. Griggs and M. Visbeck, 'Map the Interactions Between Sustainable Development Goals' (2016) *Nature* 534, 320–322.

[29] UN-DESA (2015) *Policy Integration in Government in Pursuit of the Sustainable Development Goals* <http://workspace.unpan.org/sites/Internet/Documents/UNPAN94443.pdf> accessed 26 January 2018.

national priorities and circumstances pose legitimate potential counter-considerations. This, in turn, suggests that universal analyses of pathways for implementation may not be easy to generate.

The normative commitment to 'universalism with differentiation' also complicates an assessment of how the SDGs should be placed within a context of scholarship on global justice. Here I will highlight two themes important to such an analysis. The first is whether a commitment to universalism implies or advances a cosmopolitan account of global justice. The second highlights the issue of burden sharing in a theory of global justice, and how far the SDGs identify responsibilities for all.

5.3.3 Cosmopolitanism

For theorists of global justice, these aspirational goals can be assessed in terms of their contribution to a vision of a 'future *cosmopolis*'.[30] Cosmopolitanism is both an account of moral demands beyond borders – the claim that 'human beings everywhere are the ultimate units of moral concern'[31] – and an account of how global political arrangements should go, reflecting this moral imperative.[32]

Certainly, some of the rhetoric around the SDGs seems to align with cosmopolitan accounts of global justice. A universal agenda applying to all countries is consonant with such an account of morality since it insists that SDGs do not stop at borders – notably, those of developed states. These goals are to be realised for all human beings, reflecting the commitment that the SDG framework must be 'people-centred'.[33] The High-Level Panel of Eminent Persons' 2013 report on the shape of the SDGs, a key agenda-setting moment, put this starkly: '[T]he next development agenda must ensure that in the future neither income nor gender, nor ethnicity, nor disability, nor geography, will determine whether people live or die, whether a mother can give birth safely, or whether her child has a fair chance in life.'[34] Zero-based goals are recognisably cosmopolitan in form, precisely since they suggest that

---

[30] Pogge and Sengupta, above n 2, 1.

[31] T. Pogge, *World Poverty and Human Rights* (Polity Press, 2004) 169.

[32] See, for prominent accounts of cosmopolitanism, S. Caney, *Justice Beyond Borders* (Oxford University Press, 2006); Pogge, above n 31; G. Brock, *Global Justice: A Cosmopolitan Account* (Oxford University Press, 2009).

[33] UNGA A/res/70/1, above n 10, para 2.

[34] United Nations, *A New Global Partnership: Eradicate Poverty and Transform Economies Through Sustainable Development* (UN Publications, 2013) 7. <http://www.post2015hlp.org/wp-content/uploads/2013/05/UN-Report.pdf>

membership of social and economic groups (income, gender, ethnicity, disability) or even states (geography), should not provide grounds for faring worse.

It might be thought that this will be buttressed by the injunction to 'leave no one behind' – the agenda's especial focus on vulnerable and marginalised groups. 'Leave no one behind', as I address in a later section, arguably reinforces non-discrimination and might even prove to generate a requirement to prioritise the most marginalised. All this is not to say that the SDGs should be regarded as a full account of moral cosmopolitanism though, for reasons I come to shortly.

The SDGs perhaps could also be said to advance *political* cosmopolitanism in some respects. After all, they contain targets on participatory democratic global governance and the institutions attached to the SDGs themselves – for example the HLPF – operate on relatively transparent and participatory modalities. The more that review mechanisms allow states to genuinely be held accountable for action or inaction, the more political cosmopolitanism might be said to be realised. In addition, the talk of partnerships around the SDGs means that sustainable development is a sphere of pluralism in international affairs, with NGOs, firms, and other 'stakeholders' formally acknowledged as actors.[35]

However, all this should be balanced against counter-considerations. First, the focus on differentiation, and the emphasis placed on states as the foundations and key level of reporting and implementation seems to thwart political cosmopolitan ambitions. It is by no means a surprise that a 'transformative' agenda developed by and within a state system reinforces that system. But, clearly, deferring to states on implementation and implementing a sharply limited system of global review constrains the potential for the SDGs to transform the state system and global governance in a way that political cosmopolitans might demand. A final judgement must be contingent on how the agenda is implemented over coming years and how the institutions and norms surrounding it develop.

A common critique of accounts of development is that they are underpinned by a problematic universalism that equates to Western imperialism, and that precludes consideration of other, local

accessed 13 February 2018. The High-Level Panel of Eminent Persons comprised 27 members, including heads of state, CEOs and UN officials. It was convened by the UN Secretary-General as part of the preparations for the post-2015 framework. 'Leave no one behind' is identified in their report as the first of five 'paradigm shifts'.

[35] See, Cooper and French, Chapter 12 in this volume.

approaches.[36] This kind of universalism, so this argument goes, is to be resisted. To an extent, the understanding of universalism-with-differentiation offered by the SDGs might be a *positive* aspect, helping to defuse such a charge. They are less prescriptive than the MDGs, formally according states the space to develop their own understandings of development, and eschew the prescriptive language of rights and security – though, as I address later, this can also be considered a ground for critique.

5.3.4 Global Burden Sharing

A second, reinforcing limitation bears on the extent to which the agenda is cosmopolitan. Universal application has not been translated into a principle of *fair* or *equitable* application. While there is a concern for the well-being of people and planet in a way that extends beyond state borders, there is no account of *justice* here, in the sense of how benefits and burdens should be distributed.[37] If the SDGs outline an account that identifies the urgent need of tackling global problems, it is far less specific about *who* should do *what*. It allocates very few specific or measurable responsibilities to member states, and it offers no account of how responsibilities should be allocated.

Goal 17 explicitly acknowledges actions on which developed countries should lead, for example official development assistance (target 17.2). Goal 12 again recognises differential responsibilities in a limited context (target 12.1). But while a principle of 'common but differentiated responsibilities' is invoked in the preamble in the context of climate change, this was emphatically not universally accepted. Instead, the SDGs prefer the language of a revitalised 'global partnership for development'.[38] While such a partnership could indeed be an important vehicle for realisation of the goals, partnership as a concept – with its emphasis on 'win-win' mutual benefit and voluntary action – is difficult terrain for

---

[36] See, for example, A. Escobar, *Encountering Development: The Making and Unmaking of the Third World* (Princeton University Press, 2012); G. Esteva and M. Prakash, *Grassroots Post-Modernism: Remaking the Soil of Cultures* (Zed Books, 1998).

[37] Whereas this is a constant concern of the literature around global justice, whether these be via negative responsibilities (Pogge) or positive responsibilities (Caney).

[38] See respectively, Pogge above n 32 and Caney above n 32. As invoked in the title of goal 17 and reiterated in paras 39 and 60 for example.

judgements of justice, fairness and accountability. The SDGs, then, certainly have a 'justice-based hole' at their core,[39] even as they are universal.

5.4 INDIVISIBILITY

> 17 Sustainable Development Goals with 169 associated targets which are integrated and indivisible.
>
> [The review processes] will track progress in implementing the universal Goals and targets, including the means of implementation, in all countries in a manner which respects their universal, integrated and interrelated nature and the three dimensions of sustainable development.[40]

The second commitment of the SDGs to be examined here is the indivisibility and interdependence of the goals. This can be interpreted, first, as a factual assertion – that, when considered closely, all the goals are linked. *Transforming our world* does indeed make several such assertions, both for the framework as a whole and for particular goal areas. I take aspects of this basic interconnectedness of the agenda as clearly true, perhaps even as a matter of definition.[41] But the claim to indivisibility also seems larger and more normative in character, an injunction to treat the goals holistically in implementing and reviewing them – for example, not to prioritise one and ignore another. Here, I consider these claims and commitments at two levels: a narrower focus on what they mean for implementation, and a wider perspective concerning how they shape the idea of sustainable development.

A degree of interdependence and indivisibility is certainly present in the SDG agenda. The aspects of the SDGs bearing on any particular issues are seldom wholly captured under one goal heading. For example, the recent UK parliamentary inquiry on Gender Equality in the UK context focused on SDG 5, but doing so missed specific extra targets on equal pay for men and women found in SDG 8, the wider-ranging measure of women's participation across politics demanded in SDG 16, and targets on education and sexual and reproductive health and rights

---

[39] See G. Long 'The Idea of Universality in the Sustainable Development Goals' (2015) *Ethics and International Affairs* 29(2), 203–222.

[40] UNGA A/res/70/1, above n 10, paras 18 and 74b.

[41] I am thinking, for example, of the claim that insecurity can undermine lasting sustainable development, or that gender inequality is incompatible with achievement of the agenda *for all*.

reinforced in SDGs 3 and 4. Elsewhere, overlap between SDGs might take the form of repetition, which is of relatively little importance (for example, the overlap between target 9.4 on sustainable industry, and targets under goal 12 on sustainable production). Understanding the nature and extent of the interconnectedness in the agenda is itself an important step in assessing the SDG agenda, but it is not an easy enterprise. One approach is to map interconnections between goals through analyses of word clusters,[42] though such enterprises have limitations if the context around these clusters is not also appraised. Various taxonomies have been advanced as to how targets across apparently discrete goals could be linked, positing relationships of reinforcement, duplication, compatibility and incompatibility.[43] Assessments of relationships between subsets of goals have been conducted on this basis, though they are far from complete.[44]

5.4.1 Policy Coherence and Governance

As an approach to implementation, this injunction to treat the agenda *holistically* invites certain kinds of scrutiny of both governance institutions and policies. Institutions should break down or reconfigure 'silos' within governments and across actors,[45] while policies should be assessed against a norm of 'policy coherence for sustainable development'.[46] Policy coherence for sustainable development appears in the SDG framework as a 'means of implementation' itself, under SDG 17. As

---

[42] D. LeBlanc, *Towards Integration at Last?* UN-DESA Working Paper no 141 <http://www.un.org/esa/desa/papers/2015/wp141_2015.pdf> accessed 30 July 2017.

[43] ICSU, above n 28.

[44] *Ibid.* Also see the Stockholm Environment Institute, *Cross-sectoral Integration in the Sustainable Development Goals: a Nexus Approach* (SEI Discussion Brief, 2014) <https://www.sei-international.org/mediamanager/documents/Publications/Air-land-water-resources/SEI-DB-2014-Nexus-SDGs-integration.pdf> accessed 30 July 2017.

[45] See L. Meuleman and I. Niestroy, 'Common But Differentiated Governance: A Metagovernance Approach to Make the SDGs Work' (2015) *Sustainability* 7(9), 12295–12321.

[46] For the Organisation for Economic Co-operation and Development, for example, this is a key theme of the SDGs: OECD, *Better Policies for Sustainable Development 2016: A New Framework for Policy Coherence* (OECD, 2016). G20 policies, too, have been evaluated in these terms – for example, J. Lay, C. Brandi, I. Scholz et al, 'Coherent G20 Policies Towards the 2030 Agenda for Sustainable Development' <http://www.g20-insights.org/wp-content/uploads/2017/03/TF_2030_Agenda_PolicyCoherence.pdf> accessed 30 July 2017.

a minimum, policy coherence is taken to demand that policies across different spheres – for example trade and development assistance, or economic growth and environmental protection – are not mutually contradictory or inconsistent.[47] The interconnections across the agenda might serve to identify where policy coherence yields the best results, and policy incoherence the worst.

Policy coherence invites formulation as a test, identifying ways in which certain policies might be holding back realisation of the SDGs and passing a telling judgement that such policies are 'incoherent'. Assuming that the SDGs identify valuable and meaningful ambitions to assess coherence *between* different spheres, policy coherence could be invoked as a basis for normative judgements and accountability. It offers the prospect of identifying policies that damage sustainable development, sometimes in areas apparently thematically distant. Furthermore, the idea of indivisibility also constitutes a counterpoint to the kind of 'cherry picking' and selectivity I discussed in the preceding section. While governments do have control over how to respond to the agenda, developing policy coherence as a standard might rule out responding in certain ways.

5.4.2 The SDGs as an Account of Sustainable Development

The commitment to indivisibility also addresses an important set of conceptual questions concerned with the conception of sustainable development presented by the goals. The process of agreeing the 2030 agenda combined the United Nations Conference on Sustainable Development (Rio+20), and MDG negotiation tracks, and the resulting document combines core environmental (climate change, oceans, ecosystem and species protection, sustainable consumption and production) and developmental (poverty, nutrition, education, health, water) concerns. It also extends them (for example, into issues of governance), but also through this commitment to indivisibility, *connects* them. The connection is important, since it has been charged that environmental sustainability within hard 'planetary boundaries',[48] the key concern of the 'Brundtland

---

[47] See the OECD's Framework for Policy Coherence for Sustainable Development <http://www.oecd.org/pcd/pcsd-framework.htm> accessed 31 July 2017.

[48] J. Rockström et al., 'A Safe Operating Space for Humanity' (2009) *Nature* 461, 472–475; W. Steffen, K. Richardson, J. Rockström et al, 'Planetary Boundaries: Guiding Human Development on a Changing Planet' (2015) *Science* 347, 1259855; K.A. Raworth, 'Safe and Just Space for Humanity: Can We Live Within the Doughnut? (2012) *Oxfam Policy Paper*.

account' of sustainability, has been watered down or wholly lost. In one sense, indivisibility speaks against this: it asserts that the environmental pillar is crucial. But in another, it seems to endorse a degree of watering down by pledging to *balance* these pillars – perhaps implying trade-offs or a diluted focus. The SDGs also respond with a challenge, though: perhaps instead the 'Rio track' has downplayed 'the needs of present generations' in focusing on the constraints of future ones.

Three initial considerations might be identified as important here. The first of these is the interpretation of environmental sustainability constraints on production and consumption in SDGs 9 and 12 (and around sustainable agriculture in SDG 2), and whether these go far enough. The second is the substance of the 'environmental goals' 13, 14 and 15 and how far, in practice, coherence with these objectives might constrain economic growth – in effect, whether the SDGs coherently support the ambition in target 8.4 to 'endeavour to decouple economic growth from environmental degradation'. Lastly, it should also be recognised here that the SDGs had to be framed in a way coherent with other negotiated environmental agreements.[49] The SDGs defer to the Paris Agreement on Climate Change (SDG 13 deliberately says very little that is new about mitigation and adaptation), and incorporate the Aichi Biodiversity Targets within SDG 15. As one inter-state agreement among several, it would be unrealistic – and perhaps unreasonable – to expect the SDGs themselves to bear all the burden of identifying and establishing planetary boundaries to growth.

Despite these initial remarks, it is not my intention here to go any further in investigating the impact of the SDGs on accounts of sustainable development – such an exercise goes well beyond this chapter, and is undertaken by other contributors to this volume.[50] Here, my aim has been more limited: to signal that a norm of 'indivisibility' is at the heart of an assessment of these theoretical issues. It will be interesting to see in practice, too, how far indivisibility can be meaningfully assessed and attained.

---

[49] This is from the standpoint of governments, of course; others might prefer that somehow the ambition of *this* negotiated agreement exceeded, superseded or disregarded the one reached earlier the same year, though such an approach presents its own problems.

[50] See Adelman, Chapter 2, and Kotzé, Chapter 3, in this volume.

5.5 'LEAVING NO ONE BEHIND'

> As we embark on this great collective journey, we pledge that no one will be left behind. Recognizing that the dignity of the human person is fundamental, we wish to see the Goals and targets met for all nations and peoples and for all segments of society. And we will endeavour to reach the furthest behind first.[51]

The attraction of the exhortation and apparent 'pledge' to 'leave no one behind' might be set in the context of the MDGs, where progress within countries was patchy and sometimes concentrated on 'low hanging fruit'.[52] It offers another way in which the SDGs might genuinely claim to depart from previous efforts at development. Certain components of the SDGs themselves are especially closely aligned to the demand that no one be left behind – that is, a particular focus on the poorest, most marginalised and disadvantaged. It is clearly visible in the way that SDG 10 is expressed, for example in its focus on discrimination, and in SDG 5 on gender.[53] Elsewhere in the goals, particular marginalised groups are identified by name as special focuses for efforts and review (for example, targets 2.3, 8.5, 8.8). But it is established beyond the goals too – in the preamble where the overall aims of the SDGs are established; in the principles for the review framework; and as a 'slogan' for an otherwise complex set of goals, it was the theme for the first (post-goals) HLPF in 2016.

Leaving aside for the moment potential ambiguities in exactly what it means to 'leave no one behind', it is important to consider the relevance of such a norm for policies (including development interventions) and review structures. As a 'fundamental guiding principle for SDG implementation',[54] it is possible to identify ways in which policies might leave people behind, and also which policies might do best in such respects. The UN Development Programme (UNDP), for example, undertakes such an analysis of development interventions in their contribution

---

[51] UNGA A/res/70/1, above n 10, para 4.

[52] See, for example, UN Special Rapporteur on the Human Rights of Migrants, *Report on the Human Rights of Migrants*, section III on *The Human Rights of Migrants in the Post-2015 Development Agenda* (2014) <https://documents-dds-ny.un.org/doc/UNDOC/GEN/N14/501/96/PDF/N1450196.pdf?OpenElement> accessed 30 July 2017.

[53] See Morrow, Chapter 7 in this volume.

[54] UN Division for Sustainable Development (eds), *Global Sustainable Development Report* (UN, 2016) 3–16, at 3.

to the 2016 Global Sustainable Development Report.[55] But the implications for policy responses to the goals might be broader. 'Leaving no one behind' is, like policy coherence, a test. In particular, it might seem to demand the participation of marginalised groups themselves. If so, 'leave no one behind' becomes doubly significant for the governance of the goals, creating demands not just on the policies adopted, but also on the process by which they are agreed.

'Leave no one behind' also finds expression in the data architecture around the SDGs, where it has placed a premium on the disaggregation of data. This focus on disaggregation poses a distinctive challenge for national and global statistical agencies. To the extent it is accomplished, though – and it is already informing the future thinking of such agencies – it will make inequalities, and dimensions in which particular social groups are 'left behind', clearly visible. Disaggregation reinforces the relevance of the SDGs for developed countries, too. It focuses attention not only on inequalities in how well certain social groups are faring, but also on geographical divisions and rural/urban splits,[56] and so poses ways in which targets met on aggregate might still merit policy focus. For example, in the UK context, the target on ending undernourishment (2.2) might not be considered especially relevant (compared to the issue of obesity, for example), yet close attention to statistics shows pockets of undernourishment within the UK, notably among the elderly.[57]

Lastly, attention to the poorest and most marginalised groups is identified as a guiding principle against which to assess review processes at all levels.[58] Again, a focus on vulnerable, marginalised and disadvantaged groups might offer a potent way in which to highlight inequality in different country contexts on grounds of ethnicity, gender and beyond. The more that this norm becomes something that states must report on, or must expect scrutiny from other actors against, then the greater potency it will have in this regard.

Of course, the value of 'leave no one behind' is tied to our assessment of the agenda itself. If (as Heloise Weber has charged, for example) the SDGs represent an unjust neoliberal agenda, composed of 'contentious policies which critics have shown to be highly exclusionary and therefor

---

[55] *Ibid* – see tables on pages 10; 15–16.

[56] See Aust and du Plessis, Chapter 9 in this volume.

[57] M. Elia, *The Cost of Malnutrition in England and Potential Cost Savings from Nutritional Interventions*, BAPEN/NIHR Southampton Report (2015) <http://www.bapen.org.uk/pdfs/economic-report-full.pdf> accessed 30 July 2017.

[58] UNGA A/res/70/1, above n 10, para 74.

[*sic*] unjust, and therefore also not sustainable',[59] then including everyone within the scope of this agenda is deeply troubling – and 'leaving no one behind', in effect *pulling* people into this agenda, especially so.[60] There is no denying that the SDG framework affirms capitalism. Targets variously reference and uphold private property, markets, wage labour, norms of trade and exchange, and assume the need for state and private investment to fund services for all. The SDGs are aligned with existing international agreements on trade; and they do not offer an agenda for global socio-economic equality (even as they pledge equality, or greater equality, in certain respects). However, Weber moves too quickly past aspects of this agenda which might be debated as constraining neoliberalism, or offering opportunities for resistance against it.

Weber highlights SDG targets that reference the World Trade Organization (WTO) and an apparent endorsement of microfinance, while failing to mention the targets on better regulation of financial markets, curtailing illicit flows, reform of global institutions to improve representation of developing countries, guaranteeing land rights and labour rights, adopting fiscal and wage policies aimed at greater equality, increased public spending on poverty alleviation, gender budgeting, or the emphasis on improving the trade position of least developed countries: it is not clear if she would condemn these too. Elsewhere in her critique, she cites the extreme poverty target (target 1.1), and the target on agricultural productivity of small-scale farmers (2.3) as evidence of a 'reductionist' approach to poverty and hunger, but does not acknowledge *adjacent* targets covering relative and multidimensional poverty (target 1.2) or 'ensuring access by all people to safe, nutritious and sufficient food' (target 2.1); there are systemic targets under goal 2, too, that speak to reforming agricultural and food commodity markets (though doubtless it can be charged that this reform is not sufficient). All this is not to end the debate on the merits or otherwise of this agenda, but to note that further engagement would make such critiques stronger: selectivity and cherry picking matter for academics, too.

The *prima facie* problem for wholesale rejection of the SDGs is that there is so *much* to this agenda, and so many of the aspirations seem morally desirable – whether they be on hunger, poverty, education,

---

[59] H. Weber, 'Politics of "Leaving No One Behind": Contesting the 2030 Sustainable Development Goals Agenda' (2017) *Globalizations* 14(3), 399–414, at 409.

[60] For reasons of space, I cannot engage with other important and controversial aspects of Weber's critique – for example, her understanding of SDG indicators and of what counts as a universal entitlement – here.

gender equality, access to water and energy, and beyond. There clearly are, I take it, at least *aspects or* outcomes of this agenda where we would want no one left behind – that is, where an emphasis on eliminating discrimination and identifying and helping the poorest and most vulnerable would not be morally problematic. Thus, Stenberg and others' analysis calculates that achieving *universal* SDG health coverage – i.e. coverage that 'leaves no one behind' across goal 3 and related targets – would save 97 million lives and substantially raise life expectancy in developing and middle-income countries.[61] Weber judges, though, that the SDGs might 'make the poor laws look progressive'[62] and, on the basis of five or so targets from 169, that 'dignified lives' are not the 'core' of the SDGs.[63]

5.5.1 'Leave no one behind', Human Rights and Equality

Like understandings of human rights, 'leave no one behind' is anti-discriminatory in intent.[64] And like human rights, it resists the aggregation of individuals into a larger whole for assessment of implementation strategies. The SDGs have been criticised for this – that in committing to reaching all people, even those who prove expensive to reach, they are

---

[61] K. Stenberg, O. Hanssen, T. Tan-Torres Edejer et al, 'Financing Transformative Health Systems Towards Achievement of the Health Sustainable Development Goals: A Model for Projected Resource Needs in 67 Low-Income and Middle-Income Countries' (2017) *The Lancet*, published online, July 2017 <http://www.thelancet.com/journals/langlo/article/PIIS2214-109X(17)30263-2/fulltext> accessed 30 July 2017.

[62] Weber, above n 59, 409.

[63] *Ibid*, at 410. It is possible, of course, that these references to the WTO, the encouragement of private and blended finance as a way to fund achievement of goal outcomes, the absence of a commitment to global equality (rather than less inequality) etc., *are* the core of this agenda, or else betray its real essence, with the rest merely 'window dressing' – rather than their being viewed instead as one component of a very diverse and complex (perhaps contradictory) agenda. What makes something the 'core' of this agenda is a difficult question, and the challenge for critics is to offer a compelling argument for the former interpretation over the latter (as Weber claims to have done). This criticism, it should be noted, is distinct from the charge that neoliberalism will prevent the achievement of the positive outcomes of this agenda, or that the SDGs somehow serve, by ameliorating the worst of neoliberalism, to legitimate it – each of which merits its own discussion.

[64] See also Collins, Chapter 4 in this volume.

not effective in aggregate cost-benefit terms.[65] 'Leave no one behind', then, is salient to an assessment of the SDGs in human rights terms. In making the case for the SDGs, some have explicitly linked the two: 'this is a major new commitment to everyone on the planet who feels marginalised or excluded, and to the neediest and most vulnerable people, to make sure their concerns are addressed and that they can enjoy their human rights.'[66]

The data and review agenda generated by this commitment means that such a link can be present even if not wholly explicit. If attention is focused on particular social, economic and societal groups, and inequalities in outcomes identified, we might well expect such visibility to support the universality of human rights. Furthermore, disaggregation of data can be a powerful tool in indicating the meaningful universality of targets that might otherwise be thought irrelevant. It necessarily highlights disparity and inequality, and calls attention to *who* is worst off, and *how* – and so prompting deliberation on *why*.

The SDGs have been widely criticised for missing mentions of particular vulnerable groups. The presence of an overarching commitment on this beyond the text of particular goal areas, and of a data and review agenda directed towards victims of discrimination along all nationally relevant dimensions, is surely relevant to the assessment of such critiques. El Zein and others, for example, criticise the SDGs because 'the SDGs document scarcely mentions refugees, foreign workers, non-citizens, or people who have been internally displaced', and recommend that 'countries should be required to report separately on their citizen and non-citizen populations for all relevant SDGs'.[67] But it would be uncharitable to the SDGs to assess such criticism without acknowledging 'leave no one behind' as a general underpinning principle, and the data disaggregation and review it instructs states to undertake.

---

[65] Lomborg argues that 'We should start by focusing on the 19 targets that are the most effective. It would see every dollar go about four times farther. And it would mean that in 15 years, global leaders will have done about four times more good.' B. Lomborg 'The U.N. Chose Way Too Many New Development Goals' <http://time.com/4052109/un-sustainable-development-goals/> accessed 30 July 2017.

[66] UN High-Level Panel, above n 16, 7.

[67] A. El-Zein, J. DeJong, P. Fargues et al, 'Who's Been Left Behind? Why Sustainable Development Goals Fail the Arab World' (2016) *The Lancet* 388(10040), 207–210.

Pogge and Sengupta, likewise, regard the SDGs' commitment to ending discrimination as 'tepid'.[68] They condemn the SDGs for, among other things, failing to include language on all specific groups subject to discrimination. But even if this is not at least partly addressed through an explicit target on 'ending discriminatory laws, policies and practices' (target 10.3), both these commitments (i) to review following the principle that it should be 'people-centred, gender-sensitive, respect human rights and have a particular focus on the poorest, most vulnerable and those furthest behind',[69] and (ii) for data to be disaggregated along all lines relevant for a given national context (target 17.18) are noteworthy. Pogge and Sengupta acknowledge data disaggregation only in one sentence, and say nothing on its wider potential. To be clear, the claim is not that these few lines of text in the SDGs somehow end all discrimination by *fiat*, but rather that the idea of 'leave no one behind' and the data agenda associated with it could be a resource for a human rights-based approach, especially if governments and other actors are held to it.

There remains ambiguity, though, over exactly what counts as being left behind, and over the metric for measurement. In some senses, the demand is clearly *egalitarian* in character, positively requiring equality between all, the exclusion of no one, and ruling out discrimination. But in terms of exactly what counts as being left behind, there are weaker and stronger poles of a continuum. There is a sufficientarian interpretation of leave no one behind, which interprets 'leave no one behind' as leave no one *below a certain level*. This is a promise that no one will be completely forgotten, but that beyond this point, *equality* (for example, in terms of life chances) would not be expected.[70] This interpretation might, for example, point to the way that SDG 10 on ending inequality fails to explicitly identify socio-economic inequality *between* countries or between individuals in different countries as an issue, even as it addresses other kinds and dimensions of inequality. Clearly, the socio-economic egalitarian agenda here is limited.

On the other hand, the aim to reach the 'furthest behind first' suggests a more expansive interpretation that places a priority on the worst off and

---

[68] T. Pogge and M. Sengupta, 'Assessing the Sustainable Development Goals From a Human Rights Perspective' (2016) *Journal of International and Comparative Social Policy* 32(2), 94.

[69] UNGA A/res/70/1, above n 10, para 74.

[70] Justine Greening (as former UK minister for International Development), for example, offered such an understanding in <https://www.gov.uk/government/news/greening-britain-backs-the-global-goals-for-sustainable-development> accessed 30 July 2017.

how they are faring, perhaps akin in spirit to prioritarianism as an account of socio-economic justice.[71] The meaning of a commitment to 'attempt to reach those furthest behind first' hinges, of course, on whether this refers to the 'furthest behind' globally, or in specific country contexts – another ambiguity that I cannot spend longer on here. Clearly, though, *prioritising* benefit to the most marginalised so that they benefit most or first is distinct in terms of setting outcomes and guiding policy choice – both from ensuring equal benefit, and from benefiting up to a certain point.

5.6 CONCLUSION

This chapter has aimed to draw attention to three overarching and underpinning commitments, beyond the goals and targets themselves, showing how they matter for our understanding and assessment of the SDGs. I have indicated how these norms connect the goals to wider questions in the political theory of sustainable development and global justice. I have also outlined their implications for both implementation of the SDGs, and the terms in which such implementation should be judged. Clearly, this exercise cannot be wholly comprehensive – not least, given the breadth of the framework and the inchoate nature of the institutional context for its implementation and (re)interpretation.

In identifying these elements as significant, I might be taken as contributing to a defence of the goals. My arguments here certainly indicate why the SDGs might be regarded as transformative, and offer responses to some of their critics. Universality could be a transformational development vis-à-vis the MDGs, offering a change from a narrative of 'donor' and 'recipient' to one of action for all countries. That these goals are less of a global strategy *blueprint*, and more of a *framework* in which countries can articulate their own visions of their futures might be welcome.[72] This space and support for national differentiation might, in particular, provide some kind of bulwark against a universalising conceptualisation of development, or against the dominance of certain countries. A commitment to indivisibility, as a minimum, recognises that both environmental protection and ending poverty are

[71] It might, for example, be thought to recall Rawls's difference principle – J. Rawls, *A Theory of Justice* (Harvard University Press, 1971).

[72] L. Pritchett, 'The New Global Goals Spell the End of Kinky Development' <https://www.cgdev.org/blog/new-global-goals-spell-end-kinky-development> accessed 31 July 2017.

important and related, and might provide a basis from which to judge and discourage policy *in*coherence. Lastly, for commentators dismayed by the relative absence of human rights from the goals and targets, I have shown how the idea of 'leave no one behind' might still serve to uphold and promote human rights.

But this effort to advance a richer and more involved understanding of the SDGs also contains within it the seeds of further critique. I have not denied the weakness and ambiguities present across the SDGs, and these overarching commitments are themselves in tension. Can an agenda be implemented in a way that is selective, yet integrated? Does the global pledge to leave no one behind constrain national policy space, or is it somehow traded off against it? In these respects, implementation efforts and institutions must walk an extremely fine line in balancing potentially competing considerations, just as in balancing progress on the whole agenda and across all 'three pillars' of sustainable development. If analyses of interlinkages among goals and targets are already complex, an insistence on the relevance of these wider principles adds an extra dimension to that complexity.

There is still a larger assessment to be conducted of the normative value of the goals, then – an exercise taken up in other chapters of this volume. It is clear that much hinges on how, and how far, the SDGs are taken up and used by states and other actors between now and 2030. This makes the normative evaluation of the SDGs especially difficult, since it involves assessing not just what they are, but what they might *become*. This, in turn, points to a larger question: given that our world is unjust, and a more just world is possible, what role can the SDGs play in getting *there* from *here*?

6. How the Sustainable Development Goals promote a new conception of ocean commons governance

Nadia Sánchez Castillo-Winckels*

6.1 INTRODUCTION

Areas beyond national jurisdiction (ABNJ) – often referred to as the global commons[1] – are protected by the general obligation of states to prevent, reduce and control environmental harm resulting from activities within their jurisdiction or control.[2] The ocean global commons – the high seas and its resources and the deep seabed (known in international law as the 'Area') and its resources – are also protected by specific legal regimes, including those established to regulate fishing on the high seas and deep seabed mining. However, neither the general obligation nor the

* I am grateful to Professors Nico Schrijver and Eric de Brabandere for their very helpful comments. I am also grateful to Lisa Dellmuth, Montserrat González Carrillo, Aline Jaeckel and Linlin Sun for their comments related to marine resource governance. The views expressed are strictly my own, as are any errors. All websites accessed on February 2018.

1 See, for example, K. Bosselmann, *Earth Governance: Trusteeship of the Global Commons* (Edward Elgar Publishing 2015) 71–75; N. Schrijver, 'Managing the Global Commons: Common Good or Common Sink?' (2016) *Third World Quarterly* 37(1252), 1252–1253.

2 Declaration of the United Nations Conference on the Human Environment, Stockholm, 16 June 1972, UN Doc. A/CONF.48/14/Rev.1, Principle 21; Rio Declaration on Environment and Development, Rio de Janeiro, 14 June 1992, UN Doc. A/CONF.151/26 (Vol I) ('Rio Declaration'), Principle 2. See also UN Framework Convention on Climate Change (May 1992) 1771 U.N.T.S. 107, Preamble; Convention on Biological Diversity (5 June 1992) 1760 U.N.T.S. 79, article 3; Legality of the Threat or Use of Nuclear Weapons, Advisory Opinion, I.C.J. Reports 1996, 226, at 241–242, para 29; Draft Articles on Prevention of Transboundary Harm from Hazardous Activities with commentaries, Yearbook of the International Law Commission, 2001, Vol II, Part Two, Draft article 3.

specific legal regimes have been able to prevent significant harm being caused to marine resources. The Global Ocean Commission (GOC)[3] recently concluded 'the high seas are facing a cycle of declining ecosystem health and productivity'.[4] Investigating the factors causing such decline, the GOC found that one of them is weak high seas governance.[5] In particular, it found that in the management regime for the high seas 'transparency, accountability and compliance-reporting are especially weak',[6] with 'very little accountability at the global level.'[7] Legal scholars also identify lack of effective compliance mechanisms as one of the factors contributing to degradation of the global commons,[8] and the ocean commons in particular.[9]

Public access to information and participation in global environmental governance has led to increased transparency, accountability, effectiveness and legitimacy of decision-making processes.[10] Thus, even though the engagement of civil society may decrease efficiency for being resource consuming (in terms of time and money),[11] and even may result

---

[3] Independent commission established in 2013 to raise awareness and promote action to address ocean degradation. It was conceived by the Pew Charitable Trusts and hosted by Somerville College at the University of Oxford. Members of the GOC included José María Figueres (former President of Costa Rica), Vladimir Golitsyn (President of the International Tribunal for the Law of the Sea), and Pascal Lamy (Former Director-General of the WTO).

[4] Global Ocean Commission, *From Decline to Recovery: A Rescue Package for the Global Ocean* (2014) <http://www.some.ox.ac.uk/research/global-ocean-commission/> at 16.

[5] *Ibid*, at 16–18.

[6] *Ibid*, at 7.

[7] *Ibid.*

[8] Schrijver, above n 1, 1261.

[9] D. Bhomawat, 'Shark-finning: Damage to Global Commons' (2016) *Environmental Policy and Law* 46, 56, 61; S. Kopela, 'Port-State Jurisdiction, Extraterritoriality, and the Protection of Global Commons' (2016) *Ocean Development and International Law* 47, 89.

[10] See, for example, J. Ebbesson, 'Principle 10: Public Participation' in J.E. Viñuales (ed) *The Rio Declaration on Environment and Development* (Oxford University Press, 2015); T. Kramarz and S. Park, 'Accountability in Global Environmental Governance: A Meaningful Tool for Action?' (2016) *Global Environmental Politics* 16(1), 6; T. Bernauer and R. Gampfer, 'Effects of Civil Society Involvement on Popular Legitimacy of Global Environmental Governance' (2013) *Global Environmental Change* 23, 439.

[11] C. Pahl-Wostl, 'A Conceptual Framework for Analysing Adaptive Capacity and Multi-level Learning Processes in Resource Governance Regimes' (2009) *Global Environmental Change* 19, 354, 357. See also G. Carr, G. Blöschl

in 'lowest-common-denominator solutions if decision-makers strive to accommodate as many views as possible',[12] public participation is desirable and actively promoted by the international community. Principle 10 of the 1992 Rio Declaration on Environment and Development adopted at the United Nations Conference on Environment and Development (UNCED), proclaims 'environmental issues are best handled with participation of all concerned citizens'.[13] It furthermore provides for access to information, public participation and access to justice in environmental matters. Agenda 21, the Plan of Action on Sustainable Development also adopted at UNCED, states that 'one of the fundamental prerequisites for the achievement of sustainable development is broad public participation in decision-making'.[14] Twenty years later, the UN Conference on Sustainable Development (Rio + 20) reconfirmed Principle 10 in its outcome document *The Future We Want*, underscoring participatory rights as an essential component in the promotion of sustainable development.[15] At the regional level, the Aarhus Convention on Access to Information, Public Participation in Decision-Making and Access to Justice in Environmental Matters,[16] and the Regional Agreement on Access to Information, Participation and Justice in Environmental Matters in Latin America and the Caribbean, which is currently under negotiation,[17] constitute examples of the extensive support that the international community affords to Rio Principle 10.

---

and D.P. Loucks, 'Evaluating Participation in Water Resource Management: A Review' (2012) *Water Resources Research* 48, W11401, 2.

[12] N.P. Spyke, 'Public Participation in Environmental Decisionmaking at the New Millennium: Structuring New Spheres of Public Influence' (1999) *Boston College Environmental Affairs Law Review* 26(263), 273.

[13] Rio Declaration, above n 2.

[14] Agenda 21: Programme of Action for Sustainable Development, UN Doc. A/CONF.151/26 (Vol I), Chapter 23, para 2.

[15] The Future We Want, UN Doc. A/RES/66/288, para 43. See also M. Orellana, 'Governance and the Sustainable Development Goals: The Increasing Relevance of Access Rights in Principle 10 of the Rio Declaration' (2016) 25 *Review of European Community and International Environmental Law* 50, 51–52, for an account of how the sustainable development discourse has affirmed the centrality of access rights in governance.

[16] 'Aarhus Convention' (25 June 1998) 2161 U.N.T.S. 447.

[17] The eighth meeting of the Negotiating Committee took place on 27 November to 1 December 2017 in Santiago de Chile. The eighth version of the text compiled by the presiding officers, UN Doc. LC/L.4059/Rev.8 (22 January 2018), is available at <http://repositorio.cepal.org/bitstream/handle/11362/39051/37/S1800064_en.pdf>.

The type of development envisioned by the 2030 Agenda for Sustainable Development is that it should not only be sustainable, but also inclusive. In the Agenda, states agree to foster peaceful, just and inclusive societies, declaring that this 'is an agenda of the people, by the people and for the people – and this, we believe, will ensure its success'.[18] In this chapter, I explore 'inclusiveness' from the perspective of civil society participation in the governance of marine areas beyond the limits of national jurisdiction also known as ocean global commons or ocean commons. In particular, I examine the role of the SDGs in enhancing public participation in institutions managing the ocean global commons: regional fisheries management organizations (RFMOs) and the International Seabed Authority (ISA). I focus for present purposes on two SDGs: SDG 14 'Conserve and sustainably use the oceans, seas and marine resources for sustainable development',[19] and SDG 16 'Promote peaceful and inclusive societies for sustainable development, provide access to justice for all and build effective, accountable and inclusive institutions at all levels'.[20] I argue that the SDGs promote a new conception of ocean commons governance by emphasizing civil society participation in achieving sustainable development. Prevailing practice primarily involves states and industry organizations (i.e. companies and industry associations) and restricts access to civil society. This reality is now being challenged by the SDGs, which encourage governing institutions at all levels to strengthen public participation in order to increase transparency, accountability and effectiveness of their administration. The SDGs thus promote a new understanding of ocean commons governance in which public participation is integral to the governing process and necessary to ensure institutional transparency, accountability and effectiveness for sustainable development.

The next section discusses the nature of the SDGs and their potential to influence national and international law and policy. The following section explains that public participation is not only a fundamental element in the drafting and subsequent implementation of the SDGs, but also a means to achieving the goal of building strong institutions at all levels set in SDG 16. Subsequently, section 4 provides an account of the current situation of the ocean global commons and relates it to the goal of sustainable use of marine resources envisioned in SDG 14. Section 5 examines public participation in RFMOs and the ISA and shows that

---

[18] *Transforming our world: the 2030 Agenda for Sustainable Development*, UN Doc. A/RES/70/1, 21 October 2015 ('2030 Agenda'), para 52.

[19] *Ibid*, at 23.

[20] *Ibid*, at 25.

SDG 16 provides a guiding framework for achieving SDG 14 by way of building strong institutions, *inter alia*, via ensuring public access to information and participation in decision making. The chapter concludes with the argument that through this guiding framework, the SDGs promote a new conception of ocean commons governance.

Some terminological clarification is required before continuing to the next section. First, the term 'civil society' is used as defined by the Panel of Eminent Persons on United Nations–Civil Society Relations meaning 'the associations of citizens (outside their families, friends and businesses) entered into voluntarily to advance their interests, ideas and ideologies. The term does not include profit-making activity (the private sector) or governing (the public sector).'[21] Second, the term 'public participation' refers to civil society access to information and participation in decision-making processes within governing institutions. It does not include 'access to justice' (the third 'pillar' found in Rio Principle 10). This is because no institutionalized access to justice procedure open to civil society organizations currently exists within governance structures for the ocean global commons. Finally, the terms 'marine areas beyond national jurisdiction' 'ocean global commons' and 'ocean commons' are used interchangeably and refer to the high seas and its living resources and the Area and its resources.[22]

6.2 NON-BINDING, YET INFLUENTIAL

The SDGs, contained in a resolution of the United Nations General Assembly (UNGA), are not legally biding. This does not, however, mean that the SDGs lack the capacity to influence national and international

---

[21] We the Peoples: Civil Society, the United Nations and Global Governance: Report of the Panel of Eminent Persons on United Nations–Civil Society Relations, UN Doc. A/58/817 (11 June 2004), at 13.

[22] This is based on the definitions and legal regimes established by the United Nations Convention on the Law of the Sea (UNCLOS, below n 55) discussed below. UNCLOS defines the high seas as all parts of the sea beyond national jurisdiction (article 86) and establishes a regime for the conservation and management of the living resources of the high seas (articles 116–120), which limits states' freedom of fishing (article 87). In addition, UNCLOS defines the Area as the seabed and its subsoil beyond national jurisdiction (article 1) and establishes a regime for the management of the Area and its resources based on the principle of common heritage of mankind (Part XI).

law and policy.[23] In fact, states are expected to take ownership and translate the SDGs into domestic public policies.[24] In addition, the 2030 Agenda is grounded in international human rights treaties[25] reinforcing states' international legally binding obligations to protect human rights. Furthermore, the Agenda encourages states to achieve the SDGs in accordance with existing international agreements, expressly mentioning World Trade Organization (WTO) agreements[26] and the WTO Agreement on Trade-Related Aspects of Intellectual Property Rights (TRIPS Agreement),[27] the World Health Organization Framework Convention on Tobacco Control,[28] the Convention on the Rights of the Child,[29] the United Nations Framework Convention on Climate Change,[30] and the United Nations Convention on the Law of the Sea (UNCLOS).[31] Referring states and stakeholders to existing international agreements strongly suggests consensus on combining or integrating such agreements with the SDGs, as it were, in order to achieve the overarching goal of sustainable development.[32]

It follows from this interpretation that SDG 14 does not operate in a vacuum. In fact, SDG 14 directs efforts to enhance the conservation and

---

[23] Several ways in which the SDGs could be 'non-binding yet influential' have been explored in the literature. See, for example, R.E. Kim, 'The Nexus Between International Law and the Sustainable Development Goals' (2016) *Review of European Community and International Environmental Law* 25(15), 16, arguing that the SDGs are grounded in international agreements and are best conceptualized as a '*subset* of existing intergovernmental commitments'; O. Spijkers, 'The Cross-fertilization Between the Sustainable Development Goals and International Water Law' (2016) *Review of European Community and International Environmental Law* 25(39), 40–41, stating that if states are influenced by the SDGs when applying a treaty, this could constitute relevant subsequent practice of such treaty in accordance with the Vienna Convention on the Law of Treaties; M. Orme, Z. Cuthbert, F. Sindico et al, 'Good Transboundary Water Governance in the 2015 Sustainable Development Goals: A Legal Perspective' (2015) 40 *Water International* 969, 970–971, stating that although the SDGs are not legally binding, they 'still have governing implications' because states must 'translate the SDGs into national targets, and develop and implement policies to achieve the SDGs' and 'engage not only across sectors but also across borders'.

[24] *Transforming our world*, above n 18, para 66.

[25] *Ibid*, para 10. See also Collins, Chapter 4 in this volume.

[26] *Ibid*, SDG 10, target 10a.

[27] *Ibid*, SDG 3, target 3b.

[28] *Ibid*, SDG 3, target 3a.

[29] *Ibid*, para 67.

[30] *Ibid*, SDG 13, target 13a.

[31] *Ibid*, SDG 14, target 14c.

[32] See Kim, above n 23, 16–17.

sustainable use of oceans and their resources by implementing international law as reflected in UNCLOS,[33] causing one to think that there was general agreement on combining UNCLOS and the SDGs to achieve sustainable oceans. Seen in this light, UNCLOS provides a normative framework for implementing SDG 14, while SDG 14 draws attention to priority areas regarding ocean sustainability. This potential for synergy between UNCLOS and the SDGs has been acknowledged by the ISA and is beginning to appear – albeit more timidly – in the work of the RFMOs. Indeed, the President of the ISA Council stated in 2015 that SDG 14 'goes to the heart of the responsibilities of the International Seabed Authority'[34] and that it 'will bring accountability to all organizations and agencies that play a role in the sustainability of [the] ocean's health'.[35] In addition, the Secretary-General of the ISA stated in May 2017 that 'deep seabed mining can be carried out sustainably in a manner that contributes to the realization of SDG 14'.[36] The 2030 Agenda and SDGs have also been acknowledged by member states in RFMO meetings,[37] possibly indicating that the SDGs could indeed influence the way RFMOs manage high seas fisheries.

The SDGs may not be legally binding in the strict sense of the word, but they are deeply rooted in international law and call on states to fulfil their legally binding obligations in the light of their vision and ambition

---

[33] *Transforming our world*, above n 18, target 14c.

[34] Opening Statement by President of the Council Ambassador Peter Thomson, International Seabed Authority, Kingston, Jamaica, 21st Session, 14 July 2015 <https://www.isa.org.jm/files/documents/EN/21Sess/CnclPres.pdf> at 2.

[35] *Ibid*, at 3.

[36] Statement by Secretary-General Michael Lodge at the ISA/COMRA Contract Extension Signing Ceremony, 11 May 2017, Beijing <https://www.isa.org.jm/sites/default/files/documents/EN/SG-Stats/sg-comra.pdf> at 4.

[37] See for example, Commission for the Conservation and Management of Highly Migratory Fish Stocks in the Western and Central Pacific Ocean (WCPFC), Thirteenth Regular Session of the Commission, Denarau Island, Fiji, 5–9 December 2016, Summary Report of 2 March 2017 <https://www.wcpfc.int/system/files/WCPFC13%20Summary%20Report%20final_issued%202%20March%202017%20complete.pdf> Statement by the Minister for Fisheries of Papua New Guinea, para 26, at 7–8; WCPFC, Twelfth Regular Session of the Technical and Compliance Committee, Pohnpei, Federated States of Micronesia, 21–27 September 2016, Report of 17 November 2016 <https://www.wcpfc.int/system/files/TCC12%20Summary%20Report%2017%20Nov%202016.pdf> Attachment A: Opening Remarks from the Federated States of Micronesia, at 70; Inter-American Tropical Tuna Commission (IATTC), 90th Meeting, La Jolla, California (USA) <http://www.iattc.org/Meetings/Meetings2016/June/pdf-files/IATTC-90-Minutes.pdf> Appendix 5b, Statement by Chile, at 99.

to transform our world by 2030. As shown below, the interaction between the existing legal framework applicable to the ocean commons and the SDGs could have as a result that civil society organizations join states and industry organizations as principal actors in ocean commons governance. In section 5, I propose several ways through which increased public participation in ocean commons governance could be achieved. These are (i) through making RFMO rules on non-governmental organizations (NGO) participation less restrictive, for example, via substantially reducing or eliminating NGO participation fees; (ii) through including NGO representatives in RFMO performance reviews; (iii) through developing ISA procedures to determine confidentiality of data (such procedures are currently non-existent); (iv) through providing public access to all environmental data available to the ISA; and (v) through ensuring public participation in all Legal and Technical Commission (LTC) meetings discussing environmental protection. If we agree that 'contemporary international law is often the product of a complex and evolving interplay of instruments, both binding and non-binding',[38] the interplay between the binding legal framework and the non-binding SDGs could encourage and even facilitate these proposals, thereby promoting a new conception of ocean commons governance.

6.3 PUBLIC PARTICIPATION

In contrast to the Millennium Development Goals (MDGs), which were criticized for having been drafted behind closed doors without stakeholder consultations,[39] the SDGs were envisioned to be the result of an inclusive and transparent intergovernmental process open to all stakeholders.[40] In fact, the Open Working Group on Sustainable Development Goals (OWG) had the mandate to ensure the full involvement of expertise from civil society in order to provide a diversity of perspectives

---

[38] A. Boyle and C. Chinkin, *The Making of International Law* (Oxford University Press, 2007) 210.

[39] UN System Task Team on the Post-2015 UN Development Agenda, *Review of the Contributions of the MDG Agenda to Foster Development: Lessons for the Post-2015 UN Development Agenda* <http://www.un.org/millenniumgoals/pdf/mdg_assessment_Aug.pdf> at 7; see also S. Wisor, 'After the MDGs: Citizen Deliberation and the Post-2015 Development Framework' (2012) *Ethics and International Affairs* 26, 113, 119–120; V.P. Nanda, 'The Journey from the Millennium Development Goals to the Sustainable Development Goals' (2015–2016) *Denver Journal of International Law and Policy* 44(389), 398.

[40] The Future We Want, above n 15, para 248.

and experience.[41] Accordingly, a process of public consultations took place during the elaboration of the SDGs.[42] Additionally, civil society is called on to support implementation of the SDGs together with governments, the private sector and the UN system.[43] Indeed, the process of follow-up and review of implementation of the SDGs at all levels is to be 'open, inclusive, participatory and transparent for all people and will support reporting by all relevant stakeholders'.[44] Therefore, review of implementation progress at the national level is to draw on contributions from, among others, civil society.[45] At the global level, regular reviews are to include civil society and provide a platform for partnerships, including through the participation of 'major groups and other relevant stakeholders'.[46] Civil society organizations are called to contribute not only to follow-up and review processes, but also to SDG implementation in their areas of expertise.[47] In addition to being essential to the drafting and subsequent implementation of the SDGs, public participation is a means to achieve the specific goal of building strong institutions at all levels set in SDG 16.

Sustainable Development Goal 16 is to 'promote peaceful and inclusive societies for sustainable development, provide access to justice for

---

41 *Ibid.*

42 2030 Agenda, above n 18, para 6. See also Synthesis Report of the Secretary-General on the Post-2015 Agenda, *The Road to Dignity by 2030: Ending Poverty, Transforming All Lives and Protecting the Planet* (December 2014) <http://www.un.org/disabilities/documents/reports/SG_Synthesis_Report_Road_to_Dignity_by_2030.pdf> para 37(a). For an analysis of public participation in the drafting process of the SDGs see O. Spijkers and A. Honniball, 'Developing Global Public Participation (2): Shaping the Sustainable Development Goals' (2015) *International Community Law Review* 17, 251.

43 2030 Agenda, above n 18, paras 39 and 60.

44 *Ibid*, para 74(d).

45 *Ibid*, para 79.

46 *Ibid*, paras 84 and 89. 'Major groups' refers to nine sectors of society that constitute the main channels for participation in UN activities related to sustainable development. These are women, children and youth, indigenous peoples, non-governmental organizations, local authorities, workers and trade unions, business and industry, scientific and technological community, and farmers. See Agenda 21, above n 14, Section III. 'Other relevant stakeholders' are also invited to participate in UN processes related to sustainable development. These include private philanthropic organizations, educational and academic entities, persons with disabilities and volunteer groups. See UN Doc. A/RES/67/290 Format and organizational aspects of the high-level political forum on sustainable development (23 August 2013), para 16.

47 2030 Agenda, above n 18, para 41. See also SDG 17, target 17.

all and build effective, accountable and inclusive institutions at all levels'.[48] Strong institutions (effective, accountable and inclusive) are instrumental in promoting peaceful and inclusive societies and providing access to justice for all. Therefore, this chapter specifically focuses on the goal of building strong institutions and the role of public participation in achieving such a goal in the context of the ocean global commons. Three of the targets supporting the achievement of SDG 16 directly contribute to building strong institutions. Target 16.6 is to 'develop effective, accountable and transparent institutions at all levels'; target 16.7 is to 'ensure responsive, inclusive, participatory, and representative decision making at all levels'; and target 16.10 is to 'ensure public access to information and protect fundamental freedoms, in accordance with national legislation and international agreements'.[49]

As mentioned in the introduction, public access to information and participation in environmental matters increase transparency, accountability and effectiveness of decision making and are both widely supported by the international community. SDG 16 confirms this support, drawing attention to the role that public participation plays in achieving the goal of strong institutions for sustainable management. The goal is to build strong institutions *at all levels* of governance, therefore including institutions managing the ocean global commons. In addition, according to the three relevant targets, strong institutions are to be built through effectiveness, accountability, and transparency,[50] responsiveness, inclusiveness, participation and representation,[51] and through public access to information.[52] Bearing in mind that weak governing institutions have been found to be one of the factors causing ocean degradation,[53] and that ocean commons are currently managed with minimal public participation, SDG 16 promotes a new conception of ocean commons governance. It does so by aiming at building strong institutions through, *inter alia*, ensuring public access to information and public participation in decision making. As shown below, the existing conception of ocean commons governance features states and industry representatives as primary actors with civil society organizations – and the conservation interests they represent – playing a role of secondary importance. The new conception, based on SDG 16 and intending to achieve SDG 14,

48 2030 Agenda, above n 18, at 25.
49 *Ibid*, at 25–26.
50 Target 16.6.
51 Target 16.7.
52 Target 16.10.
53 Global Ocean Commission, above n 4.

strengthens the role of civil society organizations in ensuring transparency, accountability and effectiveness of institutions managing the ocean commons.

6.4 OCEAN COMMONS AND SUSTAINABLE DEVELOPMENT GOAL 14

6.4.1 Ocean Commons

The ocean covers nearly three-quarters of the Earth's surface area.[54] The high seas, defined as 'all parts of the sea that are not included in the exclusive economic zone, in the territorial sea or in the internal waters of a State, or in the archipelagic waters of an archipelagic State',[55] constitute 64 per cent of the total surface of the ocean.[56] High seas ecosystem services include air purification, waste treatment and lifecycle maintenance, carbon capture and storage, fisheries, genetic resources, and recreational benefits.[57] The high seas also provide non-living resources such as oil, gas and minerals.[58] The 1982 UNCLOS reserves the high seas for peaceful purposes[59] and guarantees 'freedom of the high seas' for all states, coastal or land-locked.[60] Freedom of the high seas comprises, *inter alia*, freedom of navigation and overflight, freedom to lay submarine cables and pipelines, to construct artificial islands and other installations, freedom of scientific research and freedom of fishing.[61] Despite efforts made by the international community to protect the marine environment, the ocean faces several challenges. These include overfishing, acidification, pollution and biodiversity loss.

The UN Food and Agriculture Organization report *State of World Fisheries and Aquaculture 2016* (FAO Report) found that 31.4 per cent of the world's marine fish stocks were fished at a biologically unsustainable

---

[54] *Ibid*, at 4.

[55] United Nations Convention on the Law of the Sea (10 December 1982) 1833 U.N.T.S. 3, Art. 86.

[56] Global Ocean Commission, above n 4, at 4.

[57] *Ibid*, at 5.

[58] *Ibid*.

[59] Above n 55, article 88.

[60] *Ibid*, article 87.

[61] *Ibid*, article 87(a) and (e).

level and therefore overfished.[62] The report states further that most of the stocks of the 10 most productive fish species 'are fully fished with no potential for increases in production; the remainder are overfished with increases in their production only possible after successful stock restoration'.[63] In addition, the Intergovernmental Panel on Climate Change found that the ocean has absorbed 30 per cent of the emitted anthropogenic CO_2, increasing its acidity.[64] Ocean acidification has impacts on the physiology, behaviour and population dynamics of organisms, particularly those building a calcium carbonate shell (for example, molluscs and reef-building corals).[65] Moreover, the warming of the global oceans, combined with overfishing, threatens the world's richest areas for marine biodiversity.[66] Furthermore, marine litter (or debris) – mostly made up of plastic polymers, the majority of which are not biodegradable and will persist for decades and probably centuries[67] – affects habitats, ecological function, and exposes marine fauna to entanglement, suffocation, and/or ingestion of debris.[68] Finally, marine biodiversity loss 'not only impairs the ability of marine ecosystems to feed a growing human population but also sabotages their stability and recovery potential in a rapidly changing marine environment'.[69]

---

62 Food and Agriculture Organization of the United Nations, *The State of World Fisheries and Aquaculture 2016: Contributing to Food Security and Nutrition for All* (Rome 2016) <http://www.fao.org/3/a-i5555e.pdf> at 5–6.

63 *Ibid*, at 6.

64 IPCC, *Climate Change 2014: Synthesis Report.* Contribution of Working Groups I, II and III to the Fifth Assessment Report of the Intergovernmental Panel on Climate Change (Geneva 2014) <https://www.ipcc.ch/pdf/assessment-report/ar5/syr/SYR_AR5_FINAL_full.pdf> at 4.

65 *Ibid*, at 67.

66 F. Ramirez, I. Afán, L.S. Davis and A. Chiaradia, 'Climate Impacts on Global Hot Spots of Marine Biodiversity' (2017) *Science Advances* 3, 1–7.

67 UNEP and GRID-Arendal, *Marine Litter Vital Graphics* (2016) <http://staging.unep.org/docs/MarineLitter.pdf> at 7. See also D.K.A. Barnes, F. Galgani, R.C. Thompson et al, 'Accumulation and Fragmentation of Plastic Debris in Global Environments' (2009) *Philosophical Transactions of the Royal Society* B 364(1985), 1992–1993.

68 UNEP and GRID-Arendal, above n 67, at 6, 8. See also M. Eriksen, L.C.M. Lebreton, H.S. Carson et al, 'Plastic Pollution in the World's Oceans: More than 5 Trillion Plastic Pieces Weighing over 250,000 Tons Afloat at Sea' (2014) *PLoS One* 9: e111913, at 2, 11.

69 B. Worm, E.B. Barbier, N. Beaumont et al, 'Impacts of Biodiversity Loss on Ocean Ecosystem Services' (2006) *Science* 314 (787), 790. See also D.J. McCauley, M.L. Pinsky, S.R. Palumbi et al, 'Marine Defaunation: Animal Loss in the Global Ocean' (2015) *Science* 347(247), 1255641–1255643.

Concerning marine mineral resources found in the seabed beyond national jurisdiction, the so-called Area,[70] three types are commercially viable: polymetallic manganese nodules, cobalt-rich ferromanganese crusts and polymetallic sulphides.[71] Polymetallic manganese nodules are found on or just below the surface of the deep seabed and contain manganese, nickel, cobalt and copper.[72] Cobalt-rich ferromanganese crusts are deposits formed from direct precipitation of minerals from seawater onto hard substrates (rock on seamounts and active mountain chains), containing minor but significant concentrations of cobalt, titanium, nickel, platinum, molybdenum, tellurium, cerium, other metallic and rare earth elements.[73] Polymetallic sulphides are hydrothermally formed deposits of sulphides and accompanying mineral resources, which contain concentrations of metals including, *inter alia*, copper, lead, zinc, gold and silver.[74] The Area not only yields significant mineral resources, but also 'is predicted to hold millions of yet-to-be described species'.[75] As an example, the Clarion-Clipperton Zone (CCZ), located in the Eastern Central Pacific, is not only known to have the richest deposits of polymetallic nodules in terms of nodule abundance and metal concentration,[76] but also holds rich and abundant megafauna.[77]

Deep seabed mining in ABNJ is currently in the exploration phase. As of February 2018, the ISA has entered into 15-year contracts for

---

[70] UNCLOS defines the Area as 'the seabed and ocean floor and subsoil thereof, beyond the limits of national jurisdiction', above n 55, article 1(1) (1).

[71] E. Ramirez-Llodra, A. Brandt, R. Danovaro et al, 'Deep, Diverse and Definitely Different: Unique Attributes of the World's Largest Ecosystem' (2010) *Biogeosciences* 7(2851), 2882.

[72] Regulations on Prospecting and Exploration for Polymetallic Nodules in the Area, ISBA/19/C/17 (22 July 2013) hereinafter Nodules Exploration Regulations, Regulation 1(3)(d).

[73] Regulations on Prospecting and Exploration for Cobalt-rich Ferromanganese Crusts in the Area, ISBA/18/A/11 (27 July 2012) hereinafter Crusts Exploration Regulations, Regulation 1(3)(a).

[74] Regulations on Prospecting and Exploration for Polymetallic Sulphides in the Area, ISBA/16/A/12/Rev.1 (7 May 2010) hereinafter Sulphides Exploration Regulations, Regulation 1(3)(d).

[75] K.J. Mengerink, C.L. Van Dover, J. Ardron et al, 'A Call for Deep-Ocean Stewardship' (2014) 344 *Science* 696, 696.

[76] Environmental Management Plan for the Clarion-Clipperton Zone, ISBA/17/LTC/7 (13 July 2011) para 16.

[77] D.J. Amon, A.F. Ziegler, T.G. Dahlgren et al, 'Insights into the Abundance and Diversity of Abyssal Megafauna in a Polymetallic nodule Region in the Eastern Clarion-Clipperton Zone' (2016) *Scientific Reports* 6, 30492.

exploration for minerals in the Area with 28 contractors.[78] During its 22nd session (2016), the Council of the ISA approved six applications for extension of contracts for exploration,[79] four of which were signed during the 23rd session (2017).[80] Applications for exploitation licences are expected after the contracts or the extension periods expire.[81] More than half of the contracts are for exploration for polymetallic nodules in the CCZ.[82]

Nodule mining is expected to have long-lasting impacts.[83] A single nodule mining operation is projected to remove nodules and near-surface sediments from 300–700 km^2 of seafloor per year,[84] which would cause 'near total faunal mortality in the area directly mined'.[85] In addition, redeposition of sediments suspended by mining activities 'will disturb seafloor communities over an area perhaps two to five times greater'.[86] Experimental disturbances carried out to study possible impacts of mining operations showed that many nodule-attached organisms as well as mobile species 'did not reach pre-disturbance abundances decades after the disturbance took place'.[87] In addition, the biogeochemical functions of the sediments were affected, indicating impacts on the food

---

78 ISA, 'Deep Seabed Minerals Contractors' <https://www.isa.org.jm/deep-seabed-minerals-contractors>.

79 Report of the Secretary-General of the International Seabed Authority under article 166, paragraph 4, of the United Nations Convention on the Law of the Sea, ISBA/23/A/2 (5 June 2017) para 67.

80 *Ibid*, para 71. See also ISA, Selected Decisions and Documents of the Twenty-Third Session, 7–18 August 2017, available at <https://www.isa.org.jm/sites/default/files/files/documents/en_3.pdf> at 17, para 71.

81 Nodules Exploration Regulations, above n 72, Regulation 26; Crusts Exploration Regulations, above n 73, Regulation 28; Sulphides Exploration Regulations, above n 74, Regulation 28.

82 ISA, above n 78.

83 ISA, Towards an ISA Environmental Management Strategy for the Area, ISA Technical Study No. 17 (March 2017) <https://www.isa.org.jm/sites/default/files/files/documents/berlinrep-web.pdf> at 11.

84 E. Ramírez-Llodra, P.A. Tyler, M.C. Baker et al, 'Man and the Last Great Wilderness: Human Impact on the Deep Sea' (2011) 6 *PLoS One* e22588, at 11. See also ISA, Biodiversity, Species Ranges, and Gene Flow in the Abyssal Pacific Nodule Province: Predicting and Managing the Impacts of Deep Seabed Mining, ISA Technical Study No. 3 (2008) <https://www.isa.org.jm/sites/default/files/files/documents/techstudy3.pdf> at 4.

85 Ramírez-Llodra et al, above n 84.

86 *Ibid*.

87 ISA, above n 83, 11.

web of the flora and fauna found on the seafloor.[88] Notwithstanding, deep seabed ecosystems remain poorly known[89] and, as acknowledged by the Environmental Management Plan for the CCZ, 'the degree of impacts raised by potential deep sea mining is still unknown'.[90] This uncertainty calls for a precautionary approach and constitutes a main challenge in the current process of developing a legal framework to regulate the exploitation phase.[91]

6.4.2 Sustainable Development Goal 14

Sustainable Development Goal 14 (SDG 14) is to 'conserve and sustainably use the oceans, seas and marine resources for sustainable development'.[92] Several of the targets under SDG 14 direct efforts towards tackling the main challenges faced by the ocean commons described above.[93] Target 14.1 sets the objective of preventing and significantly reducing marine pollution of all kinds, including marine debris pollution. Target 14.2 aims at achieving sustainable management and protection of marine and coastal ecosystems. Target 14.3 directs actions towards minimizing and addressing the impacts of ocean acidification. Particularly relevant to the argument in this chapter are targets 14.4 and 14.6, which aim at tackling overfishing. Target 14.4 draws attention to the ineffective regulation of fishing activities, calling on governance institutions to '*effectively* regulate harvesting and end overfishing, illegal, unreported and unregulated fishing and destructive fishing practices … in order to restore fish stocks in the shortest time feasible, at least to levels that can produce maximum sustainable yield as determined by their

---

88 *Ibid.*

89 Amon et al, above n 77.

90 Environmental Management Plan for the Clarion-Clipperton Zone, above n 76, para 25.

91 ISA, Developing a Regulatory Framework for Mineral Exploitation in the Area: Report to Members of the Authority and all Stakeholders (July 2016) containing a first working draft of the Regulations and Standard Contract Terms on Exploitation for Mineral Resources in the Area <https://www.isa.org.jm/files/documents/EN/Regs/DraftExpl/Draft_ExplReg_SCT.pdf>. See also ISA, 'Ongoing Development of Regulations on Exploitation of Mineral Resources in the Area' <https://www.isa.org.jm/legal-instruments/ongoing-development-regulations-exploitation-mineral-resources-area> for a chronological list of activities undertaken and documents issued in the drafting process.

92 2030 Agenda, above n 18, at 23.

93 *Ibid*, at 23–24.

biological characteristics'.[94] Target 14.6 addresses the issue of subsidies granted to the fishing industry setting the objective of 'prohibit[ing] certain forms of fisheries subsidies which contribute to overcapacity and overfishing, eliminate subsidies that contribute to illegal, unreported and unregulated fishing and refrain from introducing new such subsidies'. Also relevant to the argument is target 14.c, which aims to 'enhance the conservation and sustainable use of oceans and their resources by implementing international law as reflected in the United Nations Convention on the Law of the Sea'. By referring to UNCLOS, SDG 14 highlights the critical role that the Law of the Sea – including the law applicable to high seas fisheries and deep seabed minerals – plays in the sustainable management of marine resources.

Regarding public participation, SDG 14 does not expressly mention public access to information and participation in decision making; however, it does contain an implicit reference by acknowledging the role of UNCLOS. As discussed below, the legal regime established by UNCLOS and its implementing agreements does include procedures – albeit modest – for the engagement of civil society in the management of the ocean global commons. In addition, target 14.a also makes an implicit reference to civil society participation by directing efforts to 'increase scientific knowledge, develop research capacity and transfer marine technology'. This calls attention to the role that civil society organizations engaged in ocean research play in improving ocean health.

6.5 PUBLIC PARTICIPATION IN OCEAN COMMONS GOVERNANCE

This section examines public participation in institutions managing high seas fisheries and seabed minerals in the Area – RFMOs and the ISA, also referred to as the Authority, respectively. Each subsection provides a brief introduction of the organization's roles, functions and competences especially regarding environmental protection, followed by a study of the legal framework for public participation and its implementation. Each subsection links this legal framework to the SDGs showing that SDG 16 provides a guiding framework for achieving SDG 14 through strong institutions.

---

[94] Emphasis added.

6.5.1 Public Participation in Regional Fisheries Management Organizations

6.5.1.1 Role of RFMOs in governance of high seas fisheries

According to UNCLOS all states have the right for their nationals to engage in fishing on the high seas provided that they observe their treaty obligations and the rights, duties and interests of the coastal states.[95] UNCLOS requires states to take measures for their respective nationals for the conservation of living resources,[96] and to cooperate with each other in the conservation and management of living resources, for instance through the establishment of fisheries organizations.[97] The Fish Stocks Agreement (FSA) elaborates states' duty to cooperate regarding two particular stocks: straddling and highly migratory fish stocks.[98] It provides for the establishment of RFMOs, which have become the principal institutions entrusted with the conservation and management of high seas fisheries at the regional level.[99]

RFMOs are intergovernmental organizations for the management of fisheries in specific areas of the high seas with a mandate to adopt measures that are binding upon their members. RFMOs essentially provide a forum for states to cooperate and adopt conservation and management measures. Where no RFMO exists for a particular fish stock, states must cooperate in order to establish one.[100] Where an RFMO does exist, states intending to fish for the resource under the jurisdiction of the RFMO must join it or, at least, follow its rules.[101] States having a real interest in the fisheries concerned are entitled to become a member of a relevant RFMO.[102] Only those states which are members of an

---

95 UNCLOS, above n 55, article 116.

96 Article 117.

97 Article 118.

98 Agreement for the Implementation of the Provisions of the United Nations Convention on the Law of the Sea of 10 December 1982 relating to the Conservation and Management of Straddling Fish Stocks and Highly Migratory Fish Stocks (4 August 1995) 2167 U.N.T.S. 3, article 2 (FSA). Straddling fish stocks occur both within a country's exclusive economic zone and in the adjacent high seas (UNCLOS article 63) for example, cod, jack mackerel and squid. Highly migratory fish stocks regularly travel long distances through both the high seas and areas under national jurisdiction (UNCLOS article 64 and Annex I), for example, tuna, swordfish and oceanic sharks.

99 *Ibid*, FSA Part III.

100 FSA, above n 98, article 8(5).

101 *Ibid*, article 8(3).

102 *Ibid*.

RFMO, or which agree to follow its rules, have access to the fishery resources to which those rules apply.[103] Most RFMOs manage specific fish stocks only, such as tuna and tuna-like species or deep-sea stocks.[104]

RFMO member states have the responsibility to agree on participatory rights such as allocations of allowable catch (fishing quotas), or levels of fishing effort (for example, fishing days),[105] ensuring that these measures maintain or restore stocks at levels capable of producing maximum sustainable yield (also referred to as 'maximum sustainable catch').[106] In addition, members must ensure that said measures are based on the best available scientific information,[107] and apply the precautionary approach.[108] Measures should also take into account the interdependence of fish stocks and dependent and associated species as well as the special requirements of developing states.[109] Furthermore, members must adopt standards for the responsible conduct of fishing operations,[110] review the status of the stocks and assess the impact of fishing on non-target and associated or dependent species.[111] They must also ensure implementation of the recommendations and decisions of the organization.[112]

Notwithstanding this legal framework, unsustainable fishing practices in the high seas constitute a persisting cause of ocean degradation. Performance reviews conducted following the 2006 UNGA Resolution on Sustainable Fisheries[113] show that RFMOs have generally 'failed to live up to expectations'.[114] They reveal common problems such as poor

---

103 *Ibid*, article 8(4).

104 Examples of RFMOs are: Northwest Atlantic Fisheries Organization (NAFO), Commission for the Conservation of Southern Bluefin Tuna (CCSBT), North Atlantic Salmon Conservation Organization (NASCO), International Commission for the Conservation of Atlantic Tunas (ICCAT).

105 FSA, article 10(b).

106 *Ibid*, article 5(b).

107 *Ibid*.

108 *Ibid*, article 5(c) and article 6.

109 *Ibid*, article 5(b).

110 *Ibid*, article 10(c).

111 *Ibid*, article 10(d).

112 *Ibid*, article 10(l).

113 Sustainable Fisheries, including through the 1995 Agreement for the Implementation of the Provisions of the United Nations Convention on the Law of the Sea of 10 December 1982 relating to the Conservation and Management of Straddling Fish Stocks and Highly Migratory Fish Stocks, and related instruments, UN Doc A/RES/61/105 (8 December 2006), para 73.

114 Global Ocean Commission, above n 4, at 9. See also K.M. Gjerde, D. Currie, K. Wowk et al, 'Ocean in Peril: Reforming the Management of Global Ocean Living Resources in Areas Beyond National Jurisdiction' (2013) *Marine*

data provision, failure to adopt appropriate conservation measures and inadequate compliance with management measures.[115] In addition, the GOC found that RFMOs are 'largely unaccountable'.[116] The above-cited FAO Report confirms that RFMOs face 'substantial challenges', including 'lack of political commitment and comprehensive compliance by members'.[117] It adds that regional fisheries bodies (including RFMOs) 'can only be as effective as member States allow' and their performance 'depends directly on their members' participation, engagement and political will'.[118] In light of this situation, and bearing in mind that public access to information and participation in decision making can improve transparency, accountability and effectiveness of governing institutions, the SDGs potentially could provide direction for achieving sustainable use of high seas fisheries. This is done, in part, through strengthening RFMOs by ensuring that civil society organizations have access to information and participation mechanisms.

6.5.1.2 Public participation in RFMOs in the light of the SDGs

Article 12 of the FSA stipulates that states must provide for transparency in the decision-making process and other activities of RFMOs.[119] It also states that representatives from NGOs concerned with straddling and highly migratory fish stocks shall be afforded the opportunity to take part in meetings as observers or otherwise.[120] NGOs must have timely access to records and reports of RFMOs, and procedures allowing their participation 'shall not be unduly restrictive'.[121] Rules of procedure on NGO participation differ from one RFMO to another. Generally, NGOs may attend meetings, make oral statements upon invitation of the presiding

---

Pollution Bulletin 74(540), 541; S. Cullis-Suzuki and D. Pauly, 'Failing the High Seas: A Global Evaluation of Regional Fisheries Management Organizations' (2010) *Marine Policy* 34(1036), 1042; M.W. Lodge, D. Anderson, T. Løbach et al, *Recommended Best Practices for Regional Fisheries Management Organizations*, 'Introduction and Overview' (Chatham House, 2007) ix.

115 Global Ocean Commission, above n 4, at 36. See also Gjerde et al, above n 114, at 542.

116 Global Ocean Commission, above n 4, at 36.

117 FAO, *The State of World Fisheries and Aquaculture 2016*, above n 62, at 95.

118 *Ibid*, at 8.

119 FSA, above n 98, article 12(1).

120 *Ibid*, article 12(2).

121 *Ibid*.

officer and distribute documents through the Secretariat.[122] Even though civil society organizations have played a role in 'pushing the RFMOs towards a more precautionary approach'[123] and 'contributed to raising political and public awareness of the need for change'[124] in the way RFMOs work, it has been documented that 'in most RFMOs [NGOs] struggle to have their views heard and discussed and are often frustrated that they are not taken seriously in the decision-making process'.[125]

The participation of civil society organizations – mostly NGOs – in RFMOs indeed tends to be constrained.[126] Some RFMOs request a participation fee from NGOs, which is perceived as 'a way to effectively discourage observer participation'.[127] For example, the rules of procedure of the Northwest Atlantic Fisheries Organization (NAFO) provide that NGOs with observer accreditation may be required to pay a fee 'which will cover the additional expenses generated by their participation'.[128] The amount of the fee is to be determined annually by the Executive Secretary.[129] Considering that lack of financial resources was found to be the main reason for poor representation of NGOs from low-income countries in international environmental institutions,[130] charging a fee, which can reach up to 500 USD to attend each meeting,[131] could be interpreted as a practice that unduly restricts access for NGOs from low-income countries, which in turn is in contravention of article 12 of the FSA. In addition, a study of more than 500 NGOs participating in procedures of five tuna RFMOs revealed that the number and access of

122 M.T. Petersson, L.M. Dellmuth, A. Merrie et al, 'NGO Participation in Global Fisheries Governance: Density, Diversity, and Volatility', paper presented at the Global and Regional Governance Workshop, April 2015, Appendix A, at 33–35 (unpublished, on file with author and available on request).

123 *Ibid*, at 13.

124 FAO Report, above n 62, at 95.

125 Report of the Independent Review, International Commission for the Conservation of Atlantic Tunas (ICCAT) PLE-106/2008, September 2008 ('ICCAT 2008 Report') at 71.

126 See for example, Gjerde et al, above n 114, at 543.

127 ICCAT 2008 Report, above n 125, at 29.

128 NAFO Rules of Procedure and Financial Regulations, December 2014, Rule 5(c).

129 *Ibid.*

130 A.N. Uhre, 'Exploring the Diversity of Transnational Actors in Global Environmental Governance' (2014) *Interest Groups and Advocacy* 3, 59.

131 Report of the Independent Performance Review of ICCAT 2016, <https://www.iccat.int/Documents/Other/0-2nd_PERFORMANCE_REVIEW_TRI.pdf> at 61.

fishing industry representatives is greater than the number and access of civil society organizations.[132] This finding suggests that conservation interests – primarily put forward by NGOs – would be under-represented, at least in five tuna RFMOs. The study also found that NGOs from high-income countries participate far more often than NGOs from low-income countries, with possible implications for representational diversity.[133] In this regard, it should be noted that the decline in fish stocks due to overfishing impoverishes coastal fishing communities in many coastal and island developing countries,[134] and that many developing countries have difficulty covering the high cost of adequate fisheries governance regimes.[135] Less restrictive participation policies could give NGOs from low-income countries the opportunity to voice their concerns within the established governance structures.

Reviews of RFMO performance confirm that NGO participation is frequently restricted.[136] As a response, some performance reviews include general recommendations to make RFMOs more inclusive with respect to NGOs. For instance, the performance review of the Commission for the Conservation of Southern Bluefin Tuna (CCSBT) recommended 'creat[ing] rules that would allow NGOs easier access to CCSBT meetings',[137] while that of the North Atlantic Salmon Conservation Organization (NASCO) recommended that NASCO 'seek ways to increase NGO involvement'.[138] In 2008, the first performance review of the International Commission for the Conservation of Atlantic Tunas (ICCAT) commented on concerns regarding 'a tendency for ICCAT to use more closed meetings with limited participation, and that this could lead to decisions that are not well understood or well considered, and could also decrease accountability'.[139] In addition, the review panel questioned ICCAT's practice of charging NGOs 500 USD for each meeting because of the 'broader role these groups have in representing special interest

---

[132] FAO Report, above n 62, at 4.

[133] *Ibid*, see also at 19–20.

[134] World Bank, *The Sunken Billions Revisited: Progress and Challenges in Global Marine Fisheries* (Washington DC, 2017) <http://hdl.handle.net/10986/24056> at 7–8.

[135] *Ibid*, at 18.

[136] FAO Fisheries and Aquaculture Circular, *The Implementation of Performance Review Reports by Regional Fisheries Bodies 2004–2014*, FIPI/C1108 ('FAO Circular').

[137] *Ibid*, at 14.

[138] *Ibid*, at 37–38.

[139] ICCAT 2008 Report, above n 125, at 29.

groups of importance in the ICCAT decision making process'.[140] The review panel recommended that ICCAT should 'review its policy on NGOs attendance at ICCAT meetings'.[141] In 2016, eight years after the first performance review, a second review found that ICCAT had not reviewed its policy on NGOs' attendance as recommended and that the participation fee, allowing attendance of two representatives, continued to apply with a supplemental 350 USD fee for each additional person in the observer delegation.[142] The reluctance to review public participation policies and the persistence of the participation fee suggest that RFMOs have little or no motivation to become more inclusive to NGOs and the public interest they represent.

A related issue is the lack of transparency in RFMO performance reviews. The 2006 UNGA Resolution on Sustainable Fisheries urged states to undertake performance reviews using transparent criteria and 'some element of independent evaluation'.[143] The GOC found that the reviews performed 'cannot be considered truly independent' because they were conducted by panels including members employed by either the RFMO or by member states.[144] Only a few RFMOs have involved NGO representatives in performance reviews.[145]

SDG 16 aims at building strong institutions, in part by ensuring 'responsive, inclusive, participatory and representative decision-making at all levels'. The FAO Report states 'governance of fisheries and aquaculture should be greatly influenced by the 2030 Agenda for Sustainable Development'.[146] In addition, the 2030 Agenda and SDGs are beginning to be acknowledged by member states in RFMO meetings,[147] indicating that the SDGs could potentially influence the work of RFMOs. I propose that the interplay between UNCLOS, the FSA and the SDGs could guide RFMOs' efforts towards making rules on NGO participation less restrictive, for instance through substantially reducing or eliminating NGO participation fees. In addition, such interplay could encourage more RFMO performance review procedures to include NGO representatives.

---

140 *Ibid*, at 71.
141 *Ibid.*
142 FAO Report, above n 62, at 61.
143 Above n 113, para 73.
144 GOC, above n 4, at 36. See also FAO Circular, above n 136, at 2.
145 FAO Circular, above n 136, at 3.
146 FAO Report, above n 62, at 7.
147 WCPFC, IATTC, above n 37.

6.5.2 Public Participation in the International Seabed Authority

6.5.2.1 Role of the ISA in the governance of seabed minerals in the Area

The Area and its resources are the common heritage of mankind.[148] Consequently, claims of sovereignty over, or appropriation of, the Area or its resources are invalid and all rights in the resources are vested in mankind as a whole.[149] In addition, activities in the Area must be carried out for the benefit of mankind and the ISA, which acts on behalf of mankind,[150] must provide for the equitable sharing of financial and other economic benefits derived from such activities.[151] Furthermore, states have the responsibility to use the Area exclusively for peaceful purposes[152] and to ensure that activities are carried out in strict conformity with UNCLOS Part XI.[153] In its 2011 advisory opinion, the International Tribunal for the Law of the Sea stated:

> [T]he role of the sponsoring State is to contribute to the common interest of all States in the proper implementation of the principle of the common heritage of mankind by assisting the Authority and by acting on its own with a view to ensuring that entities under its jurisdiction conform to the rules on deep seabed mining.[154]

The principle of common heritage of mankind is central in the current negotiations on the draft text of a legally binding instrument under UNCLOS on the conservation and sustainable use of marine biological diversity of ABNJ.[155]

---

[148] UNCLOS, above n 55, article 136.
[149] *Ibid*, article 137.
[150] *Ibid*, article 137(2).
[151] *Ibid*, article 140.
[152] *Ibid*, article 141.
[153] *Ibid*, article 139.
[154] Responsibilities and Obligations of States with respect to Activities in the Area, Advisory Opinion, 1 February 2011, ITLOS Reports 2011, 10, para 226, see also para 76. See also D. French, 'From the Depths: Rich Pickings of Principles of Sustainable Development and General International Law on the Ocean Floor – the Seabed Disputes Chamber's 2011 Advisory Opinion' (2011) *International Journal of Marine and Coastal Law* 26, 525, in particular pp. 544–546.
[155] Chair's non-paper on elements of a draft text of an international legally-binding instrument under the United Nations Convention on the Law of the Sea on the conservation and sustainable use of marine biological diversity of areas beyond national jurisdiction (2017), at 23–24. See also Chair's overview of the

States parties to UNCLOS established the ISA to 'organize and control activities in the Area, particularly with a view to administering [its] resources'[156] and entrusted it with the responsibility to adopt regulations necessary for conducting exploration and related exploitation activities.[157] Regarding the protection of the marine environment, the ISA must adopt rules, regulations and procedures for 'the prevention, reduction and control of pollution and other hazards … and of interference with the ecological balance of the marine environment'.[158] In doing so it must pay particular attention to 'the need for protection from harmful effects of certain activities such as drilling, dredging, excavation, disposal of waste, construction and operation or maintenance of installations, pipelines, and other devices related to these activities'.[159] The ISA must also provide for 'the protection and conservation of the natural resources of the Area and the prevention of damage to the flora and fauna of the marine environment'.[160] In performing these functions, the ISA must address 'the harmful effects directly resulting from activities in the Area or from shipboard processing immediately above a mine site'.[161] To date, the ISA has adopted Regulations on Prospecting and Exploration for the three above-mentioned types of commercially viable minerals: polymetallic nodules, polymetallic sulphides and ferromanganese crusts (Exploration Regulations).[162] All Exploration Regulations contain environmental provisions, including the obligation of the ISA and sponsoring states to apply a precautionary approach. The regulatory framework for the protection of the marine environment in the Area also includes the Environmental Management Plan for the Clarion-Clipperton Zone,[163] and

---

third session (2017) of the Preparatory Committee, at 4–5. Both documents are available at <http://www.un.org/depts/los/biodiversity/prepcom.htm>.

[156] UNCLOS, above n 55, article 157(1).

[157] *Ibid*, articles 160 para 2(f)(ii) and 162 para 2(o)(ii); UNCLOS Annex III, Art. 17; 1994 Agreement Relating to the Implementation of Part XI of the United Nations Convention on the Law of the Sea of 10 December 1982, 1836 U.N.T.S. 3 (28 July 1994) Annex, Section 1, para 5(f).

[158] UNCLOS, article 145(a).

[159] *Ibid.*

[160] *Ibid*, article 145(b).

[161] *Ibid*, Annex III, article 17(f).

[162] Regulations on Prospecting and Exploration for Polymetallic Nodules in the Area, above n 72; Regulations on Prospecting and Exploration for Cobalt-rich Ferromanganese Crusts in the Area, above n 73; and Regulations on Prospecting and Exploration for Polymetallic Sulphides in the Area, above n 74.

[163] Environmental Management Plan for the Clarion-Clipperton Zone, above n 76.

recommendations for the guidance of contractors in the assessment of environmental impacts arising from exploration activities.[164]

The Legal and Technical Commission (LTC), one of the organs of the ISA Council,[165] plays a crucial role in implementing the ISA's mandate to protect the marine environment. According to UNCLOS, the LTC must formulate and submit to the Council rules, regulations and procedures for exploration and exploitation activities in the Area, taking into account 'assessments of the environmental implications of [such] activities'.[166] The LTC must also keep such rules, regulations and procedures under review.[167] In addition, the LTC is required to prepare environmental impact assessments of activities in the Area and make recommendations to the Council on the protection of the marine environment.[168] These recommendations include issuing emergency orders to prevent serious environmental harm,[169] disapproving areas for exploitation when 'substantial evidence indicates the risk of serious harm to the marine environment',[170] and directing inspections of activities in the Area to ensure compliance with applicable (environmental) rules and regulations.[171] UNCLOS also requires the LTC to coordinate monitoring of the risks and effects of pollution resulting from exploration and exploitation activities.[172] The Exploration Regulations confer additional functions and competences on the LTC for environmental protection. They require the LTC to make recommendations to the Council on the establishment and implementation of environmental rules, regulations and procedures, and on the application of a precautionary approach and best environmental practices by the ISA and sponsoring states.[173] In addition, the LTC must 'develop and implement procedures for determining ... whether proposed exploration activities in the Area would have serious harmful effects on vulnerable marine ecosystems', ensuring

---

164 Recommendations for the Guidance of Contractors for the Assessment of the Possible Environmental Impacts Arising from Exploration for Marine Minerals in the Area, ISBA/19/LTC/8 (1 March 2013).

165 UNCLOS, above n 55, articles 163 and 165.

166 *Ibid*, article 165(2)(f).

167 *Ibid*, article 165(2)(g).

168 *Ibid*, article 165(2)(d) and (e).

169 *Ibid*, article 165(2)(k).

170 *Ibid*, article 165(2)(l).

171 *Ibid*, article 165(2)(m).

172 *Ibid*, article 165(2)(h).

173 Nodules Exploration Regulations, above n 72, Regulation 31(3); Crusts Exploration Regulations, above n 73, Regulation 33(3); Sulphides Exploration Regulations, above n 74, Regulation 33(3).

that 'those activities are managed to prevent such effects or not authorized to proceed'.[174] Finally, the LTC must determine whether a proposed exploration plan 'provides for effective protection and preservation of the marine environment including … the impact on biodiversity'.[175] It must not recommend approval of an exploration plan covering an area that has been disapproved for exploitation due to substantial evidence indicating the risk of serious environmental harm.[176]

In view of the significant competences invested in the LTC for the protection of the marine environment and considering that 'lack of transparency of the work of the LTC has been heavily criticized',[177] the next section pays particular attention to public access to information and participation in the LTC.

6.5.2.2 Public participation in the ISA in the light of the SDGs

Although the number of observers has increased in recent years and civil society organizations have organized side events and workshops during the ISA's annual sessions,[178] challenges exist regarding access to information and public participation in decision-making processes at the Authority. Currently, representatives of accredited organizations may attend meetings of the Assembly and the Council as observers.[179] Accredited organizations include NGOs with consultative status,[180] and upon invitation, other NGOs which have a demonstrated interest in matters under the consideration of the ISA.[181] At the Assembly, observers

---

[174] Nodules Exploration Regulations, above n 72, Regulation 31(4); Crusts Exploration Regulations, above n 73, Regulation 33(4); Sulphides Exploration Regulations, above n 74, Regulation 33(4).

[175] Nodules Exploration Regulations, above n 72, Regulation 21(4)(b); Crusts Exploration Regulations, above n 73, Regulation 23(4)(b); Sulphides Exploration Regulations, above n 74, Regulation 23(4)(b).

[176] Nodules Exploration Regulations, above n 72, Regulation 21(6)(c); Crusts Exploration Regulations, above n 73, Regulation 23(6)(c); Sulphides Exploration, Regulations, above n 74, Regulation 23(6)(c).

[177] Periodic Review of the International Seabed Authority pursuant to UNCLOS Article 154, Final Report (30 December 2016) (Seascape Consultants Ltd) <https://www.isa.org.jm/files/documents/EN/Art154/Rep/ISA154-FinalRep-3012 2016.pdf> at 2.

[178] A. Jaeckel, 'Current Legal Developments International Seabed Authority' (2016) 31 *The International Journal of Marine and Coastal Law* 706, 717–718.

[179] UNCLOS, above n 55, article 169.

[180] *Ibid.*

[181] Rules of Procedure of the Assembly of the International Seabed Authority ('ROP Assembly') <http://www.isa.org.jm/files/documents/EN/Regs/ROP_Assembly.

may sit at public meetings, make oral statements upon invitation of the President approved by the Assembly,[182] and submit written statements through the Secretariat.[183] At the Council, observers may participate in its deliberations upon invitation of the Council without the right to vote,[184] and submit written reports through the Secretariat.[185] The meetings of the LTC are held in private and are therefore closed to observers.[186] The LTC could decide to hold open meetings, for instance when discussing 'issues of general interest to members of the Authority, which do not involve the discussion of confidential information'.[187] In practice, however, the LTC rarely holds open meetings because of the confidentiality requirement.

The Rules of Procedure require LTC members to sign a confidentiality agreement before assuming their functions.[188] The obligation not to disclose confidential information remains in place after the end of their duties.[189] Confidential information includes 'any industrial secret, proprietary data which are transferred to the Authority in accordance with annex III, article 14, of [UNCLOS], or any other confidential information coming to their knowledge by reason of their duties'.[190] Article 14 of Annex III provides '[t]he operator shall transfer to the Authority … all data which are both necessary for and relevant to the effective exercise of the powers and functions of the principal organs of the Authority in respect of the area covered by the plan of work'. However, the LTC does not have procedures in place to determine which of the data provided by contractors is confidential and consequently, the contractor determines confidentiality.[191] Currently, all data contained in contract applications

---

pdf> Rule 82(1)(e); Rules of Procedure of the Council of the International Seabed Authority ('ROP Council') <http://www.isa.org.jm/files/documents/EN/Regs/ROP_Council.pdf> Rule 75.

[182] ROP Assembly, *ibid*, Rule 82(5).

[183] *Ibid*, Rule 82(6).

[184] ROP Council, above n 181, Rule 75.

[185] *Ibid*, Rule 32(2).

[186] Rules of Procedure of the Legal and Technical Commission ('ROP LTC') <http://www.isa.org.jm/files/documents/EN/Regs/ROP_LTC.pdf> Rule 6.

[187] *Ibid*.

[188] *Ibid*, Rule 11(2).

[189] *Ibid*, Rule 12(3).

[190] *Ibid*, Rule 12(1).

[191] J.A. Ardron, 'Transparency in the Operations of the International Seabed Authority: An Initial Assessment' (2016) *Marine Policy* (in press) 6, available at <https://doi.org/10.1016/j.marpol.2016.06.027>. See also *Co-Chairs Report of Griffith Law School and the International Seabed Authority Workshop Environmental Assessment and Management for Exploitation of Minerals in the Area*

and annual reports of contractors submitted to the LTC are treated as confidential.[192] As a result, environmental data provided by contractors is unavailable to the public and LTC meetings are held in private. This contravenes UNCLOS and the Exploration Regulations, which expressly provide that environmental data shall not be deemed confidential.[193]

A comparative assessment of transparency practices found that the ISA generally scored much lower than the RFMOs, especially regarding availability of information, participation in decision making and access to outcomes.[194] The same study concluded that '[p]ublic access to information, decision making, compliance reporting and justice, would greatly improve the chances of the ISA achieving long-term regulatory success'.[195] In 2016, the final report of the first Periodic Review of the ISA Pursuant to UNCLOS Article 154 (Periodic Review Report) documented the views that, although arrangements for consultation and cooperation with intergovernmental organizations and NGOs were in place, 'this is an area where improvements can be made'; that 'better dialogue and interaction with other sectoral UN agencies … is needed'; and that these efforts are 'highly relevant in the context of wider discussions related to … Sustainable Development Goal 14'.[196] The review committee made several recommendations based on the Periodic Review Report regarding transparency and access to information.[197] First, the LTC 'should be encouraged to hold more open meetings in order to allow for greater transparency in its work'.[198] Second, 'non-confidential information, such as [that] relating to the protection and preservation of the marine

(Surfer's Paradise, 23–26 May 2016) ('Co-Chairs Report') <https://www.isa.org.jm/files/documents/EN/Pubs/2016/GLS-ISA-Rep.pdf> at 23.

192 Ardron, above n 191, at 3. See also Co-Chairs Report, above n 191, at 23.

193 UNCLOS, above n 55, Annex III, article 14(2); Nodules Exploration Regulations, above n 72, Regulation 36(2); Crusts Exploration Regulations, above n 73, Regulation 38(2); Sulphides Exploration, above n 74, Regulation 38(1).

194 Ardron, above n 191, 5–6.

195 *Ibid*, at 7.

196 Above n 177, at 40.

197 Letter dated 3 February 2017 from the Chair of the Committee established by the Assembly to carry out a periodic review of the international regime of the Area pursuant to article 154 of the United Nations Convention on the Law of the Sea to the Secretary-General of the International Seabed Authority, ISBA/23/A/3 (8 February 2017). See Annex 'Final report on the periodic review of the International Seabed Authority pursuant to article 154 of the United Nations Convention on the Law of the Sea'.

198 *Ibid*, Recommendation 16.

environment, should be shared widely and be readily accessible'.[199] Third, the review committee advised that 'the sharing and accessing of environmental data collected by contractors seems to require improvement'.[200]

In addition to SDG 14, SDG 16 is highly relevant to ocean sustainability, including the sustainable management of deep seabed minerals in the Area, for it aims at building transparent, accountable and effective institutions at all levels. Because of the interplay and potential for synergy between UNCLOS and the SDGs, which has been acknowledged by the ISA,[201] SDG 16 and targets 16.6 (institutional transparency), 16.7 (inclusive and participatory decision making) and 16.10 (access to information) could guide actions towards strengthening the LTC. I propose that such actions could include (i) creating procedures to determine confidentiality of data provided by contractors; (ii) providing public access to all environmental data available to the ISA; and (iii) ensuring public participation in all LTC meetings discussing environmental matters. Such improvements would strengthen the LTC – and the ISA in general – for sustainably managing the common heritage of mankind for the benefit of present and future generations.

6.6 CONCLUSION

Civil society organizations were not only engaged in the drafting of the SDGs but also are called on to contribute expertise to follow-up and review processes. SDG 16 specifically encourages public access to information and participation in decision making as a way of strengthening institutions at all levels. Transparent, accountable and effective institutions are crucial at a time in which unsustainable fishing practices and imminent exploitation of deep seabed minerals threaten to deepen the ocean's rate of ecological decline. SDG 16 thus supports the achievement of SDG 14 – conserve and sustainably use the ocean and marine resources – providing a guiding framework to construct the institutional strength necessary to achieve ocean sustainability.

Institutions managing the ocean commons face several challenges that weaken their performance, including ineffectiveness, unaccountability and lack of transparency. Public participation can contribute to solving

---

[199] *Ibid*, Recommendation 18.

[200] *Ibid*, Recommendation 6.

[201] Opening Statement by President of the Council Ambassador Peter Thomson, above n 34 and Statement by Secretary-General Michael Lodge, above n 36.

these problems; however, both RFMOs and the ISA provide only restricted public access to information and participation in decision making. To be sure, this chapter has shown that RFMOs tend to be reluctant to include NGOs in their decision-making processes. In addition, the ISA keeps environmental information provided by contractors confidential and its LTC – the organ with the most significant role regarding environmental protection – holds most of its meetings as closed sessions. From the perspective of public participation, therefore, the existing conception of ocean commons governance is one in which states and industry organizations are the main actors and civil society organizations are relegated to a secondary role.

In line with Rio Principle 10 – and its elaboration in subsequent international agreements – and reflecting the increasing support it has gained since its adoption in 1992 (including by current negotiations on the draft text of a binding agreement on the conservation and sustainable use of marine biological diversity in ABNJ),[202] the SDGs promote a new conception of ocean commons governance through encouraging public participation in building effective, accountable and transparent institutions. In the new conception, civil society organizations join states and industry organizations as principal actors in achieving sustainable governance of high seas fisheries and deep seabed minerals in the Area. Guided by the SDGs, governing institutions could take steps towards improving existing participation mechanisms. RFMOs could make rules on NGO participation less restrictive as well as include NGOs in performance reviews. The ISA in turn could develop procedures to determine confidentiality of data provided by contractors, provide public access to all environmental data, and ensure public participation in LTC meetings discussing the protection of the marine environment. Such measures would support RFMOs and the ISA in moving much closer to achieving SDG 14.

---

[202] Chair's non-paper on elements of a draft text of an international legally-binding instrument under the United Nations Convention on the Law of the Sea on the conservation and sustainable use of marine biological diversity of areas beyond national jurisdiction, above n 155. The Chair's non-paper shows that public participation is being discussed as one of the guiding principles and approaches for the new regime (see for example, pp. 18, 37 and 70).

PART II

A selective analysis of particular goals

7. Gender and the Sustainable Development Goals

Karen Morrow

7.1 INTRODUCTION: GOALS, RIGHTS AND GENDER

This chapter examines the coverage offered by the Sustainable Development Goals (SDGs)[1] to gender issues.[2] It considers the legacy of the Millennium Development Goals (MDGs)[3] and the signal importance of the continuing reluctance of states to give substantive cognisance to links between development goals and human rights, thus ensuring that they remain confined to the political rather than the legal realm. While this approach permeates the goals, this chapter will argue that, for gender issues, with their hard-won but now established human rights-based characterisation, the mismatch is particularly acute, and the potential salience of the goals to the gender constituency is greatly compromised as a result.

[1] UNDP Sustainable Development Goals <http://www.undp.org/content/undp/en/home/sustainable-development-goals.html> accessed 15 May 2017.

[2] Discussion of gender is prominent in A/Res/70/1 *Transforming our world: the 2030 Agenda for Sustainable Development*, 21 October 2015 (Agenda 2030) <http://www.un.org/ga/search/view_doc.asp?symbol=A/RES/70/1&referer=/english/&Lang=E> accessed 10 July 2017, which features 32 references to 'women/women and girls' across a 35-page document. Notably though, while the 1995 Beijing Platform for action is listed among the UN documents that have '... laid a solid foundation for sustainable development and ... helped to shape the new Agenda' (para 11), other key documents relating to gender, such as the Convention on the Elimination of All Forms of Discrimination Against Women 1979 are not.

[3] Millennium Development Project, Millennium Development Goals <http://www.unmillenniumproject.org/goals/> accessed 29 July 2016.

7.2 GENDER AND THE UN – A BRIEF PRIMER

The United Nations (UN) has been formally committed to human equality generally, and gender equality specifically, since its inception, rejecting distinction/discrimination on grounds of sex in the Charter of the United Nations in 1945,[4] and the Universal Declaration of Human Rights 1948.[5] Women's concerns also gained fairly early specific coverage in the Convention on the Political Rights of Women 1952,[6] though it can be argued that this type of approach is not an unalloyed good as it can serve to reduce gender concerns to 'women's issues', rather than seeking to address the deeply embedded structural inequality that lies at their root.[7] The focus on gender equality in the UN's mainstream human rights instruments was reiterated in the common Article 3 provisions of the International Covenant on Civil and Political Rights 1966[8] and the International Covenant on Economic, Social and Cultural Rights 1966,[9] which refer to the 'equal right of men and women' to the enjoyment of their respective provision.

The existence of law does not of course alone ensure its efficacy, to the extent that it has been argued, with some force, that: '... women's historic hold on human rights has been both ambiguous and tenuous'.[10] It

---

[4] The preamble of which affirmed the 'equal rights of men and women' and Article 8 committing the UN to proceeding on the basis of unrestricted 'eligibility of men and women to participate in any capacity and under conditions of equality in its principal and subsidiary organs'. Charter of the United Nations <https://treaties.un.org/doc/publication/ctc/uncharter.pdf> accessed 29 July 2016.

[5] General Assembly Resolution 217 (III) A, 10 December 1948, the preamble of which refers to the 'equal rights of men and women' <http://www.ohchr.org/EN/UDHR/Documents/UDHR_Translations/eng.pdf> accessed 29 July 2016.

[6] General Assembly Resolution 640(VII) online at <https://documents-dds-ny.un.org/doc/RESOLUTION/GEN/NR0/079/83/IMG/NR007983.pdf?OpenElement> accessed 29 July 2016.

[7] S. Arora-Jonsson, 'Forty Years of Gender Research and Environmental Policy: Where Do We Stand?' (2014) *Women's Studies International Forum* 47, 295.

[8] General Assembly Resolution 2200A (XXI) of 16 December 1966 online at <http://www.ohchr.org/en/professionalinterest/pages/ccpr.aspx> accessed 7 December 2016.

[9] General Assembly Resolution 2200A (XXI) of 16 December 1966 online at <http://www.ohchr.org/EN/ProfessionalInterest/Pages/CESCR.aspx> accessed 7 December 2016.

[10] M. Pardy, 'Under Western Eyes Again? Rights Vernacular and the Gender Culture "Clash"' (2013) *Australian Journal of Human Rights* 19(1), 39.

is certainly the case that the UN's gender agenda took some considerable time to even begin to mature, and it was in the end a women-focussed approach that seeded this development, with International Women's Year 1975 and the UN Decade for Women (1976–1985) and their supporting conferences providing the impetus for the Convention on the Elimination of All Forms of Discrimination Against Women 1979 (CEDAW),[11] finally setting gender on a sound foundation within the organisation and numerous subsequent institutional developments securing the place of, and at the same time giving new prominence to, women's issues on the international stage.[12]

Acceptance in principle was, however, slow to generate headway in practice, as highlighted by the Beijing Declaration and Programme for Action 1995,[13] and the UN was ultimately forced to change tack in the search for efficacy, developing the concept of gender mainstreaming in the attempt to translate commitments on paper to progress in the real world.[14] While gender mainstreaming has not by any means proven a global panacea for the ills of gender inequality (arguably merely 'bureaucratizing the idea of gender'[15]), it has, in conjunction with other developments, such as the emergence of innovative international governance in the context of sustainable development (under the rubric of the 'social pillar'), ensured that gender is now at least (for the most part) both firmly present on the agenda and institutionalised in many of the UN's activities.

The several developments at UN level outlined above, while indicating a degree of progress at an organisational level, tend to mask the fact that gender equality remains a matter of profound disagreement and dispute among states.[16] This was very evident throughout the formation of the

---

[11] UN Women Convention on the Elimination of All Forms of Discrimination Against Women <http://www.un.org/womenwatch/daw/cedaw/text/econvention.htm> accessed 29 July 2016.

[12] Discussed in K. Morrow, 'Not So Much a Meeting of Minds as a Coincidence of Means: Ecofeminism, Gender Mainstreaming and the UN' (2006) *Thomas Jefferson Law Journal* 28(2), 185.

[13] UN Women Beijing Declaration and Platform for Action <http://www.unwomen.org/~/media/headquarters/attachments/sections/csw/pfa_e_final_web.pdf> accessed 29 July 2016.

[14] Morrow, above n 12.

[15] Arora-Jonsson, above n 7, 303.

[16] Notable laggards on women's rights include the Holy See and many Islamic States; see with reference to the SDG process S. Gabizon, I. Alvarez, S. Lovera et al, *Sustainable Development Goals and the 2030 Agenda, Women's Major Group* at UNEP, UNEP, Perspectives, Issue no. 17, October 2015,

SDGs, which exhibited constant pressure on some fronts to remove or play down references to gender in them.[17] In the end though, thanks in part to constant, coordinated and high-profile work by civil society,[18] the current (though by no means unthreatened)[19] globally prevailing recognition of gender equality won out, and gender was both accorded discrete 'headline' coverage in SDG 5 (achieve gender equality and empower all women and girls) and recognised as raising clear implications in respect to many of the others. Gender is also a recurrent feature in the regime's supporting targets.

It is also worth reflecting not only on the institutional, but also the wider (if not universal) societal climate created by the UN's largely rights-based engagement with gender over the decades. The fundamental and embedded rights-based approach to gender has generated basic expectations on how gender issues are to be addressed, with women/gender activists and institutions employing rights-talk as an established foundation to exhort action across a wide variety of spheres;[20] and many states, having signed up to (some or all of) the various agreements alluded to above, recognise (albeit to varying degrees) the force that such rights-based claims can invoke. As we shall see below, the goals-based approaches to development that have emerged first through the MDGs, and latterly the SDGs, have seen real and fundamental tensions emerge between them and rights-based approaches more generally and with marked effect in respect of gender.

Given the comparatively well-primed UN approach to gender generally, it was on balance no surprise that it featured prominently among the

---

<https://wedocs.unep.org/rest/bitstreams/10863/retrieve> accessed 12 May 2017; and, more broadly Z.F.K. Arat, 'Promoting Women's Rights against Patriarchal Culture Claims: The Women's Convention and Reservations by Muslim States' in D.P. Forsythe and P.C. McMahon (eds), *Human Rights and Diversity: Area Studies Revisited* (University of Nebraska Press, 2003).

[17] Women's Major Group: 'Women's "8 Red Flags"' Following the Conclusion of the Open Working Group on Sustainable Development Goals (SDGs)', 21 July 2014, (hereafter WMG: 'Women's "8 Red Flags"') <http://www.wedo.org/wp-content/uploads/Womens-Major-Group_OWG_FINALSTATEMENT_21July.pdf> accessed 9 August 2016.

[18] *Ibid*, 1.

[19] See, for example, J. Squires, *The New Politics of Gender Equality* (Palgrave Macmillan, 2007).

[20] See, for example, Women and Gender Constituency: 'Gender Just Climate Solutions' Women Engage for a Common Future, Utrecht (2016) <http://www.wecf.eu/english/publications/2016/ENG-WGCSolutionsPublFINALWEB.pdf> accessed 9 May 2017.

MDGs,[21] and we will consider the approach adopted therein in greater detail below as it directly sets the scene for current developments. For now, it suffices to say that, while the MDGs delivered a degree of progress on their gender-oriented objectives on the ground,[22] much remains to be done. Thus, as the shift towards gender equality remains very much work in progress, it will become apparent that gender necessarily retains a significant presence in the expanded successor regime.

A relatively short chapter cannot hope to offer full coverage of the myriad issues arising in respect of gender and international policy developments but it can illustrate the direction of travel. To that end, the chapter will focus primarily on key factors shaping the pursuit of gender equality and women's empowerment under the SDGs (not least, the legacy of the MDGs) and some of the likely impediments to their full realisation, notably the limitations of indicators-based goals and the continuing failure of the international development goals regime to engage effectively with the human rights agenda.[23]

7.3 THE MDGS' LEGACY ON GENDER

The question of how best to address gender concerns is, at best, a fraught one – and experience with the MDGs suggests that it is debatable whether it is in fact capable of a 'right' answer. The MDGs ultimately adopted a two-pronged approach: on the one hand including a specific gender goal and discrete targets; and on the other integrating gender considerations into other goals and their targets. In so doing, it arguably sought to achieve the best of both worlds.

The inclusion of the gender-oriented MDG 3 was an important development in principle, according gender a degree of prominence commensurate with other core concerns within the regime such as eradicating poverty and hunger. At the same time, there was a downside to this, as embodying gender within a discrete goal created the conceptual danger of allowing it to be/become isolated as an issue by exposing it to the risk of being siloed at this level of the MDG regime. This tendency was, however, ostensibly offset by the second approach,

[21] MDGs, above n 3.

[22] United Nations: The Millennium Development Goals Report 2015 (hereafter UN MDG Report 2015) <http://www.un.org/millenniumgoals/2015_MDG_Report.pdf> 4–9, accessed 18 November 2016.

[23] See also Collins, Chapter 4 in this volume.

ensuring that gender featured in targets falling under other goals,[24] which created opportunities to integrate and mainstream gender within the broader MDG regime. That said, it can be argued that this approach too has its dangers, as treating gender as a cross-cutting issue can create the danger that it is subsumed in other concerns.[25] Even if this was not demonstrably the case, the supporting role accorded to gender in this context arguably sent a significant signal as to its subsidiary status where it did appear. While it may have been hoped that the defects of one approach would serve to offset those of the other, this is not a given. In any event, ensuring that this would be the case would have required a very careful and coordinated eye to be given to goal and target design to this specific end – at best unlikely in the context of a highly politicised, internationally negotiated process, which is inevitably characterised by powerplays and strategic trade-offs.

The approach to gender invoked by MDG 3, as with the other goals in this regime, focussed attention on the developing world, conveniently ignoring the fact that gender issues give cause for concern globally. Its supporting targets were concentrated on indicators highlighting selected aspects of education, employment and political participation.[26] While these are laudable in themselves, this approach also served to effectively narrow the focus on gender issues[27] as in raising the profile of these

---

24 Gender features to some degree in the targets for most of the other MDGs – Goal 1: Eradicate Extreme Poverty and Hunger – Target 1A; 1B; Goal 2: Achieve Universal Primary education – Target 2.A; Goal 4: Reduce Child Mortality – Target 4A; Goal 5 Improve Maternal Health – Target 5A, 5B; Goal 6: Combat HIV/AIDS, malaria and other diseases – Target 6A (gender disaggregated data and gender differentiated impacts); and Goal 8: Develop a global partnership for development – Target 8A, <http://www.un.org/millenniumgoals/> accessed 15 May 2017.

25 E. Harrison, 'Bouncing Back? Recession, Resilience and Everyday Lives' (2012) *Critical Social Policy* 33(1), 97.

26 Target 4 – Eliminate gender disparity in primary and secondary education, preferably by 2005, and in all levels of education no later than 2015. Indicators 9 and 10, overseen by United Nations Educational, Scientific and Cultural Organization (UNESCO), focussed on the ratio of girls to boys at all levels of education and the literacy of literate women to men aged 15–24; Indicator 11, overseen by the International Labour Organization, focussed on women in waged employment outside the agricultural sector; and Indicator 12, overseen by the Inter-Parliamentary Union, focussed on the proportion of women in national parliaments <http://www.un.org/millenniumgoals/> accessed 15 May 2017.

27 See, for example, N. Kabeer, 'Gender Equality and Women's Empowerment: A Critical Analysis of the Third Millennium Development Goal' (2005) *Gender and Development* 13(1), 13.

specific issues, it arguably incentivised states to focus their efforts and scarce resources on activities that would 'count' for the purposes of the MDGs – at the expense of a broader approach to addressing gender concerns trained on deeper culture change.

That said, the key targets under MDG 3 do demonstrate progress, albeit to varying degrees. The target of eliminating gender disparity in primary education by 2005 was achieved by a majority of developing regions. Less progress was, however, made on the target to do likewise for secondary education and progress on a 2015 target for tertiary education was more limited still.[28] In terms of women's access to paid employment, while opportunities for women have slowly increased, gender remains a source of disadvantage for women.[29] Insofar as women's political representation is concerned, here again there has been progress (notably in seeing average representation increase from 11 per cent in 1995 to 22 per cent in 2015 and in developing regions[30] increasingly exceeding that in the developed world).[31] Despite these initially encouraging results, latterly it appears that progress on political representation has stalled.[32] Furthermore, the depth of change wrought is questionable and it is significant that women continue to be largely absent from leadership positions. These headlines also mask the fact that disparities in gender equality between developing regions remain at all levels,[33] though this is also the case in the developed world. With this in mind, gender equality is one area where the SDGs in rolling out regime coverage to all states, will, albeit belatedly, place the performance of the latter too under justified scrutiny.

Progress under the 8 MDG goals and targets was ultimately expressed through 21 targets which were launched by the UN Secretary-General

---

[28] UN MDG Report 2015, above n 22, 28.

[29] *Ibid*, 30.

[30] *Ibid*, 31.

[31] United Nations Development Programme (UNDP): The Path to Achieving the Millennium Development Goals: A Synthesis of Evidence from Around the World (2010) (hereafter UNDP Path) <http://www.ghd-net.org/sites/default/files/2-%20UNDP_The%20path%20to%20achieving%20MDGs_0.pdf> accessed 20 October 2016, p 27.

[32] This was observed in 2014, suggesting that the 'low hanging fruit' may now have been plucked and that further advancement may prove considerably more problematic – UN MDG Report 2015, above n 22.

[33] *Ibid*, 28–31.

and made the subject of an annual report.[34] These were fleshed out by 60 MDG Indicators,[35] which, to establish their credibility, were selected by and operated under the auspices of the Inter-Agency and Expert Group (IAEG) on MDG Indicators. The indicators, like the targets adopted, were subject to periodic review and updating.[36] Gender-based indicators provided a distinct strand for reporting within the broader suite of MDGs indicators and this proved useful in drawing them out for public consumption.[37]

In addition to the MDG regime's own treatment of gender, the United Nations Development Programme (UNDP) also observed that the law proved centrally important to progressing MDG 3, identifying it as providing a foundational '... national framework establishing the principles of gender equality' and as key in instituting practical steps to promote women's representation in legislative bodies.[38] In sum, however, the UNDP in reviewing this MDG concluded that, although progress had been made, 'parity remains a distant goal'.[39] That said, the effect of MDG 3 also needs to be considered in the context of the broader regime. Thus, it is significant that the UNDP, in charting progress on the MDGs across 34 countries, identified what it referred to as a 'catalytic' effect of action on gender equality on the other MDGs[40] and pointed to the utility of the integration of gender with other issues.[41]

---

[34] A/56/326, Road Map Towards the Implementation of the United Nations Millennium Declaration, 6 September 2001 <https://mdgs.un.org/unsd/mdg/Resources/Static/Products/SGReports/56_326/a_56_326e.pdf> accessed 9 May 2017.

[35] Millennium Development Goals Indicators: Official List of MDG Indicators <https://mdgs.un.org/unsd/mdg/Host.aspx?Content=Indicators/OfficialList.htm> accessed 17 May 2017.

[36] Millennium Development Goals Indicators https://mdgs.un.org/unsd/mdg/Host.aspx?Content=Indicators/About.htm> accessed 9 May 2017.

[37] See, for example, the eight-page-long, colourful and highly illustrated, 'Millennium Development Goals Gender Chart', 2015 <https://mdgs.un.org/unsd/mdg/Resources/Static/Products/Progress2015/Gender_Chart_Web.pdf> accessed 9 May 2017.

[38] UNDP Path, above n 31, 26–27.

[39] *Ibid*, 31.

[40] *Ibid*, 9–10.

[41] *Ibid*, 31.

7.4 GENDER, THE SDGS AND THE 2030 AGENDA FOR SUSTAINABLE DEVELOPMENT[42]

Seventeen SDGs were agreed, a substantially increased 169 targets[43] set, and a colossal 232 indicators developed under the new regime,[44] which is, beyond the basic goals, ponderous in comparison to its predecessor. The mushrooming of targets and indicators, while on the one hand speaking to expanded ambition, on the other gives pause to the viability of any claim they can offer to provide a clear steer to and simplifying the communication of the regime's progress.

The goals themselves, despite the lengthy, sophisticated and open consultative process that produced them, were in the end, perhaps inevitably given the international law and policy context, the subject of a great deal of last minute horse-trading,[45] which proved inimical to a fully reasoned outcome. That said, gender does retain the specific headline coverage in the SDGs that it enjoyed in the MDGs, specifically in Goal 5. The coverage offered here mixes top-down and bottom-up elements.[46] Also in common with the preceding regime, a cross-cutting approach, which (at least to a degree) recognises the challenges of intersectionality[47] is adopted and gender issues appear under some (but not all) other goals in their associated targets, which have significant gender dimensions and implications. In fact, women and/or gender are mentioned in some of the targets adopted under more than half of the other SDGs.[48]

---

[42] Agenda 2030, above n 2.

[43] Millennium Development Goals Gender Chart 2015, above n 37, 31.

[44] Report of the Inter-Agency and Expert Group on Sustainable Development Goal Indicators (E/CN.3/2017/2), 16 September 2016, Annex III <https://unstats.un.org/unsd/statcom/48th-session/documents/2017-2-IAEG-SDGs-E.pdf> accessed 9 May 2017.

[45] EGM/SDG Report of the Expert Group Meeting on the CSW 60 Priority Theme: Women's Empowerment and the link to Sustainable Development, 2015 (hereafter EGM/SDG Report) <http://www.unwomen.org/-/media/headquarters/attachments/sections/csw/60/csw60%20egm%20report.pdf?vs=1710> accessed 12 May 2017. See also V. Esquivel, 'Power and the Sustainable Development Goals: A Feminist Analysis' (2016) *Gender and Development* 24(1), 9.

[46] EGM/SDG Report, above n 45, 18.

[47] Defined as 'the multiple and intersecting identities (and thus exclusions) of gender, class, color, caste, creed, ability, age, sexuality, migratory status and geographic location.' *Ibid*, pp 6–7.

[48] Specifically 1 (poverty), 2 (hunger), 4 (education), 6 (clean water and sanitation), 8 (decent work and economic growth), 11 (sustainable cities and communities), 13 (climate action) and 17 (partnerships for the goals)

While there has undoubtedly been progress in this regard, there are a couple of remarkable gaps in coverage for gender in the targets set under SDG 14 (life below water) and SDG 15 (life on land), which cover areas related to reproductive activity (broadly understood as relating to human life support) such as food production, that have readily recognisable gender implications. Nonetheless, regardless of the pros and cons of each approach, on the whole coverage in targets for gender has developed significantly, as reflected in the fact that 25 per cent of the targets across all 17 goals explicitly or implicitly address gender equality/women's empowerment.[49]

An enlightening and salient analysis of the substance of the SDG approach to gender[50] emerged in the run-up to the 60th session of the Commission on the Status of Women (CSW) in 2016, which focussed on women's empowerment and sustainable development, evoking obvious opportunities to consider synergies and antipathies between the two areas of activity. The Expert Group Meeting report that fed into the CSW focussed attention on the SDGs as applied to the key areas of gender equality, women's empowerment and human rights and found them wanting in several key respects, specifically: finance; accountability; addressing power asymmetries; and data collection and monitoring.[51] The question of language in respect of the gender/sustainable development nexus was raised as a particular cause of disquiet.[52] As far as the SDGs are concerned, it seems that their habitual approach, in cutting loose from the anchor of the legal *lingua franca* of human rights and replacing it with a random mix of political, technical, donor and civil society usage, generates obfuscation, inevitably begetting confusion and adding an unwelcome further layer of complexity to an already complicated endeavour. At this point and in light of what we will consider below, it is difficult to view this as anything other than a deliberate, ongoing choice, serving to effectively defuse claims pertaining to the legal enforceability of goals.

<http://www.undp.org/content/undp/en/home/sustainable-development-goals.html> accessed 12 May 2017.

[49] EGM/SDG Report, above n 45, 18.

[50] Report of the Expert Group Meeting on the CSW 60 Priority Theme, Women's Empowerment and the Link to Sustainable Development (2015) <http://www2.unwomen.org/~/media/headquarters/attachments/sections/csw/60/csw60%20egm%20report.pdf?v=1&d=20160415T171710> accessed 29 July 2016.

[51] *Ibid*, 3.

[52] *Ibid*.

7.5 THE PROS AND CONS OF A TARGETS/INDICATORS-BASED APPROACH

7.5.1 Selection and Data Issues

The approach adopted by the MDGs and perpetuated in the SDGs arguably illustrates both the strengths and weaknesses of a target-based, indicator-driven approach to attempting to induce societal change. Among the principal limitations of such an approach is the fact, referred to above, that this type of approach tends to promote concentration on identified target areas at the expense of others.[53] Such an approach also tends to focus on targets that are easily reducible or translatable into quantitative terms. These do go some way towards generating change but are likely to have limited impact in feeding the necessary qualitative culture change that is required to address the underlying causes of societal ills such as gender inequality.[54] Nonetheless, an indicators/target-based approach, rather than being subject to interrogation and critique, has been significantly expanded upon and extended in relation to the SDGs generally,[55] and to addressing gender issues specifically[56] therein. The SDG regime then is essentially proceeding on the assumption that 'more of the same' will secure progress and will be adequate to tackle the problems that are evident in the established approach, but this seems unlikely to gain much traction in so doing.

Selection of indicators is obviously a core concern, but more fundamentally the very malleability of the medium renders it open to cynical political manipulation.[57] At heart this creates a real danger that the selected proxy or representation of progress isolated in an indicator or

---

53 As acknowledged in the UN MDG Report 2015, above n 22, 31.

54 V. Benschop and M. Verloo, 'Sisyphus' Sisters: Can Gender Mainstreaming Escape the Genderedness of Organizations?' (2006) *Journal of Gender Studies* 15, 19.

55 UN MDG Report 2015, above n 22, 13.

56 Largely reiterating the MDG approach: 'To achieve universal realization of gender equality and empowerment of women, it is critical to address the key areas of gender inequality, including gender-based discrimination in law and in practice; violence against women and girls; women's and men's unequal opportunities in the labour market; the unequal division of unpaid care and domestic work; women's limited control over assets and property; and women's unequal participation in private and public decision-making.' *Ibid*, 31.

57 See, for example, G. MacNaughton and D.F. Frey, 'Decent Work, Human Rights and the Sustainable Development Goals' (2016) *Georgetown Journal of International Law* 47, 607, pointing to an at best evasive and arguably at worst

target comes to function as a surrogate or even a substitute for broader progress. That said, the UN review of the MDGs was not blind to such problems and it did also state, more ambitiously and suggesting the need to enculturate change, that '[g]ender perspectives should be integrated fully into all goals of the post-2015 development agenda'.[58]

Centring a regime on indicators raises other important issues. Not least of these is what may be referred to as the 'data dilemma'. While it is true to say that staggering developments in information and communications technology (ICT)[59] have been instrumental to the development and functioning of the MDG regime and will prove central to the SDGs, there is a danger that preoccupation with their advances can lead to losing sight of their limitations. Data science has struggled to keep pace with the relatively modest demands of monitoring the MDG targets/indicators set, with data disaggregation, in particular, proving problematic with respect to gender throughout the duration of the MDGs.[60] Other systemic problems include lack of quality control,[61] patchy coverage, delay in release and inequalities in access to the new technologies that now permeate this area of social endeavour.[62] The more ambitious SDGs will inevitably place greater demands on data monitoring than was the case with the MDGs, and the UN itself is promoting no less than a 'data revolution' to facilitate the post-2015 agenda.[63] The latter concept is open to various interpretations: '... some emphasise citizen accountability, others new forms of social and geophysical data, new ways of sharing data and many other facets'.[64] The differences between these are crucial but, as yet, under-interrogated.

---

actively cynical treatment of decent work under the MDG and SDG regimes that ensures that they are insulated from established human rights-based protections.

58 UN MDG Report 2015, above n 22, 13.

59 *Ibid*, 10–13.

60 UNDP Path, above n 31, 30.

61 See A. Thurston, 'Can We Access and Trust Digital Records to Support Development Goals?' in Friends of Sustainable Governance (eds), *Governance for Sustainable Development* (New World Frontiers, 2015) e-book <https://www.article19.org/data/files/medialibrary/38064/Full-Governance-Book.pdf> accessed 10 July 2017.

62 See J. Espey, 'The Data Revolution for Sustainable Development' in Friends of Sustainable Governance (eds), *ibid*.

63 See the Secretary-General's Independent Expert Advisory Group on a Data Revolution for Sustainable Development (IEAG): *A World That Counts: Mobilising the Data Revolution for Sustainable Development*, online at <http://www.undatarevolution.org/report/> accessed 7 December 2016.

64 Espey, above n 62.

Even if these foundational issues of principle are not addressed, advancing the status quo that emerged under the MDGs in less fundamental ways is possible. Espey, for example, recommended four key steps to improve on existing levels of data quality, specifically: first, agreeing a limited set of global SDG indicators; second, filling in gaps in the suite of indicators; third, improving the frequency of SDG data reporting (ideally moving to an annual obligation); and fourth, establishing a new Global Partnership for Sustainable Development Data to offer leadership, foster innovation, mobilise additional resources and promulgate global standards for data harmonisation and use.[65]

That more general access to the data/information underpins sustainable development is widely recognised, for example in the 2010 Lyon Declaration on Access to Information and Development,[66] drafted under the auspices of the International Foundation of Library Associations and Institutions and enlisting the support of key information brokers in preparation for, and support of, the SDG regime. The Lyon Declaration is particularly interesting in identifying that the need to address gender issues in this regard is of central importance, notably in Article 2, which states that '[s]ustainable development must take place in a human-rights based framework', addressing inequality through 'the empowerment, education and inclusion of marginalized groups, including women …'.[67]

Indicators-based approaches clearly depend on sound data for their success or, as Thurston pithily puts it when discussing the SDGs: 'accountability benefits depend on the quality of information'.[68] This is (as discussed above) problematic in itself and, on balance, observations such as those outlined strongly suggest that, without a sound supporting regime architecture, data-driven indicators approaches are not at the present time (and are perhaps not capable of being) sufficient to secure accountability in the pursuit of the SDGs. They certainly cannot bear the burden of primacy that the current regime places on them.

In consequence of the above considerations, data defects and deficits raise several important issues, not least of which is the spectre of states 'playing the system' as the monitoring and verification of the data

---

[65] Note that Espey recommended a maximum of 100 regime indicators – considerably fewer than those eventually adopted – supported by a broader set of national indicators, *ibid*. This inevitably prompts questions as to the efficacy of the 232 regime indicators eventually endorsed.

[66] The Lyon Declaration on Access to Information and Development <http://www.lyondeclaration.org/> accessed 13 December 2016.

[67] *Ibid*, Article 2(a).

[68] Thurston, above n 61.

supplied is likely, at least in some areas, to be problematic, if not impossible. More fundamentally, as alluded to above, an indicators-based approach may also tempt states to prioritise actions which 'count' in terms of the SDG regime, to the detriment of broader coverage, including rights-based entitlements. Finally, however much supporting data science improves, the fact remains that quantitative indicators can never fully capture qualitative concerns and that too heavy a reliance on them risks institutionalising a damaging reductionism. It is therefore no surprise that the UNDP's examination of the MDGs revealed that social and cultural attitudes have a major impact on progress (the same must apply to the lack thereof) towards goals in general, and that where gender is in play, this tendency is even more marked.[69] Nothing in the determinedly indicators-based SDG regime is likely to address this.

7.5.2 Indicators, Communication and Gender

The prime appeal of indicators is that, on one level, they represent the siren call of clear communication – they can and do indicate direction of travel on headline activities – and (if well selected) they offer relative clarity and comparability.[70] That said, while indicators may communicate clearly, even if apt, they do so at the cost of the extreme simplification (with all the perils that entails as to their accuracy and efficacy) of often complex areas of societal endeavour.[71] Selection is, however, centrally important for reasons of principle and not just practicality – from a gender perspective, for example, language, and target and indictor choices are hugely significant as they can, if ill-chosen, perpetuate and even reinforce victim status.[72] Kapur points to the importance of emphasis in selective approaches to complex issues such as gender, noting that in the human rights sphere there is a danger that the prevailing emphasis on violence 'reinforces gender and cultural essentialism in the human

---

[69] UNDP Path, above n 31, 13.

[70] W. Twining, 'Globalization and Comparative Law' (1999) *Maastricht Journal of European and Comparative Law* 6(217), 240.

[71] UNEP, *Environmental Indicators for North America*, UNEP, Nairobi, 2006.

[72] R. Kapur, 'Tragedy of Victimization Rhetoric: Resurrecting the "Native" Subject in International/Post-Colonial Feminist Legal Politics' (2002) *Harvard Human Rights Journal* 51(1), 1.

rights arena'.[73] The same criticism can be levelled at targets and indicators focussed on gender-based violence.[74]

For all their disadvantages, indicators-based approaches, well deployed, can promote a degree of transparency and popularise areas of concern in the public domain. They can also allow specific issues and overlaps to be drawn out of the wider dataset, highlighting particular areas of concern, as done to promising effect with gender in the MDG regime,[75] and it is to be hoped this will continue to develop. The SDGs do offer an extended[76] and seemingly somewhat more transparent and nuanced selection[77] of (nine) targets[78] and (14) indicators[79] clustered around gender, than did the MDGs – though, as discussed above, they necessarily remain constrained by their nature, form and content as quantitative, potentially manipulatable snapshots of qualitative societal progress.

7.5.3 The Elephant in the Room – Human Rights and Development Goals

On reflection, probably the most fundamental question relating to the development goals-based approaches lies in the type of obligation they are viewed as producing. Further complexity is added to this question by the evolving nature of goals-based approaches. Specifically, while the MDGs process was arguably primed and pushed by the developed world,

---

[73] Pardy, above n 10, 41.

[74] See Report of the Inter-Agency and Expert Group on Sustainable Development Goal Indicators, above n 45, for the prominence of this issue in the SDG approach and its inclusion as a goal under SDG 5.

[75] See, for example, the Millennium Development Goals Gender Chart 2015, above n 37.

[76] Notable developments include the coverage offered to unpaid work.

[77] For coverage of discussion surrounding the selection of the indicator set, see Goal 5 – Achieve gender equality and empower all women and girls, online at <https://unstats.un.org/sdgs/files/metadata-compilation/Metadata-Goal-5.pdf> accessed 9 May 2017.

[78] Sustainable Development Knowledge Platform: Goal 5 <https://sustainabledevelopment.un.org/sdg5> accessed 9 May 2017.

[79] *Ibid.* Note that there are other indicators that touch on gender; here though the focus is only on Goal 5 as the main point of entry. Report of the Inter Agency and Expert Group on Sustainable Development Goal Indicators, above n 44, 7–8.

the SDGs have seen a more collaborative approach in partnership with the developing world in shaping coverage.[80]

In any case, states were in the MDGs and are in the SDGs willing to accept a goals-based approach as part of the political agenda, as means to revivify state ambition and augment the political prominence of state activity to address development/sustainability issues. However, the complex mix of sovereignty, resource distribution, broader democratic and specific legal obligations founded on human rights[81] inevitably begs problematic questions as to what goals can and do involve. Tensions between the goals-based approach and human rights concerns are inevitably central among these in many respects, given that the subject matter of the goals brings the concerns, interests, and very often established and/or emerging legal rights of individuals, groups and communities into play.

While on the face of things, human rights and the development approaches share obvious common ground, the nexus between them has long been contentious at best. Thus the lost opportunity to develop a synergistic approach between them in the MDGs was a consequence not only of states effectively evading the issue, but was also aided in part by the entrenched turf war between the human rights and development constituencies and a lack of vision concerning the opportunities that the MDGs offered them both.[82] The disconnect that featured in the MDG regime, between the goals and established human rights regimes and its continuation in the projected SDGs, did, however, become a bone of contention through the negotiation of the latter. In marked distinction to what had been the case with the MDGs, the porous, multi-stakeholder approach to the negotiation of the SDGs[83] saw the human rights constituency prove itself very much alive to the virtues of exploiting the potential of the development goals/human rights nexus.[84] The unprecedented public consultation that foregrounded the development of the

[80] Discussed in MacNaughton and Frey, above n 57.

[81] B. Ruis, 'The Millennium Development Goals and the Rule of Law – Round Table Dialogue' (2005) *Environmental Policy and Law* 35(2), 84.

[82] See, for example, P. Alston, 'Ships Passing in the Night: The Current State of the Human Rights and Development Debate Seen Through the Lens of the Millennium Development Goals' (2005) *Human Rights Quarterly* 27(3), 755.

[83] See, *passim* MacNaughton and Frey, above n 57.

[84] Chairpersons of the UN Human Rights Treaty Bodies Joint Statement on the Post-2015 Development Agenda, May 2013, (Hereafter, CUNHRB Joint Statement) <http://www.ohchr.org/_layouts/15/WopiFrame.aspx?sourcedoc=/Documents/HRBodies/TB/AnnualMeeting/JointStatementChairsMeetingMay

SDGs was also strongly flavoured by discussion of the connections between the goals and human rights.[85] In light of these factors, it can be said that rights-talk permeated the negotiation process.[86]

Key UN actors took the importance of the rights agenda on board in the SDG negotiating process. For example, the Secretary-General called for the SDGs to act as a 'springboard' for 'a future free from poverty and built on human rights';[87] and the High-Level Panel of Eminent Persons on the Post-2015 Development Agenda, in like vein, for them to be 'grounded in respect for universal human rights'.[88]

The human rights constituency within the UN was also vocal in signposting the SDGs/human rights nexus. A joint statement of the Chairpersons of the UN Human Rights Treaty Bodies in 2010 clearly set out the early and fundamental concern that the goals, even if achieved, '... would still fall short of what human rights treaties require, as treaties call for the realization of human rights for all, which goes beyond the reaching [*sic*] of quantified targets'.[89] The human rights bodies therefore posited the view that, in order to be 'sustainable', the development goals 'needed to be grounded in human rights, justice and the rule of law'.[90]

2013.doc&action=default&DefaultItemOpen=1> accessed 2 May 2017. Civil society took a like tack, see, for example, D. Sriskandarajah and M. Tiwana, 'Hearing the Neediest Voices, Community and Public Participation in Development: Why Civil Society and Civil Space Matter', in Friends of Sustainable Governance (eds), *Governance for Sustainable Development, New World Frontiers* (2015) e-book <https://www.article19.org/data/files/medialibrary/38064/Full-Governance-Book.pdf> accessed 10 July 2017.

[85] MacNaughton and Frey, above n 57, 644.

[86] J.H. Knox, 'Human Rights, Environmental Protection, and the Sustainable Development Goals' (2015) *Washington International Law Journal* 24(517), 524.

[87] B. Ki Moon, 'A Life of Dignity for All: Accelerating Progress Towards the Millennium Development Goals and Advancing the United Nations Development Agenda Beyond 2015 – Report of the Secretary-General', UN Doc. A/68/202, 19 June 2012, 18 <http://www.un.org/millenniumgoals/pdf/A%20Life%20of%20Dignity%20for%20All.pdf> accessed 18 November 2016.

[88] Secretary-General, High-Level Panel of Eminent Persons on the Post-2015 Development Agenda, *A New Global Partnership: Eradicate Poverty and Transform Economies Through Sustainable Development* (hereafter, SGHLPEP), 5 <http://www.post2015hlp.org/wp-content/uploads/2013/05/UN-Report.pdf> accessed 9 May 2017.

[89] CUNHRB Joint Statement, above n 84, 2.

[90] *Ibid*, 1.

In other UN processes, proponents of human rights saw the Rio+20 Outcome Document, 'The Future We Want', as hugely significant in signalling the international community's recognition of the links between the planned SDGs and human rights[91] – and indeed the document was peppered with supportive references to human rights.[92] However, the soft status of the outcome document should perhaps have sounded a note of caution both in terms of its likely heft in setting the tone for the SDGs, and as indicative of state reluctance to accept further binding obligations on sustainability.

Civil society too was widely and strongly supportive of demands to integrate human rights into the development goals process.[93] In a joint statement by 332 civil society organisations from across the globe, the aspiration for a human rights-grounded vision of the SDGs was expressed as signalling a shift from: '... a model of charity to one of justice, based on the inherent dignity of people as human rights-holders, [and] domestic governments as primary duty-bearers ...'.[94] Even if this ambition did not gain traction, the statement went on to indicate that the least that could be expected was that the SDGs would '... respect and reflect pre-existing human rights legal norms, standards and political commitments to which governments have already voluntarily agreed'.[95] However, all of this broad-based support was of little avail as the goals would ultimately have to be agreed by states and they had already, in the context of the MDGs, shown a tendency to evade associations with human rights and the legal claims that they would facilitate, which could be used as additional means to hold them to account in regard to development goals.

The Women's Major Group (WMG) took an approach towards promoting the links between the goals and human rights that was in harmony

---

[91] *Ibid*, 2.

[92] A/RES/66/288 The Future We Want <http://www.un.org/ga/search/view_doc.asp?symbol=A/RES/66/288&Lang=E> accessed 26 April 2017. For example, reference was made to human rights in general in paras 8, 9, 58(d) and 145 and to gender equality in paras 8, 31, 146 and 240.

[93] See, for example, the Joint Statement from 332 Civil Society Organizations, Human Rights for All Post-2015 (10 December 2013) <https://sustainabledevelopment.un.org/content/documents/5123joint.statement.dec10.pdf> accessed 12 May 2017 and the Vienna C+20 CSO Declaration (26 June 2013), para 57 <https://viennaplus20.files.wordpress.com/2013/04/vienna20-cso-declaration-final.pdf> accessed 9 May 2017.

[94] Joint Statement from 332 Civil Society Organizations, *ibid*, 1.

[95] *Ibid*.

with that of civil society more generally. The WMG, which comprised an impressive 500-plus civil society organisations ranging across human rights, environment and development, as well as academics and activists,[96] was also particularly active in the SDG negotiating process,[97] offering substantial input throughout.[98] The WMG stressed gender equality and achieving women's human rights as key and constant framing principles in their engagement.[99] The WMG found the negotiations open and inclusive, though not unproblematic.[100] For example, while the WMG welcomed resistance to attempts to water down gender protection; the adoption of Goal 5;[101] and the inclusion of gender in the targets set for other goals;[102] on the whole, it viewed the process and its outcomes[103] as lacking in ambition and disappointing. At a fundamental level, the SDGs in adopting 'another set of reductive goals, targets and indicators that ignore the transformational changes required to address the failure of the current development model …' (as gender activists had feared[104]) utterly missed the mark, failing to address the structural and power inequalities that underpin gender disadvantage.[105] Centrally for present purposes, in identifying what it termed 'red flags' in the SDGs,

---

96 Women's Major Group: 'Women's "8 Red Flags"', above n 17, 1.

97 See Gabizon et al, above n 16.

98 For example, Women's Major Group, *Gender Equality, Women's Rights and Women's Priorities: Recommendations for the Proposed Sustainable Development Goals (SDGs) and the Post-2015 Development Agenda*, September 2013 <http://www.wecf.eu/download/2013/FinalReportfulldocument2013-09-16_With_Covercopy.pdf> accessed 12 May 2017.

99 *Ibid*, notably, E. Blomstrom with contributions from M. Ballara, 'The case for gender equality and rights in the SDGs', 59.

100 See, for example, WMG, 'Women's "8 Red Flags"' above n 17, 1.

101 *Ibid*.

102 *Ibid*, 2.

103 WMG, On Sustainable Development and Post 2015 <http://www.womenmajorgroup.org/category/policy-statements/on-sustainable-development-and-post-2015> accessed 15 May 2017.

104 WMG, 'Feminist Visions of Structural Transformations for Achieving Women's Human Rights and Gender Equality in the 2014 [*sic*] Development Agenda' Statement adopted 21 March 2013, at the Bonn Conference 'Advancing the Post-2015 Sustainable Development Agenda' of 20–22 March 2013, reproduced *ibid*, 6–7.

105 A.I. Abelenda, 'A Feminist Perspective on the Post-2015 Development Agenda' (2014) *The Equal Rights Review* 13, 117 <http://www.equalrightstrust.org/ertdocumentbank/ERR%2013%20-%20Abelenda.pdf> accessed 10 July 2017.

the WMG took the view that human rights issues had not been adequately addressed:

> The SDGs do not fully aim to protect and fulfil human rights for all which should be at the centre of a socially just and ecologically sustainable development agenda as well as the means for achieving it. The recognition of Women's and Girls' human rights in the title of Goal 5 on gender equality, the human right to food, the right to water and sanitation as a goal, women's rights to decision making on peace and security, the rights of indigenous peoples, and the right for women to control their sexuality free of coercion, discrimination and violence ... amongst others are notably absent.[106]

In short, the SDGs as adopted perpetuate the disingenuous decoupling of states' political obligations on development from human rights protections that was begun by the MDGs. Less tangible, but just as problematic, is the fact that this approach also robs the development and human rights communities of valuable opportunities to exploit mutual reinforcement of their aims.

For gender issues, given the very direct and central rights-based coverage already in place in international law alluded to above, the lack of integration, or less charitably, deliberate disarticulation of the SDGs from this milieu is particularly significant. The human rights agenda and the views of the chairpersons of the UN human rights treaty bodies are again particularly pertinent. In 2013 they pointed to the inadequacy of the coverage proposed for gender, observing that '[t]he goal of gender equality did not ensure the elimination of discrimination against women and equality between women and men, which should be addressed as a global priority in the future agenda ...'.[107]

Despite wide-ranging expert advice[108] dispensed in the negotiation of the SDGs on the need to articulate the nexus between them and human rights provision, the ultimately ambiguous[109] treatment of the nature of the interface of the SDGs with human rights law and rhetoric represents a further deliberate choice by states to eschew an approach that would firmly moor the goals to an established legal anchor, with potential heft in terms of enforcement. Thus, the danger signalled by the Special

---

[106] WMG, 'Women's "8 Red Flags"' above n 17, 2.

[107] CUNHRB Joint Statement, above n 84, 2.

[108] See, for example, the SGHLPEP, above n 88, and the CUNHRB Joint Statement, above n 84.

[109] This was apparent in the negotiation process, see, for example, Knox, who criticised the language of the targets as insufficiently concrete and not '... closely linked to existing human rights obligations ...', above n 86, 524.

Rapporteur on Human Rights and the Environment that the SDGs would continue down the path first taken by the MDGs of '... trying to further some human rights goals without explicitly referring to them' is made manifest.[110]

Similar concerns were also evident in civil society as indicated in the Post-2015 Human Rights Caucus Open letter on the SDGs[111] and gender issues are prominent here, pointing to the imperative need for the goals to

> comprehensively support the human rights of women and girls according to international standards and agreed commitments. The future framework should ensure that gender equality and women's rights are embedded throughout all goals, targets and indicators, that robust specific funding for women's rights is in place, and that the meaningful participation by women's rights groups, organizations and movements in implementation, monitoring and accountability mechanisms is guaranteed.[112]

SDG 5, the top layer of the nested system as adopted, is expressed thus: 'Achieve gender equality and empower all women and girls',[113] pointedly not mentioning 'women's rights'.[114] Specific mention of rights under SDG 5 is scant and largely relegated to the middle layer of the nested structure – targets[115] – as is reference to eliminating discrimination.[116] Rights-based coverage also appears in the lowest tier of the regime, indicators (incidentally proving that while indicators are not normally rights based in current praxis, they are not conceptually incapable of being so) specifically under 5.A.1 and 2.[117] The choice of language is

---

110 *Ibid*, 526.

111 Post-2015 Human Rights Caucus Open letter on the SDGs, 29 September 2014 <http://www.civicus.org/images/HRs_Caucus_Letter_to_SG_-_29Sep2014.pdf> accessed 13 December 2013.

112 *Ibid*.

113 SDGs Goal 5 <http://www.un.org/sustainabledevelopment/gender-equality/> accessed 9 May 2017.

114 Gabizon et al, above n 16, 4.

115 Specifically: 5.6 'reproductive rights'; and 5.A 'equal rights to economic resources, as well as access to ownership and control over land and other forms of property, financial services, inheritance and natural resources, in accordance with national laws' (the latter clause, however, effectively neuters this provision <https://sustainabledevelopment.un.org/sdg5> accessed 12 May 2017.

116 Specifically: 5.1: 'End all forms of discrimination against all women and girls everywhere'. *Ibid*.

117 5.A.1: '(a) Proportion of total agricultural population with ownership or secure rights over agricultural land, by sex, and (b) share of women among owners or rights-bearers of agricultural land, by type of tenure' and 5.A.2:

highly significant.[118] What is at stake here is an arguable devaluation of gender issues by dissociating them from the recognised realm of human rights, diluting coverage by distancing or even divorcing gender from the established 'anti-discrimination' and 'equality' rights-based agendas, coverage of which is relegated to inclusion in two of the nine targets under the goal and the indicators nested thereunder. Gender continues to be a live topic for discussion in the SDG regime, featuring prominently in the High-Level Political Forum (HLPF) meeting in July 2017. The ensuing Ministerial Declaration is, for example, peppered with now familiar hortatory references to women/gender issues, among which states

> ... underscore that all other Sustainable Development Goals need to be implemented in a manner that delivers results for women and girls. We urge that countries fully integrate gender equality strategies into national sustainable development frameworks so as to promote greater policy coherence, recognizing that achieving gender equality will require both targeted action as well as mainstreaming gender into all our efforts.[119]

SDG 5 was subject to specific review at the forum, and predictably, the link between human rights and gender emerged as an issue [back]grounding the debate, but again, in cohortative terms.[120] If this is disappointing, it is hardly unexpected. There are, however, elements in the HLPF process that are more encouraging: not least in pointing to the need to take action on the 'gap' in the SDGs in dealing with structural aspects of gender equality;[121] and in addressing data inadequacy. The latter point may ultimately prove highly significant in forging an indirect connection between the SDGs and human rights regimes, as raised in the HLPF

'Proportion of countries where the legal framework (including customary law) guarantees women's equal rights to land ownership and/or control. *Ibid.*

[118] Gabizon et al, above n 16, 4.

[119] E/2017/L.29–E/HLPF/2017/L.2, Ministerial declaration of the 2017 High-Level Political Forum on Sustainable Development, convened under the auspices of the Economic and Social Council, on the theme 'Eradicating poverty and promoting prosperity in a changing world' <http://www.un.org/ga/search/view_doc.asp?symbol=E/HLPF/2017/L.2&Lang=E> para 17, accessed 31 July 2017.

[120] HLPF on Sustainable Development, Background Note on 2017 HLPF Thematic review of SDG 5: Achieve gender equality and empower all women and girls <https://sustainabledevelopment.un.org/content/documents/14383SDG5format-revOD.pdf> accessed 31 July 2017. This document makes one reference to CEDAW, which is in many ways illustrative of the more general approach, highlighting 'opportunity' rather than obligation, that is adopted in the discussions, at 7.

[121] *Ibid*, at 8–9.

background note on the review of SDG 5: 'Human rights monitoring and documentation methodologies, which include qualitative indicators and context-specific analysis, are critical complementary tools to indicator selection and measurement to enable a fuller understanding of whether States are meeting their human rights obligations, towards women and girls.'[122]

In the end though, states have not been convinced to volunteer change at a fundamental level that would directly and meaningfully engage human rights protection either in developing and, thus far, in progressing the SDGs and they cannot be compelled to do so. This is dispiriting not only in itself, but also because the SDGs regime as adopted and as it progresses makes it all too apparent that engagement in the debate by non-state actors on this front, at considerable cost in resources, time, effort, energy and good will, has not in the end much changed the formal agenda. The failure to commit to human rights-based coverage in principle may, however, ultimately prove to be less of a barrier in practice if the approach to data discussed at the HLPF goes on to bear fruit. The fact that, as discussed above, there are significant problems with providing adequate data to fuel the SDG process may mean that this provides fertile ground for such development.

Gender concerns, among others, will then continue to suffer the adverse consequences of a lack of acknowledgement of the connectivity between the SDGs and the machinery of international human rights law, as states continue to be reluctant to give cognisance to the fact that the goals are factually enmeshed with the latter. In the end, this intensifies the vulnerability of the SDGs to side-lining and tokenism by states and leads one to question how serious their intent is.

Hillary Clinton famously said that '... the rights of women and girls is the great unfinished business of the 21st Century'.[123] While the SDGs do represent another step (albeit a comparatively limited one) along the road towards gender equality, they will not, as they presently stand, expressed as the gift of political targets rather than as the product of legal rights, suffice to take us to that much to be desired destination. Gender equality remains at best work in (often achingly slow) progress and civil society engagement is integral to progressing it – as it is to the success of the

---

122 *Ibid*, at 9.

123 J. Fuller, 'Hillary Clinton Says Equality for Women is the 'Great Unfinished Business of the 21st Century', *The Washington Post*, 7 March 2014 <https://www.washingtonpost.com/news/post-politics/wp/2014/03/07/hillary-clinton-says-equality-for-women-is-the-great-unfinished-business-of-the 21st century/> accessed 8 August 2016.

SDGs.[124] As things stand, there is, however, a very real danger that the inherent limitations of goals/targets/indicators and their failure to engage with rights-based approaches may well lead to questions as to the continuing salience of the former relative newcomers to the global polis. It may well also be the case that goals-based approaches, if they continue on the present trajectory, will come to be viewed as otiose by the human rights and gender constituencies, prompting them to disengage and shift focus to other areas where their efforts are more likely to avail.

[124] EGM/SDG CSW 60 Report, above n 45, 6.

8. International water law and SDG 6: mutually reinforcing paradigms

Owen McIntyre

8.1 INTRODUCTION

The Sustainable Development Goals (SDGs) seek to build upon the widely acknowledged success of the Millennium Development Goals (MDGs),[1] which for the first time established at the global level a set of quantifiable, ambitious, yet realistic targets for sustainable development, which were non-binding in character and relied solely upon the political commitment of State and other actors. The SDGs came into effect on 1 January 2016 and are intended to stimulate collective action and guide the developmental decisions of State actors over the next 15 years. Of the 17 individual SDGs and 169 targets identified and agreed in the course of an extensive and participative process, SDG 6, involving a commitment to '[e]nsure availability and sustainable management of water and sanitation for all', is one of the most significant in terms of its potential impact on development outcomes. It is significant, not alone as an important goal per se, but also due to its pervasive impact on almost all other sectoral SDGs including, most notably, SDG 1 (eradication of extreme poverty), SDG 2 (eradication of extreme hunger), SDG 3 (improving health and well-being), SDG 4 (inclusive and quality education), SDG 5 (gender equality), SDG 7 (affordable and clean energy), SDG 11 (sustainable cities and communities), SDG 12 (responsible consumption and production), SDG 13 (climate action), SDG 14 (marine and coastal pollution) and SDG 15 (land-based ecosystems). Indeed, several of these SDGs make express mention of water in one or more of their associated targets,[2] indicating that sustainable management of water

[1] See, for example, J.D. Sachs, 'From Millennium Development Goals to Sustainable Development Goals' (2012) *The Lancet* 379, 2206–2211.

[2] For example, targets listed under SDG 3 aim to 'end ... water-borne diseases', and 'substantially reduce the number of deaths and illnesses from ...

resources is crucial to their achievement. However, SDG 6 is similarly dependent upon other SDGs. For example, as is the case with many of the other goals, achievement of SDG 6 will be largely dependent upon measures required to advance the non-sectoral, cross-cutting goal set out in SDG 16 (peace, justice and strong institutions) and the 'good governance' values and arrangements inherent therein.[3] Similarly, advances in responsible consumption and production in line with SDG 12 will play a significant role in achieving sustainable water management.

Although the SDGs, like the MDGs which preceded them,[4] are intended to be non-legally binding, it immediately becomes apparent upon an examination of the specific targets associated with SDG 6,[5] that efforts to achieve these targets will need to be supported by formal rules of domestic and international water law, environmental law and human rights law, which are increasingly sophisticated and prescriptive in terms of their normative implications.[6] At the same time, it is quite clear that SDG 6, and more particularly the specific targets set out thereunder, are likely to act as a strong catalyst for the continuing, progressive development of international and domestic rules for sustainable water management. The inclusive and participatory process employed for the elaboration and adoption of the SDGs, as well as the mechanisms emerging for their implementation and for monitoring compliance, enhance the relevance and legitimacy of progressive water law values and

---

water … pollution and contamination'; SDG 11 Target 4 aims to 'significantly reduce the number of deaths and the number of people affected and substantially decrease the direct economic losses … caused by … water-related disasters'; SDG 12 Target 4 aims to significantly reduce the release of chemicals and wastes to water; and targets listed under SDG 15 seek to ensure conservation, restoration and sustainable use of inland freshwater ecosystems, including in particular wetlands, in line with obligations under international agreements.

[3] On the intrinsic linkage between such 'good governance' values and realisation of the human right(s) to water and sanitation, which in turn corresponds closely with SDG 6, see O. McIntyre, 'The Human Right to Water as a Creature of Global Administrative Law' (2012) *Water International* 37(6), 654–669.

[4] On the progression from the MDGs to the SDGs, see M. Orme, Z. Cuthbert, F. Sindico, J. Gibson and R. Bostic, 'Good Transboundary Water Governance in the 2015 Sustainable Development Goals: A Legal Perspective' (2015) *Water International* 40(7), 969–983, at 970–971.

[5] These are available at <http://www.undp.org/content/undp/en/home/sustainable-development-goals/goal-6-clean-water-and-sanitation/targets/> accessed 29 January 2018.

[6] On the role of domestic normative frameworks in giving effect to the human right to water, see Cooper and French, Chapter 12 in this volume.

have the potential to have a 'transformational' effect on the interpretation and continuing development of water law frameworks. For example, the emphasis in SDG 6 on ensuring the participation of local communities in water management should promote the elaboration of more inclusive and participatory procedural and institutional arrangements for transboundary water cooperation.

Therefore, the SDGs can impact profoundly on water law in a range of ways which cohere with existing trends in the continuing evolution of water law. For example, they are likely to impact the continuing discourse in national and international law on the human right(s) of access to water and sanitation, and interpretation and application of the related concept of 'vital human needs' in international water law. The SDGs also strongly support a greater focus on ecosystem-based approaches to water management and regulation, and promote participatory water governance at both the national and international levels. At the purely international level, they support and encourage greater transboundary water cooperation. In order to highlight the possible legal implications of the SDGs, this chapter seeks to focus primarily on the multi-faceted, mutually supportive interrelationship between SDG 6 and international water law, i.e. the body of rules and principles applying to the management of international water resources shared between two or more sovereign States.

8.2 SIGNIFICANCE OF INTERNATIONAL LAW FOR THE SDGS AND LEGAL SIGNIFICANCE OF THE SDGS

It is perfectly clear from the Declaration contained in the United Nations General Assembly Resolution by means of which the SDGs were adopted[7] that the SDGs are to be informed and guided by relevant established and emerging norms of international law. In the case of water access and management in line with SDG 6, these norms will principally be found in the fields of international human rights law and international environmental law. The Declaration confirms that '[t]he new Agenda is guided by the purposes and principles of the Charter of the United Nations, including full respect for international law. It is grounded in the Universal Declaration of Human Rights, international human rights

[7] *Transforming our world: the 2030 Agenda for Sustainable Development*, UNGA Res. 70/1 (25 September 2015), UN Doc. A/RES/70/1.

treaties', etc.[8] It goes on to explain that key, seminal soft-law instruments have helped to shape the 2030 Agenda, including the 1992 Rio Declaration on Environment and Development.[9] More generally, the Declaration, as well as the targets enumerated under each SDG, are suffused with language which suggests the central relevance of the values underlying international human rights law and environmental law. For example, the Declaration envisages 'a world of universal respect for human rights and human dignity, the rule of law, justice, equality and non-discrimination' and one 'in which consumption and production patterns and use of all natural resources … are sustainable' and where environmental protection, climate sensitivity and respect for biodiversity are centrally important.[10] Of course, for a lawyer such language immediately calls to mind the existing legal frameworks which seek to promote and protect such values. These connotations are even more immediate and direct in respect of SDG 6, where the Declaration sets out a vision of '[a] world where we affirm our commitments regarding the human right(s) to safe drinking water and sanitation and where there is improved hygiene'.[11] This reference to the putative emergence in international human rights law of a human right(s) to water and sanitation, and thus to the associated intense discourse on the legal status and normative implications of such a right(s), is unmistakable.[12]

At the same time, despite its non-binding character, it appears that in adopting the 2030 Agenda the international community was aware of the potential legal significance of this solemn universal statement of formal support for what in many cases would amount to emerging and contested rules and principles of international law. For example, the Resolution adopting the 2030 Agenda, which was adopted in the General Assembly without a vote, declared on behalf of the UN Member States that '[w]e reaffirm all the principles of the Rio Declaration on Environment and Development',[13] which includes all of the key principles associated with the field of international environmental law (although the customary legal

---

[8] *Ibid*, para 10, at 4.

[9] *Ibid*, para 11, at 4–5.

[10] *Ibid*, paras 8 and 9, at 4.

[11] *Ibid*, para 7, at 3–4.

[12] For an account of this discourse, see, for example, E.B. Bluemel, 'The Implications of Formulating a Human Right to Water' (2004) *Ecology Law Quarterly* 31, 957.

[13] *Ibid*, para 12, at 5.

status of some has not been definitively established).[14] Indeed, where the Declaration states that 'we reaffirm our commitment to international law and emphasize that the Agenda is to be implemented in a manner that is consistent with the rights and obligations of States under international law', it is also careful to 'reaffirm that every State has, and shall freely exercise, full permanent sovereignty over all its wealth, natural resources and economic activity'.[15] The international community, therefore, appears to have been conscious of the possibility that Resolution 70/1 might come to be regarded as sovereign acceptance of certain contested legal paradigms, such as the human right(s) to water and sanitation.[16] This would have clear implications for the 41 States that abstained in the vote on the 2010 UN General Assembly Resolution on the matter of formal international recognition of a human right to water.[17] Even where the 2030 Agenda could not be regarded as tacit State acceptance of emerging international norms for the purposes of identifying applicable rules of customary international law, the targets set out under each SDG, as well as the various modalities being developed to assist with implementation, are likely to play a key role in informing the normative content of such emerging norms and in guiding their effective implementation, regardless of their formal source of legal authority. Consider the targets enumerated under SDG 6, which stress, inter alia, the affordability of water services,

---

[14] Take the example of the so-called precautionary principle/approach, codified in Rio Principle 15. Arguing against the principle's customary status, see, for example, D. Bodansky, 'Customary (and Not So Customary) International Environmental Law' (1995) *Indiana Journal of Global Legal Studies* 3(1), 105–119; arguing in favour of its customary status, see, for example, O. McIntyre and T. Mosedale, 'The Precautionary Principle as a Norm of Customary International Law' (1997) *Journal of Environmental Law* 9, 221–241.

[15] SDGs, above n 5, para 18, at 6.

[16] Botswana provides an example of a State that had contested the legally binding nature of a human right to water, before losing a 2011 legal battle over the San and Bakgalagadi peoples' access to water in the Central Kalahari Game Reserve. See further, C. Morinville and L. Rodina, 'Rethinking the Human Right to Water: Water Access and Dispossession in Botswana's Central Kalahari Game Reserve' (2013) *Geoforum* 49, 150–159.

[17] *The human right to water and sanitation*, UNGA Resolution 64/292 (28 July 2010), UN Doc. A/RES/64/292. States abstaining included Armenia, Australia, Austria, Bosnia and Herzegovina, Botswana, Bulgaria, Canada, Croatia, Cyprus, Czech Republic, Denmark, Estonia, Ethiopia, Greece, Guyana, Iceland, Ireland, Israel, Japan, Kazakhstan, Kenya, Latvia, Lesotho, Lithuania, Luxembourg, Malta, the Netherlands, New Zealand, Poland, Republic of Korea, Republic of Moldova, Romania, Slovakia, Sweden, Trinidad and Tobago, Turkey, Ukraine, United Kingdom, United Republic of Tanzania, United States, Zambia.

the protection of vulnerable groups, and environmental and ecosystems protection, thereby highlighting values and objectives which might be expected to guide legal measures adopted in order to realise the human right(s) to water and sanitation. Such measures might derive from international human rights law, international water law, national constitutional law or national legislation on water services, public health or environmental protection.

Although the SDGs are clearly guided by, and will operate to pursue the objectives of, the international law frameworks relevant to sustainable development,[18] they appear to embody the commitment of the international community to take action beyond the narrow and often restrictive confines of the international law-making process.[19] Therefore, the SDGs represent a novel approach emerging in international policy-making, which began with the MDGs and proceeds on the basis of political commitment rather than binding legal norms.[20] According to one leading commentator, by packaging social priorities into an easily understandable set of goals, and by establishing measurable and time-bound objectives, these goals 'help to promote global awareness, political accountability, improved metrics, social feedback, and public pressures'.[21] This permits the international community to identity goals and targets which are universal yet aspirational in nature, and which facilitate, more easily than formal international legal measures, engagement with a range of actors crucial to developmental outcomes, including civil society, the scientific community and the private sector. While the 17 goals and 169 targets are global in terms of their scope of application, they are also flexible and articulated in such a way as to be capable of taking into account different levels of national capacity and development, while respecting national policies and priorities.[22] However, it would be mistaken to assume that the SDGs are completely divorced from or immune to developments in relevant areas of international law, which are

---

[18] For example, the Preamble of Resolution 70/1; SDGs, above n 5, 1, declares that the SDGs 'seek to realize the human rights of all'.

[19] See, for example, in relation to the international environmental law-making process, O. McIntyre, 'Changing Patterns of International Environmental Law-Making: Addressing Normative Ineffectiveness' in S. Maljean-Dubois (ed), *The Effectiveness of Environmental Law* (Intersentia, 2017) 187–220.

[20] A similar approach is evident in the adoption of the 2015 Paris Agreement on Climate Change, UN Doc. FCCC/CP/2015/L.9/Rev.1.

[21] Sachs, above n 1, 2206.

[22] See United Nations Economic Commission for Europe, *A Healthy Link: The Protocol on Water and Health and the Sustainable Development Goals* (UNECE, Geneva, 2016), UN Doc. ECE/INF/NONE/2016/16, at 3.

likely both to inform the implementation of measures designed to realise the SDGs and, in turn, to be supported and enhanced by the implementation of such measures.

In order to explore further this two-way relationship between SDG 6 and relevant rules of international law, it is necessary to identify in a systematic manner the key values enshrined in the targets associated with SDG 6 and to examine how each relates to emerging and established paradigms of international law applying to access to water-related services and to management of water resources.

8.3 WATER AND SANITATION FOR ALL

The objectives set out under Targets 6.1 and 6.2 very closely reflect those encompassed by the human right(s) to water and sanitation originally set out in 2002 by the UN Committee on Economic Social and Cultural Rights (CESCR) on the basis of the Committee's progressive interpretation of the 1966 International Covenant on Economic, Social and Cultural Rights.[23] By emphasising 'universal and equitable access to safe and affordable drinking water' in Target 6.1,[24] the 2030 Agenda appears to mirror the normative content of the right to water identified in General Comment No. 15, which focuses on three key factors, i.e. availability, quality and accessibility.[25] In General Comment No. 15, 'availability' refers to a supply of water that is 'sufficient and continuous for personal and domestic uses', while 'quality' refers to the safety of the water supply in terms of being 'free from micro-organisms, chemical substances and radiological hazards that constitute a threat to a person's health'. The goal of 'accessibility' as outlined in General Comment No. 15 corresponds very closely with the requirements of equitable access and affordability contained in Target 6.1 as it comprises four overlapping dimensions, i.e. physical accessibility, economic accessibility, non-discrimination and information accessibility. 'Economic accessibility' requires that '[w]ater and water facilities and services must be affordable to all', while the requirement of 'non-discrimination' dictates that '[w]ater and water facilities and services must be accessible to all, including the most vulnerable or marginalized sections of the population,

[23] CESCR, *General Comment No. 15: The Right to Water (Arts. 11 and 12 of the Covenant)*, 20 January 2003, UN Doc. E/C.12/2002/11.

[24] Target 6.1 commits the international community to '[b]y 2030, achieve universal and equitable access to safe and affordable drinking water for all'.

[25] CESCR, above n 23, para 12, 4–6.

in law and in fact'. Of course, the equitability of access will also depend on 'physical accessibility', meaning that 'adequate water facilities and services must be within safe physical reach for all sections of the population' and, in particular, 'must be accessible within, or in the immediate vicinity of, each household, educational institution and workplace'. Similarly, equitable access will be highly dependent upon the corresponding 'right to seek, receive and impart information concerning water issues'. Therefore, the broad aims set out in Target 6.1 have already been elaborated in detail in an authoritative,[26] if contested,[27] interpretation of the normative content of a key instrument of international human rights law, and in certain instruments in the field of international environmental law.[28]

As regards the legal status of the purported human right to sanitation in international law, the aim set out in Target 6.2 to 'achieve access to adequate and equitable sanitation and hygiene for all and to end open defecation' may play a more formative role.[29] If the formal normative

---

[26] See S.C. McCaffrey, 'The Human Right to Water' in E. Brown Weiss, L. Boisson de Chazournes and N. Bernasconi-Osterwalder (eds), *Fresh Water and International Economic Law* (Oxford University Press, 2005) 93, who explains, at 94, that General Comment No. 15 constitutes a non-binding but 'highly authoritative interpretation of the Covenant and of the legal implications which flow from key relevant Covenant provisions. See also M. Williams, 'Privatization and the Human Right to Water: Challenges for the New Century' (2007) *Michigan Journal of International Law* 28(469), 475; Bluemel, above n 12, 972.

[27] See McCaffrey, above n 26, at 103; A. Hardberger, 'Life, Liberty and the Pursuit of Water: Evaluating Water as a Human Right and the Duties and Obligations it Creates' (2005) *Northwestern Journal of International Human Rights* 4(2), 331, 361–362.

[28] Notably, the 1999 Protocol on Water and Health to the 1992 UNECE (Helsinki) Convention on the Protection and Use of Transboundary Watercourses and International Lakes, UN Doc. MP.WAT/AC.1/1991/1. See further, A. Tanzi, 'Reducing the Gap between International Water Law and Human Rights Law: The UNECE Protocol on Water and Health' (2010) *International Community Law Review* 12, 267; O. McIntyre, 'The UNECE Water Convention and the Human Right to Access to Water: The Protocol on Water and Health' in A. Tanzi, O. McIntyre, A. Kolliopoulos, A. Rieu-Clarke and R. Kinna (eds), *The UNECE Convention on the Protection and Use of Transboundary Watercourses and International Lakes: Its Contribution to International Water Cooperation* (Brill Nijhoff, 2015) 345–366.

[29] Target 6.2 commits the international community to '[b]y 2030, achieve access to adequate equitable sanitation and hygiene for all and end open defecation, paying special attention to the needs of women and girls and those in vulnerable situations'.

status and justiciability in international law of the human right to water remains in doubt, then even greater uncertainty bedevils the emergence and recognition of the closely related human right of access to sanitation.[30] As a leading commentator could point out in 2010: 'As yet, there is no single resolution of the UN General Assembly on the right to sanitation and no worldwide agreement supporting this right. There is no agreed description of core obligations on sanitation and no definition of the content of the right to sanitation.'[31]

Though the UN General Assembly has since adopted a 2010 Resolution on 'The Human Right to Water *and Sanitation*',[32] Smets' telling observation that States 'in particular have not adopted a General Comment on the Right to Sanitation' remains valid.[33] Where it does include express mention of sanitation, General Comment No. 15 states that '[e]nsuring that everyone has access to adequate sanitation is not only fundamental for human dignity and privacy, but is one of the principal mechanisms for protecting the quality of drinking water supplies and resources'.[34] This suggests that it focuses primarily on problems of access to drinking water rather than the issue of access to sanitation, largely viewing the universal provision of adequate sanitation as necessary for, and ancillary to, provision of safe drinking water. However, it is worth noting that General Comment No. 15 makes special mention of 'rural and deprived urban areas' and 'the needs of women and children', a concern largely reflected in Target 6.2, which highlights the need to pay 'special attention to the needs of women and girls and those in vulnerable

---

[30] See generally, H. Smets (ed), *L'accès à L'assainissement, un Droit Fondamental* (Edn Johanet, 2010).

[31] H. Smets, 'The Right to Sanitation: A New Human Right in Developed Countries' (2010) *Environmental Policy and Law* 40(2/3), 112 (at p. 3 of on-line version).

[32] UNGA Res 64/294 (26 July 2010), UN Doc. A/64/L.63/Rev.1 (emphasis added).

[33] Smets, above n 31.

[34] Resolution 70/1, n 18, para 29, at 10. Similarly, para 1, points out that '[o]ver 1 billion persons lack access to a basic water supply, while several billion do not have access to adequate sanitation, which is the primary cause of water contamination and diseases linked to water'. In addition, when advising that State parties to the Covenant 'should adopt comprehensive and integrated strategies and programmes *to ensure that there is sufficient and safe water*', para 28 suggests that '[s]uch strategies and programmes may include … reducing and eliminating contamination of watersheds and water related ecosystems by substances such as radiation, harmful chemicals and *human excreta*' (emphasis added).

situations'. Of course, it is immediately clear that realisation of the right to sanitation would require very specific guidance on the nature of the obligations imposed and actions involved, which would be quite distinct from those associated with the right to water. For example, methods of cost recovery for sanitation services, and for measuring the affordability of any charging scheme, are likely to be quite unique.[35]

Target 6.1 is also supported by the core values inherent to international water resources law, i.e., the body of rules of international law primarily concerned with the utilisation and protection of shared international water resources, which is largely codified in, and exemplified by, the 1997 United Nations Water Convention (UNWC).[36] The cardinal and overarching rule set out in the Convention is that of equitable and reasonable utilisation, under which an equitable allocation between watercourse States of uses of an international watercourse, or of quantum share of water therefrom, is to be determined having regard to a range of relevant factors which help to characterise each State's economic, social and environmental dependence upon the shared waters in question.[37] In respect of application of this principle, while the UNWC makes it quite clear that, unless watercourse States have agreed otherwise, 'no use of an international watercourse enjoys inherent priority over other uses',[38] it also provides that '[i]n the event of a conflict between uses of an international watercourse, it shall be resolved … with special regard

[35] See, for example, African Development Bank, *Guidelines for User Fees and Cost Recovery for Urban Water and Sanitation* (AfDB, 2010), available at <https://www.afdb.org/fileadmin/uploads/afdb/Documents/Project-and-Operations/brochure%20cost%20recouvry%20urban%203_11_2010.pdf> accessed 29 January 2018. African Development Bank, *Guidelines for User Fees and Cost Recovery for Rural, Non-Networked, Water and Sanitation Delivery* (AfDB, 2010), available at <https://www.afdb.org/fileadmin/uploads/afdb/Documents/Project-and-Operations/2011_03%20Guidelines%20for%20User%20Fees%20Cost%20Recovery_Rural.pdf> accessed 29 January 2018.

[36] United Nations Convention on the Law of the Non-Navigational Uses of International Watercourses (New York, 21 May 1997), (1997) 37 ILM 700, entered into force 17 August 2014 (UNWC).

[37] *Ibid*, articles 5 and 6. See also, article V(2) of the International Law Commission's 1966 Helsinki Rules on the Uses of the Waters of International Rivers, ILA *Report of the Fifty-Second Conference* 484 (Helsinki, 1966). See further, S.C. McCaffrey, *The Law of International Watercourses* (2nd edn, Oxford University Press, 2007) 384–405; O. McIntyre, *Environmental Protection of International Watercourses under International Law* (Ashgate, 2007) 53–86 and 155–190.

[38] UNWC, above n 36, article 10(1).

being given to the requirements of *vital human needs*'.[39] This elevation in international water law of the use of water for meeting vital human needs appears to pre-empt the current discourse in international law on the human right to water and merely reflects long-established State and judicial practice confirming that certain basic needs of the population dependent on the water of a watercourse, in particular the use of water for drinking and other domestic purposes, will be accorded priority.[40] The scope of this prioritised use of shared water resources would appear to correspond closely with Target 6.1 and the related human right to water, as a Statement of Understanding on Article 10(2) was included in the Report of the UN General Assembly Working Group, which finalised drafting of the Convention, providing that, '[i]n determining "vital human needs", special attention is to be paid to providing sufficient water to sustain human life, including both drinking water and water required for production of food in order to prevent starvation'.[41] Leading commentators explain the legal significance and implications of Article 10(2) in the following terms:

> the protection of vital human needs entails a 'presumptive' priority over all the other factors listed in Article 6, such presumption being rebuttable only on the basis of the specific circumstances of the individual case. That is to say that watercourse States, in discussing the equitable allocation of shared watercourses, cannot avoid starting negotiations, taking the water supplies needed to support vital human needs as a fixed parameter.[42]

Thus, though Article 6(1) of the UNWC also includes among the '[f]actors relevant to equitable and reasonable utilization ... The population dependent on the watercourse in each watercourse State', such dependence, at least to the extent that it relates to vital human needs, appears less a factor to be considered and weighed and more a non-negotiable responsibility to be respected and fulfilled by all watercourse States. As Tanzi and Arcari note, 'this factor is likely to enhance the "human right dimension" of the use of the waters of international

---

[39] *Ibid*, article 10(2), emphasis added.

[40] See, for example, J. Lipper, 'Equitable Utilization' in A.H. Garretson, R.D. Hayton and C.J. Olmstead (eds), *The Law of International Drainage Basins* (Oceana, 1967) 60–62.

[41] Oral report of the coordinator of the informal consultations on article 10(2), UN Doc A/C.6/51/SR.57 (1997), at 3.

[42] A. Tanzi and M. Arcari, *The United Nations Convention on the Law of International Watercourses* (Kluwer Law International, 2001) 141.

watercourses'.[43] Indirectly emphasising the priority accorded to such vital human needs by Article 10(2), the International Law Commission (ILC) in its commentary to Article 7 of its 1994 Draft Articles (on the duty to prevent significant transboundary harm), which preceded and provided the basis for the Convention, makes it quite clear that '[a] use that causes significant harm to human health and safety is understood to be inherently inequitable and unreasonable'.[44] Clearly, Article 10(2) of the Convention is intended to be consistent with the aim of ensuring to all peoples access to safe and sufficient water supplies, as originally set out in Chapter 18 of Agenda 21,[45] and now most notably enshrined in SDG 6 Target 6.1. Equally, the universal adoption of SDG 6 might do much to make this presumption of priority accorded to the requirements of vital human needs irrebuttable in any circumstances and their safeguarding even more of a *sine qua non* in international water resources law.

The commitment in international water law to the aims of Target 6.1 would only appear to have strengthened in recent years. For example, the International Law Association's (ILA) 2004 Berlin Rules on Water Resources Law,[46] intended to update and replace the ILA's seminally important 1966 Helsinki Rules,[47] appear to afford clear and formal priority to vital human needs, defined to mean 'waters used for immediate human survival, including drinking, cooking and sanitary needs, as well as water needed for the immediate sustenance of a household'.[48] Article 14 of the Berlin Rules builds upon Article 10(2) of the UNWC to accord even greater emphasis and priority to the provision of adequate basic water for all by providing that:

1. In determining an equitable and reasonable use, States first allocate waters to satisfy vital human needs.

---

[43] *Ibid*, 131. See further, S.R. Tully, 'The Contribution of Human Rights to Freshwater Resource Management' (2003) *Yearbook of International Environmental Law* 14, 101.

[44] International Law Commission, Report of the International Law Commission on the Work of its Forty-Sixth Session, *Yearbook of the International Law Commission, 1994*, Vol II, Part Two, at 104, para 14.

[45] UNCED, *Report of the United Nations Conference on Environment and Development* (Rio de Janeiro, 3–14 June 1992), UN Doc. A/CONF.151/26 (Vol II) (1992).

[46] ILA, *Report of the 71st Conference on International Water Law* (2004) 337.

[47] Smets, above n 31.

[48] Article 3(20).

2. No other use or category of uses shall have an inherent preference over any other use or category of uses.

The Berlin Rules further include a distinct Chapter IV on the 'Rights of Persons', including a dedicated Article 17 on the 'The Right of Access to Water', which provides, *inter alia*, that '[e]very individual has a right of access to sufficient, safe, acceptable, physically accessible, and affordable water to meet that individual's vital human needs'.[49] Such provisions clearly reflect a growing recognition in general international water law of a human right of access to water, and of the closely related aspirations set out under SDG 6, which are to be pursued in the case of transboundary water resources by prioritisation of the need to satisfy vital human needs. Thus, while the universal adoption of SDG 6 serves to enhance the legitimacy and significance of the increasingly firmly established human right to water paradigm in international water law, the primacy afforded to vital human needs in international water law serves to assist realisation of SDG 6.

8.4 ENVIRONMENTAL AND ECOSYSTEMS PROTECTION

The environmental and ecosystems protection objectives included under Targets 6.3[50] and 6.6[51] simply reiterate and strengthen the central importance long accorded to environmental values in modern international water law, as reflected in the inclusion of the detailed and imperative environmental provisions contained in Part IV of the UNWC. Each reflects growing awareness among the international community of watercourses as complex and fragile ecosystems, providing a suite of indispensable ecosystem services to humanity and requiring holistic consideration and management of each watercourse's myriad interconnected ecological elements.[52]

---

[49] Article 17(1).

[50] Target 6.3 aims to '[b]y 2030, improve water quality by reducing pollution, eliminating dumping and minimizing release of hazardous chemicals and materials, halving the proportion of untreated wastewater and substantially increasing recycling and safe use globally'.

[51] Target 6.6 aims to '[b]y 2020, protect and restore water-related ecosystems, including mountains, forests, wetlands, rivers, aquifers and lakes'.

[52] See, for example, Tanzi and Arcari, above n 42, 8–9.

Pollution control has long been a central concern of international water law,[53] and in an attempt to codify pollution-related measures, Article 21(2) of the UNWC now provides that

> Watercourse States shall, individually and, where appropriate, jointly, prevent, reduce and control the pollution of an international watercourse that may cause significant harm to other watercourse States or their environment, including harm to human health or safety, to the use of the waters for any beneficial purpose or to the living resources of the watercourse. Watercourse States shall take steps to harmonize their policies in this connection.

Article 21(3) proceeds to make provision for the holding of inter-State consultations

> with a view to arriving at mutually agreeable measures and methods to prevent, reduce and control pollution of an international watercourse, such as:
>
> (a) Setting joint water quality objectives and criteria;
> (b) Establishing techniques and practices to address pollution from point and non-point sources;
> (c) Establishing lists of substances the introduction of which into the waters of an international watercourse is to be prohibited, limited, investigated or monitored.

In elaborating upon the significance of Article 21, the ILC, in its detailed commentary to the 1994 Draft Articles, appears to regard the due diligence obligation set out under Article 21(2) to prevent, reduce and control pollution as 'applying the general obligation of article 7 to the case of pollution'.[54] Therefore, in order to come within the scope of Article 21, the pollution in question must be of a type that 'may cause significant harm to other watercourse States or to their environment', such as the illustrative examples listed under Article 21(2), i.e. 'harm to human health or safety, to the use of the waters for any beneficial purpose or to the living resources of the watercourse'. However, the commentary also confirms that 'the principle of precautionary action is applicable, especially in respect of dangerous substances such as those that are toxic, persistent or bio-accumulative',[55] and recognises that the

[53] For detailed analysis of the emergence of environmental concerns, see generally, McIntyre, above n 37.

[54] ILA, above n 37, 122. Article 7 of the UNWC sets out the fundamental obligation of international water law not to cause significant harm to other watercourse States.

[55] *Ibid.*

pollution control framework provided by Article 21 is supported by a wealth of 'representative illustrations of international agreements, the work of international organizations, decisions of international courts and tribunals, and other instances of State practice'.[56] Thus the ILC appears expressly to recognise the critical role of the extensive body of developed practice existing in the field of international environmental law in supporting the effective implementation and application of the key pollution control obligation set out in Article 21 of the UNWC. Of course, State practice developing in light of the emerging human right to water, consistent with the stipulations of General Comment No. 15,[57] as well as practice now developing in light of the efforts of States to implement SDG 6, might also be expected to inform aspects of the due diligence required under international water law.

In relation to the ecosystem protection obligation in Article 20 of the UNWC,[58] leading commentators noted in 2001 that 'progress made in scientific research further shows that the use of watercourses can affect and be affected by processes related to other natural elements, such as soil degradation and desertification, deforestation and climate change', which 'has brought water specialists in the last decade to advocate the adoption of less economic-oriented criteria for the management of freshwater resources, following an "ecosystem approach"'.[59] Such an 'ecosystem approach' has in turn been elaborated upon in an early seminal study of the topic, which advises that

> an 'ecosystem approach' requires consideration of the whole system rather than individual components. Living species and their physical environments must be recognized as interconnected, and the focus must be on the interaction between different sub-systems and their responses to stresses resulting from human activity. Not only does interconnectedness imply management approaches that are broad-based in a spatial sense; it requires as well that human interaction with and use of the environment respect the need

[56] *Ibid*, at 123.

[57] Resolution 70/1, above n 18, paras 31–35, at 11.

[58] Article 20 of the UNWC provides that '[w]atercourse States shall, individually and, where appropriate, jointly, protect and preserve the ecosystems of international watercourses'. In addition, Article 22 requires watercourse States to prevent the introduction of alien or new species which may be detrimental to the ecosystem of an international watercourse, while article 23 requires watercourse States to take measures to protect and preserve the marine environment, thereby recognising the problem of marine pollution caused by land-based sources and helping to realise the Targets set out under SDG 14.

[59] Tanzi and Arcari, above n 52.

for maintaining 'ecosystem integrity', in other words, the system's capacity for self-organization.[60]

This evolution in scientific understanding of river basins as ecosystems has continued and is increasingly reflected in the emergence of sophisticated methodologies which can function to inform the normative implications of State obligations to protect watercourse ecosystems.[61] For example, improved understanding of the parameters for analysing environmental flows in a shared watercourse[62] has permitted judicial recognition of a corresponding legal obligation to maintain a minimum environmental flow regime.[63] Similarly, the rapidly evolving ecosystems services concept provides a methodology for the economic and social valuation of natural ecosystems which permits integration of the value of non-marketable benefits into decision-making processes.[64] Of course, lessons learned in the implementation of legal requirements arising under other environmental conventions to protect and preserve associated water-related ecosystems can also serve to inform the obligations set out under Part IV of the UNWC. It is increasingly apparent, for example, that the wealth of detailed technical guidance developed under the auspices of the 1971 Ramsar Convention[65] can play a significant role in informing the ecosystem obligations arising under the UNWC.[66] There exists obvious complementarity between these two instruments, with wetlands

[60] J. Brunnée and S.J Toope, 'Environmental Security and Freshwater Resources: A Case for International Ecosystem Law' (1994) *Yearbook of International Environmental Law* 5(41), 55.

[61] See O. McIntyre, 'The Protection of Freshwater Ecosystems Revisited: Towards a Common Understanding of the "Ecosystems Approach" to the Protection of Transboundary Water Resources' (2014) *Review of European, Comparative and International Environmental Law* 23(1), 88.

[62] See J. Gooch, *Protecting Ecological Integrity in Transboundary Watercourses: An Integrational Approach towards Implementing Environmental Flows* (Lund University, 2016).

[63] Permanent Court of Arbitration, *Indus Waters Kishenganga Arbitration (Pakistan v. India)*, Partial Award, 18 February 2013, at para 454.

[64] See Millennium Ecosystem Assessment, *Ecosystems and Human Well-being: Synthesis* (Island Press, 2005).

[65] Convention on Wetlands of International Importance especially as Waterfowl Habitat (as amended in 1982 and 1987), (Ramsar, 2 February 1971), (1972) 11 ILM 969. Today the Ramsar Convention has 169 Contracting Parties and applies to 2,260 designated wetland sites covering a total area of 215,276,293 hectares.

[66] Such guidance is now consolidated in 21 volumes of the Ramsar *Handbooks for the Wise Use of Wetlands* (4th edn, 2010).

playing a critical role in the functioning of aquatic ecosystems and in the provision of important ecosystem services, such as flood control, wildlife habitat, groundwater recharge and the 'protection, purification, retention and provision of water resources for water and food supplies … on which the well-being of people and their livelihoods depend'.[67]

There had existed for some time prior to the 1997 adoption of the UNWC a discernible trend in the practice of the environmental aspects of international water law of moving away from simple, prescriptive arrangements for the prevention, reduction or mitigation of water pollution towards a more ecosystem-oriented approach to the protection and management of shared international basins. Basin agreements, such as the 1978 Great Lakes Water Quality Agreement[68] and the 1995 Mekong Agreement,[69] have long included express ecosystems protection obligations. It has been noted that some of the earliest and most ardent support for the ecosystem approach can be found in regional water resources conventions and basin agreements adopted by developing countries,[70] which may be due to the fact that a significantly larger proportion of the populations of such States rely directly upon ecosystems and ecosystem services for their well-being and livelihoods. This trend has been equally

---

[67] Ramsar COP Resolution IX.3 on Engagement of the Ramsar Convention on Wetlands in Ongoing Multilateral Processes Dealing with Water (Kampala, 2005), at 1, para 3. In addition, the Preamble to the Convention expressly recognises the close interlinkage between wetlands conservation and water resources management by noting 'the fundamental ecological functions of wetlands as regulators of water regimes'.

[68] (Ottawa, 22 November 1978), 30 UST 1383, TIAS No. 9257, articles I and II.

[69] Agreement on Cooperation for Sustainable Development of the Mekong River Basin (Chiang Rai, 5 April 1995), (1995) 34 ILM 864, articles 3 and 7.

[70] O. McIntyre, 'The Emergence of an "Ecosystem Approach" to the Protection of International Watercourses under International Law' (2004) *Review of European Community and International Environmental Law* 13(1), 3–4. See, for example, the 1969 Treaty of the River Plate Basin, Brasilia, 23 April 1969, (1969) 8 ILM 905, article 1; the 1975 Statute of the Uruguay River, Salto, 26 February 1975, article 36; 1978 Treaty for Amazonian Cooperation, Brasilia, 3 July 1978, articles I and VII; the 1964 Convention relating to the Statute of the Senegal River, Dakar, 7 February 1964, articles 2 and 4; the 1977 Agreement Creating the Organisation for the Management and Development of the Kagera Basin, Rusumo, 24 August 1977, article 2; the 1978 Convention relating to the Status of the River Gambia, Kaolack, 30 June 1978, article 4; the 1980 Convention Creating the Niger Basin Authority, Faranah, 21 November 1980, article 4(2)(d).

apparent in regional framework agreements concerning shared transboundary basins more generally.[71] Notably, the 1992 United Nations Economic Commission for Europe (UNECE) Water Convention, the only other globally applicable framework convention relating to shared international freshwater resources, includes extensive and detailed provisions for the conservation and restoration of the ecosystems of shared basins.[72]

The somewhat less developed rules of international law relating to the use and protection of shared international groundwater resources would appear to be evolving in a similar vein. The ILC's 2008 Draft Articles on Transboundary Aquifers[73] stress 'the role of the aquifer or aquifer system in the related ecosystem'[74] and, more specifically, call upon States 'to ensure that the quantity and quality of water retained in an aquifer or aquifer system, as well as that discharged through its discharge zones, are sufficient to protect and preserve such ecosystems'.[75] Similarly, the UNECE Model Rules on Transboundary Groundwaters, which were developed under the auspices of the 1992 Water Convention on the basis of a study of the specific application of the Convention's principles and purport to 'reflect the current state of international water law with regard to transboundary groundwaters',[76] stipulate that '[t]he Parties shall use transboundary groundwaters in a sustainable manner, with a view to maximizing the long-term benefits accruing therefrom and preserving groundwater-dependent ecosystems'.[77]

---

[71] See, for example, the original 1995 Protocol on Shared Watercourse Systems in the Southern African Development Community (SADC), Johannesburg, 28 August 1995, articles 2(3), 2(11) and 2(12), reproduced in Food and Agriculture Organization, *Treaties Concerning the Non-Navigational Uses of International Watercourses: Africa* (FAO Legislative Study 61, 1997), at 146. However, the 2000 SADC Revised Protocol on Shared Watercourses (Windhoek, 7 August 2000), closely follows the approach taken under the 1997 UNWC, more or less reproducing its provisions on pollution and protection of ecosystems, at article 4(2).

[72] Convention on the Protection and Use of Transboundary Watercourses and International Lakes (Helsinki, 17 March 1992), (1992) 31 ILM 1312, articles 1(2), 2(2)(b), 2(2)(d) and 3(1)(i).

[73] International Law Commission, *Report of the International Law Commission on the Work of Its Sixtieth Session* (UN Doc. A/63/10, 2008).

[74] Article 5(1)(i).

[75] Article 10.

[76] UNECE Model Rules on Transboundary Groundwaters (UNECE, Geneva, 2014), at iii, available at: http://www.unece.org/fileadmin/DAM/env/water/publications/WAT_model_provisions/ece_mp.wat_40_eng.pdf, accessed 29 January 2018.

[77] Provision 2(1).

In addition, several river basin agreements which pre-date this general concern with ecosystem health or integrity have either been amended to incorporate some element of ecosystems protection or have been interpreted by international courts and tribunals as requiring such ecosystem protection. For example, the 1944 Colorado Treaty between the United States and Mexico[78] has recently been amended by Minute 319,[79] which identifies measures intended to 'allow both countries to better assess the long-term opportunities and cooperative measures for water conservation, management and development', including, *inter alia*, 'innovative mechanisms for … restoring environmental flows in the Colorado River down to the Gulf of California'.[80] The established water utilisation regime of the Colorado River demonstrates the need for ecosystem protection quite dramatically, with over-allocation of water having led to a reduction of wetlands in the Colorado Delta – 'once one of the world's great desert river deltas and home to dolphins, fish, birds and other wildlife' – to between 5 and 10 per cent of their historic area of 6,000 km^2.[81] Where such updating of water resources conventions to include obligations regarding ecosystems protection is neither feasible nor forthcoming, international courts and tribunals may nevertheless take an actively progressive approach to their interpretation so as to take account of prevailing ecological values.[82]

Whereas this recognition in the UNWC of the normative character and significance of ecosystem protection requirements merely reflects the continuing evolution of international environmental law more generally,

---

[78] Treaty between the United States of America and Mexico Respecting Utilization of Waters of the Colorado and Tijuana Rivers and of the Rio Grande (Washington D.C., 3 February 1944), 3 UNTS 314.

[79] International Boundary Waters Commission, Minute 319: Interim International Cooperative Measures in the Colorado River Basin Through 2017 and Extension of Minute 318 Cooperative Measures to Address the Continued Effects of the 2010 Earthquake in the Mexicali Valley, Baja California (20 November 2012).

[80] See R.M. Buono and G. Eckstein, 'Minute 319: A Cooperative Approach to Mexico-US Hydro-Relations on the Colorado River' (2014) *Water International* 39(3), 268–269.

[81] Buono and Eckstein, *ibid*, at 266. See also A.D. Tarlock, 'Mexico and the United States Assume a Legal Duty to Provide Colorado River Delta Restoration Flows: An Important International Environmental and Water Law Precedent' (2014) *Review of European, Comparative and International Environmental Law* 23(1), 76.

[82] See, for example, the *Kishenganga Arbitration*, above n 63.

notably under the 1992 Convention on Biological Diversity (CBD),[83] the universal adoption of Target 6.6 provides a hugely significant endorsement to what is rapidly emerging as a key value in transboundary water resources management. On the other hand, the increasingly sophisticated legal and technical requirements for ecosystems protection emerging in international water law provide a vital tool for realising Target 6.6 at both the international and national levels.

8.5 WATER-USE EFFICIENCY

The water-use efficiency values articulated in Target 6.4[84] have long been reflected in international water law, but are limited in their significance by the desire to strike an equitable balance between the water-use rights of developed and developing watercourse States, where the former are likely to enjoy greater technical capacity regarding water efficiency. While the UNWC requires that account be taken of the 'conservation, development, protection and economy of use of the water resources of the watercourse and the costs of measures taken to that effect' in determining equitable and reasonable utilisation,[85] and the Helsinki Rules refer to 'the avoidance of unnecessary waste in the utilization of the waters of the basin',[86] State and judicial practice suggest that the role of efficient use as a factor in determining an equitable utilisation regime for an international watercourse is rather limited.[87] In its commentary to Article V of the Helsinki Rules, the ILA took the view that '[a] "beneficial use" need not be the most productive use to which the water

---

83 (Rio de Janeiro, 5 June 1992), (1992) 31 ILM 818, article 1. In addition, article 8(f) obliges State parties to 'rehabilitate and restore degraded ecosystems'. See further S. Brels, D. Coates and F. Loures, *Transboundary Water Resources Management: The Role of International Watercourse Agreements in Implementation of the CBD* (Secretariat of the CBD, 2008).

84 According to Target 6.4, the international community is committed to '[b]y 2030, substantially increas[ing] water use efficiency across all sectors and ensure sustainable withdrawals and supply of freshwater to address water scarcity and substantially reduce the number of people suffering from water scarcity'.

85 Article 6(1)(f). The ILC commentary refers, above n 44, para 4, at 101, in the context of 'economy of use', to the avoidance of unnecessary waste of water.

86 Smets, above n 31, article V(2)(i).

87 See generally, X. Fuentes, 'The Criteria for the Equitable Utilization of International Rivers' (1996) 67 *British Yearbook of International Law* 337, at 378 *et seq.*; McIntyre, above n 37, 173–177.

may be put, nor need it utilize the most efficient methods known in order to avoid waste and ensure maximum utilization'.[88] It argued that to require otherwise would result in the dislocation of numerous productive uses and would favour more economically and technologically advanced States over less developed States, explaining that 'in its application, the present rule is not designed to foster waste but to hold States to a duty of efficiency which is commensurate with their financial resources'.[89] This approach might be regarded as an early application of the rapidly emerging international environmental law principle of 'common but differentiated responsibility', whereby the common environmental obligations of all States are recognised, but some differentiation may be permitted in respect of such obligations on the basis of the different financial and technical capacity of States.[90]

Equally, it is well established that 'no user may be wilfully wasteful or inefficient when it has the means to reduce inefficiency'.[91] The United States Supreme Court set out the nuanced nature of the requirement of efficiency in international water law in its decision in *Colorado v. New Mexico*, where the Court stated that it would only protect those rights to water which are 'reasonably required and applied', and continued that '[e]specially … where water is scarce … wasteful or inefficient uses will not be protected … Similarly, concededly senior water rights will be deemed forfeited or substantially diminished where the rights have not been exercised or asserted with reasonable diligence.'[92] The Supreme Court went on to explain that States have 'an affirmative duty to take reasonable steps to conserve and augment the water supply of an interstate stream' and that they have 'a duty to employ "financially and physically feasible" measures "adapted to conserving and equalizing the natural flow"'.[93] The Court further stated that, in such a situation, '[e]ach

---

88 Smets, above n 31, 487.

89 *Ibid.* In support of this position, see, for example, *Report of the Narmada Water Dispute Disputes Tribunal* (1979), vol 1, at 112.

90 See generally, L. Rajamani, *Differential Treatment in International Environmental Law* (Oxford University Press, 2006); McIntyre, above n 37, 260–265.

91 J. Lipper, 'Equitable Utilization' in A.H Garretson, R.D. Hayton and C.J. Olmstead (eds), *The Law of International Drainage Basins* (Dobbs Ferry/ Oceana, 1967) 47. See *Report of the Narmada Water Dispute Disputes Tribunal*, above n 89, 129.

92 459 US 176 (1982), at 184. See further, McCaffrey, above n 37, 333 *et seq.*

93 *Ibid*, at 185.

of these states [has] a duty to exercise her right reasonably and in a manner calculated to conserve the common supply'.[94]

It is readily apparent, therefore, that international water law has long had the potential to play a significant role in equitably increasing water-use efficiency, at least as regards shared international water resources, and so can function to assist in realisation of Target 6.4. However, the elevation of water-use efficiency to the level of a priority objective through its inclusion in Target 6.4, and the universal commitment of States that such inclusion represents, might over time serve to prioritise efficiency as a key factor in determining reasonable and equitable use of international waters. In this respect, once again, the SDGs might help to promote the progressive evolution of international water law to better address the challenges of an increasingly water-constrained world.

8.6 TRANSBOUNDARY COOPERATION

One of the ways in which the values set out in the SDGs cohere most markedly with those central to international water law is through the former's explicit advocacy of transboundary cooperation in governance of water resources, arguably the ultimate, defining aim of the latter body of rules.[95] Target 6.5 commits States to, '[by] 2030, implement[ing] integrated water resources management at all levels, including through transboundary cooperation as appropriate'. Though integrated water resources management (IWRM) is in essence a technical best practice paradigm of water resources management with little clear legal meaning or significance,[96] a general duty upon States to cooperate over transboundary waters is included in almost all modern water resources

[94] *Ibid*, at 185–186.

[95] See, for example, O. McIntyre, 'Chapter 15 – Water' in E. Morgera and K. Kulovesi (eds), *Research Handbook on International Law and Natural Resources* (Edward Elgar Publishing, 2016), 305–326, who describes the 'evolution of modern international water law – from a body of rules primarily concerned with the need to accommodate competing national economic interests based on territorial sovereignty, *to one which is increasingly understood as requiring meaningful inter-State engagement* in pursuit of optimal utilisation of the benefits flowing from shared water resources in a manner that is equitable as well as environmentally and socially sustainable' (emphasis added).

[96] On the legal significance of the IWRM concept, see A. Allan and A. Rieu-Clarke, 'Good Governance and IWRM: A Legal Perspective' (2010) *Irrigation and Drainage Systems* 24(3/4), 239–248.

conventions and declaratory instruments.[97] In addition to requiring watercourse States to cooperate in good faith 'in order to attain optimal utilization and adequate protection of an international watercourse', Article 8 of the UNWC encourages them to 'consider the establishment of joint mechanisms or commissions ... to facilitate cooperation on relevant measures and procedures'. The 1994 ILC commentary on draft Article 8 leaves little room for doubt as to the legal status or significance of the duty to cooperate.[98] In order to conclude that transboundary water cooperation provides an important basis 'in order to fulfil the obligations and attain the objectives set forth in the draft articles', the ILC points out that Article 8 'refers to the most fundamental principles upon which cooperation between watercourse States is founded', i.e. sovereign equality, territorial integrity, mutual benefit and good faith, before summarising the very wide range of international conventional instruments, declarations and resolutions calling for cooperation over the utilisation of international watercourses. The duty to cooperate can largely be understood as an 'umbrella' or composite obligation, consisting of a range of procedural requirements, any one or more of which might be applicable in a given situation. These notably include the duty to exchange information relevant to use of the watercourse, the duty to notify co-riparian States of planned projects potentially impacting a shared watercourse and, where necessary, duties to consult and negotiate with such States in a good faith effort to address their concerns.[99]

Beyond the general duty to cooperate over the utilisation and protection of shared water resources owed to co-riparian States, General Comment No. 15 clearly identifies a duty on States to cooperate in furtherance of realisation of the human right to water. Though it notes that the UNWC 'requires that social and human needs be taken into account in determining the equitable utilization of watercourses, that State parties take measures to prevent significant harm being caused, and [that] special regard must be given to the requirements of vital human needs',[100] General Comment No. 15 further notes, in the context of the international obligations imposed upon States by virtue of Articles 11 and 12 of the 1966 International Covenant on Economic, Social and Cultural Rights, that

---

[97] On the general duty to cooperate in international water law, see generally, C. Leb, *Cooperation in the Law of Transboundary Water Resources* (Cambridge University Press, 2013).

[98] ILC, above n 44, 105–107.

[99] As exemplified in articles 9 and 11–19 of the UNWC.

[100] *Ibid*, para 31, at 11.

> [t]o comply with their international obligations in relation to the right to water, States parties have to respect the enjoyment of the right in other countries. *International cooperation requires* States parties to refrain from actions that interfere, directly or indirectly, with the enjoyment of the right to water in other countries. Any activities undertaken within the State party's jurisdiction should not deprive another country of the ability to realize the right to water for persons in its jurisdiction.[101]

In fact, the CESCR goes so far as to include the duty to cooperate in realising the right to water as one of the 'core obligations' of States parties to the 1966 Covenant.[102] Thus, the international discourse on the human right to water had already begun to alter the focus of the fundamental duty to cooperate under international water law towards pursuit of the availability and sustainable management of water and sanitation for all, an evolutionary transformation supported in no small measure by the successive universal adoption by States of MDG 7 and SDG 6.

It should be noted that General Comment No. 15 is emphatic in linking good faith transboundary water cooperation, as required under international water law, to the realisation of the human right to water in a number of ways. For example, in listing indicative illustrations of violations of the right to water, it includes the 'failure of a State to take into account its international legal obligations regarding the right to water when entering into agreements with other States or with international organizations'.[103] Regarding the various norms requiring environmental protection of shared waters, it also advises that '[v]iolations of the obligation to respect follow from the State party's interference with the right to water. This includes, inter alia: … (iii) pollution and diminution of water resources affecting human health.'[104]

General Comment No. 15 further provides that '[d]epending on the availability of resources, States should facilitate realization of the right to water in other countries, for example through provision of water resources …'.[105] Though this provision is couched in soft terms, it could clearly be understood to recognise a requirement that, in utilising shared water resources, States ensure that adequate water is available for the realisation of the human right to water in co-basin States, once again linking human rights requirements to consideration of vital human needs

---

[101] *Ibid* (emphasis added).
[102] *Ibid*, para 38, at 13.
[103] *Ibid*, para 44(c)(vii), at 14.
[104] *Ibid*, para 44(a)(iii), at 14.
[105] *Ibid*, para 34, at 11.

in the practice of inter-State water resources allocation. Likewise, General Comment No. 15 generally suggests that

> States parties should ensure that the right to water is given due attention in international agreements and, to that end, should consider the development of further legal instruments. With regard to the conclusion and implementation of other international and regional agreements, States parties should take steps to ensure that these instruments do not adversely impact upon the right to water.

Clearly, this statement suggests that States should only conclude global or regional water resources conventions and river basin treaties that are compatible with full realisation of the human right to water in all co-basin States, and should act to further develop and adapt existing treaty regimes to ensure such compatibility. All this suggests that the CESCR envisages a particularly important role for international water law in the realisation of the human right to water and, consequently, for effective realisation of SDG 6.

Demonstrating the integrated and indivisible nature of the 2030 Agenda, some commentators link Target 6.5 to SDG 16, arguing that the former should be analysed in conjunction with the latter, which is concerned with strengthening international cooperation and transboundary good governance.[106] Clearly this aim resonates with the general objectives of the UNWC and of General Comment No. 15. For example, these authors refer to the relevance of Target 16.3, which seeks to '[p]romote the rule of law at the national and international levels, and ensure equal access to justice for all, which, in addition to promoting adherence to established rules of international water law, 'provides individuals with the ability to react to breaches of both substantive and procedural obligations in a transboundary water context'.[107] Though international water law has not traditionally concerned itself with the rights of individuals, Article 32 of the UNWC on non-discrimination regarding access to legal redress 'for the protection of the interests of persons, natural or juridical, who have suffered or are under a serious threat of suffering significant transboundary harm as a result of activities related to an international watercourse' appears to anticipate a significant role for private recourse by adversely affected legal persons to domestic

---

[106] See Orme et al, above n 4, 978–980.
[107] *Ibid*, at 978.

courts and remedies as a means for establishing effective responsibility for unlawful activities related to international watercourses.[108]

Generally, international water law appears to be developing in a manner consistent with the 'transboundary good governance' values embraced by SDG 16, such as Target 16.6, which calls upon States to 'develop effective, accountable and transparent institutions at all levels', Target 16.7, which seeks to 'ensure responsive, inclusive, participatory and representative decision-making at all levels', and Target 16.10, which aims to 'ensure public access to information and protect fundamental freedoms in accordance with national legislation and international agreements'. Regarding institutions, for example, transboundary water cooperation very often involves the establishment of some form of inter-State institutional machinery to formulate and implement common policies for the management and development of the basin,[109] an approach to managing shared water resources widely endorsed by the international community,[110] and by international bodies concerned with codification of this field of international law.[111]

While the UNECE Water Convention rather unusually imposes a general obligation upon State parties to participate in the establishment of such 'joint bodies',[112] the UNWC merely encourages watercourse States to enter into common management arrangements consistent with the requirements of the principle of equitable and reasonable utilisation, the duty to prevent significant transboundary harm, and the general duty to

---

108 Similarly, articles 69–71 of the Berlin Rules, above n 46, also provide for adversely affected legal individuals to seek recourse before a competent judicial or administrative authority in the State where the harm arises.

109 See generally, S. Schmeier, *Governing International Watercourses: The Contribution of River Basin Organizations to the Effective Governance of Internationally Shared Rivers and Lakes* (Routledge, 2013); I. Dombrowsky, *Conflict, Cooperation and Institutions in International Water Management: An Economic Analysis* (Edward Elgar Publishing, 2007); McIntyre, above n 37, 28–40.

110 See McCaffrey, above n 37, who notes, at 159, that 'well over 100 international river commissions have been established by states'.

111 Notably, Recommendation 51 of the Stockholm *Action Plan for the Human Environment*, adopted at the 1972 UN Conference on the Human Environment (UNCHE), called for the 'creation of river basin commissions or other appropriate machinery for cooperation between interested states for water resources common to more than one jurisdiction', and set down a number of basic principles by which such commissions should be guided.

112 1992 UNECE Convention on the Protection of Transboundary Watercourses and International Lakes (1992) 312 ILM 1312, article 9(2).

cooperate.[113] Incrementally, such institutions are subjected to requirements of transparency and accountability and to other rapidly evolving constraints of administrative good governance. Regarding responsive decision-making and public access to information, the practice of modern international water law has long revolved around processes of prior inter-State notification of planned measures and routine information exchange on the state of shared water resources.[114] However, in recent years such processes have begun to open up in order to facilitate or require broader engagement with the public or, at the very least, key stakeholders.[115] This can be seen in the 2010 judgment of the International Court of Justice (ICJ) in the *Pulp Mills* case, where the Court placed great emphasis on the significance of procedural requirements, and in particular the duty to conduct environmental impact assessment (EIA), in discharging the duty to cooperate over planned projects,[116] while also stressing the role of formal institutional machinery established to facilitate meaningful cooperative engagement.[117] Of course, any credible EIA process will involve significant public and stakeholder disclosure, consultation and engagement. It is clear, therefore, international water law can and must adapt in order to contribute to realisation of the 'transboundary good governance elements' of the SDGs, but equally that the SDGs have a key role in driving further progressive transformation of this body of law.

---

[113] Articles 5(2), 8(2), 9, 21, 24 and 33(2). See O. McIntyre, 'International Water Law: Concepts, Evolution and Development' in A. Earle, A. Jägerskog and J. Öjendal (eds), *Transboundary Water Management: Principles and Practice* (Earthscan, 2010) 69–70.

[114] Smets, above n 31.

[115] See, for example, article 16(8) of the 2004 Agreement on the Establishment of the Zambezi Watercourse Commission (ZAMCOM Agreement), which requires, in the context of inter-State notification of '[p]lanned programmes, projects or activities of Member States', that 'Member States shall ensure that the public in an area likely to be affected by a proposed programme, project or activity are informed thereof and are provided with the opportunity for making comments thereon or objections thereto as well as on the transmittal of such comments or objections to the Commission'.

[116] UNCED, above n 45, at paras 68–79. See further O. McIntyre, 'The Contribution of Procedural Rules to the Environmental Protection of Transboundary Rivers' in L. Boisson de Chazournes, C. Leb and M. Tignino (eds), *Freshwater and International Law: The Multiple Challenges* (Edward Elgar, Cheltenham, 2013), 239–265.

[117] *Ibid*, at paras 87–91. See generally, O. McIntyre, 'The World Court's Ongoing Contribution to International Water Law: The *Pulp Mills* Case between Argentina and Uruguay' (2011) *Water Alternatives* 4(2), 124–144.

8.7 CONCLUSION

Few would now deny that reliable access to adequate fresh water supplies has become a pressing global problem. Estimates suggest that by 2030 global water requirements will be nearly double those in 2005, and will exceed current reliable supply levels by 40 per cent.[118] The resulting water stress that many States will suffer will alter established patterns of agricultural production, adversely affect natural ecosystems and the services they provide, and generally impact livelihoods and living standards. As the fresh water crisis has come to be recognised as 'the new environmental crisis of the 21st century',[119] the recognition of water as a valuable natural resource has at last taken hold among policy-makers. Of course, this is equally true of transboundary water resources, in respect of which competition between co-basin States for the right to use shared waters has intensified. Thus, the role of international water law in promoting equitable transboundary water resources management and effective hydro-diplomacy becomes ever more critical. While the existing rules and principles of international water will clearly have a significant role to play in achieving the Targets set out under SDG 6, it is equally apparent that SDG 6 will shine an important spotlight on the need to improve transboundary water governance in order to render it 'fit for purpose' in the twenty-first century.

---

[118] See E. Brown Weiss, *International Water Law for a Water-Scarce World* (Martinus Nijhoff, 2013) 1.

[119] *Ibid.*

9. Good urban governance as a global aspiration: on the potential and limits of SDG 11

Helmut Philipp Aust and Anél du Plessis

9.1 INTRODUCTION

Goal 11 of the Sustainable Development Goals (SDGs) sets out to make cities inclusive, safe, resilient and sustainable by 2030. Together with the 'New Urban Agenda' adopted at the Habitat III conference in Quito in 2016, SDG 11 is the latest emanation of the thickening layer of international normative guidance on questions of 'good urban governance'.[1] Among the SDGs, Goal 11 occupies a peculiar place. Just like the other SDGs it sets forth a commitment by the United Nations (UN) member states which have agreed to the SDGs by consensus. At the same time, it introduces another level of governance which is situated below

[1] UN Habitat has been working on this notion for some time. In general, 'good urban governance' denotes the sum of the ways in which individuals and institutions, public and private, plan and manage the common city affairs. It is a continuing process through which conflicting or diverse interests may be accommodated and cooperative action be taken. It includes formal institutions as well as informal arrangements and the social capital of citizens. Effective urban governance is further described as being characterized as democratic and inclusive; long-term and integrated; multi-scale and multi-level; territorial; proficient and conscious of the digital age. See, in this regard, UN Habitat, <https://unhabitat.org/governance/> accessed 30 January 2018. The governance term itself is complex, especially in the urban context. As noted in the literature, 'governance refers to a particular interactive form of governing, to a normative model of how cities and states should be governed, and to a political science theory of governing', J. Pierre and B.G. Peters, 'Urban Governance' in K. Mossberger, S.E. Clarke and P. John (eds), *The Oxford Handbook of Urban Politics* (Oxford University Press, 2012) 71, at 82–83.

the level of the nation-state. In this respect SDG 11 is unique, yet expressive of several broader trends. These trends relate both to the 'disaggregation' of the nation-state,[2] as well as to the growing confidence with which cities and their governments step up to the international level. Increasingly cities view themselves as globally relevant actors.[3] The organization and objectives of the global C40 Cities Network serve as one of several prominent examples in this regard where cities collaborate to effectively share knowledge and drive meaningful, measurable and sustainable action on climate change.[4] This development is spurred by disappointment in the capacity of nation-states and their national governments to address pressing global concerns, in particular those relating to climate change, social justice and human rights.

In this chapter we aim to interrogate Goal 11 of the SDGs with specific emphasis on how it enlightens understanding of good urban governance. We commence with an introduction to what we call the urban turn in global governance, which serves to contextualize the setting in terms of which SDG 11 was developed. Subsequently we question the aspirations of Goal 11 with a specific focus on what can best be described as its inherent contradictions. Finally, we address some of the implementation risks and challenges associated with SDG 11.

9.2 THE URBAN TURN IN GLOBAL GOVERNANCE

Keen interest in the social, environmental, economic and geopolitical dynamics of cities and urban development is not new. Scholars in the fields of economics, anthropology, public and international relations, ecology, humanities, and urban studies have for decades extensively deliberated urbanization, the steady rise of cities and other urban localities, as well as their short- and long-term environmental, social and economic impacts.[5] The same cannot be said of the legal discipline which

---

[2] A.M. Slaughter, *A New World Order* (Princeton University Press, 2004) 12–15.

[3] See K. Ljungkvist, *The Global City 2.0* (Routledge, 2016) 6; see also from a legal perspective H.P. Aust, *Das Recht der globalen Stadt – Grenzüberschreitende Dimensionen kommunaler Selbstverwaltung* (Mohr Siebeck Verlag, 2017) 47–57.

[4] See more on the C40 Cities Network and its global programmes <http://www.c40.org/about> accessed 30 January 2018.

[5] For an instructive overview see C. Parnreiter, 'The Global City Tradition' in M. Acuto and W. Steele (eds), *Global City Challenges. Debating a Concept, Improving the Practice* (Palgrave Macmillan, 2013) 15–32.

is, as is often the case, lagging behind in absorbing, accommodating, and responding to new social phenomena.[6]

With the publication of the 1987 Brundtland Report and its coining of the concept of sustainable development, the 'remit of cities in addressing environmental issues was recast as central to the new [sustainable development] agenda'.[7] The Report's chapter 9 on 'The Urban Challenge' argued that since most members of the world's future population will live in urban areas, cities should be central to the pursuit of sustainable development.[8] Today it is widely agreed that the impact of urbanization will continue to bring about major global and local changes, especially with many countries in the developing world now entering the high-growth and rapid-transition features of an era of booming urbanization. This growing attention on the city level resonates with the theoretical work of Saskia Sassen, who has argued that contemporary cities are sites of the global regulatory realm, 'where policy design and implementation [are] more feasible than at the national level'.[9]

9.2.1 The Changing Context of Urban Governance

One of the predicted impacts of urbanization is its increased impact on the global carrying capacity of the Earth. This has consequences for decisions and policies on, among others, health, migration, production, natural resource use, land use, spatial planning, and environmental governance. The diffusion of governing power in, and new forms of governance relevant to, urbanization reinforces its relevance for the

---

6 Pioneering contributions include Y. Blank, 'The City and the World' (2006) *Columbia Journal of Transnational Law* 44, 868–931; G. Frug and D.J. Barron, 'International Local Government Law' (2006) 38 *The Urban Lawyer* 1–62; J. Nijman, 'The Future of the City and the International Law of the Future' in S. Muller, S. Zouridis, M. Frishman et al (eds), *The Law of the Future and the Future of Law* (Torkel Opsahl, 2011) 213–239.

7 H. Bulkeley and M. Betsill, 'Rethinking Sustainable Cities: Multilevel Governance and the "Urban" Politics of Climate Change' (2005) *Environmental Politics* 14(1), 44.

8 Critical towards proclamations of a so-called 'urban age' and the underlying statistics: N. Brenner and C. Schmid, 'The "Urban Age" in Question' (2014) *International Journal of Urban and Regional Research* 38, 731–755.

9 S. Sassen, 'A Focus on Cities Takes us Beyond Existing Governance Frameworks' in J. Stiglitz and M. Kaldor (eds), *The Quest for Security: Protection Without Protectionism and the Challenge of Global Governance* (Columbia University Press, 2013) 243.

global pursuit of sustainability, not only spatially, but also through the global economy, information flows and social networks.[10]

The SDGs denote cities as drivers of both localized urban and global transformation. Goal 11 envisions cities to be inclusive, safe, resilient and sustainable by 2030. The inclusion of this goal endorses the view that globally cities (a) contribute to unsustainable development, but (b) can also be drivers of change with respect to, among other things, basic services, accessible and sustainable transport systems, human settlement planning, the reduction of the risk of disaster, and climate change mitigation and adaptation. This duality finds itself in line with broader characterizations of cities as being simultaneously the source of pressing contemporary problems as well as the solution to these problems. On a more general level, this duality echoes a long-established parallelism between utopian and dystopian visions of urban life. It is no coincidence that Thomas More's Utopia is precisely about city life, albeit in a very idealized and – *nomen est omen* – unreachable form.[11] At the same time, one needs only to remember Charles Dickens' bleak description of urban life in the *A Tale of Two Cities*.[12]

From a legal perspective, cities are government units. Almost regardless of the political structure of the state in which they are situated, cities are micro-governments (municipalities or local authorities) overseen by state authorities. Some cities are increasingly aware of their importance and of the necessity to foster a dialogue among politically elected mayors (councils) and administrators to exchange best practices in sustainability governance. It follows that cities also increasingly advocate confronting and accommodating common interests such as climate action.[13] These local authorities or city governments are acknowledged as co-global governors to the extent that they participate directly and indirectly in matters of global governance. In fact, city governments of today have clout not only in the countries and the governments of which they are

---

[10] See further on these challenges and the role that cities might play in emerging global networks P. Khanna, *Connectography. Mapping the Global Network Revolution* (Weidenfeld and Nicolson, 2016) 49–60.

[11] T. More, *Utopia* (1516).

[12] C. Dickens, *A Tale of Two Cities* (1859).

[13] The C40 Network's Compact of Mayors is said to be the world's largest cooperative effort among mayors and city officials to reduce greenhouse gas emissions and climate risks in cities. See also H.P. Aust, 'Shining Cities on the Hill? The Global City, Climate Change, and International Law' (2015) *European Journal of International Law* 26(1), 261–265.

part, but also in a collective sense as part of international networks and global forums for cities.

Despite the noble ideas of inclusive global governance, which sees a role for cities, the challenges of effective and connected governance are real. The search for more sustainable forms of urbanization and for inclusive, safe, sustainable and resilient cities depends on political and institutional (governance) structures and decisions promoting cooperation among different governance actors operating on different scales.[14] In particular, the nation-state will remain central to any role cities can play, locally as well as globally. Despite all the talk about its demise, the nation-state remains the key player in international relations and international law.[15] After all, the regulatory freedom cities might have, and which they might use for participating in global governance processes, depends on the critical infrastructure which is provided by the state.

In addition, cities (being home to people with different legal status and being governed by politicians) cannot be expected to influence sustainability reforms in isolation from the wider global political economy in a way that is disconnected from global trends such as migration. The challenge further resides in the fact that the promotion of sustainable cities and sustainable urbanization as such cannot be dissociated from the uneven geographies of development and its consequential impact on people, the environment and places. At times, sustainability and other societal aims might clash. It has been reported, for instance, how a conflict materialized in Mumbai over the adequate use of a large public park in the city. This park was home to a large number of informal structures. Non-governmental organizations (NGOs) pressured the city administration to vacate the park so that it could be returned to its purpose as a recreational space. This attempt was eventually successful and found blessing in a decision of the High Court of Bombay.[16] As Jessie Hohmann writes, '[t]he environmental agenda is advanced as

---

[14] For scalar approaches to climate change governance and from a legal perspective see H.M. Osofsky, 'Multiscalar Governance and Climate Change: Reflections on the Role of States and Cities at Copenhagen' (2010) *Maryland Journal of International Law* 25, 64–85; H.M. Osofsky and J. Levit, 'The Scale of Networks – Local Climate Change Coalitions' (2009) *Chicago Journal of International Law* 8, 409–436.

[15] See K. Knop, 'Statehood: Territory, People, Government' in J. Crawford and M. Koskenniemi (eds), *The Cambridge Companion to International Law* (Cambridge University Press, 2012) 95, 111–114.

[16] *Bombay Environmental Action Group and another v AR Bharati and others*, 2004 (3) Bom.C.R. 244 (O.S.) (Thakker C.K., C.J. & Radhakrishnan S.J.), para 212.

"green" and presented in opposition to the "brown" needs of the poor. … In this elite discourse, the poor and their settlements are represented as pollution – a waste product that should be eliminated from India's cities.'[17] All this has taken place, as Hohmann describes, in the context of the implementation of a strategy devised by the McKinsey & Co. Consulting Company, entitled 'Vision Mumbai: Transforming Mumbai into a World Class City'.[18]

The destruction of communities and the environment are social costs of globalization that can go unmeasured by economic and market metrics. The effects of globalization on the realization of the public good at the national level is a hotly debated issue.[19] At least to some, globalization entails a diminishing capacity of national and local institutions to pursue social policy goals. At the same time, the loss in governance capability at the national level is not readily compensated at the global level. Institutions at the global level are often weak and lacking in efficiency.[20] And while national democratic institutions are weakened, global democratic institutions do not really exist. The challenge thus becomes to preserve the positive aspects of globalization while addressing its harmful effects. This, *inter alia*, requires the delegation of state functions with respect to sustainable development both upward (to global institutions) and downward to the most local of governance levels, i.e., the city.[21] The underlying message of Goal 11 of the SDGs is that globalization is not only a driving force in the growth of cities; it also facilitates at once the extension of a city's area of influence over larger geographical areas and even across national boundaries. For example, studies on urban metabolism have documented fluxes of energy, water, food and construction

---

[17] J. Hohmann, *The Right to Housing: Law, Concepts, Possibilities* (Hart, 2013) 209.

[18] *Ibid*, at 199, 207.

[19] This has materialized in various streams of the debate about global inequality and the rise of populist movements; see with respect to the former, S. Sassen, *Expulsions: Brutality and Complexity in the Global Economy* (Harvard University Press, 2014) 85 and with respect to the latter, E.A. Posner, 'The Populist Backlash to Liberal Internationalism' (2017) *Arizona State Law Journal* 49, 795–819.

[20] See further T. Pogge, 'Divided Against Itself: Aspiration and Reality of International Law' in J. Crawford and M. Koskenniemi (eds), *The Cambridge Companion to International Law* (Cambridge University Press, 2012) 373, at 390–396.

[21] See P. Streeten, 'Summary of Globalisation: Threat or Salvation?' in J.M. Harris, T.A. Wise, K.P. Gallagher et al (eds), *A Survey of Sustainable Development: Social and Economic Dimensions* (Island Press, 2001) 229, at 232.

materials. Some urban scholars such as Neil Brenner have gone as far as to coin the expression of 'planetary urbanization' in this regard, drawing attention to the fact that the growth of cities and urban agglomerations cannot be seen in isolation from the *global hinterlands*, which serve the world's urban centres with resources of the most diverse kind.[22] To date, however, little attention has been paid to (a) the locus of these resources and to the environmental and socio-economic consequences of urban growth at the local, regional and global levels;[23] and (b) the diversity and internal operation of the governance institutions responsible for sustainable development. This leaves us with limited understanding of the global–local interface and nexuses accompanying and/or contributing to so-called 'planetary urbanization'.[24] Another unknown is the impact on democratic legitimacy of (and through) local governance. With the focus on cities as particularly important actors of governance, the 'rural hinterlands' face the danger of further marginalization. In particular, they are lacking institutions which would ensure that their voices are also heard on the global level. Ideally, this situation would entail a sense of responsibility on the part of cities not to monopolize or capture the attention of global audiences. At the same time, it is not clear to what extent city governments have a mandate to concern themselves also with the needs of non-urban areas with which they are somehow economically connected. This is a further testament to the problematic division between administrative competences on the one hand, and the factual reality on the ground, on the other.

9.2.2 A Growing Role for Cities in Global Governance

Despite these concerns, cities have the potential to be at the heart of those processes governing local, national and global change. While it is true that cities currently concentrate and exemplify various sustainability problems produced by conventional development strategies, they are

---

[22] See the contributions in N. Brenner (ed.), *Implosions/Explosions – Towards a Study of Planetary Urbanization* (Jovis Verlag, 2014).

[23] R. Sánchez-Rodíquez, 'Urban Sustainability and Global Environmental Change: Reflections for an Urban Agenda' in G. Martine et al (eds), *The New Global Frontier: Urbanisation, Poverty and Environment in the 21st Century* (Earthscan, 2008) 153.

[24] See on this concept N. Brenner, 'Introduction: Urban Theory without an Outside' in Brenner (ed.), above n 22, 14, at 18; Brenner's work is influenced in this regard by H. Lefebvre, 'The Worldwide and the Planetery' in Lefebvre, *State, Space, World – Selected Writings* (University of Minnesota Press, 2009) 196.

increasingly perceived as critical in finding solutions to these global sustainability challenges. Settlement patterns, geographic and ecological location, density, and urban management practices, for example, can have an extraordinary impact on how urban growth feeds into the pursuit of global sustainability.[25]

Today, cities function in a highly complex global governance system – a 'new' governance architecture[26] that is characterized by novel forms of regulation that transcend traditional hierarchical state and inter-state activities.[27] In the normative sense, global governance in general, and more specifically in the field of sustainability, is flexible.[28] It goes beyond authoritative and formal state and inter-state structures. It brings a more inclusive circle of stakeholders and decision-makers[29] closer together in novel ways as global governance includes self-regulation by societal actors, private–public cooperation in solving environmental and other challenges, and a variety of new forms of multi-level laws and policies.[30] Global governance denotes a shift in the understanding of the co-regulation of life on Earth from (formal top-down) government to inclusive governance that recognizes and continues to restructure the roles of the public or the government sector as well as the private and other sectors.[31]

---

25 See G. Martine et al, 'Introduction' in Martine et al (eds), above n 23, 3.

26 The phenomenon, design and functioning of new governance architecture are embedded in different theoretical perspectives such as collaborative ecosystem governance and reflexive environmental law as discussed in a number of normative, explanatory and empirical studies. See C. Holley, 'Facilitating Monitoring, Subverting Self-Interest and Limiting Discretion: Learning from "New" Forms of Accountability in Practice' (2010) *Columbia Journal of Environmental Law* 35(1), 129–131.

27 Also see in general C. Holley, N. Gunningham and C. Shearing, *The New Environmental Governance* (Routledge, 2012).

28 See in general L.J. Kotzé, *Global Environmental Governance* (Edward Elgar Publishing, 2012) and Holley, above n 26, 131–132.

29 See A. Kolers, 'Subsidiarity, Secession and Cosmopolitan Democracy' (2006) *Social Theory and Practice* 32(4), 664.

30 See M.M. Betsill and H. Bulkeley, 'Transnational Networks and Global Environmental Governance: The Cities for Climate Protection Program' (2004) *International Studies Quarterly* 48(2), 472–474; Holley et al, above n 27; A.F. Sovacool and B.K. Sovacool, 'Who Governs Energy? The Challenges Facing Global Energy Governance' (2009) *Energy Policy* 37, 5241 and the published research of the Earth System Governance project available at <http://www.earthsystemgovernance.org/publications> accessed 30 January 2018.

31 See Betsill and Bulkeley, above n 30, 474.

During the past two decades a body of literature on global governance and its polycentric features has emerged that conveys ideas and an understanding that stand in stark contrast with the more traditional state-centric ontology of governance.[32] Ostrom's work, for example, explains that today we are faced with polycentric governance that conceives of a variety of centres of decision-making and action that are formally independent of each other, but that function within an interdependent system of relations.[33] From a sustainability perspective the net result, even though not yet fully understood, is that (a) the pursuit of sustainability takes place in an institutional framework that operates worldwide at and between a variety of territorial and functional scales, that (b) involve a plethora of new and familiar governance actors with varying degrees and types of authority.

It follows that novel approaches to governance are evolving that also challenge the existing knowledge base of constitutional law and of other scholars on the domestic front. These challenges concern the institutional position, role, function and powers of, and the relationships between, different governance actors, with one such actor being city governments. Cities are ordinarily situated as governed[34] and governing[35] sub-national organs of state in domestic government structures. Generally, they derive their governing power from domestic law, including constitutional, local government and environmental law.

---

[32] Traditional state-driven, top-down governance approaches predominantly anchored in the law and command and control regulation are now complemented, and sometimes even challenged, by shared public and private authority, an increased emphasis on bottom-up governance, cooperative partnerships between different actors, voluntary standards, codes of conduct, business self-regulation, etc. in a system of multi-level yet non-hierarchical environmental governance. See L.H. Gulbrandsen, *Transnational Environmental Governance* (Edward Elgar Publishing, 2010) 6, 131–132; Holley et al, above n 27, 4; Sassen, above n 9, 238–259.

[33] See the discussions by Holley et al, above n 27; B. Dente, 'The Transformations of Regional and Local Governments: Implications for Environmental Policy Integration' in A. Goria, A. Sgobbi and I. von Homeyer (eds), *Governance for the Environment* (Edward Elgar Publishing, 2010) 80.

[34] Referring to the fact that municipalities are institutions that are subject to the rules and regulations of national and provincial or state level authorities.

[35] This is with reference to the fact that they have authority over the people and actions within their allocated areas of jurisdiction.

While existing literature on global sustainability governance explicitly acknowledges a role for cities,[36] the jury is still out on the optimal performance and active participation of local actors. Cities seem to participate in global governance beyond national borders, mostly without the cloak of any tangible governing authority. Local governments, for example, enter into and participate in the sidelines deliberations and design of new regional and international environmental agreements (e.g., the Paris Climate Agreement), mainly falling back on their practical local experience and feedback capability. When traditional inter-state forms of diplomacy seem to collapse, some cities are eager to step in to remedy these deficits. This was most notable recently when United States (US) President Trump announced the withdrawal of the US from the 2015 Paris Agreement.[37] Immediately afterwards, a coalition of states and cities in the US announced that they would take it upon themselves to contribute, without federal government, to the achievement of the Paris Agreement goals.[38] Still, local authorities further participate in processes of global governance with a pervasive awareness of the power that national and sub-national authorities (for example, provinces or federal states) exercise over them. This explains why city participation in international decision-making often takes place through representative

[36] See, for example, M. Zimmermann, 'How Local Governments Have Become a Factor in Global Sustainability' in The World Watch Institute, *State of the World 2014 – Governing for Sustainability* (Washington DC, 2014) 152–153; L. Pasquini and C. Shearing, 'Municipalities, Politics, and Climate Change: An Example of the Process of Institutionalising an Environmental Agenda within Local Government' (2014) *The Journal of Environment and Development* 2; S. Sassen, 'Cities are at the Center of Our Environmental Future' (2010) *SAPIENS* 2(3), 1–8; H.P. Aust, 'Auf dem Weg zu einem Recht der globalen Stadt? "C40" und der "Konvent der Bürgemeister" im globalen Klimaschutz-regime' (2013) *ZaöRV* 73, 686; Holley et al, above n 27, 2; J.K. Binder et al, 'Towards an EU Approach to Democratic Local Governance, Decentralisation and Territorial Development', *European Commission: Background Paper Project No. 2007/147439* 15; IUCN Position Paper on the Institutional Framework for Sustainable Development for the Rio 2012 Conference (2012) available at <http://cmsdata.iucn.org/downloads/rio_20_iucn_position_on_institutional_framework_for_sd.pdf> accessed 1 February 2018).

[37] See the Statement of United States' President D. Trump of 1 June 2017, available at <https://www.whitehouse.gov/the-press-office/2017/06/01/statement-president-trump-paris-climate-accord> accessed 26 July 2017.

[38] See H. Tabuchi and H. Fountain, 'Bucking Trump, These Cities, States and Companies Commit to Paris Accord', *The New York Times*, 1 June 2017, available at <https://www.nytimes.com/2017/06/01/climate/american-cities-climate-standards.html> accessed 26 July 2017.

international local government organizations,[39] or forums such as ICLEI-Local Governments for Sustainability,[40] the C40 Cities Climate Change Leadership Group,[41] and United Cities and Local Governments. Some of these organizations are open to all interested local governments (cities), and are involved in global advocacy processes and efforts to improve global and local governance.[42] Others, such as C40, function more in the sense of an exclusive club to which 90 odd cities belong (most of them megacities), which is also meant to set them apart from more traditional city networks, which are open to any city that might wish to join (such as ICLEI with a membership base of more than 1,500 cities, towns and regions).[43] The exclusivity of a network of 'leading cities' is used as a rhetorical trope to further bolster authority of this network at the international and global levels.[44]

---

[39] 'Representative' in this context refers to the representation of members but, in a more normative sense, also to the representation of local government interests in general.

[40] Local Governments for Sustainability (ICLEI) is an international association of cities and local governments dedicated to sustainable development. It comprises 12 mega-cities, 100 super-cities and urban regions, 450 large cities, and 450 medium-sized cities and towns in 86 countries. ICLEI prides itself on the 'promotion of local action for global sustainability and its support of cities to become sustainable, resilient, resource-efficient, bio-diverse, low-carbon; to build a smart infrastructure; and to develop an inclusive, green urban economy with the ultimate aim to achieve healthy and happy communities'. See <http://www.iclei.org/iclei-global/who-is-iclei.html> accessed 30 January 2018. Partnerships exist between C40 and ICLEI regarding climate action in local government, for example.

[41] C40 is an international network of city governments that describes itself as 'a network of the world's megacities taking action to reduce greenhouse gas emissions. C40 works with participating cities to address climate risks and impacts locally and globally'. See <http://c40-production.herokuapp.com/about> accessed 30 January 2018.

[42] Zimmermann, above n 36, 153. Zimmermann also mentions other groups that offer membership to selected cities according to size.

[43] For the C40 membership list, see <http://www.c40.org/cities> accessed 30 January 2018; for ICLEI see <http://www.iclei.org/about/who-is-iclei/faq.htm> accessed 26 July 2017.

[44] For an instructive comparison between first- and second-generation city networks (ICLEI and C40 being examples of this genealogy), see D. Gordon and M. Acuto, 'If Cities Are the Solution, What Are the Problems? The Promise and Perils of Urban Climate Leadership' in C. Johnson, N. Toly and H. Schroeder (eds), *The Urban Climate Challenge – Rethinking the Role of Cities in the Global Climate Regime* (Routledge, 2015) 63, at 65–67.

As global governance actors at the national and international fronts, city governments find themselves between and among a range of actors such as state and other sub-state governments, the private sector, civil society and NGOs. What this exactly implies and entails for cities and urban development is not altogether clear. As Saskia Sassen[45] puts it: 'Cities are *de facto* components of the global environmental governance regime, though they are not so *de jure.*' The role of cities in and its immediate and tangible relevance for global governance is therefore not easily discernible, which demands new knowledge to be generated regarding, among other things: cities in relation to governance actors with traditionally more or elevated governing authority; the position and role of international local government institutions; and the relevance of the internal institutional structures and procedures of city governments.

The position of cities in global governance varies and is captured by the term 'glocalization', which was coined to refer in particular to the simultaneous presence in global governance of globalizing and localizing dynamics and to the more or less deliberate change of global models and practices within particular local contexts that in turn reshapes and redesigns these models and practices.[46] Ferguson and Mansbach describe 'glocalization' in a way that is useful to explain the multifaceted position of cities in global governance. They argue that we cannot separate the 'in here' of the city, community or locality in which we live and labour from the 'out there' of global flows of money, capital, people, power and dominance where the city serves as a geographical ambassador of space and the character of a specific place.[47] Looking into city matters in the global governance context thus depends as much on the 'infra', i.e. the below, the inferior, the underneath and the within, as the 'supra-' dimensions of (the international, the global and the transnational).

---

[45] Sassen, above n 9, 239.

[46] R. Robertson, 'Glocalization: Time-Space and Homogeneity-Heterogeneity' in M. Featherstone, S. Lash and R. Robertson (eds), *Global Modernities* (Sage, 1995) 25–44; E. Swyngedouw, '"Globalisation" or "Glocalisation"? Networks, Territories and Rescaling' (2004) *Cambridge Review of International Affairs* 17(1), 25–48.

[47] Y.H. Ferguson and R.W. Mansbach, *Globalisation: The Return of Borders to a Borderless World?* (Routledge, 2012) 138 citing Munck.

9.3 THE ASPIRATIONS OF SDG 11

In the face of climate change and other urban pressures, sub-national governments have over time become more agile as far as alliances between states, provinces and regions are concerned. Cities continue to come together in creative ways to implement actions that allegedly cannot be taken at national levels for reasons varying from political turf protection to politically delicate and protracted international negotiation procedures. The idea has taken flight that the results of city actions are often more effective, cheaper and better fitted to particular situations than international and national commitments and policies.[48] Although climate change is certainly not the only factor undermining sustainability, no other phenomenon carries such risks to the survival of planetary civilization. Climate change interacts with and exacerbates many other issues of concern for environmental integrity and human well-being – such as the availability of water, food production, biodiversity, health, disaster risk reduction, and employment. In fact, climate change has far-reaching implications for the pursuit of sustainable development and serves to show exactly what a key proactive and response role cities could and arguably should have.[49] This is part of the context which has led to the adoption of Goal 11 of the SDGs.

As indicated earlier, Goal 11 envisions that by 2030 the cities of the world must be safe, inclusive, resilient and sustainable. This goal is ambitious on a number of counts. If we look at the state of cities in the world today, the challenges arising from urbanization, especially in the Global South context, are breathtaking. The goal ultimately implies a salient agreement that the sub-national scale of intervention is necessary for sustainable development – an intervention that requires spatially targeted planning and various other actions across scales of government. The goal is broadly framed, relates to various other SDGs,[50] and speaks to all of the dimensions of sustainable development. It is highly inclusive along the lines of the view that cities are the pathways to social, economic and environmentally sustainable development. The goal's wording is thus at least potentially contradictory and causes aspirational

---

[48] World Watch Institute, above n 36, xxii.

[49] M. Renner and T. Prugh, 'Failing Governance Unsustainable Planet' in World Watch Institute, *ibid*, 4.

[50] For example, Goals 1 (no poverty), 3 (good health and well-being), 6 (clean water and sanitation), 7 (affordable and clean energy), 8 (decent work and economic growth), 9 (industry, innovation and infrastructure), 10 (reduced inequality), 13 (climate action), and 16 (peace, justice and strong institutions).

overlap, considering the meaning of notions or ideals such as inclusion, safety, sustainability and resilience. This potentially compromises the clarity and potency of Goal 11. All in all, however, given the years of arguing in favour of the more explicit recognition of cities in global governance and the pursuit of sustainable development, the inclusion of this goal is highly commendable.

SDG 11 should also be seen in connection with the adoption of the New Urban Agenda at UN-Habitat III in Quito in October 2016. The shared vision of cities expressed in this latter document partly mirrors the content of SDG 11. The specific relationship of these two documents with respect to one another is pretty much an open question. Both are not legally binding in the sense that concrete obligations for UN member states would flow from them. Both documents are aspirational in the sense that they set forth a certain vision – in the case of the SDGs, of global governance in general, in the case of the Habitat III declaration, in the context of urban governance. This might seem to imply a *lex specialis* relationship in a loose sense (as neither document is legally binding). Ideally, Habitat III could thus be used to further flesh out the content of SDG 11.[51] For example, the Heads of State and Government, Ministers and High Representatives who gathered at Habitat III announced that '[w]e share a vision of cities for all, referring to the equal use and enjoyment of cities and human settlements, seeking to promote *inclusivity* and ensure that all inhabitants, of present and future generations, ... are able to inhabit and produce just, *safe*, healthy, accessible, affordable, *resilient*, and *sustainable* cities and human settlements ...'. All four targets of SDG 11, and some additional targets, are present in this statement.

The ambition of Goal 11 arguably lies in its 10 subsidiary targets addressing matters as general as climate mitigation and adaptation, as well as matters as specific as the increased zoning and protection of open spaces and improved air quality, the preservation of cultural heritage resources, and waste management.[52] Far-ranging as the list of sub-targets

---

[51] As a side note, the practical workings of such a relationship are seriously hindered, however, by the verbose form of the Habitat III declaration.

[52] Countries of the world agreed to the following: by 2030, ensure access for all to *adequate, safe and affordable housing* and *basic services* and the *upgrading of slums*; by 2030, provide *access to safe, affordable, accessible and sustainable transport systems* for all, improving road safety, notably by expanding public transport, with special attention to the needs of those in vulnerable situations, women, children, persons with disabilities and older persons; by 2030, enhance *inclusive and sustainable urbanization* and *capacity for participatory,*

in SDG 11 appears to be at first glance, it pales in comparison to the hypertrophic 'New Urban Agenda'. In 175 paragraphs, a shared vision, principles and commitments, a call for action, an implementation plan and provisions for follow-up and review are extensively mapped out. Yet the reader cannot avoid a high level of frustration with this document: due to the great many principles and commitments expressed in this outcome document, the clear message and ultimately, the potential efficacy of this document, are severely inhibited. Virtually everything which is only remotely relevant for good urban governance today is mentioned somewhere and often in several places. This obscures rather than clarifies, and it leaves the reader puzzled as to the exact meaning of the different invocations of one and the same idea. Behind all the talk of an 'urban paradigm shift'[53] there does not seem to be much substance.

9.4 AN ATTEMPT TO SQUARE THE CIRCLE? INHERENT CONTRADICTIONS OF SDG 11

Returning the focus to SDG 11, there does not seem to be anything particularly objectionable with respect to its content. The main targets, the inclusiveness, resilience, safety and sustainability of cities come across as desirable maxims, and they seem to be in tune with general

integrated and sustainable human settlement planning and management in all countries; strengthen efforts to *protect and safeguard the world's cultural and natural heritage*; by 2030, significantly *reduce the number of deaths and the number of people affected and substantially decrease the direct economic losses relative to global gross domestic product caused by disasters*, including water-related disasters, with a focus on protecting the poor and people in vulnerable situations; by 2030, reduce the *adverse per capita environmental impact of cities*, including by paying special attention to *air quality and municipal and other waste management*; by 2030, provide *universal access to safe, inclusive and accessible, green and public spaces*, in particular for women and children, older persons and persons with disabilities; support *positive economic, social and environmental links between urban, peri-urban and rural areas* by strengthening national and regional development planning; by 2020, substantially *increase the number of cities and human settlements adopting and implementing integrated policies and plans towards inclusion, resource efficiency, mitigation and adaptation to climate change*, resilience to disasters, and develop and implement, in line with the Sendai Framework for Disaster Risk Reduction 2015–2030, holistic disaster risk management at all levels; and support least developed countries, including through financial and technical assistance, in *building sustainable and resilient buildings utilizing local materials*.

[53] Para 15.

trends of global governance. Yet one wonders whether SDG 11 and its subsidiary targets are not torn by inherent contradictions. Such contradictions will certainly pose additional hurdles for the implementation of this goal.[54] But even aside from these operational hurdles, one must also question the conceptual clarity of SDG 11. This might at first glance be a concern primarily of scholars, whereas politics and global governance are probably less concerned with conceptual clarity. However, language matters, and it often has clear normative implications: the way in which SDG 11 therefore frames the state of the art of contemporary good urban governance, or its lack of fostering of conceptual clarity, remain a concern, as we explain below.

When analysing the interrelationship between the different individual goals of SDG 11, one first and foremost notes that its four main attributes are in and of themselves rather wide and elastic notions. Inclusiveness raises primarily questions of social justice and cohesion. It may also relate to participatory matters. In comparison, resilience is a fairly novel term in the realm of global governance. Originally coined in the context of neuro-sciences, it refers to the capacity of structures to swing back after attacks and disruptions.[55] In recent years, it has gained traction as a concept addressing a blend of issues which are usually associated with safety and sustainability – the two other attributes of good urban governance raised in SDG 11. Whereas safety can be understood to refer to physical safety, and thereby also to security, the notion of sustainability is probably the broadest among all four goals. That it plays a dominant role in the construction of SDG 11 can be inferred from the fact that the entire SDG document is about sustainable development. In a sense, therefore, all SDGs flesh out a contemporary meaning of sustainable development. For SDG 11 this does not mean that the mention of sustainability is superfluous, however. For one, sustainability as it is usually understood covers economic, ecological and social dimensions. Not all of them could be subsumed under one of the other three attributes of SDG 11. What is more, the contribution of SDG 11 arguably lies less in the adoption of different substantive standards for urban governance, than in zooming in on the city as a specific site for global governance in the twenty-first century.

Beyond the elasticity of the concepts employed in SDG 11, there may also be a considerable degree of friction between its various sub-goals.

---

[54] See further the discussion below.

[55] For a thorough discussion of the conceptual implications of 'resilience' see B. Gleeson, *The Urban Condition* (Routledge, 2014) 95–107.

For instance, attempts to make a city safe might be in conflict with notions of inclusiveness. Inclusiveness might call for a maximization of participation opportunities of all individuals present in a given city, regardless of their citizenship and formal voting rights at the national and local levels. Also, security concerns can lead to a dissolution of informal settlements whose inhabitants are then pushed further out towards the margins of a given city, or even beyond. Particularly in megacities of the Global South, there is an ongoing struggle to define city limits. Informal settlements are often found not only within administrative city boundaries, but also on the margins of the city. The decision whether or not to extend city limits is often an emotionally charged political process. Legalizing informal settlements within the administrative boundaries of a given city might mean a considerable improvement in the quality of the lives of the inhabitants of these informal settlements, yet existing social and political problems in the informal settlements *extra muros* might prove to be an obstacle to the legalization of settlement structures and the granting of property titles. The image of an existing city as safe and sustainable might be tarnished if the existing governance problems no longer just pertain to an illegal settlement, but need to be addressed by formal administrative avenues.[56] This is just one example of how different sub-targets of SDG 11 might come into conflict with one another.

Another example would extend to irregular migrants who seek refuge in a city, but who are exposed as targets for security policies which, for their part, might find justification in the call to construct a safe city. In cities all over the world there is a trend towards the privatization of public spaces in the name of safety and security, which can take on various forms. Examples of privatization include the provision of security services by private actors or the creation of walled-off business and residential areas. Sometimes space which used to be public is transferred into private property, which is still open to the public. Its use, however, is then governed by private law regulation and no longer by public law principles.[57] Whereas this trend of privatization might alleviate the overstretched budgets of local governments and might help to fill urban governance gaps through forms of public–private-partnerships (PPPs), it

[56] On the inherent contradictions and challenges of such processes of legalization see L. Eslava, *Local Space, Global Life. The Everyday Operation of International Law and Development* (Cambridge University Press, 2015) 190 *et seq.*

[57] See further D. Moeckli, *Exclusion from Public Space. A Comparative Constitutional Analysis* (Cambridge University Press, 2016) 52 *et seq.*

can also lead to exclusionary politics which stand in the way of participatory processes, thus potentially curtailing the inclusiveness of city governance.

Another open question pertains to the relationship between resilience and sustainability. As already noted, resilience is the new kid on the block of global governance, and it partly overlaps with sustainability. But whereas the latter has a forward-looking tendency in order to preserve the global carrying capacity of the Earth for future generations, resilience has a more reactive character to it.[58] It is all about bouncing back after a given event, which could include anything from a terrorist attack to an environmental catastrophe. The question is how the sustainability discourse is affected by the introduction of resilience into the debate. The indicators adopted for the implementation of the SDGs do not seem to go down the route of formally including resilience as a critical consideration. In fact, resilience only appears once in the list of targets associated with SDG 11. Target 11.b sets out that by 2020 the number of cities and human settlements that have adopted and implemented integrated policies and plans, also with respect to resilience to disasters, are to be substantially increased. This is further specified both in the target and in the indicators with a reference to the Sendai Framework for Disaster Risk Reduction 2015–2030, which predominantly focuses on natural disasters.

The broader point here is that cities and their governments might find themselves confronted with a set of objectives which might not always be achievable, at least not at the same time. By referring to inclusiveness, resilience, safety and sustainability simultaneously, SDG 11 is turned into a cauldron of concepts, none of which is sufficiently defined in its own right or even delineated from the others. Moreover, as with several other SDGs interrogated in this volume, what is *not* addressed in SDG 11 is equally worrying. Human rights, for example, are not mentioned in the context of SDG 11. Instead, the vague notion of inclusiveness is deployed. It would have been more meaningful to have referred to the human rights of all city dwellers than to the less well-defined and (possibly) normatively inferior notion of inclusiveness. This ties in with the generally vague references to human rights in the 2030 Agenda for Sustainable Development.[59] Human rights are mentioned in the UN General Assembly Resolution a number of times. However, they mostly appear in the *Transforming our World* outcome document, the section

---

58 Gleeson, above n 55, 101.

59 See Collins, Chapter 4 in this volume, for a comprehensive discussion.

on means and implementation and the follow-up and review process.[60] In the SDGs themselves, there is only a single explicit mention of the trope of human rights which concerns target 4.7 ('By 2030, ensure that all learners acquire the knowledge and skills needed to promote sustainable development, including, among others, through education for sustainable development and sustainable lifestyles, human rights, gender equality, promotion of a culture of peace and non-violence, global citizenship and appreciation of cultural diversity and of culture's contribution to sustainable development'). Particularly noteworthy is the absence of human rights from Goal 16 – which mentions the rule of law at the national and international levels as a target and which sets forth that there should be equal access to justice for all. The protection of fundamental freedoms is at least mentioned in target 16.10. But if the SDGs are really built on the idea of human rights – as mentioned in the preamble and the outcome document – why not also integrate more coherently the very concept in the SDGs themselves? What is more, reference to the protection of fundamental rights is also considerably weakened by the by-line that this shall only be ensured 'in accordance with national legislation' – hardly the kind of invocation of human rights that would lend credence to the view that the SDGs are permeated by the ideals of human rights protection.[61]

9.5 THE THORNY ROAD TO IMPLEMENTATION

It is not only its conceptual lack of clarity which leads to political and operational challenges as far as SDG 11 is concerned. Some of the inherent challenges include conflicts of interest and questions surrounding the data and funds necessary for the implementation of the goal and its subsidiary objectives (as has been shown, these are hard to identify, and they could be difficult to coordinate and directly link to development interventions). Save for multi-level urban and rural planning, Goal 11 is

[60] UN Doc. A/RES/70/1, preambular para 3, op. paras 3, 8, 10, 19, 20, 29, 35, 67 and 74.

[61] See further on this N. Arajärvi, 'The Rule of Law in the 2030 Agenda', text following footnote 122, *KFG Working Paper Series*, No. 9, Berlin Potsdam Research Group 'The International Rule of Law – Rise or Decline?' Berlin, June 2017, available at <http://kfg-intlaw.de/Publications/Working_Papers/working_papers_einzel.php?ID=46> accessed 26 July 2017; for a more positive view about the relationship between the SDGs and human rights see V.P. Nanda, 'The Journey from the Millennium Development Goals to Sustainable Development Goals' (2016) *Denver Journal of International Law and Policy* 44, 389.

quiet on the fact that cities are overseen by city governments and that good urban governance critically underpins the pursuit of cities that are safe, resilient, sustainable and inclusive. This, combined with the complexity of the forces that really drive urban development outcomes, suggests that Goal 11 may not immediately be able to meet the expectations it creates; a reality which is arguably equally true for other SDGs as well. There are highly complex political and (socio) economic forces behind urban problems such as air pollution, inadequate housing, poor waste management and effective disaster risk reduction.

No Goal 11 indicators have been developed to reflect the *quality* of city policies or plans together with *quantitative* measures such as improved access to adequate housing and access to affordable and sustainable transport. Enormous differences in the challenges facing cities, and the resources available to deal with them, mean that the principles of and benchmarks for universality, integration and transformation as suggested in Goal 11 will have to be realized and met differentially within and across nations. This is arguably why no concrete global indicators have been adopted to start with. Going forward, country and city-specific targets and indicators may have to be agreed upon in a wider framework of reporting on progress with compliance with Goal 11.

9.6 CONCLUSION AND OUTLOOK

The urban reality across the world has resulted in a discourse that focuses on challenges and limitations – however, the SDGs suggest that we should not be held hostage to a discourse that limits our sense of the possible. Despite the inherent conflicts of interest and potential implementation challenges, Goal 11 calls for a very important mind shift as far as it concerns the world's understanding of the linkages between urbanization, cities and the pursuit of sustainable development. It would be a mistake to regard 'local commons' as being less important than those at national and global levels.[62] What is required is an effective linking of scales which realizes the potential of the city as a strategic site for sustainable development in the twenty-first century.

Yet, one of the difficulties with Goal 11 is that there are no standardized metrics for its inherent objectives (including measurements for good urban governance). Furthermore, the SDG process has introduced only a limited number of subsidiary urban targets and indicators for what is

[62] B.H. Weston and D. Bollier, *Green Governance* (Cambridge University Press, 2013) 236.

essentially a vast and complex domain within which states are one of many governance actors alongside the private sector and members of local communities.[63] While it is widely understood that poverty is one of the key causes of urban problems, especially cities' inability to adequately provide basic and other services and failures to secure 'the right to the city',[64] poverty does not feature in Goal 11.[65]

However, overall, the focus on cities as a spatial nexus in the global pursuit of the SDGs is an acknowledgment of the linkages between the three dimensions of sustainable development and the hybridity of global governance. It is rather curious, though, that no mention is made of the institutional dimension (especially local governance and land management and finance management capacity) – all of which are critical to meet the 10 subsidiary targets, especially in the developing world. It is here where urban challenges are often the greatest and local governance institutions the weakest. In sum, we believe that the importance of what Bulkeley and Betsill call 'the way in which local areas and economies are governed' seems to be underplayed in the SDGs.[66] One would have expected Goal 11 to be much clearer on the fact that the countries of the world may have to define, among other things, realistic institutional improvements at the city scale and in national urban development plans and budgets. Post the SDGs' adoption, changes in domestic urban law systems (and their enforcement) may now have to stimulate and facilitate reaching the Goal 11 targets. This is a tall, but attainable, order where states and their local authorities commit to good urban governance as an integral part of the global pursuit of a more sustainable and socially just society.

---

[63] Many of the provisions on which city life depends do not form part of Goal 11, e.g. massive infrastructure (e.g. electricity for elevators) and institutional support (e.g. hospitals and water purifying plants) – apartment buildings, vast sewage systems, entire electricity grids dependent on computerized management and vulnerable to breakdown. See S. Sassen, 'A Focus on Cities Takes Us Beyond Existing Governance Frameworks' in Stiglitz and Kaldor (eds), above n 9, 244.

[64] See M. Pieterse, 'Development, the Right to the City and the Legal and Constitutional Responsibilities of Local Government in South Africa' (2014) *South African Law Journal* 131, 149–177; M. Pieterse, 'The Right to the City and the Urban Environment: Re-imagining Section 24 of the 1996 Constitution' (2014) *South African Public Law Journal* 29, 175–193.

[65] Poverty is, however, the focus of Goal 1 of the SDGs.

[66] Bulkeley and Betsill, above n 7, 43.

10. The environment and the Sustainable Development Goals: 'We are on a road to nowhere'*

Werner Scholtz and Michelle Barnard

10.1 INTRODUCTION

On 25 September 2015 world leaders adopted the 2030 Agenda for Sustainable Development in the form of United Nations General Assembly Resolution 70/1. The 17 Sustainable Development Goals (SDGs) and 169 Targets embodied in the Agenda cover a broad range of sustainable development issues. The SDGs build on the advances made by the Millennium Development Goals (MDGs). Differences exist, however, between SDGs and MDGs. While the MDGs were primarily concerned with the promotion of development and the alleviation of poverty and focused on remedying developmental issues of developing nations, the SDGs focus strongly on the role of both developed and developing nations in achieving the global objective of sustainable development. As such, Agenda 2030 accordingly focuses on several key environmental, social and economic issues. The Agenda does not contain a separate or exclusive environmental goal, but SDGs 13, 14 and 15 as well as SDG 6 constitute an 'environmental cluster', which addresses several key issues in environmental law, such as climate change,[1] biodiversity,[2] the sustainable management of water resources,[3]

---

* Professor Scholtz's contribution to this chapter is based on the research supported by the National Research Foundation of South Africa (Grant Number: 106059).

[1] Goal 13.

[2] Goal 15.

[3] Goal 6. See McIntyre, Chapter 8 in this volume.

and the conservation and sustainable use of marine resources.[4] Furthermore, various other Goals include explicit references to environmental matters.[5]

At first glance it seems that the SDGs accord an important position to the 'environment' under the chapeau of sustainable development and they may constitute an important milestone for the international environmental agenda to respond to the ever-increasing environmental degradation that the Earth faces. In this regard, it is important to recall the opinion of Galizzi that 'the environment is a secondary, if not marginal, concern for the international community in the twenty-first century'.[6] This, despite efforts such as the United Nations Conference on the Human Environment of 1972 (Stockholm Conference), which put the environment centre stage as it focused specifically on environmental issues.

The introduction of sustainable development in the Brundtland Report linked environment and development, and at the United Nations Conference on Environment and Development (UNCED) of 1992 (Rio Conference) environment and development enjoyed equally important attention. The World Summit on Sustainable Development (WSSD) of 2002 'ended up focusing mainly on development and only marginally addressing environmental issues'.[7] The regression in the prominence of the importance of the environment was followed through in the Outcome Document of the World Summit of 2005,[8] where the environment is dealt with under 'Chapter II: Development', which is indicative of the lack of a strong political commitment to a robust international environmental agenda.

---

[4] Goal 14.

[5] Goal 1 (No poverty): links ending poverty with affording equal rights to the environment and improving the resilience of developing nations to environmental shocks and disasters; Goal 2 (End hunger): ecosystems must not be diminished due to unsustainable agricultural practices; Goal 3 (Good health and well-being): end water, soil and air pollution; Goal 8 (Decent work and economic growth): decouple economic growth from environmental degradation; Goal 9 (Industry, innovation and infrastructure): environmentally sound technologies and industrial processes; Goal 11 (Sustainable cities): reduce environmental impact of cities; Goal 12 (Responsible consumption and production): protect natural resources and increased environmentally sound management of waste; and Goal 17 (Partnership for the goals): transfer and develop environmentally sound technologies in developing countries.

[6] P. Galizzi, 'From Stockholm to New York, via Rio and Johannesburg: Has the Environment Lost Its Way on the Global Agenda' (2005) *Fordham International Law Journal* 29, 1002.

[7] *Ibid*, at 71.

[8] GA Resolution 60/1 of 2005.

Hence, it is important to determine how Agenda 2030 relates to the international environmental protection agenda. One must bear in mind that Agenda 2030 pursues the promotion of sustainable development and embodies goals that pertain to the environmental, social and economic pillars of sustainable development. Sustainable development implies a balancing act between the aforementioned pillars. However, it is precisely this aspect of sustainable development that attracts critique, because it is not clear how the different values should be balanced in a particular case. The relative and reconciliatory nature of sustainable development, current state practice and developmental practices, as well as the continued decay of environmental quality, imply that the predominant importance of economic interests often trumps environmental considerations.

The new agenda seemingly marks a distinct change in how common challenges are to be approached by the global community, most notably by explicitly recognizing the need to transform humankind's perception of, and interaction with, planet Earth and the components comprising our natural environment.[9] Agenda 2030 embodies a strategic approach to global environmental governance consisting of a set of common environmental indicators and targets against which progress on environmental governance is assessed. Agenda 2030's strong commitment to the environment is evident from the number of environmental Targets (89 out of 169) it contains as well as the manner in which it contextualizes the environmental dimension of sustainable development within a broader set of issues.[10] The foregoing points towards Agenda 2030 playing a significantly important role in directing current and future global environmental governance. It is therefore imperative to determine whether Agenda 2030 merely subjugates the environment to economic development or whether it provides the environment agenda with a rightful place in the promotion of international sustainable development.

In the process of exploring the foregoing a number of issues deserve attention. In the first instance the normative status of Agenda 2030 and its Goals is investigated in order to discern its potential influence on the progressive development of international environmental law. While the impact of Agenda 2030 is set to permeate global environmental politics on a broader scale, the focus of this chapter will fall exclusively on international environmental law. Following on from this, the discussion

---

[9] See <https://www.sei-international.org/2030agenda> accessed 31 July 2017.

[10] T.F. McInerney, *UNEP, International Environmental Governance, and the 2030 Sustainable Development Agenda* (United Nations Environment Programme 2017) 2.

will turn to a reflection on the nature of the relationship between international law and the SDGs – focusing specifically on international environmental law and the Goals. Accordingly, we interrogate the extent to which the so-called environmental cluster of the SDGs contains explicit and/or implicit references to specific international legal instruments, thereby not only strengthening the global application of these instruments, but also in turn providing for a firmer legal status of the SDGs themselves and ways to strengthen them. In the final instance the discussion will determine whether the focus on sustainable development is conducive to a robust international environmental agenda.

10.2 NORMATIVE NIHILISM OR ASPIRATIONAL OPPORTUNISM

The potential influence of Agenda 2030 on the progressive development of international environmental law warrants a determination of its normative status. Agenda 2030 was adopted by the United Nations General Assembly (UNGA) as a non-binding resolution. It is common cause, however, that UNGA Resolutions may (and often do) contain soft law norms that could have normative relevance.[11] Soft law has played a major role in the development of modern international environmental law.[12] The Rio Declaration on Environment and Development 1992 is exemplary of the way in which a soft law General Assembly resolution contributed to the progressive development of international environmental law principles.[13] The SDGs constitute a political declaration with mere political commitments, which, according to French, do not amount to soft law norms.[14] French offers two arguments in support of this viewpoint. The first is that in order to qualify as soft law, the SDG Agenda needs to exhibit a sense of movement of contribution to formal legality in order to facilitate the progressive evolution of international law and the intention

[11] J. Friedrich, *International Environmental Law 'Soft Law': The Functions and Limits of Nonbinding Instruments in International Environmental Governance and Law* (Springer, 2013) 23.

[12] G. Palmer, 'New Ways to Make International Environmental Law' (1992) *American Journal of International Law* 86(2), 259.

[13] *Rio Declaration on Environment and Development*, 13 June 1992, UN Doc. A/CONF.151/26.

[14] D. French, 'The Global Goals: Formalism Foregone, Contested Legality and "Re-Imaginings of International Law"' (2017) *Ethiopian Yearbook of International Law* 164–165.

to regulate in the absence of hard law.[15] He concludes that the intention to regulate and contribute to formal legality is absent. This is due to the purpose of the Goals being neither prescriptive nor regulatory, and the lack of any clear intention of becoming so. The rhetoric of the Goals is too idealized and idealistic to be easily contained within limited models of governance and regulation, and they therefore fall short of the soft law description. This speaks to the second point of criticism French levels against the SDGs as soft law constructs, namely that they do not challenge the international community, but rather embody a 'rhetorical commitment' to change, and as such the politics of their construction and implementation also disqualify their recognition as soft law.[16] Such a dismissive outcome of the normative assessment of the SDGs begs the question whether the SDGs have any legal worth in relation to international environmental law.

Persson et al seem more inclined to endow the SDGs with some form of normative value as they situate the SDGs in international law 'at the softest end of the "hard-to-soft" continuum' because the SDGs do not contain binding legal commitments to be achieved and furthermore present vague and aspirational targets rather than define specific outcomes.[17] The authors do, however, recognize that some of the Targets are relatively precise.[18] Kim also views the SDGs as political goals. He states, however, that at least some SDGs or Targets may have a soft law status.[19] He finds support for his viewpoint in the substance of the SDGs, the process, and the form in which they were adopted. He argues that the SDGs are grounded in international law and in some instances reflect international custom as well as international agreements. The intergovernmental process[20] that delivered the SDGs was adopted as a resolution of the UNGA and it is trite that these resolutions may embody soft law. Kim therefore views the SDGs and Targets as a 'subset of

---

15 *Ibid*, at 16.

16 M.E. Salomon, *Global Responsibility for Human Rights: World Poverty and the Development of International Law* (Oxford University Press, 2007) 57.

17 A. Persson, N. Weitz and M. Nilsson, 'Follow-up and Review of the Sustainable Development Goals: Alignment vs. Internalization' (2016) *Review of European Community and International Environmental Law* 25(1), 59, 60.

18 For example, Target 3.4, which relates to the reduction of premature mortality.

19 R.E. Kim, 'The Nexus between International Law and the Sustainable Development Goals' (2016) *Review of European Community and International Environmental Law* 25(1), 16.

20 P.S. Chasek, L.M. Wagner, F. Leone et al, 'Getting to 2030: Negotiating the Post-2015 Sustainable Development Agenda' (2016) *Review of European Community and International Environmental Law* 25(1), 5.

existing intergovernmental commitments' which may be used to create a framework of coordination for existing obligations.[21]

Spijkers supports Kim's assessment based on his analysis of SDG 6 as he aptly remarks that 'the SDGs will be elevated from purely political commitments to legally relevant obligations when they can be … "attached" to the norms of international water law'.[22] Spijkers argues that the SDGs, in particular SDG 6, could, for example, influence the interpretation of the Convention on the Law of the Non-navigational Uses of International Watercourses, 1997 (UN Watercourses Convention). As such the interpretation of the UN Watercourses Convention, in line with SDG 6, may constitute subsequent practice as defined in terms of Article 31(3)(b) of the Vienna Convention on the Law of Treaties of 1969.[23] Furthermore, the SDGs may be used to confirm evolving customary practice. Spijkers also views SDG 6 as a catalyst for the progressive development of the ecosystems approach in international water law.[24] Thus, it may be deducted from Spijkers' arguments that some SDGs may have some normative value and could be classified as soft law.

Lode et al consider the SDGs as soft law in their analysis of the relationship between SDGs and international air quality in international law.[25] Currently, this issue is being dealt with at a regional level and the universal nature of SDGs may elevate the issue to the global level and serve as a catalyst for a future legally binding international agreement on air pollution, and as such may contribute to the development of an international law for the atmosphere.[26]

Clearly consensus exists among scholars that SDGs are non-binding goals, but they disagree on the normative status of Agenda 2030. We are

---

[21] Kim, above n 19, 16.

[22] O. Spijkers, 'The Cross-Fertilization Between the Sustainable Development Goals and International Water Law' (2016) *Review of European Community and International Environmental Law* 25(1), 39.

[23] This provision deals with the general rule of interpretation of treaties and provides that 'any subsequent practice in the application of the treaty which establishes the agreement of the parties regarding its interpretation' shall be taken into account together with the context.

[24] SDG 6.6 and SDG 15 include references to this approach. See O. McIntyre, 'The Emergence of an "Ecosystem Approach" to the Protection of International Watercourses under International Law' (2004) *Review of European Community and International Environmental Law* 13(1), 1.

[25] B. Lode, P. Schönberger and P. Toussaint, 'Clean Air for All by 2030? Air Quality in the 2030 Agenda and in International Law' (2016) *Review of European Community and International Environmental Law* 25(1), 27, 38.

[26] *Ibid.*

of the view that at least specific SDGs may be classified as soft law norms. The reason for this is that Agenda 2030 indeed conforms to the intrinsic aspects of soft law.[27] Agenda 2030 was adopted through an intergovernmental process in the form of a UNGA Resolution and it expresses the common expectation of sustainable development for international relations between states. As such it was created by subjects of international law. Furthermore, Agenda 2030 does not stem from a formal source of law as prescribed in Article 38 of the Statute of the International Court of Justice and lacks a binding character. Very importantly, Agenda 2030 was not adopted in a normative vacuum as it affirms its commitment and is to be implemented in a manner that is consistent with the rights and obligations of states under international law.[28] It is also guided by the purposes and principles of the Charter of the United Nations, 1945 (UN Charter).[29] Agenda 2030 has a close proximity to international law and at least some of the SDGs have the potential to contribute to the development of international law as indicated by Lode et al and Spijkers. It is this interplay with international law that increases the normative influence of soft law instruments, such as the SDGs.[30]

Hence, SDGs may have normative consequences in the sense that the Goals may contribute to the development of existing international law and more specifically in how they build on their predecessors – the MDGs.[31] To this end, the SDGs may be used to clarify and develop the

---

[27] D. Thürer, 'Soft Law' in R. Wolfrum (ed), *Max Planck Encyclopedia of Public International Law* (Oxford University Press, 2012) para 3.

[28] Agenda 2030, para 18.

[29] *Ibid*, para 8.

[30] Friedrich, above n 11, 445.

[31] Both sets of Goals are widely considered to fall into the category of soft law in that neither the SDGs nor the MDGs generate any legally binding obligations on states. Some MDGs do, however, satisfy the criteria of customary international law norms, which means that while not necessarily codified in treaty form and have become sufficiently widely accepted in practice that they are arguably binding upon governments despite their original intent not to be binding. The frequent reiteration of governments' commitment to the MDGs might be seen to constitute the basis for arguing that the Goals have indeed assumed the status of a binding legal obligation. This argument correlates with the viewpoint of many commentators regarding the legal status of the Universal Declaration of Human Rights. The UDHR was adopted on the agreed basis that it did not generate any legally binding obligations but was then claimed to have attained the status of customary law as a result of being so consistently endorsed and invoked. This also speaks to the arguments put forward by among others, Boyle and French that the intention to contribute to international law-making be seen as a criterion of soft law. See B. Simma and P. Alston, 'The Sources of

meaning of treaties. The aforementioned analyses of Schrijver and Lode et al constitute examples of the manner in which SDGs may trigger further developments in relation to the ecosystems approach and the international law of the atmosphere. Thus, a determination of the normative status of the Agenda requires an investigation of specific SDGs and their potential contribution to international law. It is only in this instance that a judgement may be made on the normative influence of the SDGs.

Furthermore, the SDGs may, even in the absence of a normative value, have several consequences for the international law framework. Agenda 2030 offers an expression of objectives that affirm in various instances current international obligations in an 'unequal set of universal, integrative and ambitious aspirations that offer a shared agenda for transformation'.[32] Agenda 2030 formulates the objectives under the auspices of sustainable development and recognizes that the international development agenda must be concerned with an integrative approach to the three pillars of sustainable development and that mere development is not sufficient.

The SDGs affirm the key responsibility that national governments have for the implementation thereof in conjunction with a Global Partnership.[33] The monitoring of implementation should take place in terms of 'follow-up and review at the national, regional and global levels'.[34] A global set of 230 indicators to monitor progress proposed by the Inter-agency and Expert Group on SDGs was agreed on at the 47th Session of the United Nations Statistical Commission.[35] Furthermore, the UN High-Level Political Forum on Sustainable Development will oversee national and thematic reviews of the implementation of Agenda 2030. The review process allows for a global deliberation on the pursuit of aspirational objectives and has the potential to bolster national and

Human Rights Law: Custom, Jus Cogens, General Principles' (1988) *Australian Year Book of International Law*, 12, 82; P. Alston, 'Ships Passing in the Night: The Current State of the Human Rights and Development Debates seen through the Lens of the Millennium Development Goals' (2005) *Human Rights Quarterly* 27(3), 755, 774; A.E. Boyle, 'Some Reflections on the Relationship of Treaties and Soft Law' (1999) *International and Comparative Law Quarterly* 48(4), 901; and French, above n 14, 1.

32 Persson et al, above n 17, 59.

33 Paras 39–46. See also Cooper and French, Chapter 12 in this volume.

34 Para 47. For a discussion: Persson et al, above n 17, 59–68.

35 UN, 'UN Statistical Commission Agrees on Global Indicator Framework' (11 March 2016) <http://www.un.org/sustainabledevelopment/blog/2016/03/un-statistical-commission-endorses-global-indicator-framework/> accessed 7 February 2017.

international initiatives towards sustainable development.[36] The proposed review of the implementation of SDGs may therefore exert pressure on states to pursue 'compliance' (even if the SDGs are non-binding). The reputation of states may serve as an incentive to pursue the implementation of SDGs through national and international initiatives.

10.3 INTERNATIONAL ENVIRONMENTAL LAW AND AGENDA 2030

While the link between international law and Agenda 2030 is evident considering the nature of the relationship between them, the extent to which the Goals themselves as well as their Targets refer explicitly or implicitly to specific international legal instruments is a topic which warrants further discussion. The Agenda's declaration is guided by a number of international instruments, most notably the UN Charter,[37] the Universal Declaration of Human Rights, 1948[38] and the Rio Declaration.[39] This provision makes clear that the drafters of the declaration of Agenda 2030 had in mind that the resulting SDGs – individually and collectively – would find their legal basis in international law.

The explicit incorporation of international legal instruments in the SDGs themselves did, however, not occur to the extent that it could have. Evidence of the foregoing is that only three international conventions are mentioned explicitly in any one of the 16 SDGs and their 169 Targets. The three conventions mentioned and the Goals or Targets they pertain to are: the UN Framework Convention on Climate Change, 1992 (Goal 13); the Framework Convention on Tobacco Control, 2003 (Target 3.a) and the UN Convention on the Law of the Sea, 1982 (Target 14.c). While no reference to international human rights instruments is found in any of the SDGs,[40] it is, however, possible to 'read in' a number of international agreements that specific Targets under various SDGs reflect.

The extent or manner in which international environmental law is reflected – either tacitly or expressly – by the SDGs warrants further

---

[36] This is not a given. The vague nature of the political 'commitments' may result in uncertainty concerning what should be monitored.

[37] *Charter of the United Nations*, 24 October 1945, 1 UNTS XVI.

[38] *Universal Declaration of Human Rights*, G.A. Res. 217 (III) A, UN Doc. A/RES/3/217.

[39] *Rio Declaration on Environment and Development*, 13 June 1992, UN Doc. A/CONF.151/26.

[40] See also Collins, Chapter 4 in this volume.

attention. Here we will focus our attention on the SDGs relating to the environment or the so-called environmental goal cluster.[41] This cluster is comprised of: SDG 6 ('Ensure availability and sustainable management of water and sanitation for all');[42] SDG 13 ('Take urgent action to combat climate change and its impacts'); SDG 14 ('Conserve and sustainably use the oceans, seas and marine resources for sustainable development'); and SDG 15 ('Protect, restore and promote sustainable use of terrestrial ecosystems, sustainably manage forests, combat desertification, and halt and reverse land degradation and halt biodiversity loss'). In the absence of an overarching environmental goal, these four distinct environmental SDGs may reinforce the division of the global environment into three arbitrary components, namely the atmosphere, land and water sources.

At face value the distinct environmental SDGs operate in the absence of an overarching environmental Goal – a situation which seemingly divides the global environment into arbitrary categories. This division seems to embody a step back from the MDG framework[43] and is viewed by some scholars as counterproductive to achieving a holistic approach to the protection of the subsystems that collectively comprise the environment.[44] Despite the apparent division between the four environmental SDGs, some measure of connection/integration may be found within the Targets associated with the Goals and especially those international legal instruments they relate to.

10.3.1 SDG 13 and International Law on Climate Change

SDG 13 states that the UN Framework Convention on Climate Change (UNFCCC) is the primary international, intergovernmental forum for negotiating the global response to climate change.[45] Reciprocal acknowledgement of the SDGs by the UNFCCC regime can be found in Decision 1/CP.21 adopted at the 21st Conference of the Parties (COP) to the UNFCCC held in Paris in 2015, where the COP welcomed the adoption of the SDGs – especially SDG 13.[46] The COP of the UNFCCC

---

41 Kim, above n 19, 18.

42 For the purposes of this discussion focus will fall only on the aspect of water availability and sustainable management and not on sanitation.

43 MDG 7 pertained to environmental sustainability and did not refer to separate or specific components of the natural environment.

44 Kim, above n 19, 19.

45 Agenda 2030, above n 28, para 31.

46 UNFCCC, *Decision 1/CP.21, Adoption of the Paris Agreement* (UN Doc. FCCC/CP/2015/10/Add.1) preamble.

has played a major role in the progressive development of the international climate change regime, and the explicit acknowledgement of the UNFCCC's institutional bodies by SDG 13 necessarily implies an acceptance of the international institutions and instruments the COP and the Secretariat use to govern.[47]

10.3.2 SDG 6 and International Law on Water

SDG 6 on the other hand does not contain any explicit reference to any international legal instruments related to access to water or sustainable water management despite the existence of a number of international legal instruments on these topics. What is evident from the wording of the Targets related to the achievement of SDG 6 is that two distinct but related fields of international law, namely international human rights law and international water law, are implicitly referred to. International human rights law provides for access to water and sanitation, while international water law regulates the use of freshwater resources.[48]

Let us first consider Target 6.1, which aims to achieve universal and equitable access to safe and affordable drinking water for all.[49] This Target is reminiscent of international human rights law and more specifically the right to water as derived from Article 11(1) of the International Covenant on Economic, Social and Cultural Rights, 1966 (ICESCR).[50] In terms of General Comment No 15 of the UN Committee on Social, Cultural and Economic Rights,[51] the right to water is essential for securing an adequate standard of living, a statement which has been affirmed by the UNGA and the Human Rights Council.[52] The Committee elaborates on what should be

---

[47] These should be seen to include international institutions such as the Montreal Protocol on Substances that Deplete the Ozone Layer, 1987; the Convention on Long-Range Transboundary Air Pollution, 1979; and biodiversity-related conventions.

[48] International Institute for Sustainable Development in collaboration with the United Nations Environmental Programme, 'Summary of the First International Environmental Forum for Basin Organisations' (2014) *Basin Organisation Forum Bulletin* 227(1), 6.

[49] Target 6.2, which relates to access to sanitation, also falls under the scope and ambit of international human rights – an aspect which will be touched upon in subsequent sections.

[50] The right to an adequate standard of living.

[51] United Nations Committee on Economic, Social and Cultural Rights, *General Comment No 15: The Right to Water* (UN Doc. E/C.12/2002/11) para 3.

[52] UN Human Rights Council Resolution 15/9 (2010) para 3; UNGA Resolution 68/157 (2013) para 2; UNGA Resolution 70/169 (2015). Note that the

included under the right to water and comes to the conclusion that this right entitles everyone to sufficient, safe, acceptable, physically accessible and affordable water for personal and domestic use.[53]

In much the same way as Target 6.1, Target 6.2 ('access to adequate and equitable sanitation') also contains an implicit reference to international human rights law in the form of the right to sanitation as derived from the right to an adequate standard of living as well as the right to adequate housing and health.[54]

Target 6.3 ('reducing water pollution') implies the applicability of Agenda 21: A Programme of Action for Sustainable Development, 1992;[55] the Johannesburg Declaration on Sustainable Development, 2002;[56] the Manila Declaration on Furthering the Implementation of the Global Programme of Action for the Protection of the Marine Environment from Land-based Activities, 2012;[57] and the UNGA Future We Want, 2012 (Rio+20)[58] in relation to water pollution reduction. The Basel Convention on the Control of Transboundary Movements of Hazardous Wastes and their Disposal, 1989 (Basel Convention),[59] the Convention on the Prior Informed Consent Procedure for Certain Hazardous Chemicals and Pesticides in International Trade, 1999 (Rotterdam Convention)[60] and the Stockholm Convention on Persistent Organic Pollutants, 2001 (Stockholm Convention)[61] are implicated with reference to the release and transportation of hazardous chemicals.[62]

General Assembly and Council referred to the right to safe drinking water and sanitation as a single right until the adoption of UNGA Resolution 70/169 in 2015, which recognizes them as two rights – a right to safe drinking water and a right to sanitation.

[53] UN CESCR, *General Comment No 15*, para 2.

[54] Committee on Economic, Social and Cultural Rights, *Statement on the Right to Sanitation* (2010) para 8. UNGA Resolution 70/169 (2015) para 2; UN Human Rights Council Resolution 27/7 (2014) preambular para 21.

[55] UN Conference on Environment and Development, *Report of the United Nations Conference on Environment and Development, Vol I: Resolutions Adopted by the Conference* (United Nations, 1993) resolution 1, annex II.

[56] 2002 (UN Doc. A/CONF.199/20).

[57] 2012 (UNEP/GCSS.XII/INF/10).

[58] UNGA, *The Future We Want* (UN Doc. A/RES/66/288) (27 July 2012).

[59] 1989 (1673 UNTS 126; 28 ILM 657 (1989)).

[60] 1999 (2244 UNTS 337; 38 ILM 1 (1999)).

[61] 2001 (2256 UNTS 119; 40 ILM 532 (2001)).

[62] O. Spijkers, Y. Bian and M. Nishiumi, 'Rules and Practices of International Law for the Sustainable Management of Fresh Water Resources Towards SDG 6 on Ensuring Water and Sanitation for All' in International Law Association Committee on the Role of International Law in Sustainable Natural

Targets 6.4 ('Water use and scarcity'), 6.5 ('Water resources management') and 6.6 ('Water-related ecosystems') reflect the provisions of a wide number of international, regional and bilateral legal instruments.[63] Of primary relevance to this chapter are the environmental protection of water afforded by three specific treaties, namely the Ramsar Convention on Wetlands, 1999 (Ramsar Convention),[64] the UN Convention on the Law of the Non-Navigational Uses of International Watercourses, 1997 (UN Watercourses Convention)[65] and the UN Convention on the Protection and Use of Transboundary Watercourses and International Lakes, 1992 (Helsinki Convention).[66] How do these international legal instruments pertain specifically (although implicitly) to Targets under SDG 6? Table 10.1 highlights the various international instruments that provide a normative framework guiding international, regional and sub-regional agreements on watercourses and the achievement of SDG 6.

Table 10.1 International law on water

SDG 6 Target	International Legal Instruments
6.1 Universal and equitable access to safe and affordable drinking water for all	Committee on Economic, Social and Cultural Rights, *Statement on the Right to Sanitation* (2010). UNGA Resolution 70/169 (2015) para 2. UN Human Rights Council Resolution 27/7 (2014) para 21.

Resource Management for Development, *Sustainable Natural Resource Management for Development Final Draft* (2016) 6.

63 For a comprehensive list of these instruments see Box 2A Selected International Treaties related to SDG 6 on Sustainable Management of Water Resources and Box 2B Selected Bilateral and Regional Treaties on Sustainable Water Management in Spijkers et al, above n 62, 7–8.

64 The Ramsar Convention was agreed on 2 February 1971 in Ramsar, Iran, and includes the 1982 amendments and a 1987 protocol. See Ramsar Convention Secretariat, *The Ramsar Convention Manual* (6th edn, Ramsar Convention Secretariat, 2013) 21.

65 UN Treaty Collection, *Chapter XXVII Environment: Convention on the Law of the Non-Navigational Uses of International Watercourses* (New York, 1997).

66 UN Treaty Collection, *Chapter XXVII Environment: Convention on the Protection and Use of Transboundary Watercourses and International Lakes* (Helsinki, 1992).

SDG 6 Target	International Legal Instruments
6.2 Access to adequate and equitable sanitation	UN Conference on Environment and Development, *Report of the United Nations Conference on Environment and Development, Vol I: Resolutions Adopted by the Conference* (United Nations 1993) resolution 1, annex II. Johannesburg Declaration on Sustainable Development, Report of the World Summit on Sustainable Development, 2002 (UN Doc. A/CONF.199/20). Manila Declaration on Furthering the Implementation of the Global Programme of Action for the Protection of the Marine Environment from Land-based Activities, 2012 (UNEP/GCSS.XII/INF/10). UN General Assembly, *The Future We Want* (UN Doc. A/RES/66/288) (27 July 2012). Basel Convention on the Control of Transboundary Movements of Hazardous Wastes and their Disposal, 1989 (1673 UNTS 126; 28 ILM 657 (1989)). Convention on the Prior Informed Consent Procedure for Certain Hazardous Chemicals and Pesticides in International Trade, 1999 (2244 UNTS 337; 38 ILM 1 (1999)). Stockholm Convention on Persistent Organic Pollutants, 2001 (2256 UNTS 119; 40 ILM 532 (2001)).
6.3 Reducing water pollution	Rio Declaration on Environment and Development (1992). Johannesburg Declaration on Sustainable Development (2002). Manila Declaration on Furthering the Implementation of the Global Programme of Action for the Protection of the Marine Environment from Land-based Activities (2012). Basel Convention on the Control of Transboundary Movements of Hazardous Wastes and their Disposal (1989). Convention on the Prior Informed Consent Procedure for Certain Hazardous Chemicals and Pesticides in International Trade (1999). Stockholm Convention on Persistent Organic Pollutants (2001).
6.4 Water use and scarcity 6.5 Water resource management 6.6 Water-related ecosystems 6a Fostering international cooperation	Articles 1(1), 2, 3(2) and 6 of the Ramsar Convention. Articles 3 and 15–16 of the Helsinki Convention. Articles 11–16, 20, 21(2) and 22–27 of the UN Watercourses Convention.

From the foregoing it is clear that the three water Conventions provide a normative framework to guide international, regional and sub-regional agreements on watercourses and actively seek the achievement of SDG 6.

10.3.3 SDGs 14 and 15 and International Law of the Seas and Biodiversity

The Targets included under SDG14 ('conserve and sustainably use the oceans, seas and marine resources for sustainable development') and SDG 15 ('protect, restore and promote the sustainable use of terrestrial ecosystems, sustainably manage forests, combat desertification, and halt and reverse land degradation and halt biodiversity loss') again fall under the purview of a number of key international environmental legal instruments. In its Draft Report on Sustainable Natural Resource Management for Development, the International Law Association (ILA) Committee task team on SDG 14 noted that the scope of application of their examination would relate solely to natural resources of the ocean's high seas area and not waters under national jurisdiction.[67] The task team also duly noted that a wide range of international law relates to SDG 14; key instruments to be focused on would include the UN Convention on the Law of the Sea, 1982 (UNCLOS), the Agreement relating to the Conservation and Management of Straddling Fish Stocks and Highly Migratory Fish Stocks, 1995 (Fish Stocks Agreement),[68] and the Helsinki, UN Watercourses and Ramsar Conventions. UNCLOS is the only international legal instrument expressly referred to in the wording of the Targets related to SDG 14, with Target 14.c stating '… enhance the conservation and sustainable use of oceans and their resources by implementing international law as reflected in UNCLOS, which provides the legal framework for the conservation and sustainable use of oceans and their resources …'.[69] The extent to which various other Targets under

---

[67] D.R. Payne, 'Rules and Practices of International Law for the Sustainable Management of High Seas Marine Resources towards SDG 14 on Sustainable Management of Fisheries and Ocean Resources' in International Law Association Committee on the Role of International Law in Sustainable Natural Resource Management for Development, *Sustainable Natural Resource Management for Development Final Draft* (2016) 13.

[68] (UNTC No 37924) (UN Fish Stocks Agreement).

[69] As recalled in para 158 of *The Future We Want*, above n 58.

SDG 14 directly relate to provisions of UNCLOS and the international instruments listed above are reflected in Table 10.2.

Table 10.2 International law on the marine environment

SDG 14 Target	International Legal Instruments
14.1 Prevent and significantly reduce marine pollution of all kinds, particularly from land-based activities	Articles 197, 198, 199, 204, 205 and 206 UNCLOS (applicable to Targets 14.1, 14.2 and 14.4). Articles 6, 2(1) and 3(2) of the Ramsar Convention.
14.2 By 2020 sustainably manage and protect marine and coastal ecosystems to avoid significant adverse effects	Article 3 of the Helsinki Convention.
14.4 By 2020 effectively regulate harvesting and end overfishing, illegal, unreported and destructive fishing practices	Articles 2, 5 and 6 of the Fish Stocks Agreement.
14.5 By 2020, conserve at least 10 per cent of coastal and marine areas, consistent with national and international law and based on the best available scientific information	Articles 5, 7–9 and 20–27 of the UN Watercourses Convention.

Moving to SDG 15, it is interesting to note that the Targets listed are varied and cover a number of environmental challenges related to various ecological elements such as conserving terrestrial and freshwater ecosystems, desertification, deforestation, genetic resource sharing, addressing invasive alien species and combating the poaching and trafficking of protected species. The central theme of biodiversity conservation is evident from the aforementioned Targets and while no explicit reference can be found, the Convention on Biological Diversity, 1992 (CBD) accompanied by a host of multilateral environmental agreements (MEAs) embody the international law cluster supporting SDG 15. The link is clearer when one considers the three main aims of the CBD, which are: conservation of biological diversity;[70] sustainable use of biological

[70] The variability among living organisms from all sources and the ecological complexes of which they are a party.

resources;[71] and fair and equitable sharing of benefits arising from genetic resources.[72] In support of the central objectives and mandates of the CBD, a number of programmes, MEAs and other policy tools exist which are in direct alignment with SDG 15 Targets. The implicit linkages between SDG 15 Targets and the CBD as well as a number of supporting policy documents are contained in Table 10.3. The legal instruments in the right-hand column are applicable to all of the SDG targets.

Table 10.3 International law on biodiversity

SDG 15 Targets	International Legal Instruments
15.1 By 2020, ensure the conservation, restoration and sustainable use of terrestrial and inland freshwater ecosystems and their services, in particular forests, wetlands, mountains and drylands, in line with obligations under international agreements 15.2 By 2020, promote the implementation of sustainable management of all types of forests, halt deforestation, restore degraded forests and substantially increase afforestation and reforestation globally 15.3 By 2030, combat desertification, restore degraded land and soil, including land affected by desertification, drought and floods, and strive to achieve a land degradation-neutral world 15.4 By 2030, ensure the conservation of mountain ecosystems, including their biodiversity, in order to enhance their capacity to provide benefits that are essential for sustainable development	Convention on Biological Diversity (1992). Nagoya Protocol on Access to Genetic Resources and the Fair and Equitable Sharing of Benefits Arising from their Utilization to the Convention on Biological Diversity (2010). Convention on International Trade in Endangered Species of Wild Fauna and Flora (1973). Convention on the Conservation of Migratory Species of Wild Animals (1979). International Treaty on Plant Genetic Resources for Food and Agriculture (2001). Convention Concerning the Protection of the World Cultural and Natural Heritage (1972). International Plant Protection Convention (1951).

[71] Any biotic component of ecosystems with actual or potential use or value for humanity.

[72] Any material of plant, animal, microbial or other origin containing functional units of heredity of actual or potential value. Article 1 of the Convention on Biological Diversity, 1992.

SDG 15 Targets	International Legal Instruments
15.5 Take urgent and significant action to reduce the degradation of natural habitats, halt the loss of biodiversity and, by 2020, protect and prevent the extinction of threatened species	
15.6 Promote fair and equitable sharing of the benefits arising from the utilization of genetic resources and promote appropriate access to such resources, as internationally agreed	
15.7 Take urgent action to end poaching and trafficking of protected species of flora and fauna and address both demand and supply of illegal wildlife products	
15.8 By 2020, introduce measures to prevent the introduction and significantly reduce the impact of invasive alien species on land and water ecosystems and control or eradicate the priority species	
15.9 By 2020, integrate ecosystem and biodiversity values into national and local planning, development processes, poverty reduction strategies and accounts	

The foregoing discussion suggests that while it is true that explicit mention of all possible international legal instruments is ostensibly lacking in the wording of the 17 SDGs, and more specifically the four Goals comprising the environmental cluster, implicit and explicit references to international law in the supporting Targets are common. While the natural fit between the SDGs and international law suggests some degree of commitment on either side to combine the two approaches to achieve sustainable development, the relationship is not without its own challenges. One of the effects of the reinforcement of existing international law via the language of specific SDGs is that these Goals may encourage 'clustering' of international law within specific issues areas.[73]

[73] S. Oberthur, 'Clustering of Multi-Lateral Environmental Agreements: Potential and Limitations' (2002) *International Environment Agreements* 2(4), 317; K. Von Moltke, 'On Clustering International Environmental Agreements' in

A negative effect of deriving or linking Goals to existing international instruments is that the SDGs mirror the fragmented or compartmentalized nature of international law.[74]

In the same manner as different international agreements' objectives take different directions and sometimes even conflict, so too will some of the SDGs and their Targets compete for scarce resources. It is not inconceivable that in the absence of some internal mechanism to enhance synergies and address trade-offs, the outcome of all the SDGs being met might not have the actual effect envisaged by the 2030 Framework, namely the achievement of development that is sustainable on an economic, social and environmental level.[75]

The foregoing is especially true when considering the silo-ist approach taken in drafting of the environmental SDG. When we look at the SDGs as they currently exist, we see that the SDG framework does not include an overarching environmental goal but rather compartmentalizes the environment into separate and distinct components. While the same can be said of economic and social SDGs, the lack of a single or integrated environmental SDG is troublesome as the division of the Earth into ecological components detracts from an orchestrated international pursuit of environmental protection – one where the Earth is, or rather should be, seen as a single, complex, integrated system.[76] The closest it comes to a holistic environmental goal is the determination of the international community expressed in the preamble to Agenda 2030's declaration, which reads: 'to protect the planet from degradation … so that it can support the needs of present and future generations'. While this statement does point to a recognition of a healthy planetary environment as a prerequisite for meeting the needs of people, it is not intended as a statement of a goal. It is silent on what needs to be done and to what degree, in the sense that it does not define what the needs of present and/or future generations are or what is to be understood under degradation.[77] The latter omission is especially worrying as it has the effect of

G. Winter (ed), *Multilevel Governance of Global Environmental Change: Perspectives from Science, Sociology and the Law* (Cambridge University Press, 2006) 409.

[74] Kim, above n 19, 17.

[75] *Ibid.*

[76] *Ibid*, at 19.

[77] For an overview of the content of MDG 7 see n 43 above and for further reading see G.P. Latham and E.A. Locke, 'Self-Regulation Through Goal Setting' (1991) *Organizational Behavior and Human Decision Processes* 50(2), 212.

not clarifying the extent to which or in what ways the environment should be protected or given priority over development – a situation which is reminiscent of the failures in achieving MDG 7.[78]

In response to the perception that the SDG framework fragments sustainable development into overtly social, environmental and economic objectives (and indeed further sub-dividing these components – the environment being a case in point), Le Blanc proposes that the Goals and Targets rather be seen as a network within which links among Goals exist through Targets that explicitly refer to multiple Goals.[79] In essence the integration of the different Goals and indeed the sectors of sustainable development (social, economic and/or environment) these Goals purport to promote is to be found in the overlap in their respective Targets. Integration therefore need not be found outside the SDGs but rather within linkages among Targets.

Let us take a practical example from the Targets listed under SDGs 6, 14 and 15 as expounded in the foregoing discussion on how international law is reflected in different Goals and Targets. While these Goals refer to different ecological components of the environment (fresh water, marine life and terrestrial life), their Targets on sustainable use/management of different ecological resources overlap, thus serving as an integrative tool among the Goals. Viewed in this fashion, the overlapping SDG Targets serve to remedy the silo-ist appearance of the Goals and may further facilitate real mainstreaming of dimensions which previously did not enjoy strong sectoral anchoring in development institutions. Mapping of all the potential areas of overlap among the 169 Targets could serve to show that the SDGs indeed embody a much more integrated and coherent system of global goals than their predecessors, the MDGs, ever did.

---

[78] UNEP, *Global Environment Outlook GEO 5: Environment for the Future We Want* (UNEP 2012); UN, 'Prototype Global Sustainable Development Report' (2014) <http://sustainabledevelopment.un.org/content/documents/1454Prototype%20Global%20SD%20Report.pdf> accessed 8 February 2017); UN, *MDG Report 2014* (UN Department of Economic and Social Affairs, 2014).

[79] D. Le Blanc, *Towards Integration at Last? The Sustainable Development Goals as a Network of Targets* (UN Department of Economic and Social Affairs, 2015) 1.

10.4 SUSTAINABLE DEVELOPMENT AND SDGS: TRANSPOSITION OF A FLAWED CONCEPT?

It is important to bear in mind that although sustainable development remains an important concept in international environmental law, it is rarely conducive to global environmental protection since it does not provide an exact account of how developmental and environmental needs should be balanced.[80] In this regard, sustainable development seems ill-suited to provide a clear position in instances where there are trade-offs between environmental and economic considerations. The relative and reconciliatory nature of sustainable development implies that the predominant importance of economic interests frequently trumps environmental considerations. Uncertainty also exists concerning the exact scope and meaning of sustainable development itself.[81] Thus, although the SDGs affirm sustainable development as the *Leitmotif* in international environmental law, the aforementioned intrinsic problems associated with sustainable development may not be to the advantage of the environment. Agenda 2030 is the post-MDG development agenda which clearly provides a more integrated approach to development by virtue of its affirmation of sustainable development, but the implicit trade-offs inherent in sustainable development and the dominance of economic considerations does not necessarily take sufficient cognizance of planetary boundaries.[82] This does not imply that the authors are ignorant of the existence of grinding poverty faced by developing states and the priority to resolve this through development. However, the mere eradication of poverty via economic development could be undermined by increasing environmental pressures in the Anthropocene.[83] This raises the question whether sustainable development is a satisfactory response

---

[80] J.E. Viñuales, 'The Rise and Fall of Sustainable Development' (2013) *Review of European Community and International Environmental Law* 22(1), 3. See, however, U. Beyerlin, 'The Concept of Sustainable Development' in R. Wolfrum (ed), *Enforcing Environmental Standards: Economic Mechanisms as Viable Means* (Springer, 1996) 95–121.

[81] G. Handl, 'Sustainable Development: General Rules *versus* Specific Obligations' in W. Lang (ed), *Sustainable Development and International Law* (Graham and Trotman, 1995) 39.

[82] See J. Ntambirweki, 'The Developing Countries in the Evolution of an International Environmental Law' (1991) *Hastings International and Comparative Law Review* 14, 907.

[83] D. Vidas, J. Zalasiewicz and M. Williams, 'What is the Anthropocene – And Why is it Relevant for International Law' (2015) *Yearbook of International Environmental Law* 25, 3.

to global environmental challenges. A possible resolution could have been to include goals that relate to planetary boundaries as suggested by Rockström et al.[84] Planetary boundaries do not cap human development but rather provide a safe space for growth through the definition of a number of boundary conditions that could, if crossed, lead to a major disruption in the Earth system. As such this approach does not contradict sustainable development but rather requires an establishment of a new framework for sustainable development that will facilitate human and economic development within the boundaries of the life support system of Earth.[85] In this regard, Rockström et al recently suggested the inclusion of a Sustainable Development Trajectory, which comprises six major 'structural transformations'.[86] It is interesting to note that these transformations include the transformation to a low-carbon economy and biodiversity management transformation that would include strategies for preserving six critical biomes (Polar Regions, tropical rainforests, ocean marine systems, permafrost regions, temperate forests and savannahs).[87] Biermann suggests that the concept of planetary boundaries is useful as it provides the 'environmental target corridor' in the context of the other pillars of sustainable development.[88] Biermann, however, concedes that the political use of this approach is still limited and this caveat is even more appropriate in relation to the legal utilization of this concept and transformation to the governance arena.[89] The recognition of planetary boundaries affirms the problems associated with the current approach to sustainable development and begs the question whether the universal sustainable development framework as presented by Agenda 2030 indeed accords environmental protection with significant weight in the context of the dominance of economic growth and development.

The issue of planetary boundaries of the Earth resonates with the affirmation in the Agenda that 'planet Earth and its ecosystems are our common home and that "Mother Earth" is a common expression in a

---

[84] J. Rockström, W. Steffen, K. Noone et al, 'A Safe Operating Space for Humanity' (2009) *Nature* 461, 472.

[85] J. Rockström, J. Sachs, M.C. Öhman et al, 'Sustainable Development and Planetary Boundaries' in S. Daws and N. Samarasinghe (eds), *The United Nations – Vol VII: Poverty and Development* (Sage, 2015) 345.

[86] *Ibid*, at 346.

[87] The other are agriculture, urbanization, population and fragile states. These challenges should be addressed in conjunction with the other challenges of sustainable development such as poverty.

[88] F. Biermann, 'Planetary Boundaries and Earth System Governance: Exploring the Links' (2012) *Ecological Economics* 81, 7.

[89] *Ibid.*

number of countries and regions',[90] and that progress must occur in 'harmony with nature'.[91] The notion of Mother Earth and its linkage with environmental ethics and human rights approaches has recently attracted the attention of scholars[92] due to the 'rights for nature approach' included in Chapter 7 of the Constitution of Ecuador of 2008, which provides that 'Nature, or *Pacha Mama*, where life is reproduced and occurs, has the right to integral respect for its existence and for the maintenance and regeneration of its life cycles, structure, functions and evolutionary processes'.[93] However, although Agenda 2030 reiterates its transformative nature in several instances,[94] it does not impose a departure from an anthropocentric approach towards nature. Agenda 2030 affirms the anthropocentric nature of international environmental law and sustainable development as it declares that 'we have adopted a historic decision on a comprehensive, far-reaching and people-centred set of … Goals and targets'.[95] The anthropocentric nature of environmental law remains a major point of critique against environmental law.[96] Scholars critical of anthropocentrism have advocated for biocentrism and/or ecocentrism in order to escape from an approach that focuses on the instrumental value that nature has for human beings.[97] The 'rights for nature' approach as suggested by Stone is one of the foremost proposals to initiate a departure from anthropocentrism through the awarding of rights to nature, which could be enforced by appointed (human) guardians.[98] The inclusion of the reference to 'Mother Earth' in Agenda 2030 should be viewed against the recognition embedded in the preceding statement. The preceding sentence recognizes that 'there are different approaches, visions, models and tools available to each country, in accordance with

---

[90] Para 59.

[91] Preamble.

[92] For example, S. Borràs, 'New Transitions from Human Rights to the Environment to the Rights of Nature' (2016) *Transnational Environmental Law* 5, 136.

[93] For the English translation, see <http://pdba.georgetown.edu/Constitutions/Ecuador/english08.html> (accessed 5 October 2016).

[94] Preamble and paras 2 and 7.

[95] Para 2.

[96] It would be more correct to refer to weak anthropocentrism. C. Redgwell, 'Life, the Universe and Everything: A Critique of Anthropocentric Rights' in A. Boyle and M. Anderson (eds), *Human Rights Approaches to Environmental Protection* (Oxford University Press, 1996) 73.

[97] J. Purdy, 'Our Place in the World: A New Relationship for Environmental Ethics and Law' (2013) *Duke Law Journal* 62, 862.

[98] C.D. Stone, *Should Trees Have Standing? And Other Essays on Law, Morals and the Environment* (Oceana, 1996) 1–47.

its national circumstances and priorities, to achieve sustainable development'. As such the inclusion of 'Mother Earth' in Agenda 2030 seems to be merely rhetoric which takes cognizance of different national regimes and/or approaches to environmental protection and should not be seen as an affirmation of a rights for nature approach or a departure from the anthropocentric approach in international environmental law.

The aforementioned discussion also raises the issue of the relationship between human rights and SDGs. The MDGs did not reflect a human rights approach to development, which was viewed as one of the major flaws of the MDGs, and it was therefore seen as important to address this issue with the adoption of the post-2015 development agenda because '[r]eframing development in human rights terms is not only an ethical and legal imperative; it can also enhance the effectiveness and accountability of future development efforts. Ultimately, human rights principles ... can be building blocks of a fairer more sustainable and more just development paradigm for the 21st century.'[99] The relationship between human rights and environmental law is the result of ongoing legal discourse, especially in relation to climate change.[100] The human rights framework offers the advantages of *inter alia* universality, interdependence, accountability, equality, use of the maximum of state resources available for the enjoyment of rights, and engagement in international cooperation and assistance[101] for the field of environmental law.[102] This raises the question concerning the relationship between the human rights framework and SDGs.

---

[99] Center for Economic and Social Rights, 'A Matter of Justice: Securing Human Rights in the Post-2015 Sustainable Development Agenda' in S. Daws and N. Samarasinghe (eds), *The United Nations – Vol VII: Poverty and Development* (Sage, 2015) 324.

[100] See, for instance, J. Knox, 'Climate Change and Human Rights Law' (2009) *Virginia Journal of International Law* 50, 164; E. Cameron and M. Limon, 'Restoring the Climate by Realizing Rights: The Role of the International Human Rights System' (2012) *Review of European Community and International Environmental Law* 21(3), 204; A. Boyle, 'Human Rights and the Environment: Where Next?' (2013) *European Journal of International Law* 23(3), 613.

[101] Article 2(1) of the International Covenant on Economic, Social and Cultural Rights, 1966 (ICESCR) contains the undertaking by each Party 'to take steps, individually and through international assistance and co-operation, especially economic and technical, to the maximum of its available resources, with a view to achieving progressively the full realisation of the rights recognised in the present Covenant'.

[102] Center for Economic and Social Rights, above n 99, 322.

The Agenda explicitly states that it is 'guided by the purposes and principles of the Charter of the United Nations' and is 'grounded in the Universal Declaration of Human Rights international human rights treaties' and is 'informed by other instruments such as the Declaration on the Right to Development'.[103] Despite these references to human rights, it is evident that the SDGs in much the same way as the MDGs fail to utilize human rights in the formulation of the Goals. This is also despite the evident interlinkages and overlap between the SDGs and particularly economic, cultural and social rights. The impact of neglecting to firmly base the SDGs in and on existing and internationally accepted human rights is that it creates a governance gap and renders the SDGs a 'rhetorical tool' that lacks accountability.[104]

It is particularly the issue of what Alston referred to as the potential emergence of an 'internationalisation of responsibility' in the context of MDGs that SDGs embedded in the human rights framework could have contributed to.[105] MDG 8 specifically referred to the need to develop a Global Partnership for development. Agenda 2030 explicitly affirms that this partnership should be based on global solidarity, in particular with the poorest and the most vulnerable.[106] The affirmation of the role of solidarity[107] in Agenda 2030 adheres to the importance thereof in international environmental law.[108] The Rio Declaration on Environment and Development embodies several principles that highlight the pivotal role of solidarity.[109] It is in particular the common but differentiated responsibility (CBDR) principle, which gives effect to solidarity, that has

---

[103] Para 10. See also Collins, Chapter 4 in this volume.

[104] S. Wisor, 'The Impending Failure of the Sustainable Development Goals' (2014) <http://www.ethicsandinternationalaffairs.org/2014/the-impending-failure-of-the-sustainable-developmentgoals/> accessed 17 December 2016.

[105] Alston, above n 31, 771.

[106] Agenda 2030, above n 28, preamble and para 39.

[107] For a discussion: R. St J. Macdonald, 'Solidarity in the Practice and Discourse of Public International Law' (1996) *Pace International Law Review* 8, 259. Solidarity may be defined as a 'principle of co-operation which identifies as the goal of joint and separate state action an outcome that benefits all states or at least does not gravely interfere with the interests of other states'. See also R. Wolfrum, 'Solidarity amongst States: An Emerging Structural Principle of International Law' in P-M. Dupuy, B. Fassbender, M. Shaw et al (eds), *Völkerrecht als Wertordnung – Festschrift für Christian Tomuschat* (Engel, 1995) 1087.

[108] C.L. Riemer, *Staatengemeinschaftliche Solidarität in der Völkerrechtsordnung* (Riemer, 2003) 160.

[109] See Principles 6, 7, 9, 11, 14, 15, 18, 19 and 27.

served as the basis for framework conventions and subsequent protocols that have moved away from reciprocity of obligations between states.[110]

The internalization of responsibility entails that the responsibility for achieving the Goals should be internationalized, in the sense that developed states should assist developing states to meet the Goals where the latter show that they are unable to do so. Alston recognized that the likelihood of the existence of such an obligation was not supported by practice or consensus but did not exclude the possibility of further development. A shared responsibility pursuant to the universal promotion of human rights may be derived *inter alia* from the Declaration on the Right to Development.[111] Furthermore, the MDGs also provide examples of burden sharing based on a shared responsibility in relation to developmental goals. Shared responsibility is important since it implies that the responsibilities of richer states are limited through the division of the obligations.[112] It is accordingly important to develop the exact responsibilities of states in order to ensure that the division does not cause confusion and uncertainty concerning obligations.[113] International organizations, in particular the UN, have an important role to play in order to coordinate the residual responsibility of the international community.

The failure to link SDGs with human rights in a more explicit manner represents a missed opportunity for the clarification of the relationship

---

[110] C.D. Stone, 'Common but Differentiated Responsibilities in International Law' (2004) *American Journal of International Law* 98(2), 276.

[111] UN General Assembly Resolution 41/128 of 1986. See for a discussion S. Roy Chowdhury, E. Denters and P. de Waart, *The Right to Development in International Law* (Martinus Nijhoff, 1992). This document is, however, contested by developed countries and it is questionable whether it creates concrete legal obligations. M. Bulajic, *Principles of International Development Law: Progressive Development of the Principles of International Law Relating to the New International Economic Order* (Martinus Nijhoff, 1993) 33 *et seq.*

[112] Gibney remarks that '[t]his return to universal principles should not be read to mean that all states (particularly Western states) are responsible for all things for all people'. M. Gibney, *International Human Rights Law: Returning to Universal Principles* (Rowman & Littlefield, 2008) 3. See, for an analysis, H. Shue, 'Mediating Duties' (1988) *Ethics* 98, 687.

[113] 'Development compacts' may provide an example of a mechanism that may be used to ensure clarity concerning the division of obligations. This proposal was made by A. Sengupta (independent expert on the right to development). See A. Sengupta, 'Development Cooperation and the Right to Development' <http://www.harvardfxbcenter.org/resources/working-papers/FXBC_WP12Sengupta.pdf> accessed 30 November 2011.

between human rights and the (sustainable) development agenda and as such a lack of progress from the initial adoption of the MDGs.

10.5 CONCLUSION

In expounding upon the central question of whether and to what extent the SDGs progress the environmental agenda within international sustainable development law, a number of conclusions are evident. As to the matter of the normative contribution of the Goals in developing international law, scholarly opinion ranges between outright denial of any normative value to attributing some normative value to specific Goals.[114] The present authors position themselves in the latter category and conclude that some of the SDGs indeed hold some level of normative value and therefore have the potential to contribute to the normative development of international law. In line with the view of Spijkers, who refers specifically to the potential of SDG 6 in evolving the ecosystem approach in international water law,[115] it is the view of the present authors that the SDGs carry normative weight as they may serve to evolve customary international law. The other environmental goals in the same way contribute to the normative development of specific ecological concepts within the fields of international law they pertain to. In investigating how the Agenda reflects international law in terms of reference to international legal instruments, the authors found that only one of the four environmental cluster Goals (SDG 13) contains explicit reference to a treaty.[116] While the wording of SDGs 6, 14 and 15 does not contain any explicit reference to the relevant international legal instrument, some of their Targets do and moreover, implicit reference may be read in when considering the wording of these Goals and their Targets.[117] The authors conclude that criticism relating to the lack of international law references in the text of Agenda 2030 is not unfounded but it is necessary to add that a teleological interpretation of specific Goals and Targets indicates a myriad of implicit references. This, however, does not negate the (apparent) omission of a specific and single environmental Goal by the drafters of Agenda 2030 – an omission which solidifies the conclusion that the SDGs do little to progress the position of the environment vis-à-vis economic development within the greater

---

114 See para 2 at pp 3–4 above.

115 Spijkers, above n 22.

116 See UNFCCC. Decision 1/CP.21, above n 46, para 3.

117 See para 3 at pp 14–21 above.

sustainable development debate. The foregoing is also evident from the absence of the recognition of planetary boundaries and the lack of human rights rhetoric in the wording of the Goals and their Targets.[118] In summation, while the SDGs undoubtedly embody an extensive mandate as to what should guide international development efforts in the next 15 years, and in this sense move far beyond the MDGs, the dire state of the planet calls for a more robust global environmental agenda that is not dominated by development that too easily heeds economic interests contrary to planetary boundaries. As such, the authors are of the view that the 'development detour' in the SDGs indicates that the environment remains of secondary concern for the international community and that we are on a road to nowhere.

---

[118] See para 4 above.

11. Torn by (un)certainty – can there be peace between rule of law and other Sustainable Development Goals?

Niko Soininen

11.1 INTRODUCTION*

Within the system of Sustainable Development Goals (SDGs), SDG16 is the tag for the rule of law (SDG on Peace, Justice and Strong Institutions).[1] The rule of law encapsulates some of the most fundamental functions of the law.[2] We often accept formal conceptions of the rule of law without much consideration. Take Hayek's definition:

> Stripped of all technicalities this means that government in all its actions is bound by rules fixed and announced beforehand – rules which make it possible to foresee with fair certainty how the authority will use its coercive powers in given circumstances, and to plan one's individual affairs on the basis of this knowledge.[3]

* This study was done under the Winland Project and the BlueAdapt Project, which are funded by the Strategic Research Council of the Government of Finland.

[1] SDG 16 aims to '[p]romote peaceful and inclusive societies for sustainable development, provide access to justice for all and build effective, accountable and inclusive institutions at all levels', available at <https://sustainabledevelopment.un.org/sdg16> accessed 30 July 2017.

[2] J. Finnis, *Natural Law and Natural Rights* (2nd edn, Clarendon Press, 2011) 270 states that rule of law is '[t]he name commonly given to the state of affairs in which a legal system is legally in good shape ...'. See also, H.C. Bugge, 'Twelve Fundamental Challenges in Environmental Law. An Introduction to the Concept of Rule of Law for Nature' in C. Voigt (ed), *Rule of Law for Nature. New Dimensions and Idea in Environmental Law* (Cambridge University Press, 2013) 6.

[3] F.A. Hayek, *The Road to Serfdom* (Routledge, 2006) 75.

Few in the international or domestic arenas would disagree with this definition. Discussions at the 71st session of the United Nations General Assembly (UNGA) are a good illustration. During the debate at the Sixth Committee (Legal) on the Rule of Law, the

> General Assembly President Peter Thomson (Fiji) … reminded the delegates that they were the guardians of the international legal system. … Napoleon Beras (Dominican Republic), speaking for CELAC [Community of Latin American and Caribbean States], said that the rule of law at the national and international levels allowed for the acts of States to be foreseeable and legitimate. … Ali Nasimfar (Iran), speaking for the Non-Aligned Movement stressed that the legal rights of States under international law should be respected. … Thembile Elphus Joyini (South Africa), speaking for the African Group, said that multilateral treaties were an integral aspect of a comprehensive and robust international framework, ensuring that the rule of law governed inter-State relations. The principle processed universality, consolidated international consensus, provided certainty and accountability on rights and obligations of States, and facilitated peaceful settlement of disputes.[4]

To paint a colourful picture of the discussion, Hobbesian *bellum omnium* is only the distance of (formal) rule of law away. International order is seen to function through rules which set the playing field for inter- and intra-state actions alike. In other words, rule of law in the form of clarity, predictability and certainty is one of the few things that stands between liberty and tyranny.

In addition to the rule of law being an SDG in itself, the Sixth Committee (Legal) made an important observation stating that the rule of law was a means for achieving other SDGs, such as eradication of poverty and hunger (SDGs 1 and 2); clean water and sanitation (SDG 6); affordable and clean energy (SDG 7); climate action (SDG 13); and aquatic and terrestrial biodiversity (SDGs 14 and 15):[5]

> Napoleon Beras (Dominican Republic) said that … upholding the principle was essential in order to achieve sustained and inclusive economic growth, as well as sustainable development. … Penelope Beckles, (Trinidad and Tobago), speaking for the Caribbean Community (CARICOM) [stated that] [e]qual access to justice for all was 'essential' for translating the principle into effective mechanisms to provide protection, redress and accountability for serious crimes and violations of human rights. … Sophea Yaung Chan (Cambodia), speaking for the Association of Southeast Asian Nations

4 GA/L/3519 5 October 2016.

5 GA/L/3519 5 October 2016.

(ASEAN), said that organization's Charter embodies the fundamental principles and purposes of the rule of law, including, among others, the peaceful settlement of conflicts, good governance, and promotion and protection of human rights.[6]

Based on the discussions of the UNGA Sixth Committee (Legal), the rule of law seems to mean many, if not all, of the characteristics that could possibly be ascribed to a well-functioning system of governance, be it on the international or domestic plane. To borrow Waldron's words, a sceptic could conclude that '"[t]he Rule of Law" sounded grand, certainly; but at the end of the day, many will have formed the impression that the utterance of those magic words meant little more than "Hooray for our side!"'.[7]

To keep scepticism at bay, the first task of this chapter is to give a short account of the three main camps in the rule of law literature: formal, procedural and substantive. My argument in section two is that although these camps are scattered, and may be pitted against each other, they all have a common undercurrent flowing towards an organized functioning and development of societies. Formal and procedural rule of law (SGD 16) are prerequisites for the effective implementation of substantive rule of law (i.e. all the other SDGs). Similarly, the formal criteria of rule of law, or its procedural rules, would not amount to much were they not guided and accompanied by certain minimum conditions for *good* functioning and development of societies.

In Sections 11.3 and 11.4 I discuss the unavoidable, yet uncomfortable relationship between the rule of law and the quest for achieving the other SDGs effectively. I argue that the rule of law in all its three meanings requires certainty from the external world at such a rate that the law risks becoming the single greatest obstacle for achieving the very same goals it seeks to protect. Substantive SDGs, such as the one relating to the right to water (SDG 6), require certainty from the law. In turn, law requires

---

[6] GA/L/3519 5 October 2016.

[7] J. Waldron, 'Is the Rule of Law an Essentially Contested Concept (in Florida)' (2002) *Law and Philosophy* 21, 139. He describes the sources for scepticism: '… the lead idea of the Rule of Law is that somehow respect for law can take the edge off human political power, making it less objectionable, less dangerous, more benign and more respectful. But we disagree on how this can be done, and whether it can ever be done completely. We also disagree on the precise nature of the danger posed by human power in its unmitigated form, and on the values that would be served by introducing law into the picture. We disagree about the ailment, the medicine, and the character of the cure' (*Ibid*, at 159).

certainty from the social ecological world in which the SDGs are realized. Environmental, economic, societal and cultural uncertainties are enslaved under legal certainty, to serve legal certainty. This is the mechanism whereby law, instead of being a servant, becomes a master. And it is exactly at this point that many SDGs risk a failure of delivery.

Peace between SDGs, as it were, requires uncomfortable concessions from the (rule of) law. It requires formal and substantive uncertainty, but in a procedural setting engulfed in certainty. In Section 11.5, I will seek to reconcile the requirements of certainty and uncertainty within the rule of law, and will conclude the discussion in Section 6.

11.2 FORMAL, PROCEDURAL AND SUBSTANTIVE RULE OF LAW

Rule of law is often divided into three camps: formal, procedural and substantive. From the traditional, formal perspective, the rule of law (or the continental *Rechtsstaat*) imposes negative obligations on all state actors, restraining the use of legislative, administrative and judicial powers, and making legal actors accountable to the law.[8] Law gives its wielders great powers which must be held in check.[9] In its narrowest sense, the rule of law operates to control state actors (rule by law). This minimum condition is often complemented by further formal requirements. Fuller has stated that the rule of law requires (1) denial of *ad hoc* (purely contextual) decisions; (2) public promulgation of laws; (3) denial of retroactive legislation; (4) clarity of laws; (5) denial of contradictory rules; (6) that laws cannot require actions beyond the capabilities of the affected parties; (7) that changes to the legal system cannot be frequent; and that (8) legal norms must be implemented and enforced as they are announced.[10] According to Waldron, these criteria

---

[8] See on the early rule of law discussion A.V. Dicey, *Introduction to the Study of the Constitution* (10th edn with an introduction by E.C.S. Wade, Palgrave Macmillan, 1985) 188, 195–196 and 202 and on the continental *Rechtsstaat* discussion R. Thoma, 'Rechtsstaatsidee und Verwaltungsrechtswissenschaft' in M. Tohidipur (ed), *Der bürgerliche Rechtsstaat* (Suhrkamp, 1978) 177–194.

[9] J. Raz, *The Authority of Law: Essays on Law and Morality* (Oxford University Press, 1979) 224.

[10] L.L. Fuller, *The Morality of Law* (Rev edn, Yale University Press, 1969), 38–39.

can be summarized as requirements of generality, publicity, prospectivity, intelligibility, consistency, practicability, stability and congruence.[11]

These formal criteria establish what legal rules must look like, but they do not set any concrete criteria for the substantive content of these rules. The underlying assumption in all the formal conceptions is that the law should be organized as a system of rules which would facilitate fairly predictable interactions between legal subjects, and between the subjects and the state. The formal rule of law camp often denies the conceptual and essential linkage between the rule of law and the substance of law.[12]

Waldron has emphasized that the formal criteria for the rule of law must be separated from the procedural criteria.[13] The procedural criteria include at least the following: (1) right to a hearing by an impartial, independent and trained tribunal; (2) right to legal representation; (3) right to be present at proceedings; (4) right to confront witnesses in the process; (5) right to a fair collection of evidence by the state; (6) right to present evidence; (7) right to present arguments concerning the evidence and applicable law to the tribunal; (8) right to a reasoned decision; and (9) right of appeal.[14] Waldron's main argument is that the rule of law is essentially built on legal institutions that apply the law and the procedural rules that characterize their actions.[15] Despite the importance of procedure for the rule of law, the procedural aspects have been, according to Waldron, largely overlooked in the traditional, formal theories of the rule of law.[16]

---

[11] See J. Waldron, 'The Rule of Law and the Importance of Procedure' in J.E. Fleming (ed), *Getting to the Rule of Law* (Nomos, Yearbook of the American Society for Political and Legal Philosophy 2010) 5–6. In a similar vein Raz, above n 9, 214 has emphasized prospectivity, openness, clarity and stability of law. For F.A. Hayek, *The Constitution of Liberty* (The Definitive Edn, R. Hamowy (ed), University of Chicago Press, 2011) 312–318, the main criteria are prospectivity, predictability and equality.

[12] Raz, above n 9, 212–219. See also J. Waldron, 'The Concept and the Rule of Law' (2008) *Georgia Law Review* 43(1), 5; B.Z. Tamanaha, *A General Jurisprudence of Law and Society* (Oxford University Press, 2001) 96–106. For Hayek, above n 11, 318, injecting the rule of law with substantive requirements causes practical problems: 'But though there can be no doubt that, in order to be effective, it must be accepted as just by most people, it is doubtful whether we possess any other formal criteria of justice than generality and equality.'

[13] Waldron, above n 11, 8 and 11.

[14] These criteria are essentially based on Waldron, *ibid*, at 6.

[15] *Ibid*, at 12–14.

[16] *Ibid*, at 7–12.

In contrast, and in addition to the formal and the procedural rule of law theories, substantive theories have expanded the scope of the rule of law to include some or all of the SDGs.[17] The move towards more substantive theories of the rule of law has made the concept more vague and controversial, but from a human rights and environmental perspective one may argue that this is a positive development.[18] In this camp it is often emphasized that e.g. access to water, food and energy are of such importance that obedience to the law can hardly be safeguarded without paying attention to these fundamental requirements.[19] Following this, ecological sustainability and the rule of law have been described as the *Grundnorms* of law.[20] In this conception, substantive (sustainable development) goals are upholding the (formal and procedural) rule of law.[21]

Interestingly, neither the substantive, nor the formal and the procedural camp seem to be able to ignore the presence of one another. The substantive camp emphasizes that the achievement of the SDGs requires formal control of legislative, administrative and judicial powers.[22]

---

[17] From a substantive perspective, SDGs contain values which are ascribed essentially to a *good* legal system. See L. Kotzé, 'Sustainable Development and Rule of Law for Nature' in C. Voigt (ed), *Rule of Law for Nature. New Dimensions and Ideas in Environmental Law* (Cambridge University Press, 2013) 135.

[18] This view has been starkly criticized by the formal rule of law camp. Raz argues that the rule of law is not to be mistaken with equality or justice. Rule of law is only one of the virtues of the law, and can be sacrificed if other overriding virtues are at stake. This should not, however, be cloaked in the form of a rule of law argument. Raz, n 9, 225: 'Of course, conformity to the rule of law also enables the law to serve bad purposes.'

[19] From this perspective, the rule of law is a means for reforming and transforming environmental law, see Kotzé, above n 17, 136.

[20] K. Bosselmann, 'Grounding the Rule of Law' in C. Voigt (ed), *Rule of Law for Nature. New Dimensions and Ideas in Environmental Law* (Cambridge University Press, 2013) 83–84; D. Fisher, *Legal Reasoning in Environmental Law. A Study of Structure, Form and Language* (Edward Elgar Publishing, 2013) 433.

[21] Kotzé, above n 17, 143.

[22] Formal and procedural rule of law are prerequisites for sustainability and the management of the environment, see Bugge, above n 2, 7. See also C. Voigt, 'The Principle of Sustainable Development. Integration and Ecological Integrity' in C. Voigt (ed), *Rule of Law for Nature. New Dimensions and Ideas in Environmental Law* (Cambridge University Press, 2013) 147: 'Sustainable development can only be achieved in the context of the rule of law, requiring fair, effective and transparent international and national governance arrangements and clear and implementable environmental laws.'

Similarly, the formal and the procedural camps cannot do away with the substantive aspects. This follows partly from the fact acknowledged by Hart: law cannot be a 'suicide club'.[23] Or, as Waldron puts it: 'I believe that there is a natural overlap between substantive and formal elements, not least because … the formal elements are usually argued for on substantive grounds of dignity and liberty.'[24]

At present, the linkage between the three rule of law camps is also strongly supported by the constitutionalization (and positivization) of many of the SDGs. For instance, the Finnish Constitution (731/1999) states that it shall guarantee the inviolability of human dignity and the freedom and rights of the individual and promote justice in society (section 1). With this development, substantive goals are brought within the framework of positive law, to function as the fundamental goals which Fuller's criteria for form, and Waldron's criteria for procedure, are meant to serve. For these two reasons, it is fair to say that the law (and the rule of law) is injected with substantive considerations as an empirical matter regardless of whether one considers there to be a *conceptual* or an *essential* linkage between the law and other social ecological realities. There is a functional and empirical linkage between the formal, procedural and substantive rule of law.[25]

Based on the discussion of the UNGA Sixth Committee (Legal) on the rule of law, as well as theoretical discussions presented in this section, the formal, procedural and substantive camps link all the SDGs together. Substantive goals (SDGs 1–15) require form and procedure, which in turn require substantive goals to be meaningful. Bringing substantive aspects within the rule of law framework comes at a price, however. It forces the substantive SDGs into a framework of legal certainty that is common to all the three rule of law theories.

I will discuss next what kind of views on certainty the three rule of law camps within SDG 16 impose on the other SDGs. A useful introduction

---

23 H.L.A. Hart, *The Concept of Law* (2nd edn, Oxford University Press, 1994) 192: 'for our concern is with social arrangements for continued existence, not with those of a suicide club'.

24 Waldron, above n 11, 4.

25 Fisher, above n 20, 227. Despite this linkage, there is a need to recognize inputs stemming from the different rule of law traditions. International projects promoting the rule of law, such as the UNEP Environmental Rule of Law project, run the risk of oversimplifying the relationships between the three theories, see UNEP, *Environmental Rule of Law*, available at <http://www.unep.org/environmentalgovernance/erl/who-we-are/overview#> accessed 30 June 2017; UNEP, *Advancing Justice, Governance and Law for Environmental Sustainability* (2012) 4.

to this discussion is Raz's statement that '[t]he rule of law is essentially a negative value. The law inevitably creates a great danger of arbitrary power – the rule of law is designed to minimize the danger created by the law itself.'[26] The mechanism with which the rule of law controls is 'certainty'. Stemming from the functional linkage between all the three rule of law theories this is so regardless of which rule of law theory (or theories) one subscribes to. Ironically, the rule of law, in seeking to control arbitrary use of state powers (which is a good thing) may at times be the single greatest obstacle to the effective implementation of the SDGs (which is not so good). The linkage between form, procedure and substance within the rule of law framework may compromise the very goals for which the linkage is established. The theoretical baggage of certainty may be too much for the substantive goals to handle.

11.3 IMPOSING CERTAINTY ON AN UNCERTAIN SOCIAL ECOLOGICAL WORLD WITH THE RULE OF LAW

The reason why the rule of law pops up everywhere in theory and practice, and why it is discussed with such intensity, is that one's conception of it locks down the fundamentals for the organization of government and governance. As Hayek observes, '[t]he rule of law is therefore not a rule of the law, but a rule concerning what the law ought to be, a meta-legal doctrine or a political ideal'.[27] Against this background, the requirement of certainty – to which all the three rule of law camps subscribe – becomes one of the most fundamental and influential doctrines in legal thinking. But is it the same kind of certainty in all the three camps?

Let us begin with the formal camp. For Hayek, the rule of law consists of (1) general and abstract rules that refer 'to yet unknown cases and containing no references to particular persons, places, or objects'.[28] In addition, (2) rules must be known to the legal subjects before they are enforced.[29] Closely connected to the requirement of generality, (3) rules 'must not make irrelevant distinctions', and must 'apply equally to all, including those who govern …'.[30] Raz links the requirements of generality

---

26 Raz, above n 9, 224.
27 Hayek, above n 11, 311.
28 *Ibid*, at 315.
29 *Ibid*.
30 *Ibid*, at 317–318.

and prospectivity with (4) openness and clarity, as well as (5) stability.[31] With these additions, Fuller's criteria for the formal rule of law are more or less satisfied as well.[32]

All the five criteria are variations of certainty. The first (generality) requires that legal institutions must have an understanding of the past and the future in order to craft rules that are general enough to avoid discrimination, and specific enough to allow for the legal subjects to know their rights and obligations before their application. Legal institutions cannot say 'all that is wrong is banned, and all that is right is allowed'. Nor can they say, as a general rule, that the 'environmentally harmful operations of a specific shale gas company are banned'. The second requirement (prospectivity) denies legal institutions the benefit of hindsight and learning: they cannot frequently say 'we didn't see that coming, we'll change the rules now that we know better'. The third requirement (equality) is a variation of the first (generality). Similarly, the fourth criterion links to the second. It requires that legal institutions should not craft vague or ambiguous rules that – due to their interpretive nature – would withstand time better than clear rules. Finally, stability is a general requirement that seeks to cement legal relationships to a certain point in legal space-time with little leeway for future adjustment as new social ecological problems and answers arise. Stability is then, from a formal perspective, a desired consequence of the four previous criteria.

All the five criteria require certainty that our present knowledge of the environment, technology, societies, culture and so on will be enough, or sufficient for crafting rules that have the generality and accuracy to guide human actions. These formal criteria establish that societies boasting the rule of law must be organized with rules[33] and these rules must be able to anticipate and withstand changes and uncertainties that are presented to them. Although the formal criteria are mainly directed to the legislature, they are extended to adjudication through a formal theory of rules (adjudication is not argumentation but application of clear-cut rules),[34]

---

31 Raz, above n 9, 219.

32 Fuller, above n 10.

33 *Ibid*, at 46.

34 Waldron, above n 11, 22: 'A fallacy of modern positivism, it seems to me, is its exclusive emphasis on the command-and-control aspect of law, or the norm-and-guidance aspect of law, without any reference to the culture of argument that a legal system frames, sponsors, and institutionalizes.'

and a conception that legal interpretation is only required when authoritative legal texts are unclear.[35] Rule of law is violated when 'the norms that are applied by officials do not correspond to the norms that have been made public to the citizens or when officials act on the basis of their own discretion rather than according to norms laid down in advance'.[36]

The procedural rule of law camp subscribes to a more modest notion of certainty. The gist of the argument is that the most important aspect of the rule of law is independent and educated executive and adjudicative institutions that adhere to general, abstract, prospective, equal, open, clear and stable *procedural* rules. Waldron argues that Dicey's classical passage on the formal requirements of the rule of law[37] contains a crucial, procedural element:

> The passage I have emphasized is important. Without it, we tend to read the contrast between the rule of law and arbitrary government in terms of the application of a rule versus purely individualized application of punishment (without guidance by a rule). With it, however, the contrast between law and discretion has to do with institutions and procedures: a person must not be made to suffer except pursuant to a decision of a court arrived at in the ordinary manner observing ordinary legal process.[38]

I have illustrated Waldron's procedural rule of law criteria in Section 2. Here it suffices to say that Waldron emphasizes the argumentative nature of the law which facilitates 'living law', meaning the learning and transformation of the law to facilitate new circumstances. Law's 'living' must, however, be limited by predictable and certain procedural rules to avoid slippage towards an arbitrary system of governance.[39] Under this conception of the rule of law, certainty is not an attribute of substantive

---

[35] R.H. Fallon Jr, 'The Meaning of Legal "Meaning" and its Implications for Theories of Legal Interpretation' (2015) *University of Chicago Law Review* 82, 1299 writes: 'On this view, interpretation occurs as a response to puzzlement or uncertainty. Typically, however, no puzzlement exists. We simply understand what the law requires.'

[36] Waldron, above n 11, 21.

[37] Dicey, above n 8, 110: 'When we say that the supremacy or the rule of law is a characteristic of the English constitution, we … mean, in the first place, that no man is punishable or can be lawfully made to suffer in body or goods except for a distinct breach of law established in the ordinary legal manner before the ordinary Courts of the land. In this sense the rule of law is contrasted with every system of government based on the exercise by persons in authority of wide, arbitrary, or discretionary powers of constraint.'

[38] Waldron, n 11, 10.

[39] *Ibid*, at 18–23.

rules, but of procedural rules. The rule of law is violated if procedural rules, such as the right of appeal, are not adhered to.

Finally, I turn to substantive rule of law theories. It bears reminding that the substantive theories presented in Section 2 often accept the formal criteria for the rule of law. Substantive theories argue that the formal criteria must be complemented with substantive criteria such as rights to water, food and energy. This may, however, at times require deviations from the formal and the procedural rule of law criteria. The substantive rule of law theories state that the rule of law cannot function, and it cannot be met, without the effective implementation of social goals, in this case the SDGs. In this conception, the rule of law sets not only formal characteristics for rules generally, or procedural rules specifically, but also a requirement to respect planetary boundaries and human rights as overall goals of the legal system.[40] As Bosselmann puts it:

> If these ideas are placed in their broader jurisprudential context, it results in the assumption that the grounding of the rule of law in nature requires fundamental changes to the legal systems in international and national terms. Legal structures have to be modified so that they are constrained by ecological concerns in order, first, to prevent the further crossing of planetary boundaries and, second, to maintain environmental goods as a basis for a flourishing development of our posterity. ... This type of state differs considerably from a state solely committed ... to the rule of law.[41]

Under this conception, the substantive SDGs are not only obligations of best effort by the government, but also obligations of result.[42]

The three rule of law theories illuminate different aspects, or layers of certainty, moving from less to more demanding. The formal theories set general criteria for the crafting of rules, mainly for the legislature and the courts in *creating* rules. In this conception, certainty is a recipe for what general ingredients legal rules must contain, but not a recipe for what the rules are about, or what they should regulate substantively. Formal

---

[40] Kotzé, above n 17, 135–136.

[41] K. Bosselmann, 'A Normative Approach to Environmental Governance: Sustainability at the Apex of Environmental Law' in D. Fisher (ed), *Research Handbook on Fundamental Concepts of Environmental Law* (Edward Elgar Publishing, 2016) 42.

[42] See on the distinction, J. van Kempen, 'Obligations of Result or Best Efforts: Dealing with Problems of Interpretation' in M. Peeters and R. Uylenburg (eds), *EU Environmental Legislation. Legal Perspectives on Regulatory Strategies* (Edward Elgar Publishing, 2014) 149–151.

theories do not require democracy, separation of powers, or any other criteria that are presently ascribed to good governance. Singer's rule would easily meet the formal requirements for the rule of law:

> It is easy to create completely determinate legal rules and arguments. For example, an absolutely determinate private law system could be based on the rule that no one is liable to anyone else for anything and that everyone is free to do whatever she wants without government interference. Relentless application of this rule would produce a state-of-nature legal system that would be fully determinate: The plaintiff would always lose. The problem is that this or any other determinate system bears no relation to anything anyone would consider to be just or legitimate.[43]

In contrast, the procedural conception of certainty requires independent and trained courts that apply the law equally to all, and that carefully follow the recipe of the adjudicative due process presented in Section 2. The procedural camp can live with any adjudicative outcome as long as it is the outcome of a due process. In further contrast, the substantive conception is the most demanding of the three. In addition to, and sometimes conflicting with, the formal and the procedural requirements, the most important characteristic for the substantive rule of law is to achieve goals that are fundamental to functioning societies, such as the rights to water, food and energy (SDGs 6, 2 and 7).

One of the main problems shared by all the three rule of law theories is that they all build on variations of certainty that may be at odds with the uncertainty of the social ecological world.[44] The main problem caused by formal certainty is that it places fundamental weight on the insight and knowledge of the law-creating institutions, even though they can never fully predict the future when issuing a rule. As Hart puts it, the relative ignorance of fact introduces and imposes the relative indeterminacy of (legal) goals.[45] The procedural certainty camp faces problems with, for

---

[43] J. Singer, 'The Player and the Cards: Nihilism and Legal Theory' (1984) *Yale Law Journal* 94(1), 11.

[44] This point is echoed by Justice Benjamin in his call for the increased role of science in legal reasoning: 'Environmental law, however, calls for a new ethic that takes science into account and goes beyond traditional boundaries and local contexts to encompass the needs of all living organisms and the Earth as a whole.' UNEP, above n 25, 9.

[45] See Hart, above n 23, 128: 'If the world in which we live were characterized only by a finite number of features, and these together with all the modes in which they could combine were known to us, then provision could be made in advance for every possibility. We could make rules, the application of which to particular cases never called for a further choice. Everything could be

example, overtly rigid rules on the evaluation of evidence, or too high a standard for legal justification banning consequentialist evaluations, which may in turn prevent the evolution of the law to new social ecological realities. Finally, the main problem of the substantive camp is that the law-creating institutions must know *ex ante* what is in the public good now and in the future, and how the public good develops and can be achieved. Substantive rule of law locks in the goals, requires certainty in their realization, and presupposes that it is politically possible to set a coherent set of substantive goals or prioritize those that have the most social ecological merit when they are applied.

Despite the criticism, certainty under the rule of law has much merit to it. Many of the SDGs call for preventive action, or abstaining from the use of certain geographical areas, environmental media and natural resources. Clean water (SDG 6) and aquatic biodiversity (SDG 14), and the broader water security require that water resources are used sustainably, and that point-source and non-point-source pollution is controlled to the effect that water resources maintain their utility for households, irrigation, industry and ecosystems.[46] Climate change mitigation (SDG 13) requires minimizing the use of hydrocarbons, increasing the role of renewables in the energy mix (SDG 7), and changes in global consumption patterns (SDG 12).[47] Many of the social ecological drivers and consequences behind the lack of water, loss of aquatic biodiversity and harmful human-induced climate change are known. The certainty that the law provides undeniably plays an important part in achieving these SDGs.

Notwithstanding this, there is also considerable uncertainty as to the social ecological drivers and consequences of environmental changes and harm that neither yesterday's nor today's environmental laws can predict. Uncertainty of the social ecological world is caused mainly by the lack of scientific data and understanding of biological systems, economic and

---

known, and for everything, since it could be known, something could be done and specified in advance by rule. This would be a world fit for "mechanical" jurisprudence. Plainly this world is not our world; human legislators can have no such knowledge of all the possible combinations of circumstances which the future may bring. This inability to anticipate brings with it a relative indeterminacy of aim.'

[46] UN Water, *Water Security & the Global Water Agenda* (A UN-Water Analytical Brief. Revised version 2013) 1–5, available at <http:// www.unwater.org/fileadmin/user_upload/unwater_new/docs/analytical_brief_oct2013_web.pdf> accessed 24 April 2017.

[47] IPCC, *Climate Change 2014: Synthesis Report* (2014) 4–6.

social risks, and the dynamic and complex nature of social ecological systems.[48] First, uncertainty results from data gaps that are due to new technology that is yet to be studied (such as new waste water treatment technologies or new energy technologies). Second, uncertainty may result from lack of historical data, which makes it difficult to establish reference points against which to measure present environmental changes. The third source of uncertainty is complexity.[49] Single drivers of climate change, declining biodiversity and changes in biogeochemical cycles may be scientifically predictable. 'Wicked' uncertainty is not, however, visible until one observes all the interlinked phenomena at all the ecosystem scales. Different local phenomena interacting together can lead to unpredictable consequences at the global level. For this reason, one of the most pressing problems in ecology is to understand how changes in local or regional ecosystems will alter emergent patterns or mechanisms at other levels of biological organization.[50] Scientific models and quantifications involve considerable uncertainty in predicting the future of ecological and social systems, and their interactions. Both gradual changes and external perturbations may cause radical and random shifts in social material relations and interaction patterns.[51] Complex adaptive systems are fundamentally characterized by this non-linearity.[52] Hence, obtaining scientific certainty of the effects that human actions have had or will have on ecosystems, the biosphere, the economy, and social and cultural systems is at present impossible. If science cannot be (reasonably) certain of how the social ecological world operates or will

---

[48] J.B. Ruhl, 'Thinking of Environmental Law as a Complex Adaptive System: How to Clean Up the Environment by Making a Mess of Environmental Law' (1997) *Houston Law Review* 34, 132; L. Rist, A. Felton, L. Samuels, C. Sandström and O. Rosvall, 'A New Paradigm for Adaptive Management' (2013) *Ecology and Society* 18(4), 63–71.

[49] A. Wiersema, 'The Precautionary Principle in Environmental Governance' in D. Fisher (ed), *Research Handbook on Fundamental Concepts of Environmental Law* (Edward Elgar Publishing, 2016) 451.

[50] See G. Hartvigsen, A. Kinzig and G. Peterson, 'Use and Analysis of Complex Adaptive Systems in Ecosystem Science: Overview of Special Section' (1998) *Ecosystems* 1, 429.

[51] J. Nordberg and G.S. Cumming, 'Complexity Theory for a Sustainable Future' in J. Nordberg and G.S. Cumming (eds), *Complexity Theory for a Sustainable Future* (Columbia University Press, 2008) 277–293.

[52] P. Perez and D. Batten, 'Complex Science for a Complex World: An Introduction' in P. Perez and D. Batten (eds), *Complex Science for a Complex World: Exploring Human Ecosystems with Agents* (ANU E Press, 2006) 8.

operate, neither can the (rule of) law that seeks to regulate the human–environment interface.

The uncertainties of the social ecological world in which the SDGs – such as those dealing with clean water, food and energy, maintenance of biodiversity, and mitigation of climate change – are implemented demerit any effort of imposing legal certainty onto an otherwise uncertain world. There is genuine uncertainty concerning some of the drivers, consequences, and equitable and effective responses to these environmental problems. The (rule of) law needs to acknowledge this uncertainty to stay relevant for addressing these sustainability challenges. In the next section, I will discuss briefly some familiar regulatory and adjudicative strategies for reconciling the fundamental (societal) need for certainty with the uncertainty of the social ecological world.

11.4 ADJUDICATIVE AND REGULATORY STRATEGIES FOR NAVIGATING UNCERTAINTY IN SCIENCE AND LAW

> The Wind and the Sun were disputing which was the stronger. Suddenly they saw a traveller coming down the road, and the Sun said: 'I see a way to decide our dispute. Whichever of us can cause that traveller to take off his cloak shall be regarded as the stronger[.] You begin.' So the Sun retired behind a cloud, and the Wind began to blow as hard as it could upon the traveller. But the harder he blew the more closely did the traveller wrap his cloak round him, till at last the Wind had to give up in despair. Then the Sun came out and shone in all his glory upon the traveller, who soon found it too hot to walk with his cloak on.[53]

Much like the Wind in the classic story above, the rule of law cannot force absolute certainty upon itself, nor upon the scientific and social practices in which legal debates unfold. There are two main strategies for navigating the uncertainty of the social ecological world, and reconciling it with the (rule of) law: (1) crafting regulation along the lines of adaptive law theories, and/or (2) interpreting existing laws considering the precautionary principle and the golden rule (teleology).

In addressing the social ecological uncertainty and effectively achieving the SDGs, the more salient of these strategies is to craft legislation that acknowledges the permanent and chronic outdatedness of the law as

[53] J. Jacobs, 'Æ. Fables' (1909–1914) *The Harvard Classics* XVII(1) (P.F. Collier and Son).

soon as it is passed, and seeks to bridge the gap between science and governance. Such approaches have been extensively discussed under the banner of adaptive management and law, as well as resilience theories.[54] The guiding paradigm of these theories is that there are always significant gaps in the understanding of the legislature, which hinders the achievement of even the most plausible of environmental or other goals. For this reason, legislation generally, and environmental legislation specifically, should contain procedural mechanisms that would allow constant monitoring of the environment and human actions influencing it, as well as a periodical re-evaluation of the legality of human actions. Law should be connected to the best scientific knowledge available, and directly linked to the goals (hopefully good ones) set in legislation.

In practice, adaptive law builds upon an adaptive management cycle, which consists of assessing the condition of environmental media and pressures affecting them, designing mechanisms (e.g. licence conditions) for achieving legislative targets, implementing these mechanisms, monitoring their effectiveness, evaluation of the mechanisms, and never-ending adjustment of environmental management. The adaptive management cycle is based on learning, iteration and sensitivity to new scientific knowledge.[55] Much of the European Union's environmental legislation – such as the Water Framework Directive (2000/60/EC) and the Marine Strategy Framework Directive (2008/56/EC) – is based on this approach.[56]

As adaptive law leaves many substantive issues unregulated (uncertain), and places significant societal power in the hands of scientists and

---

[54] See for example, Ruhl, above n 48, 101–164; C.A. Arnold and L.H. Gunderson, 'Adaptive Law and Resilience' (2013) *Environmental Law Reporter* 43, 10428; A.E. Camacho and R.L. Glicksman, 'Legal Adaptive Capacity: How Program Goals and Processes Shape Federal Land Adaptation to Climate Change' (2016) *University of Colorado Law Review* 87(3), 722.

[55] C.S. Holling, *Adaptive Environmental Assessment and Management* (John Wiley and Sons, 1978); C.J. Walters, *Adaptive Management of Renewable Resources* (Macmillan, 1986); M.H. Benson, 'Integrating Adaptive Management and Oil and Gas Development: Existing Obstacles and Opportunities for Reform' (2009) 39 *Environmental Law Reporter* 10962; Rist et al, above n 48.

[56] See L. Squintani and H. Van Rijswick, 'Improving Legal Certainty and Adaptability in the Programmatic Approach' (2016) *Journal of Environmental Law* 28, 443–445; N. Soininen and F.M. Platjouw, 'Resilience and Adaptive Capacity of Aquatic Environmental Law in the EU – An Evaluation and Comparison of the WFD, MSFD, and MSPD' in D. Langlet and R. Rayfuse (eds), *The Ecosystem Approach in Ocean Planning and Governance* (Brill, 2018, forthcoming).

environmental managers, there is a fundamental need to hold these powers in check with procedural mechanisms contained in due process generally, e.g. access to justice and the obligation to give reasons for decisions that may impact the environment.[57] But considering the unavoidability of environmental management,[58] and the uncertainties contained in it, it would be a mistake to abandon adaptive law for the threats it poses for the rule of law. These threats can be largely compensated for by a rigorous application of procedural rules. Moreover, it is unlikely that any other regulatory strategy could respond to the uncertainties of the social ecological world more effectively. And if environmental law cannot effectively facilitate the achievement of environmental targets, such as the SDGs, then what is it for? Certainty for the sake of certainty does not sound very promising, or legitimate.

The second strategy is much more traditional, and less effective in reducing certainty and adapting law to changing circumstances within the rule of law. This strategy employs the precautionary principle in reversing the burden of proof in evaluating the legality of activities with major potential for environmental harm. This strategy seeks to counter the scientific uncertainty present in environmental management, and counter the deficiency that the legal framework does not contain adaptive mechanisms for minimizing scientific uncertainty.[59]

The precautionary principle is often coupled with an interpretive or argumentative attitude towards the law. Legal provisions are interpreted as leaving discretion for the executive branch and the courts for (re)evaluating environmentally harmful projects. It is constantly observed in the adaptive law literature that globally many of the environmental regulations targeting pollution control, extraction of natural resources, and

---

[57] See on the discretionary problems B. Pardy, 'The Pardy-Ruhl Dialogue on Ecosystem Management Part V: Discretion, Complex-Adaptive Problem Solving and the Rule of Law' (2008) *Pace Environmental Law Review* 25, 354; and the requirement to control environmental managers, B. Pardy, 'Towards an Environmental Rule of Law' (2014) *Asia Pacific Journal of Environmental Law* 17, 174–175.

[58] This is a somewhat contested claim as the Pardy–Ruhl debate demonstrates, see B. Pardy, 'Changing Nature: The Myth of the Inevitability of Ecosystem Management' (2003) *Pace Environmental Law Review* 20, 675–692; J.B. Ruhl, 'The Myth of What Is Inevitable Under Ecosystem Management: A Response to Pardy' (2004) *Pace Environmental Law Review* 21, 315–323; Pardy, 'The Pardy-Ruhl Dialogue' above n 57, 341–354.

[59] P. Sands and J. Peel, *Principles of International Environmental Law* (3rd edn, Cambridge University Press, 2012) 222; Wiersema, above n 49, 450–461.

nature conservation have been drafted with a fairly stable social ecological environment in mind.[60] As this premise is increasingly criticized, existing and often scientifically outdated environmental regulations merit a more teleological interpretation, which facilitates the achievement of environmental goals contained in old laws, or the goals of more recent legal instruments that may be located at the domestic, regional or international levels.[61] Here, the interpretive and argumentative nature of the law is a mechanism which allows the law to breathe and adjust to new social ecological circumstances, and stay relevant for societies in achieving desirable goals contained within existing domestic legislation, or international agreements.[62] Waldron argues that the argumentative nature of law is often ignored and marginalized in traditional legal positivistic theories, which often go hand in hand with the formal rule of law theories:

> When positivists in the tradition of H. L. A. Hart pay attention to this aspect of interpretation and argument, they tend to treat it as an occasional and problematic sideline. The impression given is that, in most cases, the authoritative identification of legal norms using a rule of recognition is sufficient; once it is recognized, a legal norm can become a straightforward guide to official action. But, it is said, occasionally the language is unclear –

---

60 Ruhl, above n 48, 107: 'Complex adaptive systems, because of their highly collectivized, nonlinear, dynamic behavior, defy prediction through classical reductionist method, or any other known method for that matter. Yet we have not designed our environmental law system with this underlying property in mind. Rather, it is mired in a reductionist, linear, predictivist mentality ignorant of underlying complex system behaviors. We find ourselves as a result constantly befuddled when the intended benefits of environmental regulation fail to materialize or, worse, when consequences contrary to the intended effects materialize.'

61 See on the international plane the *Danube Dam* case: 25 September 1997 (*Hungary v. Slovakia*) ICJ Rep., 37 *International Legal Materials* (1998), and its analysis in N. Soininen, 'The Structure, Form and Language of International Environmental Norms – from Absolute to Relative Normativity' in D. Fisher (ed), *Research Handbook on Fundamental Concepts of Environmental Law* (Edward Elgar Publishing, 2016) 257; and on the plane of the European Union C-525/12 *Commission v. Germany* para 43: 'It should be borne in mind, as a preliminary point, that in accordance with the Court's settled case-law, the interpretation of a provision of EU law requires that account be taken not only of its wording and the objectives it pursues, but also its context and the provisions of EU law as a whole.' See also generally, Fisher, above n 20, 277–278.

62 Waldron, above n 11, 20–21: 'So we cannot just brush the argumentative aspect of law's procedures aside so far as the Rule of Law is concerned. I believe this tension in the Rule of Law ideal is largely unavoidable, and we should own up to the fact that the Rule of Law points, as it were, in both directions.'

> because words have open texture or because our aims are indeterminate or because for some other reasons there is a hiccough in the interface between words and the facts that they apply to – and then, unfortunately, we have no choice but to argue the matter through. … But this account radically underestimates the point that argumentation (about what this or that provision means or about the effect of this array of precedents) is business as usual in law. We would be uneasy about counting a system that did not exhibit it and make routine provision for it as a legal system.[63]

Furthermore, a strict textual interpretation of (environmental) regulation that is based on discredited scientific knowledge does not allow for the effective achievement of regulatory goals (often prevention of environmental harm in one way or another).[64] Justice Benjamin argues for instance that property laws 'must be reinterpreted to incorporate concepts of environmental stewardship and sustainability'. In other words, certainty of property law must sometimes be sacrificed for adapting it to new scientific knowledge on the functioning of social ecological systems.[65] Turning a blind eye to consequentialist evaluations in adjudication, and overemphasizing the legal certainty and adjudicative mechanisms that deliver it (e.g. strict textual interpretation of an outdated statute), risk turning law from a servant to master, and marginalizing law in the instrument mix of environmental governance.[66]

By way of conclusion, it is clear that environmental laws need to be effective to achieve the SDGs. This in turn requires certainty from the law, but it also requires adaptivity to adjust to new social ecological realities, and to new scientific knowledge. Law must at times operate like the Sun, leaving substantive freedom for the environmental managers to adjust the legality of environmentally harmful projects in light of the

---

63 *Ibid*, at 22.

64 This is a standard criticism of the formal rule of law theories, see T.R.S. Allan, 'Freedom, Equality, Legality' in J.R. Silkenat, J.E. Hickey Jr and P.D. Barenboim (eds), *The Legal Doctrines of the Rule of Law and the Legal State (Rechtstaat)* (Springer, 2014) 160.

65 See UNEP, above n 25, 9.

66 This is also acknowledged by the formal rule of law theorists, see Raz, above n 9, 228: 'It [the rule of law] has always to be balanced against competing claims of other values … Conformity to the rule of law is a matter of degree, and though, other things being equal, the greater the conformity the better – other things are rarely equal. A lesser degree of conformity is often to be preferred precisely because it helps realization of other goals.' Raz would, however, claim that these 'other goals' do not belong to the realm of the rule of law at all. As I discussed in Section 2, the separation of form and substance is difficult in practice, although it may be discussed in theory.

most recent science. Wind is, in turn, required to hold the managers and the adjudicative procedure in check.

11.5 CONCLUSIONS

I began this chapter by dividing the rule of law into formal, procedural and substantive camps. In a nutshell, the formal camp emphasizes controlling arbitrary public powers. This is done by setting formal criteria for what legal rules and their application must look like. These theories rest on certainty and predictability in all legal relations. The procedural rule of law theories make a more modest claim. They emphasize the role of law-applying institutions such as the courts. At the core of procedural rule of law is adherence to due process, which means, among other things, access to justice and limits to the evaluation of evidence, legal reasoning, and statement of reasons. Finally, the substantive rule of law camp requires that goals, such as the SDGs, should guide both the legislature and the courts in all their actions.

I then argued that the formal rule of law requires substance because otherwise law would risk transforming into a 'suicide club'. The procedural rule of law theories would, in turn, be meaningless if they had no substantive goals to serve. Similarly, the substantive rule of law theories require the formal and the procedural theories as substantive goals cannot be realized without institutional structures or any formal criteria for what the legal rules should look like. There is accordingly a functional and empirical linkage between the rule of law theories.

One of the main problems with all the rule of law theories is that they impose certainty on an uncertain social ecological world. The formal camp requires the legislature to craft rules that can withstand unforeseen environmental, social, economic and cultural changes. The procedural camp requires adherence to strict procedural rules in evaluating evidence and dealing with the burden of proof, as well as strict criteria for legal argumentation. The substantive camp claims to know the goals that should be subscribed to in legislation and adjudication, and in which order of priority the often conflicting goals should be placed. All these three rule of law theories require different kinds of certainty that is at odds with the uncertainty of the social ecological 'real' world discussed in Section 4. The uncertainty, in turn, is a result of, among other things, ever-developing technology, and gaps in scientific knowledge. The clash between (legal) certainty and social ecological uncertainty may at times be the single greatest obstacle to effectively achieving environmental goals such as the SDGs.

Finally, I turned to two categories of legal mechanisms that may be used to reconcile the (rule of law's) need for certainty, and the uncertainty of the social ecological world. The first mechanism is regulatory, and aimed at the legislature. The second is adjudicative, and aimed at the law-applying institutions. In the first line of inquiry, environmental regulations should be designed to alleviate scientific uncertainty. Law can facilitate this by establishing iterative and adaptive management processes that facilitate a functioning science/policy interface. A recent example includes the European Union's water and marine legislation. In the second line of inquiry, courts are required to exercise their discretion in evaluating the factual effects of environmentally harmful projects considering the precautionary principle. Statutory and agreement-based legal requirements must be interpreted and evaluated considering the golden rule, i.e. the aims of the provisions under application, rather than looking categorically at the textual formulations of applicable provisions. The golden rule facilitates consequentialist inquiries, which, if done right, should be based on the best available science that informs of the effects of environmentally harmful projects. Recent decisions incorporating climate change considerations are early testimony of courts' ability to undertake this.

Overall, the required substantive freedom of environmental managers to adjust human activities having a significant individual or cumulative effect on the SDGs is a significant concession from the rule of law. But it need not be a disaster for the rule of law. This, however, requires that the procedural mechanisms and safeguards that the legal system provides take centre stage. Control of administrative and judicial powers under the rule of law trickles down to questions like how well (a sound factual and legal basis) and openly the decisions are reasoned. Placing less emphasis on the substantive and the formal, and more on the procedural, is the best combination of all the rule of law worlds for the SDGs.

12. SDG 17: partnerships for the Goals – cooperation within the context of a voluntarist framework

Nathan Cooper and Duncan French

12.1 INTRODUCTION

International cooperation in matters of development is recognised as a *sine qua non* of any meaningful international development strategy.[1] International cooperation has never been accurately – or precisely – defined and on its own terms is value neutral in terms of the objective to be achieved. Nevertheless, as the principal means by which development assistance and resources (be that technical, financial, human or knowledge) are transferred invariably to the global South, international cooperation is a vital process. However, what that cooperation actually entails, between whom, and to what ends, has never been straightforward and is one of the most contentious aspects of developmental policy. Issues such as voluntarism versus obligation, bilateralism versus multilateralism, and aid versus trade, interact with broader questions of project ownership and sovereignty, institutional oversight and political accountability, as well as general matters of effectiveness, local implementation and sustainability, among others. These ensure that cooperation is both a politically loaded concept and, equally problematic, an indeterminate instrument of development policy. In normative terms, whether international cooperation is – or should – be viewed as a mandatory aspect of the function of a State, and from where any such obligation arises, also remains hugely contested. Nevertheless, as a cornerstone of international

[1] 2000 Millennium Declaration, United Nations General Assembly Resolution 55/2, 2000, para 32: 'We solemnly reaffirm, on this historic occasion, that the United Nations is the indispensable common house of the entire human family, through which we will seek to realize our universal aspirations for peace, cooperation and development.'

strategy, cooperation in its increasingly myriad variations and guises (State-to-State, private, charitable, commercial and, more often than not, amalgams of these approaches) continues to be both a stated objective of, and an accepted pathway to, development. Indeed, it is the very conflation of ends and means that provides much of the ongoing political debate in this area.

As with almost every United Nations (UN) document on development and global strategy for the past 70 years, *Transforming our world*, which adopted the Sustainable Development Goals (SDGs) in 2015, places international cooperation at the heart of its achievement.[2] Indeed, to identify where and how cooperation features in the Global Goals would be to take an unduly granular approach to the 17 Goals, 169 targets and more than 300 indicators of progress. Cooperation runs through each pervasively and, at times, rather noticeably. Thus, to say that each of the Global Goals, wholly or in part, depends on numerous forms of cooperation, is a blatant and consequently unhelpful, truism. The purpose of this chapter is therefore more limited, namely to focus on the global Goal, SDG 17, specifically given over to international partnerships, and recognising the overlap, but by no means synergy, between such 'partnerships' and international cooperation as it is perhaps more generally understood.

After broadly outlining the scope and stated ambition of SDG 17, the chapter will provide a critique of the Goal, broadly around three discrete aspects of the partnerships idea. First, on their own terms, how far are the targets identified likely to support the Global Goals and contribute, in particular, to the implementation of effective partnerships? Significantly, what are some of the policy obstacles and legal challenges to this occurring? Secondly, how far does the formulation and implementation of such partnerships reflect – within a normative context – the existence of a putative international duty to cooperate in developmental affairs (recognised by some as *lex lata* while rejected by others with equal determination as divisive and dystopian)? Thirdly, in developing further this line of argument, what does the multiplicity of partnerships identified in SDG 17 say, not only about the broadening understanding of international cooperation, but also about the changing normative structure of the international system? Attention will be given to the role of civil society in developing such partnerships, with particular reference to SDG 6 on the sustainable management of water and sanitation. The chapter will conclude by noting that critiquing the content and context of

---

[2] *Transforming our world: the 2030 Agenda for Sustainable Development*, United Nations General Assembly Resolution 70/1, 2015.

SDG 17 is not the same as questioning the importance of international cooperation, as more generally understood. What it does require, however, is to develop and articulate a much clearer framework on how international cooperation supports development; not to head back to the bipartisan politics of North versus South, but in recognising that even within a voluntarist system of cooperation, a normative framework is much more than simply useful: it is essential.

12.2 COOPERATION IN DEVELOPMENT AND SDG 17

The expectation of international cooperation runs throughout the international community's attempt to tackle the challenges of global development. As the UN Charter states, '[a]ll Members pledge themselves to take *joint and separate action in co-operation with the Organization* for the achievement of the purposes set forth in Article 55'.[3] Those purposes include 'higher standards of living, full employment, and conditions of economic and social progress and development' and 'solutions of international economic, social, health, and related problems; and international cultural and educational cooperation'.[4] The General Assembly more recently in the 2005 World Summit Outcome emphasised 'the need for the United Nations to play a fundamental role in the promotion of international cooperation for development and the coherence, coordination and implementation of development goals and actions agreed upon by the international community'.[5]

The international community has thus, over the decades, sought to operationalise such ideas, primarily through the establishment of multilateral structures (e.g. the World Bank), international programmes (e.g. the UN Development Programme (UNDP)) and other legal and non-legal regimes (e.g. the Organisation for Economic Co-operation and Development (OECD) work on aid effectiveness), as well as encouraging more *ad hoc* (including bilateral) cooperation between States. Thus, ever since the international community has recognised and sought to promote development as a valid global objective – namely, something worthy of attention and resource – international cooperation has been the cornerstone of its development strategy.

Such cooperation – even when structured through established multilateral processes – has rarely been unproblematic or not subject to

[3] Charter of the United Nations, 1945, art. 56. Emphasis added.

[4] *Ibid*, art. 55.

[5] United Nations General Assembly Resolution 60/1, 2005, para 38.

complex, and indeed occasionally overt, political contestation. States have invariably viewed the support they give in the area of development as ranging widely in purpose and almost more often than not beyond the strictly humanitarian. Strategic, economic and political considerations are equally important, and not only to the donor; the receiving State is equally aware of the importance of receiving the 'right' form of cooperation. Nevertheless, the idea, if not the ideal, of cooperation on matters of development between States persists. Whether there exists a general legal *duty* to cooperate (beyond those mandated by a specific treaty) is a particularly divisive issue in international law, historically dividing many developed States (which rejected anything but a voluntarist approach) and developing States (which argued broadly in favour of the existence of a wider normative obligation).[6]

It is within this overall context that attempts to give meaningful shape to cooperation within successive international development strategies have had to take place. It is beyond the scope of this chapter to outline the role and utility of international cooperation and assistance in such strategies over the decades.[7] Much attention would undoubtedly focus on, among other things, the Bretton Woods Institutions (BWIs), the changing nature and purpose of official development assistance (ODA) and, more latterly, moves on debt relief and preferential treatment in trade relations. Others might point to UN 'decades of development', the bipartisan debates in the UN General Assembly during the 1970s, and the debates over permanent sovereignty over natural resources and the attempt to establish a New International Economic Order (NIEO). Still others would rightly opt to focus on more recent shifts in private finance and investment, both foreign direct investment (FDI) and portfolio investment.

---

[6] It is interesting to note that in relation to the Millennium Development Goals (MDGs), it was commented that 'it can be observed that the case [for normative status] would be most easily made in relation to the first six of the Goals' (P. Alston, 'Ships Passing in the Night: The Current State of the Human Rights and Development Debate Seen Through the Lens of the Millennium Development Goals' (2005) *Human Rights Quarterly* 27, 774). Significantly, MDG 8 on the establishment of a global partnership was omitted even from this putative list. Also omitted was MDG 7 ('ensuring environmental sustainability'), which perhaps in light of the naming of the 2015 Goals as the *Sustainable Development Goals* suggests just how far the debate has come.

[7] For a general discussion of these issues, see M. Boas and D. McNeill (eds), *Global Institutions and Development: Framing the World?* (Routledge, 2003). See Sam Adelman, Chapter 2 in this volume.

Each has, of course, been extremely important in its own way, and has undoubtedly led to the current situation that the international community has now reached as regards global development: significant moral injunction yet, in the main, legal voluntarism. Others would want to focus on the human rights implications of development, be that at the level of the individual (economic, social and cultural rights); (more controversially) at the group and/or State level (the right to development);[8] or operationally (for instance, the ongoing debates over the role of human rights in the work of the BWIs).[9] Both proponents and critics of international development strategies would argue that the development debate now includes many new issues – in the last 20 years, this would surely include an increased focus on good governance, gender, sustainability, access to technology and the Internet, etc – but the old frustrations are the same, namely that cooperation is often fulfilled more in the rhetoric than in reality, and that imagining new international strategies is still necessary because of the failure of real political will to implement past attempts.

Despite the inevitable truth in such arguments, something does seem to have changed. Since 2000 there has been a new approach to development in the UN and more widely among global governance actors. Through the identification of aspirational goals, a wide group of actors – States, international organisations, the private sector and civil society – have been encouraged to act in a more coordinated fashion to support, promote and contribute to their attainment. Fragmentation invariably remains, but both at a higher (conceptual) level and at a lower (operational) level, there is undoubtedly increasing coherence in approach. From 2000–2015, such goals were contained in the Millennium Development Goals (MDGs) and, for the next 15 years, they are to be found in the Sustainable Development Goals (SDGs), or the 'Global Goals' as they are more commonly referenced. Of course, it would be naïve to presuppose that development is now prioritised above, or necessarily even mainstreamed within, everyday economic transactions or international diplomacy. Collapse in world trade talks, ongoing discussions on plurilateral trade and investment agreements, unilateral shifts in aid policies,

[8] UN Declaration on the Right to Development, United Nations General Assembly Resolution 41/128, 1986.

[9] 2015 Report of the Special Rapporteur on extreme poverty and human rights (4 August 2015) UN Doc. A/70/274, para 68: 'For most purposes, the World Bank is a human rights-free zone. In its operational policies, in particular, it treats human rights more like an infectious disease than universal values and obligations.'

as well as the political pushes and pulls of such major challenges as climate change, all reveal the often transitional and contested nature of development in international relations.

12.2.1 Partnerships for the Goals

Of specific interest for this chapter is SDG 17, which is entitled 'Partnerships for the Goals'. It reflects a pattern set by the MDGs, where the last Goal was also the most instrumental, in that case MDG 8: 'a Global Partnership for Development'. The difference in what the two Goals are called (and other differences in content and tone) are arguably more than merely symbolic and thus will be considered below. As with each of the other goals, SDG17 has set against it a number of targets, which are worth setting out below in full:

Finance

Strengthen domestic resource mobilization, including through international support to developing countries, to improve domestic capacity for tax and other revenue collection

Developed countries to implement fully their official development assistance commitments, including the commitment by many developed countries to achieve the target of 0.7 per cent of ODA/GNI [official development assistance/gross national income] to developing countries and 0.15 to 0.20 per cent of ODA/GNI to least developed countries ODA providers are encouraged to consider setting a target to provide at least 0.20 per cent of ODA/GNI to least developed countries

Mobilize additional financial resources for developing countries from multiple sources

Assist developing countries in attaining long-term debt sustainability through coordinated policies aimed at fostering debt financing, debt relief and debt restructuring, as appropriate, and address the external debt of highly indebted poor countries to reduce debt distress

Adopt and implement investment promotion regimes for least developed countries

Technology

Enhance North-South, South-South and triangular regional and international cooperation on and access to science, technology and innovation and enhance knowledge sharing on mutually agreed terms, including through improved coordination among existing mechanisms, in particular at the United Nations level, and through a global technology facilitation mechanism

Promote the development, transfer, dissemination and diffusion of environmentally sound technologies to developing countries on favourable terms, including on concessional and preferential terms, as mutually agreed

Fully operationalize the technology bank and science, technology and innovation capacity-building mechanism for least developed countries by 2017 and enhance the use of enabling technology, in particular information and communications technology

Capacity building

Enhance international support for implementing effective and targeted capacity-building in developing countries to support national plans to implement all the sustainable development goals, including through North-South, South-South and triangular cooperation

Trade

Promote a universal, rules-based, open, non-discriminatory and equitable multilateral trading system under the World Trade Organization, including through the conclusion of negotiations under its Doha Development Agenda

Significantly increase the exports of developing countries, in particular with a view to doubling the least developed countries' share of global exports by 2020

Realize timely implementation of duty-free and quota-free market access on a lasting basis for all least developed countries, consistent with World Trade Organization decisions, including by ensuring that preferential rules of origin applicable to imports from least developed countries are transparent and simple, and contribute to facilitating market access

In addition, and unlike the other goals, SDG17 also lists what it refers to as 'Systemic issues', which are structural in nature, attention to which is central to the attainment of the SDGs. The necessity of including such a list – as most of the themes are reflective of the ingrained problems and structural tensions that have bedevilled the attainment of long-term development for decades – immediately highlights the complexity of many of the issues under SDG 17. The notion of partnerships within the Global Goals would thus seem to span the whole gamut of the most intractable and contentious issues within international economic relations, notably trade, finance, investment, and technology transfer. The 'systemic issues' are:

Policy and institutional coherence

Enhance global macroeconomic stability, including through policy coordination and policy coherence

Enhance policy coherence for sustainable development

Respect each country's policy space and leadership to establish and implement policies for poverty eradication and sustainable development

Multi-stakeholder partnerships

Enhance the global partnership for sustainable development, complemented by multi-stakeholder partnerships that mobilize and share knowledge, expertise, technology and financial resources, to support the achievement of the sustainable development goals in all countries, in particular developing countries

Encourage and promote effective public, public-private and civil society partnerships, building on the experience and resourcing strategies of partnerships

There is a final section on data, monitoring and accountability, which recognises the importance of statistical data. Moreover, there is seemingly recognition of the limitation of gross domestic product (GDP) as a metric, though any progress on the identification of new measurements to record wider success is very much complementary to GDP, and by no means a replacement for it.

12.2.2 Constrained Idealism and Real Constraints in SDG 17

Before identifying some of the specific problems arising under the targets and systemic issues which are set for SDG 17, it is worth noting that, whether by intention or design, many of the issue areas that could have fallen (or partially do fall) under SDG 17 are actually mentioned elsewhere in the Global Goals. Equally, other important issues get little mention at all (or only by implication), including, for instance, intellectual property rights, tax evasion,[10] and the value of undertaking sustainability impact assessments of trade agreements. Indeed, it might validly be argued that as an agenda, *Transforming our world* is paradoxically relatively narrow and purposely circumscribed.

In relation to issues mentioned in other Goals, specific reference should be made to SDG 10 ('Reducing Inequalities') and SDG 16

[10] Target 17.1 mutedly refers to '[s]trengthen[ing] domestic resource mobilization, including through international support to developing countries, to improve domestic capacity for tax and other revenue collection'.

('Peace, Justice and Strong Institutions'). Within each of their admittedly broad remits, there are some notable inclusions. SDG 10, for instance, includes (rather randomly sitting next to targets on migration, welfare protections and equal opportunities promotion) such targets as to '[i]mprove the regulation and monitoring of global financial markets and institutions and strengthen the implementation of such regulations'; to '[e]nsure enhanced representation and voice for developing countries in decision-making in global international economic and financial institutions'; and to '[i]mplement the principle of special and differential treatment for developing countries, in particular least developed countries, in accordance with World Trade Organization agreements'.

As regards SDG 16, which is primarily centred on national rule of law and justice matters, there is a similar disjunction as in SDG 10 between domestic and truly global priorities – in this case to '[b]roaden and strengthen the participation of developing countries in the institutions of global governance'. If this sounds familiar, many of the targets have appeared in various forms in earlier global strategic documents over the decades.[11] The lack of progress so far and the need to relist them is as dispiriting as it is unsurprising.

Thus, the first fallacy that must be rejected is that SDG 17 is the exclusive 'international cooperation' Goal. First, as noted, many instances of cooperation are found elsewhere within the Global Goals. Secondly, as the saying goes, there is nothing new under the sun; most of the targets are reformulated versions of earlier (and yet still unachieved) objectives of the international community. But thirdly, and much more on the substance, the content of the Goal itself extends beyond what many might consider development cooperation to be, namely focusing on supporting poverty alleviation and other immediate development goals. Indeed, it perhaps strains the normal meaning of 'partnerships' to include such issues as tax and revenue collection, investment promotion and the operation of a technology bank. Defining cooperation is itself, of course, a superficially easy – yet ultimately problematic – endeavour. As Wolfrum notes, '[t]he term "co-operation" has never been defined by an international treaty or a resolution of an international organization'.[12]

---

[11] See, for instance, Millennium Declaration, n 1, para 5: 'These efforts must include policies and measures, at the global level, which correspond to the needs of developing countries and economies in transition and are formulated and implemented with their effective participation'.

[12] R. Wolfrum, 'International Law of Cooperation' in *Max Planck Encyclopedia of Public International Law* (Oxford University Press, 2013) para 2.

Moreover, cooperation per se 'has no inherent value'[13] – it is descriptive of a process – and much relates to the objective to be achieved. Though he dismisses its general legal force (an issue returned to in the next section), Wolfrum accurately notes that cooperation, when used in the context of development (which he rather circularly calls the 'law of co-operation'), means 'co-operation among States for the purposes of development to increase the social welfare of the world community'.[14] Of course, this again only takes the debate so far as it says very little about the means and forms of cooperation.

Therefore, beyond the debate as to *how* cooperation can occur (e.g. bilaterally, via multilateral institutions, through treaties, or voluntarily), there is the more substantive question as to its *purpose*. Should cooperation for development, for instance, be about improving formal equality between States or ensuring preferential treatment for developing countries to overcome their development challenges (and other means of achieving substantive equality), or should it be primarily focused on humanitarian assistance, or a combination of these and many other objectives?[15] Indeed, why focus on States at all; should the focus not be on the *lived* experience of peoples and communities?

The fact that the global South – and broadly sympathetic scholars – prefer to discuss these matters in terms of 'international solidarity' would seem to push the debate away from being simply about formal equality and procedural fairness, and towards substantive fairness and equity.[16] As Wolfrum again notes (but disagrees with on a point of normative principle), 'solidarity means the intensification of co-operation for development' as well as invariably relying upon greater 'institutionalized co-operation'.[17] The extent to which the Global Goals can be viewed as an expression of solidarity must, however, be viewed with significant scepticism. If intensification and institutionalisation are key criteria on which to assess the impact of developmental targets, the Global Goals are

[13] *Ibid.*

[14] *Ibid.*

[15] On the issue of fairness generally, see T. Franck, *Fairness in International Law and Institutions* (Clarendon Press, 1995).

[16] Report of the Independent Expert on Human Rights and International Solidarity (1 April 2014) UN Doc. A/HRC/26/34, 16: 'International solidarity is a broad principle not limited to international assistance and cooperation, aid, charity or humanitarian assistance, and that it includes sustainability in international relations, especially international economic relations, the peaceful coexistence of all members of the international community, equal partnerships and the equitable sharing of benefits and burdens'.

[17] Wolfrum, above n 12, para 3.

singularly weak textually in both respects – an issue we again pick up on in the conclusion of this chapter.

In particular, those developmental critics of the Global Goals who have pointed out, more generally, the limitations and/or paradoxes in many of the Goals would invariably see SDG 17 as being the ultimate contradiction. They would argue that it manifestly sustains and reaffirms the overarching liberal economic paradigm built around world trade rules and traditional financial flows. How can a system that created many of the global problems now be relied upon to remedy the same situation? More specifically, in relation to the Goals themselves, how far will such economically focused targets contribute to the achievement of individual social and environmental targets?

To give one example, Target 17.5 under finance, one of the apparently clearer targets, is to adopt and implement investment promotion regimes for least developed countries. Investment has long been a contentious element of development strategy. And while the Goal talks of investor promotion and notably not the more controversial issue of investor protection,[18] most assume that the former would almost certainly incorporate (at least) elements of the latter at the insistence of developed States (and their investors) and the BWIs. Even putting to one side the fundamental question of how far FDI contributes positively to development (at least not without appropriate host and home State coordination), a more nuanced but equally important question is how well investor promotion fits with, and contributes to, the other Goals and targets to ensure a coherent and mutually supportive package of actions. So, for instance, how will investment contribute to equality (SDG 10), clean water and sanitation (SDG 6), and biodiversity protection on land (SDG 15)? The advancement of investment promotion per se as a development tool (as just one example) seemingly ignores the need for joined-up and comprehensive action across all Goals concurrently. At the very least, the selective choice of – and within – the Goals raises an intrinsically politico-economic, and indeed polemical, discourse around such questions as effectiveness, fairness and ultimately whose vision of development is being espoused in the Global Goals.

Nevertheless, to the extent that SDG 17 presents a coherent picture of international cooperation – itself a debatable proposition – there are some

---

[18] Investor protection relates to the implementation of such rules as expropriation, fair and equitable treatment and full protection and security, and, of course, enforcement through investor–State arbitration.

very important themes. First, as noted above, the targets are a juxtaposition of attempting to identify (if not rectify) formal inequalities and (to a lesser extent) promote a rather shallow type of substantive equality. So, for instance, significant emphasis is placed in Target 17.10 upon – as it always is – a 'universal, rules-based, open, non-discriminatory [yet] equitable multilateral trading system' while adding 'timely implementation of duty-free and quota-free market access … for all least developed countries'. This hides innate tensions between the North and South on world trade, with any general preferences for developing countries *en masse* being increasingly marginalised in favour of specific aspirations for least developed countries. In one regard, Target 17.10 is already in significant jeopardy as the World Trade Organization (WTO) Ministerial Conference, held later in 2015, accepted the deprioritisation of the completion of the Doha Development Agenda,[19] notwithstanding the sentiments of the Global Goals, adopted merely three months earlier.

A similar example relates to transfer of technology, with the usual ambiguous rhetoric in Target 17.7 of 'on favourable terms, including on concessional and preferential terms, as mutually agreed', the latter clause generally recognised as cancelling out any moral (or pseudo-solidarity) imperatives contained in the former. Transfer of technology has been an agenda item for various UN fora for over 40 years – if not longer – and yet we are seemingly still entrenched between a transactional and communitarian approach to the sharing of technology. Benefit sharing as a form of partnership is also noticeable by its general absence in the Global Goals.

Of course, the very nature of such targets means that they leave significant scope for flexibility and variation to be achieved over the 15-year time span between 2015 and 2030. Moreover, as a UN document with broad endorsement, it reflects the concerns and priorities across the developmental spectrum. More generally, the South is not as unified as it once was, and its interests are notably more fragmented than in previous decades. To the extent that the international community has historically viewed development as being achieved both through equality in some matters and inequality in others, the Global Goals are no different. And yet, in the juxtaposition between the two, there is little sense of an overarching rationale for the respective balance between them. As indicated above, it would seem that each target is unrelated to the other;

---

[19] 2015 WTO Nairobi Ministerial Declaration, para 30, available at <https://www.wto.org/english/thewto_e/minist_e/mc10_e/mindecision_e.htm> accessed 13 May 2017.

all being drawn from a menu-like list of strategies that has been advanced (and mostly tried) before. At this point it is useful to note that while the Global Goals are more numerous and, in many ways, more comprehensive than the MDGs, there is a similar critique as to their internal coherence and linkage. Moreover, the expansion of the MDGs to the much more overt Sustainable Development Goals has simply compounded the difficulties of identifying what is the overarching rationale of sustainable development. To the extent that SDG 17 is concerned with the necessary partnerships to achieve such goals, it would seem to fail to reflect the complexity and richness of the objectives in the previous 16 Goals.

12.2.3 The 'Systemic Issues': A Critical Analysis

Thus, it was perhaps a rather honest approach to include within SDG 17 so-called systemic issues, recognising the implementation challenges that countries will face moving these Goals and targets forward in the years to come. But to the extent that it is a positive that such a list of issues is included, it is also merely question-begging as to how they will be resolved or, less ambitiously, reconciled. Three pairs of systemic tensions seem particularly apparent within SDG 17. First, how to balance the necessity of effective global governance with sovereign discretion. Or, in the words of SDG 17, how to 'enhance global macroeconomic stability, including through policy coordination and policy coherence' while simultaneously 'respect[ing] each country's policy space'. Second, how to reconcile the intergovernmental, largely public and indeed, in some cases, rather bureaucratic objectives contained in the Global Goals, with the more limited capacity of States to 'nudge' private behaviour and corporate interests that lie behind many of these pressures. And third, what role for civil society, which is both promoted within the Global Goals, but whose role is curiously muted, perhaps in the face of those countries yet to accede to a free and open presence of civil society, domestic or foreign, within their political and socio-economic life. Section 4 of the chapter returns specifically to this issue of civil society as a partner in the achievement of the Goals.

We take each one of the pairs of tensions in turn. The first set of systemic issues revolves around the respective balance between beneficiary States (which are now uniformly recognised in UN policy-speak as having primary responsibility in the achievement of their own development),[20] and the increasingly complex and diffuse global economic

---

20 World Summit Outcome, above n 5, para 22.

architecture of which they form part, and yet to which they are also subject. The history of this relationship is, of course, well known and characterised largely through economic control and international oversight. Practices of the World Bank and the International Monetary Fund (IMF) were particularly critiqued as asserting dominion over developing countries, notwithstanding each having political neutrality clauses in their Articles of Agreement.[21] The so-called Washington Consensus of market liberalism and deregulation may have been the extreme limit of this imbalance between global institutions, on the one hand, and individual countries of the global South, on the other, and yet even 20 years on, the notion of sovereign control in matters of development remains far from a reality. States recognise that their 'policy space' is severely constrained by the external environment of investment rules, trade relations, the need for a positive credit score, as well as access to the more traditional forms of international economic assistance via the BWIs. There is something truly paradoxical in the fact that the non-binding nature of much of the economic system – through the variety of ways that global monitoring and convergence occur – is as (if not more) prescriptive on the actions of States than the most binding legal rule. True, States do diverge on many aspects, but in matters of economic importance, references to 'policy coordination and policy coherence' fail to capture just how pervasive the global system is on the internal dynamics of the State.

The second set of systemic issues is no less problematic, namely squaring the very public characterisation of the Global Goals as objectives of social welfare with the limited capacity of States to socially engineer their achievement in the face of the market economy. SDG 17 has a lot of fine words about multi-stakeholder partnerships 'that mobilize and share knowledge, expertise, technology and financial resources' as well as promoting 'effective ... public-private' partnerships, and yet the role of the State *qua* territorial regulatory sovereign is supplanted by a more open-textured role of the State as facilitator and promoter of voluntary progress. The Goals, generally, say little about domestic implementation per se; as with many international treaties, the choice of form of implementation is an example of sovereignty in action. Nevertheless, the seemingly complete absence of references to the role of regulation in the achievement of sustainable development, and rather

[21] See, for instance, article IV, sec. 10 IBRD [World Bank] Articles of Agreement: 'The Bank and its officers shall not interfere in the political affairs of any member; nor shall they be influenced in their decisions by the political character of the member or members concerned.'

more banal language in SDG 17 about State leadership and 'building on the experience and resourcing strategies of partnerships' suggests an understanding of development that subjugates law to secondary importance, ensuring compatibility with market imperatives. As one of us has recently noted, '[l]aw is a given, a constraint or, where change is mooted, voluntary and soft. To change the structure, the law – the "rules of the game" themselves – is often viewed as a return to the partisan, and divisive, days of the New International Economic Order.'[22] Thus, attainment is to be through softer means. Corporate social responsibility comes immediately to mind, as does improvement in corporate reporting mechanisms.[23] Multinational corporations and other private sector actors undoubtedly do play an important role in achieving (or jeopardising) a country's sustainable development plan.[24] What is noticeable here is how little regard is paid to any meaningful role for regulation and other forms of the exercise of territorial jurisdiction in that relationship.

The third set of systemic issues is also the most noticeable, and arguably political, omission in the Global Goals, namely the centrality of the role civil society plays in the achievement of sustainable development – across all issue areas – and yet the cursory manner in which it is dealt with. As noted above, different countries' approaches to the place and operation of civil society within their territory surely affected the language on this point. Though it does not do so, the insertion of a reference to civil societies playing a full part 'in accordance with national law' would not have been surprising. Indeed, *Transforming our world* does indeed use such language when discussing SDG 5 on gender equality: 'Undertake reforms to give women equal rights to economic resources, as well as access to ownership and control over land and other forms of property, financial services, inheritance and natural resources, *in accordance with national laws*.'[25]

As we note later in this chapter, civil society often plays a hugely instrumental and catalytic role in development, working to bring together

---

[22] D. French, 'The Global Goals: Formalism Foregone, Contested Legality and "Re-imaginings" of International Law' in *Ethiopian Yearbook of International Law 2016* (2017) 161.

[23] See Target 12.6: 'Encourage companies, especially large and transnational companies, to adopt sustainable practices and to integrate sustainability information into their reporting cycle.'

[24] R. Scheyvens, G. Banks and E. Hughes, 'The Private Sector and the SDGs: The Need to Move Beyond "Business as Usual"' (2016) *Sustainable Development* 24, 371–382.

[25] Target 5.a. Emphasis added.

different communities and public and private agencies.[26] And yet, the contingent nature of their work is often seen as simply an 'occupational hazard'; the nature of being an NGO. It is easy to fall into that trap. As the European Union (EU) Commission noted in 2012:

> the relationship between states and CSOs [civil society organisations] is often delicate. A limited tradition of dialogue still prevails in many countries and far too often the space for civil society remains narrow or is shrinking, with severe restrictions applied. In many contexts, CSOs focused on human rights and advocacy, including women's organisations, face limitations in their opportunities to work and to secure funding.[27]

But as the Commission went on to note, despite the challenges being very real for civil society in many situations, they should not be accepted as inevitable. In particular, the role of civil society within host countries needs to be more firmly embedded in accordance with underlying principles of clarity of purpose and mutual trust:

> Wherever possible, [CSOs acting as service providers] should be framed in collaborative *multi-actor partnerships* coordinated with national authorities, with the long term objective of promoting more accountable, effective and sustainable systems at the service of populations. In addition, CSOs' initiatives can be supported when addressing issues that do not receive adequate consideration within national policies but are key to social progress and reflect human rights concerns as well as sustainable development issues.[28]

It is unfortunate that such positive language, or ideas, did not find their way into *Transforming our world*, indicating perhaps the more positive perspective of the EU as donor than others as host countries.

All told, the overarching complexity of the systemic issues gives little hope for optimism in the achievement of the Global Goals, though again one must probably distinguish between progress against individual targets and more difficult questions of overall synergy and coordination. Indeed, this may prove more difficult in the case of the Global Goals than the

---

[26] J.C.N. Paul, 'Law and Development and Peter Slinn' in J. Hatchard and A. Perry-Kessaris (eds), *Law and Development: Facing Complexity in the 21st Century* (Cavendish Publishing, 2003) xv.

[27] EU Commission Communication 'The Roots of Democracy and Sustainable Development: Europe's Engagement with Civil Society in External Relations' (COM (2012) 492 final) 3–4. Available at <http://eur-lex.europa.eu/LexUriServ/LexUriServ.do?uri=COM%3A2012%3A0492%3AFIN%3AEN%3APDF> accessed 12 May 2017.

[28] *Ibid*, 6.

MDGs. To a not unreasonable extent, the MDGs were developmental goals that were more metric driven. Improvements in GDP could, on the whole, contribute to, improve or meet many of the targets – not all but certainly a good number of them. In the case of the Global Goals, such incidental progress is much less likely as many of the Goals are more socially nuanced and dependent on shifts in policy (and indeed culture). Targets around equality, rule of law, and gender are not attainable through the perpetuation of global economic trends. Indeed, as the above discussion on investment promotion implied, there is a risk of divergence between the economic and socio-political Goals.

Thus, it might be thought surprising that SDG 17 did not give greater thought to exactly what it was creating partnerships for. Moreover, might one not go further and suggest whether, in light of such policy challenges, it is not almost perverse to include within the list of systemic issues something so fundamental as to '[e]nhance policy coherence for sustainable development'? True, that must be an ongoing process. But is it not policy coherence that setting the Global Goals was meant to achieve, at least in part? And if that has not yet been achieved – and rather the Goals are simply viewed as being a wish-list of every public and social good considered desirable and (more importantly) acceptable through intergovernmental negotiation – it is frankly difficult to see how coherence and coordination will be any further strengthened in the years ahead. Of course, the annual High-Level Political Forum, *inter alia*, at the global level may, over time, provide some guidance in this regard. But coherent policy-making and implementation between regimes, between global priorities and national implementation, and within national institutions seeking to reconcile differing priorities, remains as distant in this area as they ever have been. All this and notwithstanding *Transforming our world*'s warm (yet hollow) words in its preamble that '[t]he interlinkages and integrated nature of the Sustainable Development Goals are of crucial importance in ensuring that the purpose of the new Agenda is realised'.

12.2.4 What Place for International Solidarity?

And this must be a real risk; that the Goals and targets – especially those in SDG 17 – are not simply aspirational, they are utopian. Not in the sense of 'to be strived for', but utopian in the sense that without a sea-change in political priorities and business practices, they are almost unachievable; we have already seen the Doha Development Agenda invariably fall from the table only a few months after the Global Goals were adopted.

More generally, there is a mismatch between the targets included – however important each is individually – and the wider object of the Goal itself of creating partnerships. SDG 17 operates instrumentally in identifying particular means of implementation rather than normatively in securing structural global change. But what the targets are not, and what they do not achieve, is a global partnership *properly conceived*. Such targets, however utile, are far removed from the ambitious idealism inherent within international solidarity. As the Independent Expert on Human Rights and International Solidarity, who has been working on a draft declaration on this matter to be put to the General Assembly, has noted:

> International solidarity shall be understood as the convergence of interests, purposes and actions between and among peoples, individuals, States and their international organizations in order to preserve the order and ensure the very survival of international society and to achieve common goals which require international cooperation and collective action, based on the international normative system of duties which they implement and practise to foster peace and security, development and human rights.
>
> International solidarity shall be made evident in the collective actions of States that have a positive impact on the exercise and enjoyment of human rights by peoples and individuals within and outside of their respective territories, notably in the ratification of the United Nations international human rights treaties and international labour standards and the adoption of commitments and decisions agreed upon voluntarily between and among States at the regional and international levels.[29]

It is high rhetoric and unsurprisingly finds connections with much of the preambular references in *Transforming our world*: ideas of co-existence, collaboration and common good. In particular, the Independent Expert's views on solidarity move away from voluntarism towards a clearer sense of legal obligation and legal entitlement. On the other hand, within the *substance* of the Global Goals, there are noticeably fewer linkages.

Moreover, in the move away from the singular in MDG 8 ('Global Partnership') to the plural ('Partnerships for the Goals') there is arguably a wider context, namely a fragmentation of purpose, less focused on the advancement of key social ideals and shared interests – in other words, with less of a focus on solidarity. Perhaps this is best reflected in the published goal for SDG 17: that by 2030 everyone will have access to

---

[29] Report of the Independent Expert on Human Rights and International Solidarity, above n 16, 17–18.

the Internet.[30] A good thing (perhaps?) but by what stretch of the imagination is this relevant to the attainment of global partnerships? And if this seems an unduly textual analysis, one only needs to look back a little earlier – to 1992 – to note how the terminology has shifted even further. In the Rio Declaration on Environment and Development, the relevant objective was outlined as the 'goal of establishing a new and equitable global partnership through the creation of new levels of cooperation among States, key sectors of societies and people'.[31] Grand words, and indeed only words. Utopian in themselves perhaps, but words carry meaning. Moreover, as the 1992 Rio Declaration stated immediately afterwards: '[w]orking towards international agreements which respect the interests of all and protect the integrity of the global environmental and developmental system'. In this case, partnership, cooperation and the advancement of international law are intricately connected. And as lawyers, we would seek to argue that international rules provide one of the principal tools by which such meaning is communicated into actual practice. Thus, the next section reconsiders whether the Global Goals would be better understood as cementing a duty in international law to cooperate in developmental matters.

12.3 GLOBAL GOALS AND A NORMATIVE DUTY TO COOPERATE?

If the Global Goals were to be viewed, and were to be constructed, as legal norms, how might things look differently? It is important to recognise that despite the mainstream rejection of legality, there is nevertheless a strongly held viewpoint – if by no means majority consensus – prepared to acknowledge wider normative obligations on States in this area. On superficial appearances, SDG 17 is very much part of a historical legacy of the attempt to establish a duty to cooperate on matters of development, which proponents would see as stretching back (at least) to the UN Charter, which had development as one of its core purposes. In particular, Article 1(3) recognises the Organisation's pivotal role 'in solving international problems of an economic, social, cultural, or humanitarian character', as well as articles 55 and 56, which further gave meaning to that purpose.

---

[30] Available at <http://www.globalgoals.org/outcomes/proportion-of-internet-users/> accessed 13 May 2017.

[31] UN Doc. A/CONF.151/26 (Vol. I), available at <http://www.un.org/documents/ga/conf151/aconf15126-1annex1.htm> accessed 13 May 2017.

For proponents, there exists a very real legal duty in this area, and arguably more than that, one which has meaningful content. Others would point to the political and policy nature of much of the documentation in this area. Many are perhaps willing to accept a putative norm.[32] Nevertheless, one cannot escape the polemic and dogmatic history surrounding such a duty, notably the attempt by the global South to create an NIEO in the 1970s, and the equal attempt by developed States to refute it. As Schwebel commented,

> I see those documents as very mixed, containing progressive elements, but regressive elements as well. The resolutions of the NIEO were forced through the General Assembly in a lamentable atmosphere. They were not negotiated solutions but a partisan set of demands … As for the [1974] Charter of Economic Rights and Duties of States [CERDS], it is not international law, and happily so, for in some respects it is sound, but in other respects, quite nationalistic and unsound.[33]

One way for the North to undermine the NIEO was to deny it any form of legal status. And while some of its supporters were talking in terms of a 'new branch of international law' – an 'international law of development' – critics argued that any action taken by developed States towards assisting developing States was purely voluntary and that the rules contained within such declarations as the CERDS 'had not yet crossed the threshold of lex lata'.[34] By arguing that it was not representative of customary international law, developed States were able to control the nature and extent of much of the reform of the general economic system. The effect of this was to ensure that the NIEO became little more than an aspiration, and the resolutions adopted little more than a series of platitudes.

Of course, this lack of enthusiasm for economic reform coincided with a general reversal in the social and economic situation of many States, particularly at the end of the 1970s and in the early 1980s. Thus, the NIEO as a wholesale movement of change was dead. However, despite a

---

[32] D. French, '"From Seoul with Love" – The Continuing Relevance of the 1986 Seoul ILA Declaration on Progressive Development of Principles of Public International Law relating to a New International Economic Order' (2008) LV *Netherlands International Law Review* 23 '[such principles] remain either *de lege ferenda* or "soft" law at best'.

[33] S. Schwebel, 'A Commentary' in T.M.C. Asser Institute (ed.), *International Law and the Grotian Heritage* (T.M.C. Asser Institute, 1985) 142.

[34] G. Abi-Saab, 'Whither the International Community?' 1998 *European Journal of International Law* 9, 264.

general failure to implement the NIEO, there were nevertheless subsequent developments which, at least, appeared to recognise more explicitly the needs and situation of developing countries, such as the General Agreement on Tariff and Trade's (GATT) 1979 Decision on Differential and More Favourable Treatment, Reciprocity and Fuller Participation of Developing Countries;[35] the conclusion of international commodity agreements; the (admittedly failed) attempts to negotiate international codes of conduct for transnational corporations and technology transfer; and the increasing reference to the interests of developing countries in multilateral conventions, arguably most conspicuously in the negotiation and conclusion of the 1982 Law of the Sea Convention.

In part as a response to the political criticism of such attempts, an alternative approach premised on human rights considerations emerged, relying on such seminal texts as the International Covenant on Economic, Social and Cultural Rights (ICESCR).[36] Article 2(1) of the 1966 Covenant, for instance, requires all States Parties 'to take steps, individually and through international assistance and cooperation, especially economic and technical, to the maximum of its available resources, with a view to achieving progressively the full realization of the rights recognized ...'. This received further elaboration by the Committee on Economic, Social and Cultural Rights (CESCR) in 1990 when it said 'international cooperation for development and thus for the realization of economic, social and cultural rights is an obligation of all States. It is particularly incumbent upon those States which are in a position to assist others in this regard.'[37] Significant support for such an idea was found in the earlier 1986 UN Declaration on the Right to Development, which noted: 'the right to development is an inalienable human right by virtue of which every human person and all peoples are entitled to participate in, contribute to, and enjoy economic, social, cultural and political development, in which all human rights and fundamental freedoms can be fully realized'.[38]

It was with such legal provisions in mind that Alston talked, in the midst of the MDGs, of the emergence of an 'internationalization of

---

[35] Decision of 28 November 1979 (L/4903). GATT BISD 26th Suppl. (1980) 203.

[36] United Nations, Treaty Series, vol 993, p. 3.

[37] Committee on Economic, Social and Cultural Rights (1990) General Comment 3 ('The Nature of States Parties Obligations (art. 2, para 1)') (14 December 1990) UN Doc. E/1991/23, para 14.

[38] UN Declaration on the Right to Development, above n 8, art. 1.

responsibility'.[39] Nevertheless, Alston, while acknowledging the MDGs had the potential to change the tone of the debate, remained circumspect as to the likelihood, recognising that there is little practice, never mind consensus, to support the 'proposition that any given country is obligated to provide specific assistance to any other country'.[40] In part, such realism is itself historical, reflecting the divisions and politicisation of development within the UN, notably though not exclusively around attempts to formalise development assistance, to establish a right to development, to realign the workings of the BWIs, and indeed the attempts to create a whole NIEO.

Despite attempts to identify and enunciate relevant legal principles, the notion of a duty to cooperate in international development remains inchoate and we remain very much in the area of contested and putative legality. Solidarity as a legal principle has yet to be fully operationalised or sufficiently captured in legal form. Thus for many international lawyers, accepting the existence of a mandatory duty to cooperate on development issues is simply premature. Others cannot accept that international law would stretch that far into matters of welfare.[41] For precisely the same reason, others argue it must. In earlier work, one of us sought to identify common ground:

> A sounder argument is to consider [international development principles] … as containing useful pointers – if not, in some instances, also measurable signposts – towards the achievement of longer-term goals, in this case arriving 'at a just balance between converging and diverging interests and in particular between the interests of developed and developing countries', which must be considered foundational to the functioning not only of an equitable economic system but also, in the light of changing expectations, a sustainable international community, more generally. But being longer-term makes such objectives no less important.[42]

This is, in many ways, an old fight between different legal camps; its relevance to the Global Goals, however, is a new arena to revisit underlying contestations. But beyond the conceptual and the polemic,

---

[39] Alston, above n 6, 775.

[40] *Ibid*, 777.

[41] Wolfrum, above n 12, para 40: 'The attempts to develop a general international obligation to co-operate for development, which in effect would have had redistributive effect, have failed to meet the necessary acceptability in all groups of States … If an obligation to co-operate has been established, even an obligation to co-operate for development, this obligation is treaty-based. The ensuing consequences cannot be generalized.'

[42] French, above n 32.

does uncertainty in the overarching normative framework matter? In the final section, the chapter looks at one example – the role of civil society in developing such partnerships – to reflect on how legal certainty, domestically and internationally, is pivotal to the operation of even the smallest community-focused partnerships.

12.4 COMMUNITY-FOCUSED PARTNERSHIPS

As SDG 17 acknowledges, the broad scope of the Goals generally will require a similarly broad coalition of 'Governments, civil society, the private sector, the United Nations system and other actors [in order to mobilise] all available resources'. Emphasis within the Global Goals on the importance of civil society involvement – even if, as noted above, it is largely rhetorical – follows recent trends in acknowledging civil society as a 'crucial and integral component of any democracy', which can 'foster … pluralism and contribute to more effective policies, equitable development and inclusive growth'.[43] Indeed, the EU specifically noted the positive potential of civil society to extend into development-related areas due to its 'capacity to empower, represent, defend and reach out to vulnerable and socially excluded groups, including minorities' and in so doing, catalyse 'economic and human development, as well as social cohesion and innovation'.[44] On this basis, increased acknowledgment of civil society rightly emphasises its pivotal role in achieving wider developmental objectives, including combating malnutrition, improving healthcare and education, reducing inequalities and tackling climate change, among many others.[45]

One area where civil society is actively involved, in coalition with government and private actors, is the water sector, and in relation to efforts to 'ensure availability and sustainable management of water and sanitation for all', as set out in SDG 6. More specifically, targets 6.1 and 6.2 aim respectively to 'achieve universal and equitable access to safe

[43] EU Commission Communication, above n 27, 3. For further examples of the rising acknowledgment of civil society as a key development actor, see the World Economic Forum Schwab Foundation Report 'Beyond Organizational Scale: How Social Entrepreneurs Create Systems Change'. Available at <http://reports.weforum.org/schwab-foundation-beyond-organizational-scale/> accessed 10 May 2017.

[44] *Ibid.*

[45] Global Goals 2, 3, 4, 5, 10 and 13 respectively. See <http://www.globalgoals.org/> accessed 27 June 2017.

and affordable drinking water for all by 2030', and to 'achieve access to adequate and equitable sanitation and hygiene for all and end open defecation, paying special attention to the needs of women and girls and those in vulnerable situations' also by the same year. Therefore this section looks to the water sector, and to efforts to improve access to water in one geographical area, in order to consider what such partnerships described in SDG 17 may look like in practice, in the context of one substantive Goal, namely SDG 6.

Recent research undertaken by one of the authors in Blantyre, Malawi, observing and interviewing various stakeholders involved in water governance, provides a contemporary illustration of such a coalition of actors, working together to achieve the aims encapsulated in SDG 6. In Malawi 57 per cent of the population live below the national poverty line.[46] The World Health Organization (WHO)/United Nations Children's Fund (UNICEF) Joint Monitoring Programme Report[47] estimates that 96 per cent of people in urban areas and 89 per cent in rural areas have access to safe water (designated as either water piped on to premises, or water from other improved source). But these statistics have been criticised as considerably inflated.[48] *Water for People*, a water NGO based in Blantyre, Malawi's second city, estimates that only 38 per cent of people living in the 21 low-income peri-urban areas of the city have access to water that meets government standards. In the rural district of Chikhwawa only 42 per cent have access to safe drinking water. Access to sanitation in these areas is estimated to be 22 per cent in peri-urban Blantyre, and 8 per cent in Chikhwawa using improved sanitation facilities.[49] *WaterAid* estimate that with a total population of 15 million people, 2 million lack safe access to water, and 10 million are without access to adequate sanitation.[50] Suffice to say that access to water is a challenge for many, and water poverty is a daily reality, which throws the fulfilment of SDG 6 into sharp relief.

---

[46] United Nations Development Programme country information. Available at <http://www.mw.undp.org/content/malawi/en/home/countryinfo/> accessed 12 May 2017.

[47] WHO/UNICEF Joint Monitoring Programme (JMP) for Water Supply and Sanitation, 2015. Available at <http://www.wssinfo.org/documents/?tx_displaycontroller%5Btype%5D=country_files> accessed 12 May 2017.

[48] *Water for People*, Country Report, Malawi. Available at <https://www.waterforpeople.org/where-we-work/malawi> accessed 12 May 2017.

[49] *Ibid.*

[50] See *WaterAid* website <http://www.wateraid.org/where-we-work/page/malawi> accessed 12 May 2017.

Water for People has been working in Malawi for over a decade. One particular focus of its efforts can be seen on the outskirts of Blantyre, supporting local communities to develop community-owned Water Users' Associations (WUAs), in order for people to gain sustainable access to clean, affordable water. Here a rich mixture of local, national and international connections can be seen at work, spanning the public sector, private enterprise, and civil society, and reflecting the type of partnerships articulated in SDG 17.[51] Established in 1991 by the American Water Works Association, *Water for People* is a United States-based not-for-profit charity, working in nine countries across three continents.[52] In Malawi, as elsewhere, *Water for People* utilises international donor funds to support WUAs in partnership with local communities, in order to develop appropriate administrative structures for water governance, which ultimately aim to ensure universal, sustainable access to water. The NGO also trains 'sanitation entrepreneurs' (small private companies) to dig pit latrines for improved sanitation, and partners with local (municipal) government to connect infrastructure and monitor water quality.

In the Blantyre area, water is purified and pumped from a municipal plant to multiple standpipes (called water points) in each community. Access to water at each water point is controlled by the local WUA. The purpose and scope of this initiative is explained in the following extract from an interview conducted by the co-author, Nathan Cooper (NC), with Andrew (A), a representative from *Water for People*:

> A: We train the communities to maintain their own laws without having support from somewhere but the community within should know how to manage their water points if they break down: Management training.
>
> NC: So when you say manage, do you include repair or any sort of infrastructure or is it just management of who gets the water?
>
> A: Both repair and management … and also how they can contribute funds …
>
> A: At the moment, all the households will have access to that water point, and access to the water point if they pay enough of the tariff, they don't pay per use, they pay a monthly tariff so the water point committee goes around to collect that monthly tariff. For the people that don't have that tariff, an

[51] 'A successful sustainable development agenda requires partnerships between governments, the private sector and civil society. These inclusive partnerships built upon principles and values, a shared vision, and shared goals that place people and the planet at the centre, are needed at the global, regional, national and local level'. See <http://www.un.org/sustainabledevelopment/globalpartnerships/> accessed 12 May 2017.

[52] See <https://www.waterforpeople.org/about> accessed 12 May 2017.

> agreement is met, so they can pay in the future. It's a community based management so they understand which people have problems and when they can pay, but they agree the amount to be paid per household no matter how much quantity they draw from the water point.[53]

Andrew's explanation clearly emphasises that management of water resources in the communities where *Water for People* partners is community-based. Embedding the governance of water resources within the very communities being served allows those administering the water points to hear, evaluate and respond to both the needs of community members, and to their ability to contribute. Undoubtedly, this is helping to facilitate affordable access to sufficient safe water for many in the Blantyre area, and in so doing, the efforts of *Water for People*, the WUAs and their private and public sector partners are already contributing towards greater realisation of SDG 6. In this respect, such a partnership represents a pragmatic solution to water poverty, in keeping with the NGO's vision of a world where everyone has access to reliable and safe water and sanitation services.[54] This is also an apt illustration of the kinds of partnerships that SDG 17 seeks to promote, and which it is claimed are crucial to strengthening the implementation of Goals 1–16: 'effective public, public-private and civil society partnerships, building on the experience and resourcing strategies of partnerships'.[55]

12.4.1 Partnerships Towards a *Right* to Water

The seminal role played by the ICESCR during the UN development decades in grounding development aims within the language and obligations of rights has already been alluded to above. It is instructive to note that *Water for People*'s website makes no mention of water as a human right, but does include a specific section on SDG 6, and on their efforts to align their own monitoring of water and sanitation projects with that Goal's requirements.[56] But, arguably, without claiming that safe water and sanitation are rights, such pragmatic solutions to water poverty lack a

---

[53] From interview 16: 7 April 2014, Soche community, near Blantyre, Malawi.

[54] Note that there is no reference to a (human) right to water in the vision and mission statements: <https://www.waterforpeople.org/about#mission> accessed 12 May 2017.

[55] See SDG 17: Partnerships: <http://www.globalgoals.org/global-goals/partnerships-for-the-goals/> accessed 27 June 2017.

[56] This is in contrast to other water NGOs, including *WaterAid*, which continue to frame their fundraising and promotional work with reference to the

normative foundation upon which to build a firmer base for project, programmatic and partnership responses. The normative and logistical issues arising from such uncertainty are considered below, after a brief explanation of the human right to water.

General Comment 15[57] from the Committee on Economic, Social and Cultural Rights (CESCR) of the UN Economic and Social Council (ECOSOC) provides the primary basis on which a human right to water is asserted.[58] That is that such a right is derived from, and is required for, the rights to an adequate standard of living (dignified life) and to the highest attainable standard of health (Articles 11 and 12 ICESCR). Therefore the elements that constitute the human right to water must be sufficient to meet these requirements of dignified life and health. Paragraph 2 describes the human right to water as entitling 'everyone to sufficient, safe, acceptable, physically accessible and affordable water for personal and domestic uses'.

Requiring that water is physically and economically accessible (namely, affordable) is crucial to addressing some of the most pressing challenges facing water-poor people, including in the area of Malawi where *Water for People* works. Nevertheless, the lack of clarity in the normative architecture will invariably raise daunting challenges for both local communities and partnering organisations. In what is a common situation, partnerships, where they exist, are not sufficiently anchored within an appropriate governance framework to operate effectively and rights, even when correctly identified, are rarely enforceable. In Malawi, as elsewhere, the absence of law (or the absence of a sufficiently clear appeal to or application of the law) can be inhibitive to successful partnerships and development. Gains achieved are far from guaranteed. Such uncertainty can particularly affect the role of civil society in supporting development

right to water. See *WaterAid* briefing note: <http://www.wateraid.org/uk/google-search?query=human+right+to+water> accessed 12 May 2017.

[57] See Committee on Economic, Social and Cultural Rights, General Comment No. 15 ('The Right to Water') (26 November 2002) UN Doc. E/C.12/2002/11.

[58] Note the absence from the International Bill of Human Rights of a legally binding human right to water has meant that General Comment 15 has come to play a particularly important part in stating the nature and scope of the human right to water. As McCaffrey observes, General Comment 15 'is the first recognition by a United Nations human rights body of an independent and generally applicable human right to water'. See S. McCaffrey, 'The Human Right to Water' in E. Brown Weiss, L. Boisson de Chazournes, and N. Bernasconi-Osterwalder (eds), *Fresh Water and International Economic Law* (Oxford University Press, 2005) 93 at 101.

due to its ambivalent legal status, ambiguities around how it interrelates to the governing apparatus and the innate political context of its social licence to operate. By depending on good will, normative uncertainty and the self-promulgation of technical expertise, the role of civil society in such partnerships is very often contingent on the (sovereign) acquiescence of the State. This can be appropriate when there are no challenges. But even limited obstacles can present real legal issues.

The following extract, illustrating some people's experience of economically inaccessible water, takes place between the co-author (NC), 'Jennifer' (J), an assistant at the Soche Water Users' Association, and 'Andrew' (A), previously introduced as a representative from *Water for People*. Despite the specific context of the issue, the wider problems of governance are also very evident:

> NC: So what do you charge for water, how much is the water per litre or 20 litres?
>
> J: The tariff? 20 litres is 12 kwacha [£0.015], 40 litres is 24, and 60 litres is 36 kwacha, and that's our tariff.
>
> NC: Do you ever have any problems with people not being able to pay?
>
> A: Do you have people that collect water from the kiosks but they don't have money?
>
> J: Yeah … some people they do … run away from our kiosks and go to bore holes, there are bore holes in some regions – they pay 100 kwacha and draw out for the whole month.
>
> NC: Sorry what do they do, they pay at the bore hole?
>
> J: Yeah.
>
> A: They bore holes with hand pumps, they pay once for a month, they go to that side and pay a hundred kwacha, so they can draw the whole month, go to a kiosk where they pay per fetch.
>
> NC: The water quality, is it different?
>
> A: Very different.
>
> NC: What are the problems with the water from the bore hole?
>
> J: The problem, they are not treating it.
>
> NC: Do you actually see people in the community getting sick?
>
> J: Yeah, they do get sick.[59]

[59] From interview 16: 7 April 2014 Soche community, near Blantyre, Malawi.

Clearly, despite the unit price for water from the Water Users Association being less than that charged elsewhere by private providers, even this cost proves sufficiently prohibitive for some people, who instead risk their health for cheaper, untreated water. This link between inadequate water and health is particularly important to note. Not only does it affirm the rationale offered in General Comment 15 for recognising a right to water as derived from ICESCR Article 12, but the lack of (economically) accessible water also compromises the realisation of other Covenant rights.[60] Crucially, the response by the partnership of *Water for People*, the WUAs and others to the economic disenfranchisement experienced by those unable to afford clean water is invariably constrained due to the project-limited focus of their partnership and the lack of an underpinning normative framework in which it is located. But the consequences of such a project-limited focus for those affected can be profound, constituting – in the language of human rights – a violation not only of the right to water, but also of the right to an adequate standard of living, and the right to enjoy the highest attainable standard of health.

Though just one example, it does represent something of the risks of a normative vacuum, which, arguably, the non-legal character of the Global Goals has created. Of course, it is perhaps too early to tell what the consequences may be for the effectiveness of partnerships to meet the SDGs, but at the least it leads to uncertainty regarding the expectations and obligations of the partners involved, which risks hindering the realisation of development opportunities, in this case SDG 6, in contexts where multiple partners are connected, but without an adequate normative framework. The fact that experiences like those above are not located within, or problematised in relation to, human rights standards simultaneously points to an absence of normative vocabulary within the partnership – and indeed within the Goals themselves – and to an absence of effective remedy (or, at the least, an accessible avenue towards remedy) for those people affected.

We are not arguing that (re)framing essential development Goals, like access to safe and affordable water, within the language of human rights will automatically guarantee their greater realisation. Sticking with the Malawian context, the Universal Declaration of Human Rights is now accepted as part of domestic law[61] and the Constitution of Malawi contains a broad and explicitly justiciable right to development, which

---

[60] Contrary to General Comment 15, Para 12 (c)(i), above n 57.

[61] See the case of *Chihana v. Republic*, Criminal Appeal No. 9 of 1992 (MSCA). Note: The Republic of Malawi is also party to the ICESCR, having ratified in 1993.

allows for a right to water to be implied.[62] So there already exists a framework of internationally derived, and nationally entrenched, rights, the concomitant obligations to which should support the realisation of universal access to water (and therefore the fulfilment of SDG 6). But this is clearly not the case, as *Water for People* country director, Kate Harawa, confirmed: 'They have committed themselves to certain international agreements in terms of water, so the Malawi government is obligated to provide that 27 litres of water per person per capita for the people of the low income areas. But it doesn't always meet that obligation.'[63]

However, the degree to which partnerships encourage the pursuit of Goals, such as SDG 6, separately from such Goal's rights-based counterparts – thereby eschewing legal form – raises serious concerns. The degree to which partnerships between government (that is obliged to 'take all necessary measures' to fulfil their rights-based commitments),[64] and civil society and the private sector (that carry no such positive rights-based obligations) might continue to work productively over the long term, without a shared normative framework beyond (or beneath) the aspirations of the SDG targets, must be questioned, particularly in the face of geo-political volatility and (relating to the above examples) NGO and government vulnerability to donor fatigue.

Faced with such potential weaknesses to the integrity of partnerships for development, it is appropriate to give fresh consideration to rights-based approaches to development, and of the *lex ferenda* that human rights law may yet represent. One important aim of taking steps to reconnect rights-based law in development with the Global Goals may be to emphasise the moral claim that should be implicit in all rights-based approaches. In spite of the limited effectiveness of rights in action (as

---

62 Malawian Constitution sec. 30 '(1) All persons and peoples have a right to development and therefore to the enjoyment of economic, social, cultural and political development and women, children and the disabled in particular shall be given special consideration in the application of this right. (2) The State shall take all necessary measures for the realization of the right to development. Such measures shall include, amongst other things, equality of opportunity for all in their access to basic resources, education, health services, food, shelter, employment and infrastructure. (3) The State shall take measures to introduce reforms aimed at eradicating social injustices and inequalities. (4) The State has a responsibility to respect the right to development and to justify its policies in accordance with this responsibility.' See <http://www.cssr.uct.ac.za/sites/cssr.uct.ac.za/files/Constitution%20Malawi.pdf> accessed 13 May 2017.

63 Interview 15: 6 April 2014, *Water for People* offices, Blantyre, Malawi.

64 See Malawian Constitution, n 62, sec. 30(2).

evinced by the above examples in Malawi), such a morally sensitised vision of human rights could override resistance of legal domestication. In so doing – specifically regarding SDG 17 – it retains some potential to provide a coherent normative framework, within which both clear and bold claims can be pursued, and partnerships to implementation can be adopted.

Undoubtedly the formality of law lends itself to making such claims more effectively than do non-legal formations. Certainly in the water sector, some NGOs continue to adopt the language of rights, framing their efforts as not just contributing to the fulfilment of a development priority, or goal, but to the realisation of a human right to water.[65] The reassertion of a rights-based normative framework for the Global Goals could make a significant contribution to strengthening its current, fragile frame on which the Goals are based. Indeed, the connection between human rights and the Goals is there – if inchoate – in *Transforming our world*: 'We envisage a world of universal respect for human rights and human dignity, the rule of law, justice, equality and non-discrimination.'[66] What better way to encourage respect for human rights, than by weaving them within the fabric of the Global Goals agenda, and reconnecting them to the Goals in ways that will inspire and galvanise the all-important partnerships envisaged in SDG 17?

12.5 CONCLUSION

Partnerships are essential to the achievement of the Global Goals. As *Transforming our world* says boldly in its preamble:

> We are determined to mobilize the means required to implement this Agenda through a revitalised Global Partnership for Sustainable Development, based on a spirit of strengthened global solidarity, focussed in particular on the needs of the poorest and most vulnerable and with the participation of all countries, all stakeholders and all people.

It is therefore supremely surprising that partnerships have been subject to such limited analysis. To be clear, the modes of cooperation identified have been subject to endless debate and critique over the decades; in particular, the positive and negative contributions of international trade,

65 *WaterAid*, above n 56.
66 *Transforming our world*, above n 2, para 7.

finance and overseas aid to development. What is less apparent is how far the exact *utility* of such partnerships in achieving the specifics of the SDGs (and before that the MDGs) has itself been considered. Revisiting traditional strategies is a non-contentious way of international diplomacy. But there is little recognition or discussion as to whether such strategies are appropriate or likely to be successful. Moreover, as this chapter has indicated, the individual forms of cooperation and the idea of a global partnership are noticeable in their disjointed characterisation. The instrumentality of the targets under SDG 17 gives little sense of how a more comprehensive and coordinated approach to global development will take shape. The very inclusion of 'systemic issues' is an unusually honest acceptance of that.

The chapter has also sought to reflect on how SDG 17 is captured by ongoing debates as to the normative divide between obligation and voluntarism, between legally binding solidarity and weaker, optional, variations. As Wolfrum indicated, solidarity suggests both an intensification and institutionalisation of cooperation. Both are noticeably lacking in the Global Goals. In terms of intensification, it is simply more of the same. And in terms of institutionalisation, there is little appetite – from either donor or beneficiary States – to co-opt or pool sovereign discretion. What is perhaps most apparent in the Global Goals – clearer than in the MDGs – is the priority given to the private sector in implementing the Goals. But, as the chapter notes, how far States can 'nudge' private behaviour when such little scope is given to States to adopt a regulatory response suggests effective and meaningful implementation remains at best, aspiration, and at worst, utopian in its reach.

Within this, there is an age-old debate as to the active versus passive role of the State itself in the achievement of its own development. One of the principal changes (at least in rhetoric but also to some extent in reality) over the last 20 years has been an increasing acceptance of the need for host State ownership of its development strategy to maximise welfare and to ensure coherence in activity. Nevertheless, as noted above, the reality is that sovereign control remains illusory; many developing countries have struggled, and will continue to struggle, to capitalise on that ownership in the face of global pressures outside of their control. SDG 17 provides little solace in this regard. Moreover, in the new era where civil society has a meaningful role to play, normative uncertainty and the absence of a rights-based approach to service provision in development operations jeopardises progress. Even where the Global Goals promote effective partnerships, they have not given sufficient guidance to States to affect them. Thus, even within an increasingly voluntarist system of cooperation, a normative framework is much more than simply useful; it is essential.

Index